Operation Welcome

How Strasbourg Remained a Seat of European Institutions, 1949-1979

P.I.E. Peter Lang

Bruxelles • Bern • Berlin • Frankfurt am Main • New York • Oxford • Wien

Claudia Leskien

Operation Welcome

How Strasbourg Remained a Seat of European Institutions, 1949-1979

Multiple Europes
No. 55

Cover picture: private collection.

All manuscripts in this series are subject to a critical review by the book series editors as well as external peer review.

Éditions scientifiques internationales
Brussels, 2016
1 avenue Maurice, B-1050 Brussels, Belgium
www.peterlang.com; info@peterlang.com

Printed in Germany

ISSN 1376-0904
ISBN 978-2-87574-316-9
eISBN 978-3-0352-6595-8
D/2016/5678/04

CIP available from the Library of Congress and the British Library, GB.

Bibliographic information published by "Die Deutsche Nationalbibliothek"

"Die Deutsche Nationalbibliothek" lists this publication in the "Deutsche Nationalbibliografie"; detailed bibliographic data is available on the Internet at <http://dnb.d-nb.de>.

Table of Contents

List of Illustrations and Tables 11

Abbreviations 13

Preface 15

Introduction 19

Section 1.01 Siting European institutions 23
Section 1.02 Siting institutions – not only a political issue 27
Section 1.03 Currency of the seat question 31
Section 1.04 Conceptualisations 33
Section 1.05 Structure of this book 37

Chapter 1. Strasbourg, seat of European institutions 41

(a) Alsatian history 41
(b) National political support for Strasbourg 45
(c) Local politics and European institutions 48
(d) Urban development after 1945 52
(e) Economic impact of the European institutions 54

Section 1.06 Attracting European institutions (1949-1952) 58

(a) Siting the Council of Europe 59
(b) Siting the institutions of the Schuman Plan 63

Chapter 2. Hosting Europe 79

Section 1.07 Constructing Strasbourg's European mission 80
Section 1.08 Central Actors 87

(a) City/departmental administration 88
(b) Private organisations 105
(c) Other actors 128

Section 1.09 The start-up phase: 1949-1956 131

(a) Activities and accommodation 133
(b) Promotion of Strasbourg as seat 137
(c) Informing the public about European institutions 139

Section 1.10 The implementation phase: 1956-1959 140

(a) Using session frame programmes to increase renown as a host 143
(b) Competition with other seat cities 147

Section 1.11 The business-as-usual phase: 1960-1979 160

(a) Session frame programmes 163
(b) Developments threatening Strasbourg's position 1960–1979 168

Section 1.12 Concluding Remarks 172

CHAPTER 3. *L'Europe vient à Strasbourg* 175

Section 1.13 Central Actors 178

(a) City/departmental administration 178
(b) Other actors 182
(c) Cooperation between actors 184

Section 1.14 Long-distance transport 186

(a) Air links 187
(b) Chauffeuring service 204

Section 1.15 Local transport 207

(a) Public transport 208
(b) Taxis 214

Section 1.16 Concluding Remarks 220

CHAPTER 4. Building Capacity to Cope 223

Section 1.17 Central Actors 227

(a) City/Departmental Administration 227
(b) Other actors 230
(c) Cooperation between actors 233

Section 1.18 Creating a European infrastructure: 1949-1964 234

(a) Constructions 235
(b) Accommodation 244

Section 1.19 The Palais de l'Europe 249

(a) Planning 251
(b) Affirming Strasbourg's European mission 257
(c) Construction phase 258
(d) Summary 259

Section 1.20 The Immeuble Parlementaire Européenne (IPE) 260

(a) Planning the IPE 261
(b) Planning the construction 264
(c) Construction phase 265

Section 1.21 Concluding Remarks 267

Conclusion 269

Section 1.22 Mapping the local group of actors 270
Section 1.23 Strategies to consolidate the seat status 274

(a) Keeping it local 276
(b) Conditioning elements 278
(c) The competitive factor 280
(d) Promoting Strasbourg 282

Section 1.24 Perspectives 283

References 285

Section 1.25 Unpublished Sources 285

(a) ABR – Archives Départementales du Bas-Rhin, Strasbourg, France 285
(b) AC – Archive of the Council of the European Union, Brussels, Belgium 286
(c) ACE – Archive of the Council of Europe, Strasbourg, France 287
(d) AS – Archives de la Ville de Strasbourg et de la Communauté Urbaine, France 288
(e) CARDOC – Archive of the European Parliament, Luxembourg 296

Section 1.26 Published Sources 297
Section 1.27 Literature 298
Section 1.28 Web sites and online sources 303

Article XI. Appendixes 311

Section 2.01 Appendix I: Most active multipositioned actors 311
Section 2.02 Appendix II: Examples of Hosting Programme costs .. 321

The first EP session 19.-21.3.1958 322
PACE and EP session 19.-29.9.1961 323

Index 327

List of Illustrations and Tables

1. The inner circle of actors 100
2. Structure of the Comité Strasbourgeois pour le Mouvement Européen 107
3. Structure of the Cercle des Amitiés Européennes 119
4. Structure of the Cercle Européen de Strasbourg 125
5. Post-mark "Strasbourg, Siège du Conseil de l'Europe" (1957) 145
6. "Do not leave me"-post card (1964) 170

Abbreviations

CAE	Cercle des Amitiés Européennes
CCI	Chambre de Commerce et d'Industrie de Strasbourg et du Bas-Rhin
CES	Cercle européen de Strasbourg
CoE	Council of Europe
COREPER	Committee of permanent representatives
CSME	Comité Strasbourgeois pour le Mouvement Européen
CTS	Compagnie des Tramways/Transports Strasbourgeois
CUS	Communauté Urbaine de Strasbourg
DATAR	Délégation interministérielle à l'aménagement et à l'attractivité régionale
DNA	Dernières Nouvelles d'Alsace
EC	European Community
ECSC	European Coal and Steel Community
EEC	European Economic Community
EP	European Parliament
EU	European Union
EURATOM	European Atomic Energy Community
FIAT	Fonds d'intervention pour l'aménagement du territoire
IGC	Intergovernmental Conference
INSEE	Institut national de la statistique et des études économiques
IO	International Organisation
MEP	Member of the European Parliament
MP	Member of Parliament
OEEC	Organisation for European Economic Co-operation
PACE	Parliamentary Assembly of the Council of Europe
UN	United Nations

UNESCO	United Nations Educational, Scientific and Cultural Organisation
WEU	Western European Union

Key to Archives

ABR	Archives Départementales du Bas-Rhin, Strasbourg, France
AC	Archive of the Council of the European Union, Brussels, Belgium
ACE	Archive of the Council of Europe, Strasbourg, France
AS	Archives de la Ville et la Communauté Urbaine de Strasbourg, France
CARDOC	Archive of the European Parliament, Luxembourg, Luxembourg

Preface

This book is based on my PhD-dissertation *Operation Welcome. The Municipal Politics of Consolidating Strasbourg's Position as European Institution Host from 1949 to 1979* which is the product of my doctoral studies from 2010 to 2014 at Aarhus University, Denmark. It is an independent study within the research project *Institutions of democracy in transition. Transnational fields in politics, administration and law in Denmark and Western Europe after 1945* conducted by Associate Professor Ann-Christina Lauring Knudsen which ran from 2010 to 2013. The thesis investigates which local agents in the city of Strasbourg attempted to consolidate the city's position as European institution host, as well as which measures and strategies they employed to achieve this aim.

The intergovernmental decision process of determining the host, or seat city, of the institutions of the European Communities is well known. The institutions of the Schuman Plan were provisionally located in Luxembourg and Strasbourg, while Brussels from 1958 started to house the new organisations following the Treaties of Rome the year before. My initial point of entry into the issue were the questions, whether actors on other levels than the intergovernmental one were involved and what occurred in the time spans between decisions of the foreign ministers of the European Communities. In a survey of available literature, it seemed as if Pierre Pflimlin, long-term mayor of the city from 1959 to 1983, was nearly singularly responsible for Strasbourg staying European institution seat.[1]

For a first brief research stay in the local archive in Strasbourg, I was interested in confirming or disproving my hypothesis that Pflimlin was the most important local actor in relation to consolidating the city's position as institution seat. After the perusal of this brief search, it appeared that there seemed to have been a myth-building present in literature, because the mayor by no means was the only highly active actor. After a longer, more thorough research stay in the local archive, I can conclude that Pflimlin

1 E.g. Clark, Stephen and Priestley, Julian, Europe's *Parliament. People, Places, Politics*, London, John Harper, 2012, p. 47 or Hein, Carola, *The Capital of Europe. Architecture and Urban Planning for the European Union*, Westport, Praeger, 2004, p. 100 or De Groof, Roel, "Promoting Brussels as Political World Capital. From the National Jubilee of 1905 to Expo 58", in De Groof, Roel (ed.), *Brussels and Europe – Bruxelles et l'Europe*, Brussels, ASP, 2008, p. 119.

was important for Strasbourg, but also on a more abstract level. As my research shows, a small number of highly active and well-connected city administration politicians and civil servants, supported by various local associations were instrumental to Strasbourg's consolidation efforts. While Pflimlin was not always as actively involved in day-to-day business, he was an important coordinating instance. Taking his importance to a more abstract level, his presence, political network and activity in lobbying for Strasbourg in national and European political circles was an essential element of consolidation efforts. However, in contrast to how available literature portrays him, he was by no means the only, most important actor. Those others can only be found if one looks within the city itself.

Therefore, due to the lack of previous studies concerned with local efforts of consolidating the host status of European institutions, my study is almost exclusively based on primary sources. I collected them from the Archive of the European Parliament in Luxembourg, the Archive of the Council of the European Union (EU) in Brussels, the Municipal Archive of Strasbourg, the Archive of the Council of Europe in Strasbourg and the Archive of the Département du Bas-Rhin in the same city. I predominantly use documents from the local archive, supported by those from the departmental archive of Bas-Rhin. The fact that most sources are in the municipal archive demonstrates that most activity occurred on the local level. The institution archives commonly contain information corroborating the 'accepted narrative' of intergovernmental efforts to determine seats of European organisations without including a local dimension, although the archive of the Council of Europe also contains some sources on collaboration with actors in Strasbourg.

The placement of European institutions not only touches political issues as debates between nation states of which country should host the Community institutions, but also whether their placement makes the location a European capital in the sense that it executed the same functions as a national capital. These different forms of scholarship are all intertwined to varying degrees, although they are rarely covered comprehensively, but rather according to topic areas. Additionally, a double blind angle is present in these kinds of literature. Many focus on the present and do not provide much historical analysis; historical studies commonly do not cover the local level, especially in the case of Strasbourg.

One major issue that is not present in this collection of relevant literature from various fields that each discuss aspects of the seat question, is the comprehensive and encompassing study of local actors in an institution host city, their composition and their strategies to consolidate their position. Some works mention local actors in (prospective) seat cities such as Strasbourg and their initiatives, but the brief description of interaction generally remains on the intergovernmental and supranational levels by presenting either the member states or the European Communities as focal actors.[2] Additionally, literature exists on Brussels or Luxembourg, but these only occupy themselves with one issue at a time, such as only political activity or infrastructure as will be presented below. Another gap is concrete consolidation efforts. In European integration histories, a concentration on the initial (provisional) sitings and subsequent decisions to finalise them, is apparent. This book aims to fill these lacunae with a case study of all ranges of local actors' activities in the city of Strasbourg.

It draws on a mix of aspects from several disciplines that form the context of Strasbourg's local actors and their strategies. Even though only the case of the Alsatian city is analysed, it was not isolated and influenced by the outside, such as the competitive situation with the other seats of the European Communities. This research fills the lacuna in European integration literature, which focuses nearly exclusively on the intergovernmental decision processes of determining the seat, with a comprehensive case study of local activity in one seat city of European institutions. In addition, it also combines the institutions of the European Communities with the Council of Europe[3] that remain separate in European integration literature that generally concentrates on the former.

2 E.g. Hein, Carola, *The Capital of Europe. Architecture and Urban Planning for the European Union*, Westport, Praeger, 2004, p. 100.

3 As will be shown in this study (especially in chapter 2), local actors in Strasbourg concentrated until the late 1950s nearly exclusively on the Council of Europe which had its permanent seat in the city since 1949.

Introduction

With the increasing creation of international organisations (IOs) following the Second World War, the issue where and how to site them emerged as a new political theme, as well. Central concerns included the political and juridical status of their headquarter buildings and the areals they were constructed on. Next to the practical application with newly founded IOs, theoretical considerations were made, such as reflections on the status and the administration of its territory.[1] In most cases, negotiations on these aspects occurred between the organisation or representatives of its member states with the government of the prospective host country. They did not seem to have resulted in protracted discussions.

One example constitutes the regional organisation Council of Europe (CoE), founded in 1949, whose siting in the city of Strasbourg, France, proceeded in that manner. In material issued by the organisation, such as the various editions of the procedure and practice of the Parliamentary Assembly of the Council of Europe (PACE),[2] a description of its founding process is included. From the matter-of-fact statement that its seat is in Strasbourg without any specification of the decision process,[3] it becomes apparent that it must have been a relatively undisputed decision.

In contrast, the political question where to site institutions of the different European Communities has been a highly symbolic and contested matter with recurring discussions and attempts for a permanent solution. The treaty of the European Coal and Steel Community (ECSC) specified that a seat should be found in common accord by the member states.[4] From the Schuman declaration in 1950 until the Edinburgh European Council

---

1 E.g. Jenks, Clarence, *The headquarters of international institutions: a study of their location and status*, London, The Royal Institute of International Affairs, 1945, pp. 53; 44.

2 Only the acronym of the present name, PACE, will be employed in this book. In 1974, the designation changed from Consultative to Parliamentary Assembly (cf. "Secretariat memorandum on the name of the Assembly of the Council of Europe (Strasbourg, 26 February 1975)." Centre Virtuel de la Connaissance sur l'Europe. <http://www.cvce.eu/content/publication/2005/4/19/f98114c5-8da8-4d43-b7be-daa5b96b3ed2/publishable_en.pdf> (accessed 29.08.2013)).

3 Council of Europe, *The Consultative Assembly, Procedure and Practice*, Strasbourg, 1965, p. 22.

4 "Treaty establishing the European Coal and Steel Community (Paris, 18 April 1951)." Centre Virtuel de la Connaissance sur l'Europe. <http://www.cvce.eu/content/

in 1992 and the Treaty of Amsterdam in 1997 in which the long-standing provisional distribution of institutions between Brussels, Luxembourg and Strasbourg was inscribed into the treaty basis, the question where to site permanently the European Communities was a protracted process with many debates.[5] The seat question is relevant today, since discussions still occur despite the protocol in the treaty and the preceding decision at the Edinburgh Council in 1992. For example, the campaign for a single seat of the European Parliament (EP) was founded in 2010 with the participation of Members of the European Parliament (MEPs) and other politicians, for example its chair British MEP and Vice-president of the EP Edward McMillan-Scott.[6] The main arguments are different types of expenses that could be avoided in regard to the EP.[7] This issue will be returned to below.

For the endeavour of studying these phenomena, the French city of Strasbourg[8] constitutes an eminently suitable example of dynamics of local initiatives to retain the status as seat of European institutions. It has been the permanent seat of the CoE since 1949 and has hosted the EP and its predecessor assemblies from 1952 onwards. It has become synonymous with the EP and PACE; the designation 'assembly of Strasbourg' is a common moniker for both.[9] It is also home to further European institutions, both affiliated to the CoE and independent. These include, among others, the European Human Rights Court, the Assembly of European Regions or the European Science Foundation.[10] During the 1950s, other European and international organisations met in the city, as

publication/1997/10/13/11a21305-941e-49d7-a171-ed5be548cd58/publishable_en.pdf> (accessed 24.04.2014), p. 34.

5 "Annex 6 to Part A, Decision taken by common agreement between the Representatives of the Governments of the member states on the location of the seat of the institutions and of certain bodies and departments of the European Communities, Edinburgh European Council 11 - 12 December 1992." European Parliament. <http://www.europarl.europa.eu/summits/edinburgh/a6_en.pdf> (accessed 27.6.2014), p. 51 and "Treaty of Amsterdam, Protocol on the location of the seats of the institutions and of certain bodies and departments of the European Communities and of Europol." <http://old.eur-lex.europa.eu/en/treaties/dat/11997D/htm/11997D.html> (accessed 25.06.2014).

6 "Who we are." Single Seat Campaign <http://singleseat.eu/9.html> (accessed 26.06.2014).

7 "The price of a multi-seat European Parliament." Single Seat Campaign. <http://singleseat.eu/10.html> (accessed 26.06.2014).

8 The city is located on the river Rhine in the East of France, in the Département du Bas-Rhin and in the region Alsace.

9 E.g. Houdard, Geneviève, "Strasbourg: la vocation européenne", in *Moniteur du Commerce International*, 607, 1984, p. 37.

10 Muller, François, *The European Quarter, Strasbourg*, Regensburg, Schnell & Steiner, 2010, p. 30.

well. For instance, the European Parliamentary Union[11] in the early or the Assembly of Captive European Nations[12] in the latter half of the decade held several meetings in the city.[13]

The objective of this book is to investigate two central aspects of local activity regarding Strasbourg as European institution host. Firstly, the different local agents who were concerned with the European institutions in Strasbourg will be identified, as well as the nature of their involvement. Secondly, their activities will be discussed, namely what their strategies to consolidate Strasbourg's position as seat were and how they employed them. The focus will be on the two organisations that were most important to local actors; the European Communities, as well as the Council of Europe.

This study is based on an extensive analysis of documents from the city administration and other organisations from the municipal archive of Strasbourg, supported by material from the departmental archive of Bas-Rhin. Through this investigation, three important themes have been identified, which are measures to host European parliamentarians during sessions, optimisation of the transport network and building infrastructure. The actors and their strategies that fall into each of these three areas will be discussed in a chapter that will highlight how the city of Strasbourg sought to consolidate its position as host of European institutions.

The analysis commences with the siting of the first European institution, the Council of Europe, in 1949, which was joined by the Common Assembly of the ECSC in 1952. The processes of locating these two institutions in Strasbourg are not the focus of this study. They will be outlined briefly in chapter 1 to provide the context for the efforts of local

11 Richard Coudenhove-Kalergi, the founder of the Pan-European Union (1923), formed this assembly in 1947. It was composed of supporters of European federalism from parliaments of various countries, but especially the Netherlands, Belgium, France and Italy (cf. "The post-war European idea and the first European Movements (1945-1949) – Introduction", Centre Virtuel de la Connaissance sur l'Europe, <http://www.cvce.eu/obj/the_post_war_european_idea_and_the_first_european_movements_1945_1949_introduction-en-987cf261-b707-4ca1-8de7-d61ab4f445a5.html> (accessed 03.02.2015)).

12 The assembly was headquartered in New York, was active from 1954-1972 and its members were former government and cultural leaders of Albania, Bulgaria, Czechoslovakia, Estonia, Hungary, Latvia, Lithuania, Poland and Romania. Its goals were to educate about the situation behind the Iron Curtain, peaceful liberation from the Soviet Union and integration into a united Europe. From 1956, annual special sessions were held in Strasbourg (cf. "Assembly of Captive European Nations, Records, 1953-1972" Immigration History Research Center University of Minnesota. <http://www.ihrc.umn.edu/research/vitrage/all/am/GENassembly.htm> (accessed 13.02.2015)).

13 Archives de Strasbourg (AS), 235 MW 267, *Extrait du Nouvel Alsacien 2.7.1951*; Archives du Département du Bas-Rhin (ABR), 544 D 208, *2e session spéciale 12.-15.4.1956.*

agents to consolidate their position. The activities of local agents to remain institution host was of a different nature than efforts to attract them. Apart from differing policies, the dimension of relations between the local and supranational levels would be much deeper had European organisations already been sited in a city. This connection could be employed strategically to consolidate the seat position by concentrating on a well-functioning relationship. Most academic literature focuses on the process of locating European institutions, or in the case of the European Community (EC) to re-decide or confirm the sitings, and not on concrete efforts to consolidate a (provisional) seat's position.

The ending date of 1979 for this study has been chosen because of two main reasons. Firstly, local archive material shows that directly after this year, activity of local agents towards the European institutions began to decline, a stronger activity only redeveloped towards the end of the 1980s. Secondly, most local agents who had been involved from the beginning or the early stages during the 1950s, retired from politics in the course of the 1970s, completing a generation change. Mayor Pierre Pflimlin, in office from 1959 to 1983, was the last of this type of agents to leave. Nevertheless, when ongoing processes continued into the early 1980s, these will be included or an overview of further events will be given. This was especially the case with the construction of buildings for the EP after the first direct election that commonly ran from circa 1977 to 1981 and 1982. However, aspects following the tenure of Pflimlin as mayor will not be included in the analysis, since a wholly new set of actors began to operate the city's consolidation efforts.

In European integration literature, the ECSC is already recognised as important in other seat cities such as Luxembourg, but the combination of its study with the CoE allows for a new perspective. Furthermore, this research constitutes a new contribution, as it is looking at the siting of the institutions but at the efforts to consolidate these placements. By doing this, a historical depth is added to the ongoing debate of the seat question which is another important addition. Especially in the early 1950s, local actors seemed to have concentrated on the CoE, as city administration documents suggest. Additionally, the CoE shared its facilities and especially the plenary hall with the assembly of the European Communities.[14]

[14] Soldwisch, Ines, "Die Gebäude des Europäischen Parlaments in Straßburg, Luxemburg und Brüssel als Orte der Kommunikation und Repräsentation 1979-2004", in Schulz, Andreas and Wirsching, Andreas (eds.), *Parlamentarische Kulturen in Europa. Das Parlament als Kommunikationsraum*, Düsseldorf, Droste Verlag, 2012, p. 426.

Section 1.01 Siting European institutions

The standard narrative in European integration history is that determining and consolidating the seats of the various Community institutions was either shaped by intergovernmental or national actors.[15] Furthermore, scholarship on single institutions generally briefly covers political events regarding the siting of the particular organisation.[16] Hardly any scientific attention has been paid to the aspect of local involvement in the processes of siting European Community institutions.[17] Although the decision power to site the European institutions lay on the intergovernmental level, this must have been conditioned by other political activities. It is likely that the local level figured in a capacity, as well.

Although existing scholarship on political agency in the seat question hardly discusses local Strasbourgese involvement, if certain aspects are incorporated, they generally focus on Pierre Pflimlin, mayor of Strasbourg from 1959-1983, and long-term advocate of the city as European institution seat. They portray him as the only or most important local actor responsible for Strasbourg's status as institution host. Pierre Pflimlin was a prolific political figure in French and European politics, but also an important local politician in Strasbourg.[18] Among others, he was mayor

---

15 E.g. Dinan, Desmond, *Europe Recast*, Basingstoke, Palgrave, 2004. It contains one paragraph on the political solution and difficulties to provisory site the institutions of the Schuman Plan in 1952, while the rest of the book concentrates on the formation of the administrative structures, their functioning, their members and their political issues (pp. 54-55). Other examples include Dinan, Desmond, *Ever Closer Union. An Introduction to European Integration*, Basingstoke, Palgrave, 2010 or Croisé-Schirtz, Edmée, "La bataille des sièges (1950-1958)", in Trausch, Gilbert *et al.* (eds.), *Le Luxembourg face à la construction européenne – Luxemburg und die europäische Einigung*, Luxembourg, Centre d'Etudes et de Recherches Européennes Robert Schuman, 1996, pp. 67-104. In addition to such publications, several Master theses dealing with the seat question of the European Communities exist, as well. They commonly cover this general narrative of siting the institutions, but also some local political efforts (e.g. Reymund, Phillipe, *La Question du siège de l'Assemblée des Communautés Européennes*. Master thesis, Université des Sciences Juridiques, Politiques, Sociales et de Technologie de Strasbourg, Institut Hautes Etudes Européennes, 1981 or Van Lierde, Claire, *La querelle des sièges des institutions des Communautés Européennes*, Mémoire présenté en vue de l'obtention du grade de licenciée en Affaires Publiques et Internationales, Université Catholique de Louvain, 1993).

16 E.g. Olivier Costa's publication on the European Parliament includes a chapter on its seat, where mostly the political decisions are analysed, although a hint to infrastructural difficulties of Strasbourg was given (Costa, Olivier, *Le Parlement Européen, assemblée délibérante*, Brussels, Ed. de l'Université de Bruxelles, 2001, pp. 228-250).

17 E.g. Clark, Stephen and Priestley, Julian, *Europe's Parliament. People, Places, Politics*, London, John Harper, 2012, pp. 43-72.

18 Cf. Appendix I for more information on the political posts Pflimlin held in the city of Strasbourg, the *Département du Bas-Rhin* and the French state.

of Strasbourg from 1959 to 1983.[19] His importance and political influence in connection with consolidating Strasbourg's position as seat is one of the few instances of local agency in Strasbourg that scholarship and biographies consistently acknowledge. These descriptions and analyses could be characterised as facilitating a myth of Pierre Pflimlin.

In one example, the analysis of the French stance during the first ECSC seat application round in 1952 includes the following, "Schuman was opposed to Paris, because it would have outraged Strasbourg and its mayor, Pflimlin."[20] Apart from the fact that local actors were reduced to the head of administration, this statement bore another common characteristic of how Pflimlin's involvement was centralised in a way that a myth about his agency seems to have been created. Pflimlin only became mayor in March 1959, at the time of the initial attempt to site the institutions of the Schuman Plan; he was president of the departmental assembly, the *Conseil Général du Bas-Rhin*.[21] Local archive sources from 1952 show that he strongly participated in local efforts during this period, but was not an executive member of the municipality. He did not participate as municipality actor during the entire debate how to facilitate the candidature for the single seat as the quote suggests. In contrast, the material from Strasbourg's municipal archive displays a more nuanced situation. While Pflimlin was the representative of the city after he became mayor and chiefly communicated with actors outside of Strasbourg on its behalf, a host of actors was highly active behind the scenes. Since Pflimlin appeared to be the most visible one due to his position, his political activity towards consolidating Strasbourg's seat position was likely reproduced in literature and mythicised.

In a similar manner to European integration history regarding the issue where to locate community institutions, scholarship on the CoE's development does not devote much space if any to the question where to site it.[22] As with European integration literature regarding the European Communities, such accounts tend to focus on policy issues, political

---

19 "Pierre Pflimlin en quelques dates." Strasbourg, l'Européenne. Centre d'information sur les Institutions Européennes. <http://www.strasbourg-europe.eu/pierre-pflimlin,14544,fr.html> (accessed 20.03.2013).

20 De Groof, Roel, "Promoting Brussels as Political World Capital. From the National Jubilee of 1905 to Expo 58", in De Groof, Roel (ed.), *Brussels and Europe – Bruxelles et l'Europe*, Brussels, ASP, 2008, p. 119.

21 Pflimlin, Pierre; Pflimlin, Édouard; Monmarché, Carole, *Pierre Pflimlin: Les choix d'une vie*, Strasbourg, Editions du Signe, 2001, pp. 162; 164.

22 For instance, Klaus Brummer does not mention the placement of the CoE at all, while Birte Wassenberg dedicates one of circa 600 pages on the history of the CoE to a brief description of Strasbourg as seat city (Brummer, Klaus, *Der Europarat. Eine Einführung*,

developments and administrative structures. The concrete activity of physically locating its headquarters is only briefly covered and then only regarding the intergovernmental level, while omitting public or private actors on other political levels. This book aims to fill this lacuna by presenting a comprehensive case study of the various local actors in Strasbourg and their modes of activities.

Especially the municipal government of a (temporary) IO host city must have a vested interest in keeping them in the city, because it would benefit the city economically, among others. Additionally, the practical organisation of the functioning of international institutions must have been at least partly organised locally. Such questions of relations between supranational and local levels, interactions between international organisations and their host cities, have not been covered in European integration history literature either. These aspects form part of this book, since they all were related to local activities to consolidate the position as host for IOs.

How prospective seat cities dealt with or campaigned for European institutions has never been studied for the city of Strasbourg. For its closest competition, Brussels and Luxembourg, some studies exist, which treat parts of the issue.[23] In addition to political decisions and urban planning, the issue of welcoming European parliamentarians and civil servants in seat cities played a role in hosting international organisations. However, hardly any scholarship exists on it in connection to the European institutions. It is possible to transfer aspects from international congresses or organisations, since the necessary organisational steps remain the

---

Wiesbaden, Verlag für Sozialwissenschaften, 2008 and Wassenberg, Birte, *Histoire du Conseil de l'Europe (1949-2009)*, Brussels, Peter Lang, 2012, pp. 57-58).

23 For instance, the edited volume *Luxemburg und die europäische Einigung* (Trausch, Gilbert *et al.* (eds.), *Le Luxembourg face à la construction européenne – Luxemburg und die europäische Einigung*, Luxembourg, Centre d'Etudes et de Recherches Européennes Robert Schuman, 1996) contains an article by Edmée Croisé-Schirtz dealing with the political efforts of actors to become seat of ECSC institutions from 1950 to 1958, although it mostly concentrates on the national level. Based on archival research, it presents a rendition of Luxembourg's political efforts to locate the institutions of the ECSC and to consolidate its provisional position (Croisé-Schirtz, Edmée, "La bataille des sièges (1950-1958)", in Trausch, Gilbert *et al.* (eds.), *Le Luxembourg face à la construction européenne – Luxemburg und die europäische Einigung*, Luxembourg, Centre d'Etudes et de Recherches Européennes Robert Schuman, 1996, pp. 67-104). Other scholarship contains a variation from the common narrative of intergovernmental decision processes without concisely or comprehensively focusing on one country or even candidate city. Generally, it concentrates on Brussels and especially urban planning for European institutions in the Belgian capital.

same.[24] It bears similarities to corresponding efforts of Strasbourg's local actors to welcome the CoE and EP in municipal governments. This could help to identify possible patterns of dealing with the presence of European institutions that might be transferable to similar cases.

While this study focuses on the city of Strasbourg, it is important to note that the aspect of competition with other prospective and provisional seat cities of the European Communities constituted a strong influencing factor for the environment in which the city's local agents organised strategies to consolidate Strasbourg's position as European institution host. Over time, the other two host cities of European institutions, Brussels and Luxembourg, presented the biggest threat. During the 1950s, when the seat question was much more open with ten official applicants, other cities, such as the national capital Paris also constituted close rivals.

However, this book is a case study concentrating on the actors within city of Strasbourg and their strategies to consolidate Strasbourg's position without a comparative element. This methodological choice has been made in order to investigate succinctly all aspects of local agency to cover all facets of the involvement. The archive material from the municipal archive of Strasbourg shows a rich collection of documents which did not only touch political manoeuvring, but also elements of infrastructure and city development. In a comparative study, it would have been more feasible to evaluate a selection of these aspects across several seat cities. Only parts of local involvement, predominantly in Brussels, such as impact of European institution on city development have been the subject of scientific studies. Studies of the entirety of a seat's involvement should be produced before comparing cases. Nevertheless, the competitive aspect will remain an issue and appear recurrently throughout the empirical chapters.

In this connection, that this study is based on sources from the municipal archive of Strasbourg contains certain issues that have to be kept in mind. Firstly, this focus includes the limitation that the efforts and successes of local actors might be overstated. Secondly, it cannot be excluded that decisions about Strasbourg's status were taken outside the city and that documentation about them had not been sent to the city administration. However, the nature of local agency in Strasbourg regarding European institutions is underexplored in academic literature.

---

24 For example, an archival study on hosting efforts of local actors in The Hague for the Congress of Europe in 1948 presents the actors and necessary efforts in order to receive the attendants and make their stay pleasant (Beers, Marloes, "Hosting Europe. Local Organisation of the Congress of Europe", in Guieu, Jean-Michel and Le Dréau, Christophe (eds.), *Le "Congrès de l'Europe" à La Haye (1948-2009)*, The Hague, Brussels, Peter Lang, 2009, pp. 137-149).

Therefore, it is important to map this activity comprehensively before cooperation with, for example, the French state is investigated.

Additionally, the sources in the municipal archive allow for the conclusion that most activity regarding the themes of hosting transport and building infrastructure occurred in the city. Material shows no obvious gaps and a low number of forwarded documents on Strasbourg's position from the French state show that the bulk of decisions were made by local actors. This is corroborated by the fact that the *Département du Bas-Rhin*, the local representative of the state, only played a supporting role to the municipality, as archive sources suggest. Nevertheless, it has to be kept in mind that the concentration on local sources in this study might contain the above limitations.

Section 1.02 Siting institutions – not only a political issue

The issue of housing European institutions also impinges on other areas, such as city development. In European integration literature, the focus lies on political decisions and processes, but providing adequate facilities constitutes an important prerequisite to be able to house an international organisation and has economic impacts, as well. In general, this issue is located between two disciplines, because urban planning and architectural literature focussing on the construction aspect only marginally deals with political processes which conditioned this activity.

Looking at these two academic disciplines, it becomes apparent that scholarship about the placement of European Institutions not only touches debates between nation states of who should host the Community Institutions, but also whether their placement would constitute the specific city as a European capital, or how such a capital city of Europe should look like. The bulk of scholarship in this field has been produced by Carola Hein. She predominantly focuses on urban planning and architectural issues and implications in connection with determining the host of European institutions.[25] Commonly, this kind of urban studies literature focuses

25 Cf. e.g. Hein, Carola, "Choosing a site for the capital of Europe", in *Geo Journal*, 51:1-2, 2000, pp. 83-97 and Hein, Carola, "Bruxelles et les villes sièges de l'Union Européenne", in Plissart, Marie-Françoise (ed.), *Change. Brussels Capital of Europe*, Brussels, Prisme Editions, 2004, pp. 118-122 and Hein, Carola, "Hoofdstad Europa: over de vestigingsproblematiek van de Europese Unie/A Capital for Europe: Where to House the European Union", in *Archis*, 11, 1995, pp. 62-73 and Hein, Carola, "Hauptstadt Europa," PhD Fachbereich Architektur der Hochschule für bildende Künste Hamburg, 1995 and Hein, Carola, *The Capital of Europe, Architecture and Urban Planning for the European Union*, Westport, CT, Praeger, 2004, and Hein, Carola, "The polycentric and opportunistic capital of Europe, A new model for the siting and reallocation of EU headquarters and the design of European districts in Brussels and other host cities,"

on Brussels its development regarding the European and international organisations. Central topics are, for example, the development of *Quartier* Léopold, the area where most headquarters, such as the Commission, are located in that city.[26]

Next to evaluating the effects the presence of European institutions has on town planning in Brussels, various studies analyse economic impacts of them by using contemporary data without adding a comprehensive historical dimension.[27] Aspects, such as how civil servants of the European institutions influence the housing and rental market, exist, as well.[28] In the case of Strasbourg, especially financial gains and the impact of the European institution's presence of economic development only began to be analysed in the late 1980s in the form of studies by civil servants or economic associations.[29]

Apart from the literature focussing on the impact of European institutions, general literature on urbanism in Strasbourg aids to situate construction activities for the CoE and EP which are described in municipal archive sources in the context. For example, the edited volume *Strasbourg, chroniques d'urbanisme* provides analyses of town planning

---

Brussels Studies, 2 (2006), pp. 1-8, as well as the two books she edited, Hein, Carola (ed.), *Bruxelles l'Européenne, Capitale de qui? Ville de qui?* Brussels, La Lettre Volée, 2006, and Hein, Carola, and Pierre Laconte (eds.), *Brussels, Perspectives on a European Capital*, Brussels, Editions Aliter, 2007.

26 Kuhk, Annette, "Facilitating the Integration if Discourses about the European Quarter: How Can Inclusive Policies for Complex Urban Issues be More Professional?", in Hein, Carola (ed.), *Bruxelles, l'Européenne. Capitale de qui? Ville de qui?* Brussels, La Lettre Volée, 2006, pp. 155-171, or Papadopoulos, Alex, *Urban Regimes and Strategies; Building Europe's Central Business District in Brussels, The University of Chicago Geography Research Paper No. 239*, Chicago, University of Chicago Press, 1996.

27 Degadt, Jan, "The Impact of the Presence of European and International Institutions on the Regional Economic Fabric in Brussels", in De Groof, Roel (ed.), *Brussels and Europe – Bruxelles et l'Europe*, Brussels, ASP, 2008, pp. 219-234 or Vandermotten, Christian and Biot, Valérie and Van Hamme, Gilles, "L'économie et la socio-démographie de la Région de Bruxelles-Capitale et la présence européenne et internationale", in De Groof, Roel (ed.), *Brussels and Europe – Bruxelles et l'Europe*, Brussels, ASP, 2008, pp. 255-268.

28 Bernard, Nicolas, "L'impact de l'Union européenne sur les prix de l'immobilier à Bruxelles et la configuration spatiale de la ville", in De Groof, Roel (ed.), *Brussels and Europe – Bruxelles et l'Europe*, Brussels, ASP, 2008, pp. 269-281.

29 Villain, Claude. "Rapport sur le renforcement durable du rôle européen de Strasbourg, 31.3.1989", *Ministère des Affaires Européennes*, or Groupement EDR, City Consult, and Médiascope. "Impact économique de la présence des Institutions européennes à Strasbourg." Alsaeco – le portal de l'économie alsacienne. <http://www.alsaeco.com/etudes/impact-economique-de-la-presence-des-institutions-europeennes-a-strasbourg,36941850.html> (accessed 06.02.2014).

activity and the local organisations and associations concerned with it.[30] Since some of these were involved in the construction of buildings for the European institutions in Strasbourg, this kind of scholarship forms a contribution to the analysis.

Specific publications on building infrastructure in Strasbourg, or even Luxembourg, is mostly included in studies of all three provisional EC seat cities, although literature on Brussels by itself is still the most prevalent. In the field of urban planning and architecture, Hein analyses the three provisional seat cities Brussels, Luxembourg and Strasbourg as a polycentric capital structure, although the decision where to site them remained a political one, which is also stressed by her.[31] In the early stages, the two ECSC seat application rounds of the 1950s presented such a conditioning political activity. For instance, during the initial attempt to site the institutions of the Schuman Plan in 1952, Hein analyses that urban planning processes were influenced by the political indecision regarding the seat.[32] Similarly, in 1958, when the European Communities had instituted a committee of urbanism experts to evaluate a new batch of seat city candidates on common criteria, they virtually had no impact on political discussions.[33] That allows for the probability that in kind, European integration literature did not focus on urban development regarding the institutions of the EC.

Additionally, discussions how and in which form institution buildings should be integrated in the host city, was prevalent within the European Communities, especially in the early 1960s. Most scholarship deals with districts of international organisations, of which Hein also presents a comprehensive picture in her works. This constitutes an important aspect for siting European institutions from an architectural perspective, because its buildings are symbols for its values, which has to be included in the planning process.[34] Regarding the institutions of the European communities, Hein analyses this as difficult due to their provisional presence in their seat cities.[35]

---

30 Cullier, Francis (ed.), *Strasbourg. Chroniques d'urbanisme*, La Tour d'Aigues, éditions de l'aube, 1994.

31 Hein, Carola, *The Capital of Europe. Architecture and Urban Planning for the European Union*, Westport, Praeger, 2004, p. 67.

32 Hein, Carola, "Hauptstadt Europa", Arbeit zur Erlangung des Grades Doktor-Ingenieur am Fachbereich Architektur der Hochschule für bildende Künste Hamburg, 1995, p. 58.

33 *Ibid.*, p. 157.

34 Hein, Carola, *The Capital of Europe. Architecture and Urban Planning for the European Union*, Westport, Praeger, 2004, pp. 1; 37.

35 *Ibid.*, p. 9.

Especially organisations' headquarter buildings as symbols or physical representatives of their aims are prominent. Such aspects are studied by political architecture, which also concerns European institutions, such as the European Parliament.[36] Another text on its buildings in Brussels, Luxembourg and Strasbourg adds that in the case of the assembly to express this was difficult, since the provisional nature of its siting had repercussions on its buildings. Due to the fact that it had no final placement and moved between the three cities, it could not create a local identity.[37] Additionally, the dynamics regarding building construction between the three seats was covered as well, which towards the end of the 1970s had an impact on Strasbourg's actors' strategies to consolidate their position.[38]

One also might consider the concept of Europeanisation as relevant for this study. It largely focused on politics between European, national and local institutions and the impact of European aspects on those. However, it contains a concept of a general transformation of processes by such a dimension that is not relevant in this context. Furthermore, it is vague. Different definitions of this notion, its occurrences, what it influences, exist in the scholarship and is conditioned by how the concept and how the processes occur.[39] Moreover, most literature about the impact of Europeanisation on administrations focuses on how changes were implemented by ordinary structures of government.[40] However, as will be shown in this book, a separated 'bubble' of actors formed itself within the city administration that was not integrated in the day-to-day running of the municipality. Therefore, the concept of Europeanisation and its impact on various government structures will not be considered here.

---

36 E.g. Biesenbender, Jan and Grösch, Julia, "European Identity trough Architecture? Examining the European Parliament Buildings in Brussels and Strasbourg", in Hein, Carola (ed.), *Bruxelles l'Européenne. Capitale de qui? Ville de qui?*, Brussels, La Lettre Volée, 2006, pp. 112-129.

37 Soldwisch, Ines, "Die Gebäude des Europäischen Parlaments in Straßburg, Luxemburg und Brüssel als Orte der Kommunikation und Repräsentation 1979-2004", in Schulz, Andreas and Wirsching, Andreas (eds.), *Parlamentarische Kulturen in Europa. Das Parlament als Kommunikationsraum*, Düsseldorf, Droste Verlag, 2012, p. 423.

38 *Ibid.*, pp. 435-437.

39 Cf. e.g. Featherstone, Kevin and Radaelli, Claudio M. (eds.), *The Politics of Europeanization*, Oxford, Oxford University Press, 2003.

40 Dussauge Laguna, Mauricio I., "El proceso de integración europea y sus efectos en las administraciones públicas nacionales: ¿hacia la convergencia administrativa?", in *Foro Internacional*, 45.1 (2005): 293-314.

Section 1.03 Currency of the seat question

Although the location of EU institutions has been formally decided in the 1990s, it is still debated by various actors. Additionally, seat cities capitalise on their statuses. As argued in this book, the various local actors in (prospective) seat cities played an important role with both directly openly and secretly, as well as indirectly influencing the decision holders. An example is Roland Ries, the present mayor of Strasbourg, writing to the newly designated Secretary of State for European Affairs of France Harlem Désir in April 2014 which was published on the web page of the regional newspaper *Dernières Nouvelles d'Alsace (DNA)*. He demanded Désir to consolidate the status of Strasbourg in order to strengthen the role of France and Europe and cited historic developments regarding European institutions in the city which would give it a European mission.[41]

Arguments of the *Single Seat*-campaign concerned Strasbourg. For instance, figures included that the city administration would have overcharged rent of 80 million Euros in recent years and that hotel rates would increase by 150 percent during EP sessions, but also that the presence of the assembly contributed with 20 million Euros to the local economy.[42] During a seminar held by the single seat campaign in 2012, one of its members, British MEP Ashley Fox pointed out that historically, Strasbourg had been a symbol of peace and Franco-German reconciliation, but that it now would be a signpost of negative elements within the EU.[43]

In this context, another research possibility would be how Strasbourg and other similar cities employ the history of the involvement with the European institutions today. For example, in 2014, the new permanent exhibition *Lieu d'Europe* opened in Strasbourg, financed by the city, the department, the region and the state with a contribution by the EP and CoE.[44] Its objectives include familiarising people with general European culture and other elements, but its primary mission constitutes informing about the European institutions and European history in connection

---

41 "Lettre de Roland Ries à Harlem Désir – Strasbourg: Défense du siège du Parlement européen: Roland Ries écrit à Harlem Désir 10.4.2014." Dernières Nouvelles d'Alsace. <http://www.dna.fr/actualite/2014/04/10/defense-du-siege-du-parlement-europeen-roland-ries-ecrit-a-harlem-desir> (accessed 5.06.2014).

42 *Ibid.*

43 "Seminar, Single Seat Campaign, Towards 2014: A single seat and the European Parliament Election, 10/2012 (Video)." ALDE Youtube Channel. <http://www.youtube.com/watch?v=vDthJzUQxXc> (accessed 12.03.2014), 7:14-8:20 min.

44 "Partenaires." Lieu de l'Europe. <http://lieudeurope.strasbourg.eu/partenaires/> (accessed 20.05.2014).

to Strasbourg.[45] The mission statement, "le choix de Strasbourg comme capitale européenne au lendemain du second conflit mondial n'est pas le fruit du hasard mais le symbole de la réconciliation entre les peuples et l'avenir de l'Europe."[46] Moreover, promotion material of the city administration throughout time employed the presence of the European institutions as a matter of cause as in "l'Europe se construit et se construira à Strasbourg."[47]

Furthermore arguments with historic events or the display of them frequently occur in Strasbourg. Since its beginning as European institution host in 1949, the city of Strasbourg identified itself strongly with the presence of the European Institutions, as it designated itself as *capitale européenne*. One of the most visible instances where this is used includes the official letterhead that is also found on the municipality's homepage.[48] The fact that the site does not use the country code 'fr' for France, but 'eu' which is also used by EU institutions such as the Commission or the EP, is another sign for some form of bond with Europe and a possible entitlement of European elements.

From 1 January 2015, Strasbourg has had the status of a *Eurométropole*, which also includes the three most populated agglomerations in France.[49] In the press release, Guy-Dominique Kennel, *Président du Conseil Général du Bas-Rhin*, states that the city deserves this merit due to its historic role in European integration and the fact that it is the capital city of Europe.[50] Likewise, such indicators are used in current local politics. The 2014 re-election campaign of Ries not only prominently contained a picture of the European flag on the website, but the slogan "un engagement total en faveur de la vocation européenne de Strasbourg", as well.[51] Strasbourg as host of European institutions with a history of European significance is

45 "Missions." Lieu de l'Europe. <http://lieudeurope.strasbourg.eu/le-lieu-deurope/> (accessed 20.05.2014).

46 "Strasbourg et l'Europe." Lieu de l'Europe. <http://lieudeurope.strasbourg.eu/strasbourg-et-leurope/> (accessed 20.05.2014).

47 AS, 958 W 73, *Architecture*, p. 3.

48 Cf. http://www.strasbourg.eu.

49 Kennel, Guy-Dominique, "Strasbourg Eurométropole et Collectivité Territoriale d'Alsace: une ambition partagée", Département du Bas-Rhin. <http://www.bas-rhin.fr/eCommunityDocuments/BB9FAA02-A33D-4E64-9176-BA6926CD4D2B/582/document_communique-presse-bas-rhin-tribune-GDK-eurometrople.pdf> (accessed 3.02.2015).

50 *Ibid.*

51 "Home page Roland Ries 2014," Roland Ries. <http://rolandries2014.eu/pionniere-rayonnante/engagement-total-faveur-vocation-europeenne-strasbourg/> (accessed 06.06.2014).

still highly visible in contemporary presentations of the city, as visible in the examples above. Therefore, it is relevant to investigate the origins of this and how it was used in history.

Section 1.04 Conceptualisations

This section will cover how certain terms regarding local consolidation activity in Strasbourg are used in this book. The word 'strategy' will mean any action of actors in order to improve their image as seat city. 'Hosting measures' or 'arrangements' constitute umbrella terms for all activities to welcome parliamentarians except infrastructure, as will be analysed in chapter 2.

All individual local or departmental politicians and civil servants, organisations or collectives of those involved in welcoming European institutions are 'actors'. This study focuses on the kinds of persons and organisations in the city of Strasbourg who were actively attempting to consolidate the city's seat status by using various strategies to achieve this aim. Therefore, their agency will be concentrated on. As a general rule, whenever designations such as 'mayor', 'local actors' or 'city administration' without any further locative specification are employed, the city of Strasbourg is referred to. The standalone expression 'local actors' is an unspecific mention of all involved actors. Similarly, 'city', 'city administration' and its synonyms denote those of its members concerned with European institutions without an allusion to a particular actor, as does 'private organisations' for all associations.

The involved actors operated within a bubble-like structure within the city administration. This term is employed to describe certain features of this actor group, first and foremost that it was hardly subjected to outside influences, such as elections or that it alone stood for the bulk of the organisation regarding strategies to consolidate Strasbourg's seat status. Additionally, the term 'bubble' is applicable, because local agents involved in dealing with the European institutions in the city were removed from the normal operations of local government. They did exert influence on decision bodies of the city administration such as the municipal council when decisions they had taken needed to be confirmed officially. However, also in these fora, actors within the bubble structure dominated the discussion. Generally, this bubble structure of involved actors, who commonly occupied higher ranks within the municipality operated outside the ordinary politics of the city administration and was not subjected to any outside influence. This will be discussed further in the 'local politics'-section in chapter 1.

Throughout the chapters, where sums in French Francs are given, the present approximate rounded value in Euros is included as a reference point. These numbers stem from the French national statistics institute *Institut national de la statistique et des études économiques (INSEE)* that offers a currency converter. It calculates the current purchasing power of an amount of Francs from any year in Euros.[52] Although it considers inflation, the value in Euros is an approximate amount, but it is included to give a general idea of the expenses of local actors.

The city administration did not differentiate between the CoE and EC and grouped them under the term 'European institutions'. In this book, the wording will be used in this manner, as well. Additionally, 'European parliamentarians' refers to delegates of both PACE and the EP, as well as members of other transnational assemblies meeting in Strasbourg.

In urban planning literature, Carola Hein and others point out in an edited volume on Brussels as the "Capital of Europe" that a dichotomy between the designations 'seat' and 'capital' exists. The former would only encompass the institution buildings, while the latter would extend this definition with culture and leisurely offers.[53] A capital would also denote political, economic and cultural functions that arose from the presence of the government.[54] Moreover, these cities serve as identification for the political structures they represented. For example, Brussels is often employed as a synonym or synecdoche for matters pertaining to the European Communities.[55] In the same manner, in relation to PACE or the EP the terminology "the assembly of Strasbourg" was and is common.[56]

Most ideas about a 'capital of Europe', both projects for purpose built cities and seats appropriating this expression draw upon the concept of a state capital in the sense that it is the political administrative centre.[57] In regard to the transferral of these principles, Hein argues that a fundamental difference exists in the architecture of a national and a European capital. In the former, the government would have manifested its power in built symbols, while the European institutions lack such power.

---

52 "Convertisseur franc-euro: pouvoir d'achat de l'euro et du franc." INSEE. <http://www.insee.fr/fr/themes/calcul-pouvoir-achat.asp> (accessed 02.06.2014).

53 Hein, Carola, "Brussels and the Capital of Europe", in Hein, Carola (ed.), *Bruxelles, l'Européenne. Capitale de qui? Ville de qui?* Brussels, La Lettre Volée, 2006, p. 26.

54 *Ibid.*

55 Corijn, Eric, *Building the Capital of Europe as a Heterotopia*, in Hein, Carola (ed.), *Bruxelles, l'Européenne. Capitale de qui? Ville de qui?* Brussels, La Lettre Volée, 2006, p. 52.

56 E.g. Biedermann, Alfred, "Périr ou s'unir", in *Vers l'Europe*, 1:6-7, 1950, p. 5.

57 Leary, Robert, "Capital on the Ottawa", in *Town Planning Review*, 41:1, 1970, pp. 3-14, p. 4.

Instead, local and national actors capitalise this potential for themselves.[58] Additionally, in the literature, it is hypothesised that the capital of Europe should be conceptualised as a post-national capital, rather than on the basis of a national one.[59] This encompasses the partly supranational and intergovernmental nature of the EU. Thus, its possible capital would be different from the capital of a country. This trend is observable with both the seats of European institutions and proposals for new capital cities that principally occurred in the 1950s.

Examples of a first category of cities constituted seats that appropriated the designation 'capital of Europe'. It likely constituted a strategy to create association to the general conception of a capital city as governmental centre of a nation in order to strengthen the position as host for European institutions. A second group constituted planned capital city-proposals for a general unified Europe.

In regard to the first category, the seats of the EC, no specific conceptualisations of them as European capital(s) existed during the period of study.[60] For example, Hein analyses that in Brussels uniform office blocks for the European institutions dominated rather than architectural symbolism as most national capitals expressed towards the government they housed.[61] Especially Strasbourg and Brussels claimed the term 'capital of Europe' for themselves in connection to the presence of various European institutions in those cities. In the case of Strasbourg, this designation was already in use in 1949, also by people outside the city. For instance, in a letter to Pierre Pflimlin, the president of the General Council of Bas-Rhin on 18 August 1949, Ernest Bevin, the British secretary of state for foreign affairs thanked him for the welcome during the PACE session, which would have been "worthy" of the capital of Europe.[62] Judging by the sources, local actors seemed to have employed this appellation in context of a strategy to confirm Strasbourg's alleged European mission

58 Hein, Carola, "The polycentric and opportunistic capital of Europe: A new model for the siting and reallocation of EU headquarters and the design of European districts in Brussels and other host cities, in *Brussels Studies*, 2, 2006, p. 2.

59 Calay, Vincent, *"Capitale de l'Europe" ou "siège des institutions européennes"? Quels termes pour quels espaces imaginaires?*, in Hein, Carola (ed.), *Bruxelles, l'Européenne. Capitale de qui? Ville de qui?* Brussels, La Lettre Volée, 2006, p. 69.

60 Corijn, Eric, *Building the Capital of Europe as a Heterotopia*, in Hein, Carola (ed.), *Bruxelles, l'Européenne. Capitale de qui? Ville de qui?* Brussels, La Lettre Volée, 2006, p. 61.

61 Hein, Carola, *Brussels and the Capital of Europe*, in Hein, Carola (ed.), *Bruxelles, l'Européenne. Capitale de qui? Ville de qui?* Brussels, La Lettre Volée, 2006, p. 19.

62 AS, 198 MW 83, *Lettre du Bevin au Maire 18.8.1949.*

as yet another marker how suitable the city would be to host European institutions.

Additionally, the form of the EU's capital city is a new feature that was created by the structural conditions of the organisation, namely a polycentric and partially itinerant form.[63] It manifested differently from the most common mode of country capitals which usually is a single city.[64] This decentralisation, which has been present from the founding of the ECSC, could be one of the catalysts for the competitive situation between the three EP seats, as well. In the case of the EC and especially judging by sources from the municipal archive of Strasbourg, 'seat' and 'capital' seem to have been used interchangeably as synonyms without any discernible distinctions in the manner Hein makes. She notes on this issue that it would be feasible that Brussels developed from a seat to a true capital in the future, even if the polycentric distribution remained in practice.[65]

In the case of Strasbourg, both pro and contra arguments exist for the city as European capital after her definition. Politically, the presence of the CoE and EP did have a cascading effect, judging by the many different European organisations housed in the city. The issue of additional cultural elements seems slightly more controversial. An extensive hosting programme directly resulted from the presence of the organisations, but the majority of them were restricted to session periods of the assemblies. It is debatable whether this constituted as a qualifier for the designation 'capital' due to its temporality. From the 1980s, economic activity increased that could be directly linked to the presence of the European institutions. A prime example included a three-year-contract to improve its transport and building infrastructure concluded between the French state, the department and the city in 1980 which specifically emphasised that it had been concluded to equip Strasbourg with "les moyens nécessaires à l'exercice de sa fonction de capitale de l'Europe démocratique."[66] Thus, it is argued that Strasbourg is positioned between 'seat' and 'capital', since it exhibits several elements of not just housing institution buildings, although not all of them were permanent or manifested relatively late in the process, such as increased economic functions.

---

63 Hein, Carola, *Brussels and the Capital of Europe*, in Hein, Carola (ed.), *Bruxelles, l'Européenne. Capitale de qui? Ville de qui?* Brussels, La Lettre Volée, 2006, p. 20.

64 *Ibid.*, p. 27.

65 Hein, Carola, *Collaboration for Europe and Brussels* in Hein, Carola (ed.), *Bruxelles, l'Européenne. Capitale de qui? Ville de qui?* Brussels, La Lettre Volée, 2006, p. 282.

66 AS, 114 W 284/1, *Contrat*, p. 1.

Section 1.05 Structure of this book

As final part of the introduction, the structure of this book will be presented. The aim of this study is to investigate which kinds of local actors were concerned with the European institutions in Strasbourg and which strategies they employed to consolidate the position of the city as host of European institutions from 1949 to 1979. The analysis commences with the first European institution, the Council of Europe, sited in Strasbourg in 1949. There will be no focus on the processes of initially locating those organisations in Strasbourg except a general overview in chapter 1. The activities of local actors to retain the position as institution host was of a different nature than activity to initially attract them. Apart from differing policies, the dimension of relations between the local and supranational levels would be much deeper had IOs already been sited in a city. This connection could be employed strategically to consolidate the seat position by concentrating on a well-functioning relationship.

Following chapter 1, which offers historical background regarding Strasbourg and the siting processes of the CoE in 1949 and Common Assembly of the ECSC during the 1950s, the study is structured around three main themes hosting the assemblies during session periods, improvement of transport systems and creation of a building infrastructure. Based on the archival research, they constituted the central areas of local actors' efforts and each will be treated individually in chapters 2 to 4.

Based on the amount of attention paid to single aspects in city administration documents, each of the three themes was important or the main focus of the city actors' efforts during different times, which is reflected in the order of the chapters. Strategies investigated in chapter 2, *Hosting Europe*, were the dominant issues of the 1950s. The 1960s constituted a transitional period from local actors' focus from soft to hard infrastructure matters, also visible in the fact that the hybrid of these two areas, transport, became the focus of their efforts during that decade. Chapter 4 investigates building infrastructure which was the central focus of the 1970s, mostly in the form of two major construction projects. It is illustrated well by the manner the term *accueil* was employed in city administration documents. While it nearly exclusively referred to leisure activities during European sessions in the 1950s, it alluded to the provision of buildings and other infrastructure during the 1970s. The fact that each of these enjoyed a period of principal focus did not mean that the other two were disregarded by local actors during this period. They were only comparatively paid less attention to.

Why local actors concentrated on different aspects during each decade cannot be conclusively analysed from the available archive material, however, it is likely that focuses changed due to outside factors framing the entire process of determining seat cities of the European Communities. During the 1950s, the seat question was much more open in terms of possibilities, visible not only in the ten official candidates of the 1957-1959 application round, but also in the various other suggestions for European capitals and/or hosts. During the 1970s, the situation had changed in the way that only the three provisional EC seat cities, Brussels, Luxembourg and Strasbourg, remained viable candidates and increased the pressure due to the increased competition between only three cities already housing European institutions. This could be a reason why infrastructure constituted the main concern of the 1970s for Strasbourg's local actors, in order to be on the same, if not better level than the other two provisional seats.

The mapping of local actors is separated according to the three themes and it will contain an investigation of the relevant actors at the beginning of each empirical chapter 2 to 4. Subsequently, how actors employed different measures as strategies will be analysed in the chapter proper. That the two main objectives of this book build upon each other is reflected in the make-up of the chapters. Although a select group of actors from the city administration was involved in all three cases, there is a clear distinction between those involved in hosting and infrastructure matters. Additionally, grouping activities and the concrete actor groups concerned with those together allows for a comprehensive study of events within the city. Chapters 2 to 4 share the same format, starting with an introduction, the actor description, the analysis of strategies in various sub-chapters, as well as a final part with concluding remarks which both summarises the entire chapter and covers aspects common to all activities regarding the particular theme analysed in the chapter.

The first of them, hosting, which will be analysed in chapter 2, contains the formation of structures that were partly present as fully functioning entities regarding processes connected to the two infrastructure topics. Central elements were the soft infrastructure measures including orchestrating a general 'European atmosphere' in the city, reception arrangements and leisure activities for the European parliamentarians during PACE and EP sessions, as well as assisting civil servants of the institutions with housing and other matters. It is important to note that this period was not homogenous in terms of city actors' activities. Based on available city administration documents, this decade is partitioned into two phases. From the placement of the CoE in 1949 until 1956, hosting activities were characterised by unstructured efforts, when various different actors were involved in an uncoordinated manner and specialised structures first had to be developed. In 1956, the city administration started to institute specialised committees which were exclusively occupied with all aspects of welcoming European institutions, although a strong focus remained on welcoming European institution parliamentarians and civil servants with a wide selection of leisure activities. This circumstance characterised these activities from the second half of the 1950s, when arrangements were centrally organised through the specialised committees, mainly with the aim of supporting Strasbourg's candidature for the single seat of the three European Communities from 1957 onwards.

The element of the European mission of Strasbourg will precede the analysis of hosting activities, since it was mostly intrinsic to them. One of its main characteristics was that all actors, outside and inside the city, accepted it. The available sources commonly indicated that Strasbourg not only possessed such a European mission from 1949 with the placement of the CoE, but had always been European, by drawing on several historic events. In the case of Strasbourg, the concept was also combined with the city being the symbol for Franco-German reconciliation.

Chapter 3 investigates the improvement of traffic infrastructure, the second case of local actors' involvement. Improvement of the transport system was on the one hand a matter of receiving parliamentarians in an effective manner and on the other hand an issue of possessing adequate infrastructure to provide such services. Chapter 4 principally deals with the two large construction projects of the 1970s, the *Palais de l'Europe* for the CoE and the *Immeuble Parlementaire Européen (IPE)* for an enlarged EP following the first direct election. The building of the latter edifice, which commenced in the second half of the 1970s, was regarded as especially important by the city administration, also in terms of the competition Brussels and Luxembourg, in order to provide the best working conditions of the three seat cities. A sub-chapter analysing and summarising construction efforts from 1950 to 1970 precedes this.

The structure of the appendixes loosely reflects the order of the chapters and they contain contextual or further information to the single aspects discussed during the empirical part. These are an overview of the most involved multipositioned local actors and their different positions in appendix I and examples of costs of hosting arrangements during sessions in appendix II.

A specialised committee of the city administration dealing with the presence of the European institutions in the city used the term *opération accueil* as designation regarding certain arrangements for leisure programmes during session periods.[67] The English version, 'Operation Welcome', is employed as main title for this book, since it is applicable to the character of all efforts of Strasbourg regarding the European institutions in the city. *Accueil* has two translational equivalents in English, 'welcome' and 'reception'. The former possibility is used here, as it fits the overall character of local activities, whose spectrum exceeded elements commonly associated with receiving guests such as offering dinners or accommodation. It has to be noted that the term carries a double entendre with an illusion to how municipal actors concretely received them.

By focussing on all these aspects during the analysis, it will become apparent that other levels than the intergovernmental one, which held the formal decision power regarding the seat, comprised important activity in this matter. Furthermore, it will not only focus on political aspects, but also include other issues, such as building facilities for the institutions. It will be a contribution to academic European Studies literature concerning this aspect of European integration, both due to the comprehensive exploration of other types of actors and the focus on both the European Communities and the Council of Europe. This latter aspect is usually studied separately as well, with an emphasis on the EU and its predecessor organisations.

67 AS, 235 MW 273, *Minutes of the Bipartite Committee, 21.2.1958*, p. 3.

Chapter 1

Strasbourg, seat of European institutions

This chapter serves as a contextual chapter to the subsequent three chapters on each of the three main themes of Strasbourg's efforts to consolidate its position as seat. It introduces key events of Alsatian history which were especially pertinent to the promotion of Strasbourg as European and symbol for Franco-German reconciliation. Subsequently, general urban developments in Strasbourg from 1945 will be outlined to illustrate the environment mainly infrastructural processes to welcome European institutions were imbedded in. In a sub-chapter, the siting of the CoE in 1949, the Common Assembly in 1952 and further activities of the European Communities to determine a permanent seat during the 1950s will be briefly investigated and summarised.

(a) Alsatian history

In order to analyse some of the strategies of local actors, it is necessary to draw on recent Alsatian history. The conflict between France and Germany over the region from 1871 onwards was often employed to rationalise Strasbourg's status as symbol for reconciliation following the Second World War by local actors. Strasbourg portrayed itself as the symbol of Franco-German reconciliation to justify the validity of their application for the single seat. This description also is a staple element of the general narrative of the history of the European integration process.[1] Recent Alsatian history is important to consider in this context, as the actors in Strasbourg appropriated it by stylising themselves as 'the victim' of the power struggle between France and Germany. In this context, they argued that they should be the seat due to the symbolism that was attached to the city in the early European integration process. Therefore, it is important to take the history of this conflict into account to understand why this played a significant role.

1 Trunk, Achim, *Europa, ein Ausweg: Politische Eliten und europäische Identität in den 1950er Jahren*, München, Oldenbourg, 2007, p. 117.

This section will predominantly deal with Alsatian History from 1871 to 1945 with a focus on the period until 1920 in order to provide the background and context to the actor constructions that will be investigated in chapter 2.1 with the construction of Strasbourg's European mission. In connection to continuing changes of ownership, France and Germany each developed the myth of Alsace as an integral part of their nation, while Alsatians themselves predominantly identified with their region.[2] Such sentiments might also have contributed to the construction of Strasbourg as a symbol for Franco-German reconciliation, as the historic conflict was both ingrained in Alsatian history and identity as an experience common to the entire region.

After the Franco-Prussian war of 1871, Alsace-Lorraine[3] had to be ceded to the newly founded Germany according to the Treaty of Frankfurt. In the reasoning of the German Empire, as analysed in a contemporary journal article from 1918, this annexation had historic reasons, because they claimed, Alsace had been unlawfully taken from the Holy Roman Empire and been given to France as spoils of the Thirty Years-War in 1648.[4] Other, more prominent reasons would have been the strategic military importance of the region and economic advantages such as natural resources of Alsace.[5] Within the Empire, it was placed under direct command of the emperor as a *Reichsland* and therewith not part of the federation.[6] Strasbourg as the regional capital experienced a construction boom which tripled the size of the city due to the German effort of signalling their power through buildings.[7] Alsace's political influence was restrained to local affairs until the introduction of an Alsatian constitution in 1911 when it gained three seats in the *Bundesrat*, but remained without any real decision power.[8]

---

2 Eckhardt, Carl, "The Alsace-Lorraine Question", in *The Scientific Monthly*, 6:5, 1918, pp. 433; 441.

3 From the annexations of the two regions in 1871 by Germany, they were often talked about in tandem, although they had somewhat separate histories. As this section is to provide historical context to the local actors' constructions of Strasbourg as a European city, the focus will be on Alsace, the region of which the city was the capital.

4 *Ibid.*, p. 433; 432.

5 *Ibid.*, p. 433.

6 *Ibid.*, p. 435.

7 "Carnets de Ville No. 1, novembre 2013, Le patrimoine, une mémoire pour le futur." Ville de Strasbourg. <http://www.strasbourg.eu/developpement-rayonnement/urbanisme-logement-amenagement/la-formation-du-territoire/histoire-ville-quartiers-communes/carnets-de-ville> (accessed 19.06.2014), p. 4.

8 Eckhardt, Carl, "The Alsace-Lorraine Question", in *The Scientific Monthly*, 6:5, 1918, pp. 431-443, pp. 435-436.

During the war years, martial law was in effect in Alsace, which led to a high number of denunciations and preventive detentions without trial.[9] On the French side, already in February 1915, a *Conférence d'Alsace* had been convened with members of the French Alsatian population in order to prepare for a return of the region (and Lorraine) to France by studying how French law could be quickly adapted.[10]

A phenomenon of the war years that was not restricted to the region was the publication of articles and books that dealt with the issue of Alsace-Lorraine and overwhelmingly argued in favour of the region being a part of France. The book *Alsace-Lorraine; a study of the relations of the two provinces to France and to Germany, and a presentation of the just claims of their people* written by Daniel Blumenthal for an American audience and published in New York in 1917 presents such an example.[11] It depicted Alsace as being unlawfully taken from France in 1871 and that the region was inherently French.[12] Additionally, the publication pleaded for the return of Alsace to France, its "rightly home" and pointed out that America would be instrumental in bringing about this result.[13] Apart from such texts which had an agenda of promoting Alsace's 'return' to France, other publications occupied themselves with a more objective evaluation of the annexation process and historical events from 1871 to the First World War.[14]

In the cease-fire agreement of the First World War, Alsace was specified as part of France and treated like this by the French, although it technically remained German territory occupied by French troops until the signing of the Treaty of Versailles, which officially returned it.[15] After the war, triage commissions were created to handle the expulsion of Germans and their

9 Harvey, David, "Lost Children or Enemy Aliens? Classifying the Population of Alsace after the First World War", in *Journal of Contemporary History*, Vol. 34:4, 1999, p. 542.

10 Grünewald, Irmgard, *Die Elsass-Lothringer im Reich 1918-1933: ihre Organisationen zwischen Integration und "Kampf um Seele der Heimat"*, Frankfurt am Main, Peter Lang, 1984, pp. 14; 16.

11 Blumenthal, Daniel, *Alsace-Lorraine; a study of the relations of the two provinces to France and to Germany, and a presentation of the just claims of their people*, New York, G.B. Putnam's Sons, 1917.

12 *Ibid.*, pp. 1-30.

13 *Ibid.*, pp. 50; 60.

14 E.g. Starr Jordan, David, "Alsace-Lorraine: a study of conquest", in *Atlantic Monthly*, 113:, 1914, pp. 688-702.

15 Zind, Pierri, *Elsass-Lothringen – Alsace-Lorraine: une nation interdite*, Paris, Copernic, 1979, p. 94.

sympathisers in order to re-integrate the region into the country.[16] Many denunciations to the commissions were not motivated by patriotism, but also by personal feuds, or Germans who were unemployed or regarded as causing Alsatians to be unemployed were also investigated.[17]

These panels, composed of members from the military and civilians in a more minor capacity, specifically examined persons with a doubtful loyalty to France and had powers to place suspects under surveillance, in detention or to expel them from the country.[18] The triage commissions started their work in December 1918 and from February 1919 operated according to a standardised system – either taking no action in case of acquittals, ordering surveillance on those with questionable loyalties, or detaining/deporting those suspected of a pro-German stance.[19] These panels functioned until October 1919, when their work was discontinued.[20]

Another measure was the introduction of category A to D identity cards which denoted the owner's nationality and ancestry.[21] Someone with Alsatian or French parents would receive the A-card, those in category B had one Alsatian parent, C was for foreigners of non-German or Austrian ancestry and Germans (or Austrians), even those born in Alsace, received the identity card D, which led to various restrictions in daily life.[22] This classification was discontinued when the triage commissions were disbanded. It can be regarded, together with the panels, as an attempt of French authorities quickly to integrate Alsace back into France.[23]

Based on the developed myth in France of Alsace as an integral part of the nation, the French authorities attempted to impose Frenchness and to remove instances of pro-German influence in the region, which mainly occurred without requesting the participation of local elites.[24] Politically,

---

16 Boswell, Laird, "From Liberation to Purge Trials in the "Mythic Provinces": Recasting French Identities in Alsace and Lorraine, 1918-1920", in *French Historical Studies*, 23:1, 2000, pp. 140; 145.

17 Harvey, David, "Lost Children or Enemy Aliens? Classifying the Population of Alsace after the First World War", in *Journal of Contemporary History*, Vol. 34:4, 1999, pp. 544; 546.

18 *Ibid.*, p. 541.

19 *Ibid.*, p. 542.

20 *Ibid.*, p. 550.

21 *Ibid.*, p. 548. These documents were individual and in one family, members could have identity cards of different categories.

22 *Ibid.*, pp. 548-549.

23 *Ibid.*, pp. 551; 553.

24 Boswell, Laird, "From Liberation to Purge Trials in the "Mythic Provinces": Recasting French Identities in Alsace and Lorraine, 1918-1920", in *French Historical Studies*, 23:1, 2000, pp. 132-137.

the interwar years were characterised by a struggle between different political leanings in Alsace, as for instance the autonomists.[25] In 1940, the region was re-annexed by Germany until shortly before the Second World War ended.[26] Immediately after the occupation, 'unwanted' persons were expulsed and for example street names returned to their German names that had been in use prior to 1918.[27] This was accompanied by an ordinance from 1943 which required everyone to change French forenames and names to German ones.[28] Thus, the opposite of what occurred in 1918 after the First World War took place, to erase indicators of the French or respectively German culture.

(b) National political support for Strasbourg

As will be shown later in this chapter, Strasbourg's actors held a marginal role in the siting of European institutions. In contrast, consolidation endeavours predominantly seem to have been a local affair. Pierre Pflimlin, Mayor of Strasbourg from 1959 to 1983, stated in 1974,

> Si la ville de Strasbourg a assumé avec ferveur et détermination la mission européenne qui lui était confiée, si elle a bénéficié de l'appui constant du Conseil Général du Bas-Rhin, qui participe notamment à toutes les dépenses d'accueil, il faut dire que longtemps elle n'a guère reçu d'encouragement venant de Paris.[29]

This remark hints at the fact that the assumptions of a form of local activity regarding the city's seat status seem to have been applicable and that this issue also touches on relations between a host city and its national government. Notably, sources show that until the 1970s, the French state was hardly involved in city actors' activities to strengthen Strasbourg's position as seat. From then on, participation still remained somewhat marginal and concentrated itself on assisting financially with specialised air links and other infrastructure, while the planning thereof largely was executed by the municipality.

Since this study only considered local and departmental archive sources, it is possible that the French national archives contain material that was not transmitted to the city administration of Strasbourg. However,

---

25 Zind, Pierri, *Elsass-Lothringen – Alsace-Lorraine: une nation interdite*, Paris, Copernic, 1979, pp. 153-196.

26 *Ibid.*, p. 684.

27 Baechler, Christian, "Espoirs et désillusions: l'entre-deux-guerres et l'occupation nazie (1918-1944)", in Livet, Georges and Rapp, Francis (eds.), *Histoire de Strasbourg*, Toulouse, Privé/Dernières Nouvelles d'Alsace, 1987, p. 441.

28 *Ibid.*

29 AS, 9 Z 192, *Strasbourg et le Conseil de l'Europe, 11.4.1974*, p. 3.

the lack of correspondence or common meetings of the municipality and the state allow for the conclusion that the French state was not involved in a significant manner in the activities of the city administration to consolidate the seat.

It is interesting to note in the French case with a strongly centralised state that most planning appeared to have been carried out by the city administration and other local associations. The Département du Bas-Rhin and its head, the prefect, the local representative of the state, were involved, but not in a principal role. Sources in the municipal and regional archive show only this picture, which leaves it unclear whether the state was participating indirectly, for example in unofficial dealings with local actors which were set apart from official city politics. A contributing factor to the state's apparent non-involvement could have been Pierre Pflimlin. A book on the EP described him regarding the competition between Brussels, Luxembourg and Strasbourg as "[...] political force in his own right."[30] Thus, his strong political weight might have contributed to Strasbourg's success.

Next to academic literature, books on Pflimlin's political career, mostly in the form of interview books and a Festschrift perpetuate this myth further. In one of these publications, *Itinéraires d'un Européen*, Pflimlin is portrayed as the epitome of a European, starting with the introduction where other local politicians are quoted on his local political career, before his entire bibliography with a special emphasis on his political career is discussed between him and the authors.[31] In this vein, the introduction specifies, "Pflimlin – l'Européen: c'est un pléonasme."[32] One chapter especially concentrates on the European institutions in Strasbourg, where Pflimlin emphasises that Strasbourg had become a symbol for Europe or that it housed many different European institutions, such as the *Commission Centrale du Rhin* which would be the oldest of such organisations whose creation in 1868 could be traced back to the Congress of Vienna in 1815.[33]

This interview book is a local publication, since the two interviewers are editors with the regional newspaper *Dernières Nouvelles d'Alsace*.[34] A similar publication which contains an interview between Pflimlin, Édouard

30 Clark, Stephen and Priestley, Julian, *Europe's Parliament. People, Places, Politics*, London, John Harper, 2012, p. 47.

31 English, Jean-Louis; Riot, Daniel, *Itinéraires d'un Européen. Entretiens avec Pierre Pflimlin*, Strasbourg, La Nuée Bleue, 1989.

32 *Ibid.*, p. 21.

33 *Ibid.*, pp. 313; 317.

34 *Ibid.*, back cover.

Pflimlin and Carole Monmarché, titled *Les choix d'une vie*, focuses less on the local aspect of his political career, but still covers his positions in European politics.[35] Several questions pertain to Pflimlin's aims, such as what his objectives for his presidency of PACE from 1963 to 1966 were.[36] Highlighting the European aspect of his career is also mirrored in the main title of Pflimlin's autobiography with *Mémoires d'un Européen de la IVᵉ à la Vᵉ République*, which covers all aspects of his political career.[37] Pflimlin's European political activities are presented in other forms, such as a Festschrift edited by the *Cercle Pierre Pflimlin*, entitled *Pierre Pflimlin Alsacien & Européen.*[38] It had been published to honour his centenary in 2007 in memory of his engagements, notably regarding European integration and Franco-German reconciliation.[39]

These publications with a strong focus on Pflimlin's European political career and the emphasis of its importance, might have contributed to the fact that he became to be regarded as the one essential local actor. Although he, according to local archive documents, was not the only active local politician who was involved in efforts to consolidate Strasbourg's seat position, some documents hinted at an elevated role, as well, which will be covered during the empirical part. This might present an indication that the myth of the universality of Pflimlin's involvement could in part be founded on how his contemporaries in the political arena constructed his involvement. Furthermore, it is an indicator that a local level of agency regarding the siting of European institutions was active and could have presented a decisive factor in especially the consolidation process after a decision to locate the seats provisionally was made. It is the central aim of this book to investigate which kind of local level was present in the city of Strasbourg and which strategies were used in order to expedite the consolidation of Strasbourg's seat status of the Common Assembly of the ECSC and other European institutions after the decision to locate them in the city was made.

Such possible influence is not explicitly mentioned in city administration documents, but it could have acted behind the scenes. All in all, from the sources, it is likely that national support, except general political activities

35 Pflimlin, Pierre; Pflimlin, Édouard; Monmarché, Carole, *Pierre Pflimlin: Les choix d'une vie*, Strasbourg, Editions du Signe, 2001.

36 *Ibid.*, p. 110.

37 Pflimlin, Pierre, *Mémoires d'un Européen de la IVᵉ à la Vᵉ République*, Paris, Fayard, 1991.

38 Cercle Pierre Pflimlin (ed.), *Pierre Pflimlin: Alsacien & Européen*, Strasbourg, Editions Coprur, 2007.

39 Jung, Louis, "Pierre Pflimlin, l'Europe à cœur, Strasbourg", in Cercle Pierre Pflimlin (ed.), *Pierre Pflimlin: Alsacien & Européen*, Editions Coprur, 2007, p. 7.

in the European Communities, was at best minimal until the 1970s. One example for this would be the matter of air links. The city administration's more modest efforts of the 1960s were dwarfed by the numerous specialised connections of the 1970s with state assistance.[40] Sometimes, issues arose, such as in 1967, when the city had reached an accord with the airline *Lux Air* to prolong its Brussels-Luxembourg connection to Strasbourg.[41] The national *Aviation Civile* prohibited this, since it did not allow a foreign carrier to operate from Strasbourg's airport.[42] Only in 1980, the French state declared Strasbourg as open airport for all airlines from EC member states.[43]

That the city had to rely on its own (financial) means is also asserted by Carola Hein.[44] However, she continues that only from 1989, with the architectural competition for the new Human Rights Court building, local actors had been able to take action in construction matters due to the progressing decentralisation of the French state.[45] As will be investigated in chapter 4, the city actively planned and partly financed or acquired investors for several building projects before this date, most notably the C block housing offices for the EP in 1959, the original Human Rights Court from 1961 and the *Immeuble Parlementaire Européen* from 1978. Additionally, they supported the CoE in its construction efforts for the *Maison* and *Palais de l'Europe* by, among others, liberating prospective building sites and providing them to the organisation at very advantageous prices.

(c) Local politics and European institutions

As mentioned before, the activities of politicians and civil servants concerned with consolidating Strasbourg's seat status in the city administration remained to a large degree separate from its ordinary structures. They formed bubbles of a tight-knit group on which outside influences such as municipal elections were virtually imperceptible. Throughout the other three empirical chapters, this enclosed space within the actor group of Strasbourg will be concentrated on. Therefore, the ordinary running of the municipality will not be presented in this book.

40 This issue will be treated in chapter 3.2 in the section on air links.

41 AS, 236 MW 24/1, *Minutes of the Bipartite Committee session, 1967*, p. 2.

42 AS, 236 MW 24/1, *Minutes of the Bipartite Committee session, 1967*, p. 2.

43 Nonn, Henri and Livet, Georges and Fuchs, René, "Livre VII. Les grandes mutations contemporaines (1945-1980)", Livet, Georges and Rapp, Francis (eds.), *Histoire de Strasbourg des origines à nos jours. Tome 4: Strasbourg de 1815 à nos jours, XIXe et XXe siècles*, Strasbourg, Éditions des Dernières Nouvelles d'Alsace, 1982, p. 517.

44 Hein, Carola, "Brussels and the Capital of Europe", in Hein, Carola (ed.), *Bruxelles l'Européenne. Capitale de qui? Ville de qui*, Brussels, La Lettre Volée, 2006, p. 29.

45 *Ibid.*

Of the 37 elected politicians in the municipal council during the 1950s, approximately one third was occupied with welcoming the European institutions in the city, mostly outside this administrative body. For example, 13 of the 37 mandate holders elected on 8 March 1959 when Pflimlin became mayor, were involved in this; a number that remained stable from previous occasions.[46] These actors commonly remained continuously active into the 1970s regarding the European institutions.

Based on empirical sources, the following structural composition of those involved in consolidating Strasbourg's seat position is extracted. In the local group of actors, smaller structures existed with different functions that either complimented each other or overlapped. Concerning actors in the municipal government, politicians and civil servants, they remained somewhat separate from ordinary city or departmental administration structures. Elections did not seem to have been a factor either and the most active actor group remained relatively stable over time. Therefore, these actors operated within a bubble in the municipal government. They did not seem to adhere to ordinary decision processes, but formed a group of actors that came from different areas of the city administration pertinent to facilitate dealings with the European institutions' presence. 'Outsiders' of this set of actors were only marginally involved if a task was delegated to them. Thus, this bubble has to be understood as the decision centre which was nearly impenetrable from the outside, while actors inside it involved administrative structures outside of it whenever necessary.[47] For example, city administrations cooperated with private organisations which also had the goal of welcoming the European institutions in Strasbourg.

The only ordinary city administration structures outside this close group which were regularly involved were the deliberating bodies *Conseil Municipal (municipal council)* and *Conférence des Adjoints*, the assembly of the deputy mayors, whenever a decision needed to be made official. Items concerning European institutions usually constituted one of the last points on the agenda and discussions were very brief, where commonly only those who also were members of one or more of the specialised

[46] Nonn, Henri and Livet, Georges and Fuchs, René, "Livre VII. Les grandes mutations contemporaines (1945-1980)", Livet, Georges and Rapp, Francis (eds.), *Histoire de Strasbourg des origines à nos jours. Tome 4: Strasbourg de 1815 à nos jours, XIXe et XXe siècles*, Strasbourg, Éditions des Dernières Nouvelles d'Alsace, 1982, pp. 578; 573 – The list of the 37 members on this page was compared to those politicians appearing in the relevant files in the municipal archive to reach this number.

[47] The actor descriptions in the subsequent three chapters will focus on actors within this bubble, since they constituted the main decision holders.

structures actively participated. During the most intensive phase of the second seat application round from 1957 to 1959, only respectively seven and four meetings dealt with matters regarding Strasbourg's candidature.[48] They were only concerned with officially implementing or presenting key decisions. One example of such activity was a resolution for the second seat application in October 1957.[49] A reason for this circumstance could be that the mayor, especially under Pflimlin's tenure, who with the deputy mayors constituted the executive organ of the city,[50] was a highly active actor among the parts of the local administration that were concerned with European institutions. Additionally, several deputy mayors, among them long-time *Premier Adjoint au Maire* (first deputy mayor) Paul Wach, belonged to this structure.

The actors within the bubble of those concerned with the European institutions can be partitioned into two different categories. The 'technical group' comprises public, but also private sector actors that were occupied with tasks related to the presence of European institutions, because they fell into their area of expertise. Within the city government, mostly civil servants who implemented the political consolidation measures belonged to this category. They were a small number of highly involved actors, also over longer periods and in several positions

The other group is comprised of actors who had a form of 'European' agenda, meaning that they were focussing on the European idea or policy issues of the European institutions. City administration actors of this category were mainly politicians who drafted all strategies and measures. They generally focussed on making parliamentarians and institutions feel welcome in the city, while the 'technical' group rather focussed on hard infrastructure like transport and building facilities. Additionally, purpose-founded private organisations responded to the European presence, for instance to organise activities for accompanying spouses of parliamentarians belonged to the 'European' group.

Actors of these two categories of 'technical' and 'European' were not separate from each other but closely cooperated. Another important

---

48 AS, 208 MW 7 and 208 MW 278 and 208 MW 285 and 208 MW 21 and Conseil Municipal de la Ville de Strasbourg, *Débats du Conseil Municipal de l'Année 1957*, Strasbourg: Société d'Édition de la Basse Alsace, 1958 and *Débats du Conseil Municipal de l'Année 1958*, Strasbourg: Société d'Édition de la Basse Alsace, 1959 and AS, 208 MW 267 and 208 MW 21 and 235 MW 271 and 209 MW 18.

49 AS, 235 MW 268, *Résolution du 19.10.1957.*

50 "Présentation, Fonctionnement." Ville de Strasbourg. <http://www.strasbourg.eu/fonctionnement-ville-cus/mairie-de-strasbourg/presentation-fonctionnement> (accessed 23.04.2014).

feature of this constellation was that many actors in this structure were multipositioned, as they simultaneously or subsequently held different public and private functions regarding the welcoming of European institutions. Appendix I contains an overview of all of them and their positions. Through this, the connection between these two groups of actors was further increased. Regarding the 'European' group, a connection is clearly visible due to their creation in response to the European institutions' presence, but with the 'technical' actor group, such features to ascertain belonging are fuzzier. For instance, although the *Conseil Municipal* was regularly involved in decision-making, it is not considered as part of the special structure in this book, since the majority of its members discussing issues regarding European institutions were members of the other group, as well.

The criteria for the members of this category are defined in the following two ways: multipositioned, namely membership in public or private purpose founded entities, and/or active involvement over a long time in several issues concerning the CoE or EP. One such example would be the secretary-general of Strasbourg during the 1960s, Albert Fix, who was heavily and continuously involved in building projects of that decade and moreover the director of the municipal agency responsible for their constructions. Such actors were stakeholders in the process of creating infrastructure for the European institutions and an integral part of the bubble structure. Just as the concept of a 'Brussels bubble' was created in European integration literature, it is argued that a European bubble was present in the city of Strasbourg that contained a – to the outside – closed political/technocratic world of those concerned with consolidating the city's seat position.

Apart from forming a virtually impenetrable group, the actors concerned with consolidating Strasbourg's seat status brushed aside opposing opinions in the rare instances they occurred. One example was the contrary position of communist municipal councillor Alphonse Boosz in connection with Strasbourg's seat candidature from 1957-1959. He stated that the European presence in Strasbourg would lead to internationalisation, negate 'Frenchness' and allow for the infiltration of the administration by the Germans who would dominate the ECSC.[51] The city administration sources leave the impression that Boosz's concerns were regarded as irrelevant, because after his speeches in the *Conseil Municipal*, Mayor Charles Altorffer immediately dismissed his points,

51 AS, 208 MW 7, *Interpellation de M. Boosz, 30.12.1957* and 208 MW 13, *Note sur l'interpellation de M. Boosz*; Ville de Strasbourg, *Débats du Conseil Municipal de 1957*, pp. 310-311.

sometimes in a patronising manner such as "votre interpellation est basée sur un malentendu."[52] Such rebuttals were often commented with "bravo" from other members of the city council.[53] Such opposing views remained negligible due to the self-contained structure within the municipal administration of the operation to welcome the European institutions and further Strasbourg's chances during the seat question.

(d) Urban development after 1945

The early phases of the presence of European institutions coincided with a reconstruction period that also informed the manner in which local actors dealt with their presence. After the end of the Second World War, 20 percent of Strasbourg had been destroyed.[54] Urban development until the mid-1950s included this factor of devastation. Damages were distributed over the entire city and during reconstructions, Strasbourg was modernised, for example with wider streets.[55] It was declared as *ville sinistrée* in 1947, which meant that a plan to repair all damages had to be drawn up for the entire parish.[56]

Housing for the population constituted a major concern with an influx of people after the war and over 7,000 lodgings destroyed.[57] In the following decades, the population steadily increased; from 175,515 in 1946, it reached 200,000 by 1954 and grew to 257,303 in 1975.[58] All in all, 12,000 houses and flats were estimated to be lacking in the city in

52 AS, 208 MW 7, *Interpellation de M. Boosz, 30.12.1957*, p. 16.

53 AS, 208 MW 7, *Interpellation de M. Boosz, 30.12.1957*, p. 16.

54 "Une ville en transformation et préservée (depuis 1945)." Ville de Strasbourg. <http://www.strasbourg.eu/developpement-rayonnement/urbanisme-logement-amenagement/la-formation-du-territoire/histoire-ville-quartiers-communes/etapes-formation-territoire/une-ville-en-transformation-et-preservee-depuis-1945> (accessed 19.06.2014).

55 Bachofen, Charles, "La reconstruction", in Cullier, Francis (ed.), *Strasbourg. Chroniques d'urbanisme*, La Tour d'Aigues, éditions de l'aube, 1994, pp. 25-26.

56 "Une ville en transformation et préservée (depuis 1945)." Ville de Strasbourg. <http://www.strasbourg.eu/developpement-rayonnement/urbanisme-logement-amenagement/la-formation-du-territoire/histoire-ville-quartiers-communes/etapes-formation-territoire/une-ville-en-transformation-et-preservee-depuis-1945> (accessed 19.06.2014).

57 *Ibid.* and Bachofen, Charles, "La reconstruction", in Cullier, Francis (ed.), *Strasbourg. Chroniques d'urbanisme*, La Tour d'Aigues, éditions de l'aube, 1994, p. 25.

58 Nonn, Henri and Livet, Georges and Fuchs, René, "Livre VII. Les grandes mutations contemporaines (1945-1980)", Livet, Georges and Rapp, Francis (eds.), *Histoire de Strasbourg des origines à nos jours. Tome 4: Strasbourg de 1815 à nos jours, XIXe et XXe siècles*, Strasbourg, Éditions des Dernières Nouvelles d'Alsace, 1982, p. 511.

1945.[59] Apart from redistributing existing living space and construction, barracks were erected and parts of the population were accommodated in Kehl until the early 1950s, the German town on the opposite bank of the Rhine.[60] Reconstructions also included big complexes, *cités*, such as the *Cité Rotterdam* in 1951 with 800 flats for some of the 6,000-8,000 Strasbourgese who had to be housed in Kehl.[61] By 1955, most of the housing damaged by the war had been restored.[62]

Towards the end of the 1950s, a new urban development process started with the decommission of military grounds throughout the city. Notably, the local administration bought the military terrain Esplanade in 1958 on which a university campus and apartments were built.[63] Some European institution buildings along the river Ill were erected on former military grounds, as well.[64] Other construction efforts concentrated on hotels, although a stagnant period was visible during the 1950s, when the lack of capacity in luxury and simple hotels was especially evident.[65]

The European institutions were implanted in Robertsau and Wacken. Robertsau had its origin as living space for fishermen, dredgers and shipwrights, but from the 18th century, it developed as quarter for nobles and bourgeois outside city walls, since Strasbourg became more populated and unsanitary during this period.[66] Following the Second World War, the area was strongly urbanised, for example with expansions of residential

59 Bachofen, Charles, "La reconstruction", in Cullier, Francis (ed.), *Strasbourg. Chroniques d'urbanisme*, La Tour d'Aigues, éditions de l'aube, 1994, p. 29.

60 *Ibid.*

61 "Histoire du Quartier Conseil des XV – Rotterdam." Ville de Strasbourg. <http://www.strasbourg.eu/territoire/les-quartiers/conseil-des-xv-rotterdam/decouvrir-quartier-rotterdam/histoire-quartier-rotterdam> (accessed 19.06.2014) and Nonn, Henri and Livet, Georges and Fuchs, René, "Livre VII. Les grandes mutations contemporaines (1945-1980)", Livet, Georges and Rapp, Francis (eds.), *Histoire de Strasbourg des origines à nos jours. Tome 4: Strasbourg de 1815 à nos jours, XIXe et XXe siècles*, Strasbourg, Éditions des Dernières Nouvelles d'Alsace, 1982, p. 510.

62 Bachofen, Charles, "La reconstruction", in Cullier, Francis (ed.), *Strasbourg. Chroniques d'urbanisme*, La Tour d'Aigues, éditions de l'aube, 1994, p. 29.

63 "Histoire du Quartier Bourse – Esplanade – Krutenau." Ville de Strasbourg. <http://www.strasbourg.eu/territoire/les-quartiers/bourse-esplanade-krutenau/decouvrir-quartier-bourse/histoire-quartier-bourse> (accessed 19.06.2014).

64 E.g. AS, 752 W 11, *Note pour M. le Maire, 3.10.1978.*

65 Nonn, Henri and Livet, Georges and Fuchs, René, "Livre VII. Les grandes mutations contemporaines (1945-1980)", Livet, Georges and Rapp, Francis (eds.), *Histoire de Strasbourg des origines à nos jours. Tome 4: Strasbourg de 1815 à nos jours, XIXe et XXe siècles*, Strasbourg, Éditions des Dernières Nouvelles d'Alsace, 1982, p. 522.

66 "Histoire du Quartier Robertsau, Wacken." Ville de Strasbourg. <http://www.strasbourg.eu/territoire/les-quartiers/robertsau-wacken/decouvrir-quartier-robertsau/histoire-quartier-robertsau> (accessed 19.06.2014).

areas in the 1960s.[67] This coincided with several more minor construction projects for the European institutions in the same decade before the two grand projects of the 1970s. Wacken housed both mansions built during the 1920s and the exposition grounds from 1927.[68] In the 1970s, an administrative complex was erected close to the European institutions, as well as a congress centre.[69] Parts of the international organisations were also located in the *Quartier* Conseil des XV, which received its name from the governing body that ruled Strasbourg from 1433 to 1789.[70] Until 1880, it was located outside the fortified city area and saw an increase of constructions in this time, as well as after 1945, when many lodgings were built.[71] The European institutions were located outside the city centre, mostly in an upper-class neighbourhood.

(e) Economic impact of the European institutions

A peculiar circumstance characterises the documents from the municipal archive of Strasbourg, namely that hardly any documentation on the economic stakes regarding the presence of the European institutions is available. Given the peripheral position of the city in France and the sustained war damages, it could be surmised that such monetary interests would have been at the heart of local actors' efforts. While sources on measures to remain seat of international organisations referred to the matter of prestige for the city, economic ramifications were not present and at best only occasionally hinted at. Nevertheless, they must have constituted an important factor, not only because of the revenue attained from what institution civil servants and parliamentarians spent while staying in the city, but also due to the potential for an accelerated development resulting from Strasbourg's seat status. As a study on the economic impact of institutions in Brussels denotes, the costs to run them would almost fully be spent in their seat city.[72]

Towards the outside, the municipality, mostly in the form of the mayor, seemed to propagate an image of idealism regarding the housing

---

67 *Ibid.*

68 *Ibid.*

69 *Ibid.*

70 "Histoire du Quartier Conseil des XV – Rotterdam." Ville de Strasbourg. <http://www.strasbourg.eu/territoire/les-quartiers/conseil-des-xv-rotterdam/decouvrir-quartier-rotterdam/histoire-quartier-rotterdam> (accessed 19.06.2014).

71 *Ibid.*

72 Degadt, Jan, "The Impact of the Presence of European and International Institutions on the Regional Economic Fabric in Brussels", in De Groof, Roel (ed.), *Brussels and Europe – Bruxelles et l'Europe*, Brussels, ASP, 2008, p. 225.

of European organisations. For example, Pierre Pflimlin wrote in the conclusion to *Histoire de Strasbourg des origines à nos jours*, a multi-volume publication on the history of the city that the factor of institution expenditure and economic advantages would not be important; only that Strasbourg stayed true to its European mission[73] assigned by geography and history.[74] Therefore, economic implications will not be referred to in the subsequent three analytic chapters of city actors' efforts in hosting, as well as transport and building infrastructure, since this book is concerned with the actual strategies and deliberations of the municipality and local private organisations. However, it has to be kept in mind that reasons such as economic self-interests must have been at stake, although at best only hinted at in the available sources. Other comparable cases seem to indicate such processes, for instance after the completion of the Euro-tunnel connecting Great Britain and France, the border city of Lille experienced growth due to its presence. It and the Département Nord-Pas de Calais implemented projects to profit from it.[75]

More concise and structured endeavours of national authorities to study or improve economic impacts of European institutions on Strasbourg only seem to have been undertaken from 1980 onwards. In this case, agency did not originate from the city administration, but from the French state. One example presents a three-year contract between the state, department and Strasbourg to help it develop its potential which was signed in the same year.[76] In that period, the city administration seemed to have occupied itself more increasingly with such questions, as well. In a note to the Secretary-General from 1982, monetary figures were given regarding the possible spending power of the approximately 1,100 permanent staff from the European institutions, embassies and circa 8,000 guests during sessions.[77]

Prior to the 1970s virtually no references to gained revenue were made by local actors. In that decade, tentative beginnings of explicitly including the economic factor in strategies to consolidate the city's seat status are

---

73 How local actors employed an alleged European mission of Strasbourg as an argument for it being a suitable choice as seat will be investigated in chapter 3.

74 Pflimlin, Pierre, "Conclusion: Strasbourg et l'Europe", in Livet, Georges and Rapp, Francis (eds.), *Histoire de Strasbourg des origines à nos jours. Tome 4: Strasbourg de 1815 à nos jours, XIXe et XXe siècles*, Strasbourg, Éditions des Dernières Nouvelles d'Alsace, 1982, p. 734.

75 Levine, Myron, "The transformation of urban politics in France. The roots of growth politics and urban regimes", in *Urban Affairs Quarterly*, 29:3, 1994, p. 396.

76 AS, 114 W 284/1, *Contrat Métropole Européenne.*

77 AS, 752 W 108, *Note pour le Secrétaire-Général, 24.11.1982.*

visible. In the sources of the municipal archive, although hardly any explicit mentions of economic gains were made, but it can be inferred from the expenditure of city actors to welcome the European institutions that they had a vested interest in keeping the EP and CoE in the city and that they presented a factor of economic development. The relative obscurity of economic factors as strategies to remain host of European institutions could have been caused by the long-time concentration on symbolic matters. It can be assumed that local actors considered economic incentives in connection to the European institutions, although municipal sources only showcased a focus on presenting the city as European.

Next to the general existence of the European institutions, the attendant parliamentarians during sessions constituted an implicit important economic factor as can be inferred from the following case. In 1977, several complaints about opening hours of shops and restaurants reached the city administration. One of the main problems was that most restaurants were closed on Mondays – commonly the first day of meeting periods.[78] Raymond Leissner, *Adjoint au Maire chargé des affaires européennes*, notified the President of the *Syndicat des Hôteliers-Restaurateurs et Débiteurs de Strasbourg* that this went against the efforts of the city to welcome the European parliamentarians. "Cette situation étant ressentie désagréablement par nos hôtes européens, je suis d'avis qu'elle est aussi préjudiciable aux efforts que nous faisons pour rendre le séjour dans notre ville de ces personnalités européennes aussi attrayant que possible."[79] Leissner added that the present opening hours would not contribute to finding a definitive seat and that it would be in the interest of the European mission of Strasbourg if an alternative solution was found.[80]

Leissner addressed a similar letter to the President of the *Association des Commerçants Détaillants de Strasbourg*, since the opening hours of shops with early closing times and a mid-day closure from 12:00-14:00 hours would not coincide with the parliamentarians' spare time.[81] The city's strategies of creating a pleasant stay for the European guests also had economic connotations. Not only the concrete spending power of the visitors was at stake, but more importantly the image of Strasbourg as a competent host with all possible conveniences, as well. On a more abstract level, these factors had repercussions for the competitive environment of

78 AS, 614 W 63, *Lettre de Leissner à Clauss, 29.6.1977.*

79 AS, 614 W 63, *Lettre de Leissner à Clauss, 29.6.1977.*

80 AS, 614 W 63, *Lettre de Leissner à Clauss, 29.6.1977.*

81 AS, 614 W 63, *Lettre de Leissner à Amos, 29.6.1977.*

the seat question. As Leissner argued in the letters, this had the potential to be detrimental to Strasbourg's chances.[82]

In practice, both commercial associations were reluctant to change opening hours, as they raised concerns about staff compensation and the uniqueness of a possible change. In November 1978, the shop owner association finally suggested a model which contained a minor concession towards the parliamentarians' requests, but insisted that they needed to be legalised by a prefectural decree.[83] Although Mayor Pierre Pflimlin had phoned the *Préfet du Département du Bas-Rhin* (Prefect of the Department of the Lower Rhine) regarding this matter, the latter maintained that the commerce needed to solve this issue amongst themselves and referred to the law on the powers of his position from 22 December 1789 which would specify that he had not any competences in the matter.[84] Efforts of the city to account for possible economic incentives were hampered by administrative functions, as well. Only in 1980, the *Association des Commerçants* wrote to Pflimlin, stating that they would do their part to assist Strasbourg's endeavour to remain institution seat.[85] However, it is unclear from the sources in the municipal archive whether and how much the association relented in their stance on opening hours.

A more institutionalised approach to determine and support economic developments caused by the presence of European institutions in Strasbourg, came from a state incentive. All of these started in the 1980s. After a proposal of the President of the French Republic, a three-year contract between the state, department and the city had been signed in 1980 to focus on infrastructure development suitable of a European capital. Already in July 1979, Pierre Pflimlin, Raymond Leissner, Secretary-General of Strasbourg Daniel Adam and a city administration civil servant, Roger Hannsler, met with the *Préfet* to discuss their wishes. The prefect would transmit them to the national government.[86] These elements included the improvement of all modes of transport, though especially air links, financial assistance for construction activities, as well as development of culture with aid to the municipal orchestra, opera and theatre and the development of international schools.[87] In 1982, shortly before the expiration of the contract, the opinion was voiced that it needed

82 AS, 614 W 63, *Lettres de Leissner à Clauss et Amos, 29.6.1977.*

83 AS, 614 W 63, *Lettre d'Amos au Préfet, 21.11.1978.*

84 AS, 614 W 63, *Lettre du Préfet au Maire, 9.1.1979.*

85 AS, 752 W 114, *Lettre de L'Association des Commerçants au Maire, 26.3.1980.*

86 AS, 114 W 284/1, *Compte-rendu du 26.7.1979.*

87 AS, 114 W 284/1, *Contrat Métropole Européenne.*

to be prolonged with certain additions due to the economic situation.[88] Since that date, it has been continuously renewed, a more recent edition, running from 2012 to 2014, still contains largely the same points as the initial document.[89]

The triennial contract with its focus on the improvement of infrastructure and the strengthening of the city's economy encompassed strong symbolic notions. An article in the regional newspaper *DNA* which analysed the initial contract when it was signed in February 1980 summarised these circumstances quite well, "La vocation européenne. Trois ans pour se doter des moyens de ses ambitions."[90] It was not only a device to improve infrastructure for the European institutions, but was a continuation of city actors' rhetoric of Strasbourg as European city with a mission which had been strategically employed since the implantation of the CoE in 1949 (see chapter 2.1).

Next to development aid, the French state began to commission studies on the economic impact of the European institutions on Strasbourg. One of the earliest examples was a report from 31 March 1989 on how to reinforce durably the European role of the city. It had been commissioned by the Prime Minister in December 1988 and it included an evaluation by using statements of MEPs, civil servants and politicians, both from the EC and the city of Strasbourg.[91] This degree of state involvement only developed from 1980, before, local actors with few selective instances of support had nearly exclusively driven the action of Strasbourg.

Section 1.06 Attracting European institutions (1949-1952)

The vantage point of this study is to analyse consolidation efforts of local actors in Strasbourg regarding the presence of European organisations in their city. In order to understand this, the siting processes of the two main European institutions in the Alsatian capital, the Council of Europe and the Common Assembly of the ECSC, will be described with a specific concentration on how municipal actors figured in these developments. Compared to the scale of activity of local actors later on, this involvement was very limited.

---

88 ABR, 1130 W 904/1, *Eléments de réflexion.*

89 "Contrat triennal Strasbourg, capitale européenne 2012-2014 entre l'Etat, la Ville de Strasbourg, la Communauté Urbaine de Strasbourg, le Département du Bas-Rhin, la Région Alsace." Préfet de la Région Alsace. <http://www.alsace.pref.gouv.fr/medias/fichiers/Contrat_Triennal_2012_2014.pdf> (accessed 22.05.2014).

90 AS, 114 W 284/2, *Extrait des DNA, 12.2.1980.*

91 Villain, Claude, "Rapport sur le renforcement durable du rôle européen de Strasbourg, 31.3.1989", *Ministère des Affaires Européennes*, p. 4.

(a) Siting the Council of Europe

In the following, the siting of the Council of Europe in Strasbourg in 1949 will be described to give an overview of the political efforts leading to this result. The idea for such an organisation had already been proposed by Winston Churchill in 1942 and was further concretised during the 1948 congress in The Hague, among others.[92] Most of the discussion of siting it occurred during the founding conference in London, while the Preparatory Commission of the Council of Europe, which formulated rules and regulations and prepared for the first sessions of the Committee of Ministers and the organisation's assembly in August 1949, played a minor role. The location of the CoE in Strasbourg presents background information to the activities of local actors, who started their activities regarding the European institution after this decision.

(i) London Conference, May 1949

The "Conference for the establishment of a Council of Europe" was held in London from 3 to 5 May 1949 with the participation of Belgium, Denmark, France, Ireland, Italy, Luxembourg, the Netherlands, Norway, Sweden and the United Kingdom, whose Secretary of State for Foreign Affairs, Ernest Bevin, was the chairman of the meeting.[93] In the proceedings each of the different articles of the proposed statute were discussed, of which the name of the organisation were among the items debated for a longer time.[94] This section will concentrate on the discussions where to locate the organisation.

The premise of the discussion regarding the siting of the new organisation was that, as Schuman expressed it, Bevin had "spontaneously proposed Strasbourg."[95] In principle, none of the delegations openly disagreed to this option and no interlocutors disputed the assertion that the city would have a symbolic importance, since the region it was located in, Alsace, had long been a matter of territorial conflict between France and Germany.[96] The use of history later constituted one of the central strategies of local actors in Strasbourg to consolidate their position as CoE

---

92 Wassenberg, Birte, *Histoire du Conseil de l'Europe*, Brussels, Peter Lang, 2012, p. 17.

93 Archive of the Council of Europe (ACE), 13/16/1/1949, *Conference*, pp. 3; 4.

94 The discussion was whether to call the new organisation European Union or Council of Europe. The decision for the latter was made because it was feared that European Union might not totally fit the institution's aims. The Swedish Foreign Minister Östen Undén also claimed the first option would sound too pompous (cf. ACE, 13/16/1/1949, *Conference*).

95 ACE, 13/16/1/1949, *Conference*, p. 6.

96 ACE, 13/16/1/1949, *Conference*, p. 6.

and EP seat, especially in hosting matters which will be analysed in the subsequent chapter.

The Swedish Foreign Minister Östen Undén and his Danish colleague Gustav Rasmussen voiced reservations regarding facilities, transport options and the geographic centrality, but did not insist on their objections, since the majority was in favour of Bevin's suggestion.[97] Symbolic considerations seemed to have taken precedence over infrastructural capabilities, which often was the case regarding local actors' strategies especially during the 1950s. Schuman reassured Rasmussen after the latter stated he would either prefer a smaller, easily accessible country like Belgium or the Netherlands, or Paris if the decision fell for France, since he was uncertain of infrastructure in Strasbourg and the hot climate in late summer.[98] Schuman replied that facilities in the Alsatian city would be sufficient, as it had been seat of the provincial parliament for 50 years, before emphasising the attached symbolism and that it would fulfil the aim of achieving closer unity in Europe.[99]

The selection of Strasbourg as seat of the Council of Europe on the initiative of Bevin had had symbolic reasons and it was not strongly opposed by its critics, seeing that the conference agreed to designate the city as seat.[100] The British Foreign Minister emphasised this in the statement he made at the signature of the statute on 5 May 1949 with, "the really vital and symbolic moment in this business will come when the Council of Europe first meets on the historic soil of Alsace-Lorraine in a few months' time."[101] This symbolism played a crucial role in the strategies of local actors regarding relations with the CoE and in the seat question of the European Communities, as well, which will be presented in the following chapters. For instance, city administration actors drew on the fact that Bevin had suggested Strasbourg and had ascribed it its symbolic status as validation for their strategies to present themselves as a European city and ideal institution seat.

(ii) Preparing for the first session of PACE

The choice of Strasbourg remained uncontroversial in the setting up of the organisation. Following the London Conference, the Preparatory Commission of the Council of Europe was convened to prepare rules and

97 ACE, 13/16/1/1949, *Conference*, pp. 6-7.

98 ACE, 13/16/1/1949, *Conference*, p. 6.

99 ACE, 13/16/1/1949, *Conference*, p. 6.

100 ACE, 13/16/1/1949, *Conference*, p. 7.

101 ACE, 13/16/1/1949, *Conference*, p. 26.

regulations in time for the first session of its assembly and Committee of Ministers in August 1949. It was composed of one and in the case of the UK two representatives from each country. Most of them were either politicians or civil servants, such as the Belgian representative Fernand Dehousse for the first category, or the Dutch member Posthumus Meyjes, who later signed the general agreement on privileges and immunities of the CoE for the Netherlands for the second.[102] The panel met 25 times from its creation on 5 May until 13 July 1949.[103] In the archive of the European organisation, numerous drafts of the report of the commission were archived and they show that the installation in Strasbourg virtually drew no discussion. For example, one version of the report denoted that the special agreement between the CoE and the French government relating to the seat did not "[...] call for specific comment."[104] This agreement was signed on 2 September 1949 and it regulated the legal aspects regarding the seat. The CoE had taken the seat agreement between the United Nations (UN) and the United States as inspiration and tailored it to its needs.[105]

Next to creating the legal and administrative basis for Strasbourg's seat status, the commission was tasked with preparing the first session of the Committee of Ministers and the assembly in August 1949. For this objective, they made a study visit to the city from 13 to 14 May 1949, during which they evaluated facilities, established what was required and how to organise the session.[106] As will be analysed further in chapter 2, they decided in cooperation with the city administration to hold the assembly meetings in the main hall of the university and the Committee of Ministers sessions in the town hall.[107] In the announcement of this decision, the preparatory commission expressly thanked the mayor, prefect of the department and the rector of the university for their assistance in the process.[108] Additionally, the commission arranged for a CoE organisation of hotel accommodation. Some national delegations to PACE had already made their own arrangements, but interested members could transmit

[102] ACE, 21/0016/1-4/1949, *3e séance du 18.5.1949*, p. 1 and Council of Europe, *The General Agreement on Privileges and Immunities of the Council of Europe of 2nd September 1949, together with the Supplementary Agreement of 18th March 1950, the Protocol to the General Agreement of 6th November 1952, the Second Protocol of 15th December 1956, the Third Protocol of 6th March 1959, and the Fourth Protocol of 16th December 1961*, Strasbourg, Council of Europe Publications Section, 1983, p. 12.

[103] ACE, 17/16/5-6/1949, *Covering letter.*

[104] ACE, 17/16/5-6/1949, *XIII – Draft special agreement.*

[105] ACE, 17/16/5-6/1949, *XIII – Draft special agreement* and 044/00120, *Special agreement.*

[106] ACE, 20/0016/10-12/1949, *Report of the visit.*

[107] ACE, 20/0016/10-12/1949, *Communiqué du 21.6.1949.*

[108] ACE, 20/0016/10-12/1949, *Communiqué du 21.6.1949.*

their accommodation needs to the executive secretary until 15 June 1949, who would then make reservation arrangements.[109] The activity of the city administration was characterised by ad hoc decisions rather than long-term strategies that were visible after the establishment of the CoE.

The organisational process for the first session had been conducted between the institution and local actors without any further involvement of the French state, a characteristic which repeated itself during the following years. Other than a note addressed to Schuman regarding facilities and hosting measures in Strasbourg after discussions with the *Institut d'Etudes Européennes de Strasbourg* and the *Comité Alsacien d'Etudes et d'Informations*, the national government did not seem to have been involved.[110]

Judging by the source material in the municipal archive, the hosting programme and building efforts were organised by local actors with no or very little involvement of the state until the 1970s. Nevertheless, this note shows the different issues the decision to site the CoE in Strasbourg entailed. In regard to transport facilities, the situation was characterised as poor for the three main modes railway, air and road, of which the latter was given the most optimistic assessment.[111] Especially the train link between Basel and Brussels was described as very slow and the note specified that no air traffic of note occurred in the local airport which meant the nearest airport close to Mulhouse 120 kilometres away was the only possibility to reach Strasbourg by air.[112]

The state of possible lodgings was described as desolate as well, since war damages had not been entirely removed and hotel resources would be of a provincial character, among others.[113] The evaluation of the hospitality sector of Strasbourg led to a similar bleak result, for example, the note stated there had not been anything of semblance for visitors during the summer of 1948 and that the only option would have been cinemas.[114] As a final point the note expressed that Strasbourg needed to be transformed into a great French city with an international flair in order to welcome the CoE adequately, where it still would lack in some aspects, for example, German nationals were not allowed to sojourn in the city at the time.[115]

109 ACE, 21/0016/1-4/1949, *7e compte-rendu du 9.6.1949*, pp. 2-3.

110 ACE, 044/00120, *Note pour M. Schuman*, p. 1.

111 ACE, 044/00120, *Note pour M. Schuman*, p. 3.

112 ACE, 044/00120, *Note pour M. Schuman*, p. 3.

113 ACE, 044/00120, *Note pour M. Schuman*, p. 4.

114 ACE, 044/00120, *Note pour M. Schuman*, p. 4.

115 ACE, 044/00120, *Note pour M. Schuman*, p. 6.

The content of this report emphasised the fact that Strasbourg had mainly been chosen by the London Conference due to symbolic considerations that could be inferred from the city's history. As will be shown during the course of the analysis, these infrastructural issues took time to overcome despite the efforts of local actors. This could have been another reason why activities in the 1950s largely focussed on this symbolic aspect and the creation of a welcoming environment (see chapter 2). Nevertheless, although among others Rasmussen and Undén had voiced tentative concerns about Strasbourg's infrastructure, they had not played a role in the political process to locate the institution in the Alsatian city.

The only aspect of the siting of the CoE which attracted more attention was the question of where and how in Strasbourg to house it. Prior to the custom headquarters, the *Maison de l'Europe*, had been constructed in 1950, efforts to install the organisation in an existing building that fit or could be adapted to its requirements were made until the custom building was chosen as the best option. This issue will be discussed during the analysis of pre-1970 infrastructure for the European institutions in chapter 4.

(b) Siting the institutions of the Schuman Plan

In the following, events of the initial attempt of the European Communities to designate a permanent seat will be. In the beginning of the siting process, the municipality exhibited the same hesitancy as with the placement of the CoE and it only started to be active later in the political process. This section is based both on primary sources from archive research, as well as municipal documents from other candidates available online from the *Centre Virtuel de la Connaissance sur l'Europe*. As described in the introduction, scholarships on political aspects of Brussels and Luxembourg's efforts to consolidate their position as seat exist, from which information to the primary sources will be supplemented.

The attempts to find a location for the institutions of the ECSC following the Schuman declaration on 9 May 1950 were characterised by confusion regarding definitions, conflicting proposals, behind-the-scenes horse-trading and national politics. The number of official candidates seems to have been such a matter, as well, judging by the fact that also academic texts mention different ones. The Hague, Liège, Luxembourg, Strasbourg and Saarbrucken were commonly named, while other texts also referred to Maastricht, Brussels, Paris and Turin as candidates for the seat of the

ECSC.[116] For instance, before a foreign ministers conference in July 1952 Turin had not been mentioned in the political arena, but apparently only in a newspaper.[117]

The main actors in the matter generally were the foreign ministers of the six member states, who held the formal decision power of siting the institutions of the Schuman Plan, but occasionally also heads of the national governments. They were Dirk Stikker (Netherlands), Paul van Zeeland (Belgium), Joseph Bech (Luxembourg), Robert Schuman (France), Carlo Sforza and Alcide de Gasperi (Italy), as well as Walter Hallstein and Konrad Adenauer (Germany).

Next to the conferences they held, diplomatic endeavours were undertaken, as well. For example, in a letter from 30 October 1950 to Bech, Albert Wehrer, the representative of Luxembourg in Bonn, stressed that the minister should approach Schuman in order to obtain his support, because then it would be easier to attain the approval of the others.[118] He added that "il faut absolument gagner cette bataille", since expenses of the High Authority were estimated at 400 million Belgian Francs, which would in part benefit the Grand Duchy if it housed the seat.[119] Additionally, further cities announced their candidatures, for example in May 1951, Liège.[120] The mayor of Saarbrucken transmitted the city's candidature in a letter to Schuman in June 1951, citing its connections to the steel industry and the centrality in relation to transport and distances.[121]

---

116 E.g. Trausch, Gilbert, "Robert Schuman, le Luxembourg et l'Europe", in Trausch, Gilbert *et al.* (eds.), *Le Luxembourg face à la construction européenne – Luxemburg und die europäische Einigung*, Luxembourg, Centre d'études et de recherches européennes Robert Schuman, 1996, p. 33.

117 Croisé-Schirtz, Edmée, "La bataille des sièges (1950-1958)", in Trausch, Gilbert *et al.* (eds.), *Le Luxembourg face à la construction européenne – Luxemburg und die europäische Einigung*, Luxembourg, Centre d'Etudes et de Recherches Européennes Robert Schuman, 1996, p. 73.

118 "Rapport de Albert Wehrer sur la question du siège des institutions européennes (Luxembourg, 30 octobre 1950)." Centre Virtuel de la Connaissance sur l'Europe. <http://www.cvce.eu/obj/report_by_albert_wehrer_on_the_question_of_the_seat_of_the_european_institutions_luxembourg_30_october_1950-en-4b115ba2-c37b-423d-9115-a89281e11868.html> (accessed 13.06.2014), p. 2.

119 *Ibid.*

120 Croisé-Schirtz, Edmée, "La bataille des sièges (1950-1958)", in Trausch, Gilbert *et al.* (eds.), *Le Luxembourg face à la construction européenne – Luxemburg und die europäische Einigung*, Luxembourg, Centre d'Etudes et de Recherches Européennes Robert Schuman, 1996, p. 69.

121 "Lettre de candidature de la ville de Sarrebruck aux institutions communautaires (Sarrebruck, 11 juin 1951)." Centre Virtuel de la Connaissance sur l'Europe. <http://www.cvce.eu/obj/lettre_de_candidature_de_la_ville_de_sarrebruck_aux_institutions_

As Croisé-Schirtz analyses in her assessment of political sources from Luxembourg, around 1951, the German delegation seems to have been in favour of the Grand Duchy as institution host, except for the Court of Justice which they wanted in The Hague.[122] As a contrast, the French, especially Jean Monnet, seemed to prefer any other choice than Luxembourg, while Italy seemed to support Paris, although they would probably choose the geographically closer Luxembourg, should a choice remain between it and Liège.[123] The Netherlands and Belgium seemed to prefer the institutions in their own candidates, The Hague and Liège. In relation to the latter, the authorities in Luxembourg evaluated this application as antagonistic towards their country.[124] They analysed that without this applicant, the Benelux states and Germany would probably have supported them and Italy and France might have agreed to the Grand Duchy, as well.[125] In addition, Luxembourg's delegation attempted to profit from the fact that the Belgian government had not officially proposed Brussels as candidate, of which the other delegations, especially Germany, might have agreed in order to curry instead the favour of the other national delegations.[126]

Next to these efforts, the Interim Committee of the ECSC had instituted a committee composed of lawyers and economists to compose a report on all applicants, to which all but Saarbrucken responded.[127] Such factors of changing support and national politics might have constituted the reason that a provisional solution was only found on 25 July 1952, around the time the treaty of the ECSC came into force. It had been made on the Foreign Ministers Conference from 23 to 24 July 1952, which meant a tight timeframe for the temporary seats, since the institutions, the High Authority and Court of Justice, were supposed to function from 10 August, while the assembly would hold its first session from 10 September.[128]

---

communautaires_sarrebruck_11_juin_1951-fr-6f8eec29-6f25-4da2-b48a-3eb54c32092e.html> (accessed 13.06.2014).

122 Croisé-Schirtz, Edmée, "La bataille des sièges (1950-1958)", in Trausch, Gilbert *et al.* (eds.), *Le Luxembourg face à la construction européenne – Luxemburg und die europäische Einigung*, Luxembourg, Centre d'Etudes et de Recherches Européennes Robert Schuman, 1996, p. 69.

123 *Ibid.*

124 *Ibid.*, pp. 69-70.

125 *Ibid.*, p. 70.

126 *Ibid.*, p. 72.

127 *Ibid.*

128 Archive of the Council of the EU (AC), CM1/1955 48, *Communiqué du 25.7.1952.*

(i) The Seat Question, July 1952

During the July conference, which was chaired by Schuman and attended by Adenauer, De Gasperi, Van Zeeland, Stikker and Bech,[129] the climate of differing, essentially national positions continued, mixed with changing patterns of support. One major example for this was that Schuman suddenly proposed Saarbrucken, which apparently had not counted among principal candidates, as permanent seat and to give the Saarland a European statute, while Strasbourg could become interim seat until this plan could be implemented.[130] It pended the approval of the population through a referendum.[131] Adenauer did not approve of this solution and proposed The Hague as seat for all ECSC institutions, or any other neutral city, which found the approval of Benelux.[132] In the early morning hours of 24 June, an accord was apparently found for a dual seat, with the High Authority and the court in Turin and the assembly in Strasbourg, although the motion failed to be carried due to the veto of Monnet who surprisingly proposed Luxembourg as provisional seat.[133]

This situation apparently characterised the entire conference, which named even more candidates that commonly gained all but one vote. An internal note from the ministry of foreign affairs in Luxembourg recounted in 1954 how the final accord for Luxembourg and for the assembly, Strasbourg, had been reached.[134] Brussels constituted the next promising candidate, but the only vote it failed to attain was of its own country, since Van Zeeland vetoed and insisted on Liège as the only Belgian option.[135] Adenauer's proposal of designating The Hague as temporary seat to gain time for further discussion met with the same situation, this time Van Zeeland disapproved because he claimed an applicant for

---

129 Croisé-Schirtz, Edmée, "La bataille des sièges (1950-1958)", in Trausch, Gilbert *et al.* (eds.), *Le Luxembourg face à la construction européenne – Luxemburg und die europäische Einigung*, Luxembourg, Centre d'Etudes et de Recherches Européennes Robert Schuman, 1996, p. 73.

130 *Ibid.*

131 AC, CM1/1955 48, *Proposition de M. Schuman du 23.7.1952.*

132 Croisé-Schirtz, Edmée, "La bataille des sièges (1950-1958)", in Trausch, Gilbert *et al.* (eds.), *Le Luxembourg face à la construction européenne – Luxemburg und die europäische Einigung*, Luxembourg, Centre d'Etudes et de Recherches Européennes Robert Schuman, 1996, p. 74.

133 *Ibid.*, p. 75.

134 "Note interne du ministère des Affaires étrangères luxembourgeois (14 décembre 1954)." European Navigator (Centre Virtuel de la Connaissance sur l'Europe). <http://www.ena.lu/internal_note_luxembourg_foreign_ministry_14_december_1954-2-12732.pdf> (accessed 15.02.2011).

135 *Ibid.*, p. 4.

the permanent seat could not become the provisional host.[136] The note reported that upon this statement, a furious Stikker left the room and slammed the door behind him.[137] In the resulting intermission, Adenauer approached Bech to ask him to withdraw Luxembourg's candidature for the definitive seat, so that it could become the interim location instead.[138] The Foreign Minister agreed and proposed this after the session had been resumed, which Van Zeeland consequently could not disapprove of, and Luxembourg gained the approval of all delegations as temporary seat for the High Authority and the court.[139] The assembly was located in Strasbourg, so that it could share facilities with the CoE.[140] However, the secretariat of the parliament was located in Luxembourg in order to avoid confusion with the corresponding institution of the CoE and to allow for physical closeness to the ECSC decision centre.[141]

(ii) The Seat Question 1952-1957

The majority of activity following this tentative accord regarded Schuman's proposal of Saarbrucken as permanent seat and the Europeanisation of the Saarland. An agreement between France and Germany on the Saarland's statute from 23 October 1954 cemented this decision. It proposed the governing of the state under a European statute and recommended the permanent siting of all European institutions in its capital.[142]

Its biggest supporter seems to have been France, because public opinion in Germany was not favourable and also the governments of Benelux opposed, because they saw it as an expression of the dominance of the big states in the ECSC.[143] For example, Luxembourg's government stated in an internal note, "la ville s'est adaptée à sa nouvelle mission et ce

---

136 *Ibid.*

137 *Ibid.*

138 *Ibid.*

139 *Ibid.*, pp. 4-5.

140 Dinan, Desmond, *Europe Recast*, Basingstoke, Palgrave, 2004, p. 55. In the same sentence it is mentioned that Council meetings would be held in Brussels. However, this city was not an option during 1952, when the Belgian government presented Liège as the country's only candidate. The decision for Brussels was only made in 1958.

141 Göldner, Markus, *Politische Symbole der europäischen Integration. Rechtshistorische Reihe, Bd. 62*, Frankfurt am Main, Peter Lang, 1988, 163.

142 "Accord conclu entre le gouvernement de la République fédérale d'Allemagne et le gouvernement de la République Française sur le statut de la Sarre 1954." Digithèque de matériaux juridiques et politiques, Université de Perpignon. <http://mjp.univ-perp.fr/defense/sarre54.htm> (accessed 09.06.2014).

143 Croisé-Schirtz, Edmée, "La bataille des sièges (1950-1958)", in Trausch, Gilbert *et al.* (eds.), *Le Luxembourg face à la construction européenne – Luxemburg und die*

serait un pur scandale si, après tous ces efforts, la Communauté quitterait maintenant Luxembourg pour aller s'installer dans des villes qui avouent n'avoir rien d'autre à offrir que des champs pour construire."[144] Thus, the Saarland decision went against the Grand Duchy's efforts to consolidate its provisional position, which is also asserted by Croisé-Schirtz.[145]

The referendum in Saarland was held on 23 October 1955, and since 67.7 percent rejected the European statute,[146] Saarbrucken as the permanent ECSC seat ceased to be an option. According to Croisé-Schirtz, no further activity regarding the designation of a permanent seat was visible until 1957, when the second ECSC seat application round began.[147] Despite the fact that it was not popular, Saarbrucken was one of the closest attainments of a political decision to site permanently the institutions of the ECSC. For example, the internal 1954 note from Luxembourg quoted German civil servants of the High Authority, "also die Herren von der neuen Europaunion [WEU] wählen sich Paris und London zum künftigen Sitz und uns reserviert man eine Strafversetzung nach Saarbrücken, nur um den Saarbrücker einen Gefallen zu machen."[148]

(iii) Local activity

In the immediate years following the highly provisional placement of the High Authority and the court in Luxembourg, its government worked hard to consolidate its position, not only with political means, but also with

europäische Einigung, Luxembourg, Centre d'Etudes et de Recherches Européennes Robert Schuman, 1996, p. 79.

144 "Note interne du ministère des Affaires étrangères luxembourgeois (14 décembre 1954)." European Navigator (Centre Virtuel de la Connaissance sur l'Europe). <http://www.ena.lu/internal_note_luxembourg_foreign_ministry_14_december_1954-2-12732.pdf> (accessed 15.02.2011), p. 6.

145 Croisé-Schirtz, Edmée, "La bataille des sièges (1950-1958)", in Trausch, Gilbert *et al.* (eds.), *Le Luxembourg face à la construction européenne – Luxemburg und die europäische Einigung*, Luxembourg, Centre d'Etudes et de Recherches Européennes Robert Schuman, 1996, p. 83.

146 "Die saarländische Sonderrolle bis 1955. Sitzverteilung im ersten saarländischen Parlament." Landtag des Saarlandes <http://www.landtag-saar.de/DerLandtag/langerWeg/Seiten/VTSonderrolle.aspx> (accessed 09.06.2014).

147 Croisé-Schirtz, Edmée, "La bataille des sièges (1950-1958)", in Trausch, Gilbert *et al.* (eds.), *Le Luxembourg face à la construction européenne – Luxemburg und die europäische Einigung*, Luxembourg, Centre d'Etudes et de Recherches Européennes Robert Schuman, 1996, p. 87.

148 "Note interne du ministère des Affaires étrangères luxembourgeois (14 décembre 1954)." European Navigator (Centre Virtuel de la Connaissance sur l'Europe). <http://www.ena.lu/internal_note_luxembourg_foreign_ministry_14_december_1954-2-12732.pdf> (accessed 15.02.2011), p. 7.

measures in the city. The fact that the decision for the siting fell on 25 July and that the institutions needed to be operational from 10 August 1952 meant that the Grand Duchy did not have a long preparation time. The High Authority moved in the building of the direction of *Chemins de fer Luxembourgeois* at Place de Metz, which just had two weeks to move and the court was placed in the *Villa Vauban*, for which the museum it housed had to make way, as well.[149] A leisure activities programme apparently figured as well, whose functionality was also evaluated by the competition.

In 1954, after a government change in Belgium, the tourism association of Brussels made overtures to push for a candidature of the city. During a meeting on 26 May, its president listed reasons why the organisation should push this, but also mentioned facilities in Luxembourg, such as that it only had four cinemas and added, "les gens de la C.E.C.A. qui sont à Luxembourg m'ont dit: C'est épouvantable à Luxembourg nos femmes ne savent pas où prendre le thé. C'est un désastre!"[150] Being able to host the staff of European institutions was important, as well. The city administration of Strasbourg concentrated much of its early efforts on this area and used special events for parliamentarians strategically to strengthen their position as permanent CoE and provisional EP seat, which will be the focus of chapter 2.

During the first ECSC seat application round in 1952, local actors in Strasbourg were hardly involved when compared to later phases. Next to concrete efforts regarding the siting of the institutions of the Schuman Plan, the city administration exhibited some activity on the local level by involving the CoE. Actors could best be analysed as sending mixed signals. The *Conseil Municipal* session on 25 February occupied itself with this matter. Mayor Charles Frey stated that Strasbourg would not apply from its own initiative, but would not be disinterested either.[151]

Nevertheless, the assembly declared it would be highly interested in an extraordinary session, with the reasoning that the Schuman plan institutions should be in a French city and that there seemed to be a consensus that they should be grouped together with the CoE.[152] In this discussion, Pflimlin seems to have been the driving force, who pushed

---

149 Nies-Berchem, Martine, "L'administration luxembourgeoise et les débuts de l'administration européenne (1952-1967)", in Trausch, Gilbert *et al.* (eds.), *Le Luxembourg face à la construction européenne – Luxemburg und die europäische Einigung*, Luxembourg, Centre d'études et de recherches européennes Robert Schuman, 1996, p. 156.

150 ena.lu, *Position du Syndicat d'Initiative de Bruxelles, 26.5.1954*, p. 6.

151 Conseil Municipal de la Ville de Strasbourg, *Débats du Conseil Municipal de 1952*, Strasbourg, Imprimerie Alsacienne, 1953, p. 68.

152 *Ibid.*, pp. 68-69.

for the publishing of the resolution on the seat.[153] This resolution just made a recommendation to the above argument, to locate all European institutions in the same city.[154] Apart from that, the city and departmental administrations seemed to have allowed the national political level to decide, a stark contrast to the period from the mid-1950s to the late 1970s. Then, the local level constituted the driving force of strategies to consolidate Strasbourg's position, with the national government only playing a minor role with sporadic assistances regarding infrastructure and political interventions at the European Communities.

In January 1952, Mayor Charles Frey had sent a letter to Jacques Camille Paris, the Secretary-General of the CoE, asking what he thought the needs for the European institutions were. Although he stated that Strasbourg had not offered its candidature officially, it would give French negotiations all the leeway needed.[155] The European organisation stood in contact with several involved actors, such as the Belgian Minister of Foreign Affairs sending a letter to Paul Lévy, the Director of Information at the CoE to inform him of his opinions on the form of the seat.[156] In general, the institution favoured the grouping of other European institutions at its seat, as for example expressed in the answer of J.C. Paris to Frey to the missive the latter sent in January.[157]

The fact that the city administration did not appear particularly active during the first ECSC seat application round did not seem to have been a singular occurrence, as Luxembourg did not drive a publicity campaign either. Bech reasoned that the siting of the institutions would be an important political issue that should not be accompanied with a raucous campaign.[158] This could have been a contributing factor apart from the apparent main reason that local actors in Strasbourg principally focused on the CoE until 1957.

In contrast, a private organisation founded in response to the siting of the CoE, the *Comité Strasbourgeois pour le Mouvement Européen (CSME)*, strongly promoted Strasbourg in 1952. In its journal *Vers l'Europe* it advertised the city as the best possibility, as well as the question of the

---

153 *Ibid.*, pp. 70; 72.

154 ACE, 3153/2409, *Résolution du Conseil Municipal de la Ville de Strasbourg du 25.2.1952.*

155 ACE, 3153/2409, *Lettre du M. le Maire à Paris, 30.1.1952.*

156 ACE, 3153/2409, *Lettre de Maurice à Lévy, 22.2.1952.*

157 ACE, 3153/2409, *Lettre de Paris au Maire, 1.2.1952.*

158 Croisé-Schirtz, Edmée, "La bataille des sièges (1950-1958)", in Trausch, Gilbert *et al.* (eds.), *Le Luxembourg face à la construction européenne – Luxemburg und die europäische Einigung*, Luxembourg, Centre d'Etudes et de Recherches Européennes Robert Schuman, 1996, p. 72.

European capital and its form, namely concentration or dispersion of institutions, the issue of general European integration and its form was also raised. For example, the entire April 1952 issue had been devoted to these matters, publishing pro-Strasbourg answers of an opinion poll the *CSME* had conducted among PACE delegates, national politicians and journalists, as well as a book which argued for the same.[159]

(iv) The Seat Question, 1957-1959

In this section, an overview of key events of the second seat application round will be given. The attempt to locate the European institutions permanently in a city encompassed all three European Communities, ECSC, European Economic Community (EEC) and the European Atomic Energy Community (EURATOM), but in the sources, a focus seemed to have been on the initial organisation. Therefore, it will mostly be referred to it as the second application round of the ECSC.

This second attempt to determine a definitive seat started following the Treaties of Rome in 1957 and spanned the rest of the decade and the early 1960s, although no official decision was taken until 1965.[160] The most active phase lay between 1957 and 1959; therefore, this period will be concentrated on. During it, the indecision about seat locations continued. The formal decision power lay with the foreign ministers who regularly met during this period to find a solution. Next to the councils of the three communities, the permanent representatives and the Intergovernmental Conference (IGC) were involved, for example, the IGC on demand of the former elaborated a report on the progress of finding a seat in 1959 and 1960.[161]

The Foreign Ministers Conference from 6-7 January 1958 was the first attempt of the European Communities to find a solution during this application round. It did not lead to any results, other than that the ministers decided to institute a committee of European urbanism experts in order to evaluate candidates according to common geographic,

159 Comité Strasbourgeois pour le Mouvement Européen, "Notre enquête des personnalités européennes de tous pays et de toutes tendances se prononce sur la concentration des autorités spéciales autour du Conseil de l'Europe", in *Vers l'Europe*' 3:26' 1952, pp. 1-8 and Comité Strasbourgeois pour le Mouvement Européen, *Strasbourg, capitale européenne, siège du Conseil de l'Europe, doit devenir le siège des autorités européennes*, Strasbourg, Impressions Strasbourg, 1952.

160 Croisé-Schirtz, Edmée, "La bataille des sièges (1950-1958)", in Trausch, Gilbert *et al.* (eds.), *Le Luxembourg face à la construction européenne - Luxemburg und die europäische Einigung*, Luxembourg, Centre d'Etudes et de Recherches Européennes Robert Schuman, 1996, pp. 87; 103.

161 AC, CM2 1965 245, *Entwurf eines Berichts.*

infrastructural and symbolic criteria.[162] Each of the ECSC member states designated a member, which were recruited from universities or civil servant positions[163] with a relation to urbanism.[164] This *Comité européen d'experts en urbanisme* visited all candidates that had applied within the set deadline of 31 March 1958, by official transmission from their national governments. The committee composed its report between 10 March and 30 April 1958.[165] The foreign ministers decided to discuss the committee's results at a meeting on 1 June 1958.[166]

Additionally, the Council of the three Communities, ECSC, EURATOM and the EEC, decided on 25 February 1958 to accept only candidatures that had been transmitted or presented by their national government authorities until 31 March 1958.[167] The French Ministry of Foreign Affairs only confirmed by letter to the Presidents of the Committee of Permanent Representatives (COREPER) and the Council of the European Communities on 27 and 28 March 1958 that they presented the candidature of Strasbourg and would likewise transmit the proposals of Paris, the Département de l'Oise[168] and Nice.[169] Therewith, these four applications had been officially accepted by the European Communities. Strasbourg had originally announced its candidature on 25 July 1957, and had sent out an additional notice with a resolution at the end of October 1957, but that the French government only gave the necessary endorsement days before the deadline. It was a significant indicator for that local authorities had to promote their candidature themselves.

---

162 AC, CM2/1958 0201, *Note du 6.2.1958.*

163 The members were: Belgium (chair) – Victor Bure (Directeur Général de l'Administration de l'Urbanisme, Ministère des Travaux Publics et de la Reconstruction); Germany – Johannes Rossig (Ministerialdirigent, Bundesministerium für den wirtschaftlichen Besitz des Bundes); France – Pierre Randet (Contrôleur Général au Ministère de la Reconstruction et du Logement); Italy – Cesare Valle (Presidente di Sezione del Consiglio Superiore dei L.L.P.P., Professore di Urbanistica presso l'Università di Roma); Luxembourg – A. Luja (Architecte urbaniste au Service d'Urbanisme d'Etat, Ministère des Travaux Publics); Netherlands – J.P. Thijsse (Conseiller Général Urbaniste, Rijksdienst voor het Nationale Plan) (cf. AC, CM1/1958 0120, *Bericht der europäischen Fachkommission für Städteplanung*, p. 4).

164 AC, CM2/1958 0201, *Note du 6.3.1958.*

165 AC, CM2/1958 0205, *Ausschuss von Fachleuten.*

166 AC, CM2/1958 0222, *Extrait du Procès-verbal du 6/7.1.1958*, p. 2.

167 AC, CM2/1958 0204, *Lettre de Calmes au Ministère Affaires Etrangères Françaises, 1.4.1958.*

168 The Département de l'Oise had already announced its candidature in November 1957, as well.

169 AC, CM2/1958 0203, *Lettre de la Ministère des Affaires Etrangères / Ministre aux Présidents COREPER/Comité des Ministres des Communautés Européennes, 27./28.3.1958.*

Other French cities, which applied directly to the Council of the three European Communities, or where the French government transmitted them after the deadline, were not accepted. These were, among others, Arc et Senans, Versailles and Fontainebleau.[170] The proposal of Lyon to function as the seat of European institutions, which its mayor sent to the French government on 26 March 1958, was only transmitted to the European Communities on 1 April, which meant that it was not accepted due to the passed submission deadline.[171] The mayor of the city later claimed in a letter to the President of the Committee of Ministers, where he advocated his city as a new choice to break the nondecision regarding the seat, a technical error had caused the late submission of his candidature.[172]

In a resolution of Lyon's *Conseil Municipal* on 28 July 1958, which had been sent to the European Communities, the willingness of the city to become single seat was reconfirmed.[173] Next to indicating infrastructural advantages, such as closeness to Marseille, a major port, and Geneva, the seat of numerous international organisations, Lyon's *vocation européenne* was employed as an argument.[174] History was used in the same manner as Strasbourg's actors constructed their past to state why the city should house European institutions. Lyon, founded 2,000 years ago, was, due to having been the capital of the Gauls, the perfect candidate as single seat, since their territory once encompassed much of Western Europe.[175] Furthermore, because of the French engagement in the Common Market, a city of this country should become capital of Europe. The resolution argued that Paris was not suitable and that Lyon, the second metropolis after the national capital, would constitute the ideal candidate.[176]

Since Lyon was one of the never officially endorsed candidates, it was a footnote in the intra-national competition of French applicant cities. However, it illustrates the competitiveness regarding the seat question from 1957 to 1959. Furthermore, it shows that the use of an alleged

---

170 AC, CM2/1958 0204, *Maire Arc et Senans aux "Six"* and Hein, Carola, "Hauptstadt Europa", Arbeit zur Erlangung des Grades Doktor-Ingenieur am Fachbereich Architektur der Hochschule für bildende Künste Hamburg, 1995, p. 112.

171 AC, CM2/1958 0204, *Lettre du Maire de Lyon au Président du Comité des Ministres des Communautés Européennes, 25.6.1958* and *Lettre de Calmes au Ministère des Affaires Etrangères Françaises, 1.4.1958.*

172 AC, CM2/1958 0204, *Lettre du Maire de Lyon au Président du Comité des Ministres des Communautés Européennes, 25.6.1958.*

173 AC, CM2/1958 0204, *Conseil Municipal de la Ville de Lyon, 28.7.1958.*

174 AC, CM2/1958 0204, *Conseil Municipal de la Ville de Lyon, 28.7.1958.*

175 AC, CM2/1958 0204, *Conseil Municipal de la Ville de Lyon 28.7.1958*, pp. 1-2.

176 AC, CM2/1958 0204, *Conseil Municipal de la Ville de Lyon 28.7.1958*, p. 1.

European mission as in the case of Strasbourg (see next chapter) was not unusual, although the acceptance of the city's narrative did present an exceptional case.

Sources show that the endorsement of the French government oscillated between supporting Paris and Strasbourg, however, the official candidature transmission letter named Strasbourg as the principal applicant.[177] In the same manner, as Paris constituted serious competition due to its infrastructure and central location, Brussels shared these arguments in its favour as well. Many member states seemed to prefer the Belgian city.[178] Moreover, different versions of what a member state preferred as seat solution seem to have been circulating. For instance, a member of the German parliament *Bundestag* stated in a letter to Paul Lévy, the Director of Information of the CoE, in December 1957 that Germany would only officially support Strasbourg, if the German town of Kehl on the opposite bank of the Rhine from Strasbourg also received institution buildings.[179] However, a CoE report from January 1958 stated that the German chancellor Konrad Adenauer would continue to support Brussels.[180] Therefore, an unclear situation of who supported whom, contributed to the threat scenario of Strasbourg falling out of favour, as well. This situation seems to have been based on rumours or hearsay that nevertheless tended to be treated as concrete facts by the city administration which always almost immediately countered them by actions or verbal promotion of the capabilities of Strasbourg.

The report of the urbanism expert committee was intended to be an objective evaluation of all official candidates according to common evaluation criteria. However, the foreign ministers conference mandated that no comparisons should be drawn between applicants, as this would not be the objective of the committee.[181] The aspects, each city was evaluated on were grouped into three categories – features of the city regarding European factors, special features of the city and features of the proposed sites for the construction of European buildings and if need be for the establishment of an European district.[182] These three

177 AC, CM2/1958 0203, *Lettre de la Ministère des Affaires Etrangères au Président du COREPER, 27.3.1958.*

178 ACE, 3153/2409, *Siège, rapport, 1.-31.1.1958*, p. 2.

179 ACE, 3153/2409, *Lettre à Lévy, 4.12.1957.*

180 ACE, 3153/2409, *Siège, rapport, 1.-31.1.1958*, p. 3.

181 AC, CM1/ 1958 0120, *Bericht der europäischen Fachkommission für Städteplanung*, p. 7.

182 AC, AC, CM1/ 1958 0120, *Bericht der europäischen Fachkommission für Städteplanung*, pp. 13; 14; 17. The report was published in all official languages of the ECSC (French, Dutch, German and Italian), the English translation is based on the German version

categories encompassed everything from a European mission of the city, geographical position, state of transport and building infrastructure and cultural life.[183]

The city of Strasbourg had counted among the first applicants to announce its candidature before this conference by letter in July 1957. They sent it to the French Minister for Foreign affairs, the President of the Committee of Ministers of the CoE, the President of PACE, the Secretary-General of the CoE, as well as the president of the High Authority of the ECSC, among others.[184] The application was reconfirmed by a resolution from 19 October 1957, which had similarly been widely dispersed.[185] At first, Luxembourg had been reluctant to submit its candidature for the second seat application round, since its government was only interested in consolidating its position as host for the ECSC High Authority and the Court.[186] In order to retain these institutions, Luxembourg City eventually applied for the single seat on 7 March 1958, which the Grand Duchy's government transmitted to COREPER on 15 March 1958.[187] This hesitation might also have contributed to the fact that Strasbourg's actors rather saw Paris and not Luxembourg as most dangerous competition after Brussels until the Merger Treaty.

All in all, there were ten official candidate cities in total; Brussels, Luxembourg, Strasbourg, Paris, Département de l'Oise, Nice, Milan, Turin, Stresa and Monza.[188] Despite these developments, no further decisions, except adjournments were made in seat matters until the mid-1960s. In the meantime, the institutions of the by now three communities, ECSC, EEC and EURATOM, remained provisionally distributed between Strasbourg,

---

and translated by the author. The originals are: *Merkmale der Stadt unter europäischem Gesichtspunkt*, *Besondere Eigenschaften der Stadt* and *Merkmale der für den Bau der europäischen Gebäude und gegebenenfalls für die Einrichtung eines europäischen Komplexes vorgeschlagenen Gelände.*

183 AC, CM1/ 1958 0120, *Bericht der europäischen Fachkommission für Städteplanung*, pp. 13-17.

184 AS, 209 MW 6, *Note du 16.10.1963*, p. 1.

185 AS, 235 MW 268, *Résolution du 19.10.1957.*

186 Croisé-Schirtz, Edmée, "La bataille des sièges (1950-1958)", in Trausch, Gilbert *et al.* (eds.), *Le Luxembourg face à la construction européenne – Luxemburg und die europäische Einigung*, Luxembourg, Centre d'Etudes et de Recherches Européennes Robert Schuman, 1996, pp. 97-98.

187 *Ibid.*, p. 102.

188 AC, CM2/1958 0205, *Siège des Institutions.*

Luxembourg and Brussels. The latter city had been designated as interim host for EEC and EURATOM institutions.[189]

Additionally, the EP voted on their favourite applicants on 23 June 1958. In a first vote, each MEP elected five favourites, with five being the highest preference.[190] Overall, the most preferred candidates were Brussels, Strasbourg, Milan, Nice and Luxembourg.[191] Of these options, the MEPs had to vote for their three favourites in a second ballot, which resulted in Brussels, Strasbourg and Milan.[192] Both the urbanism expert committee's report and the opinion of the MEPs did not seem to have been taken into account by the European Communities which repeatedly postponed decisions until 1965.[193]

In the Merger Treaty, signed on 8 April 1965, Brussels, Luxembourg and Strasbourg were confirmed as provisional seats.[194] Finally, drawing on this decision, the Edinburgh European Council in December 1992 decided this as a permanent solution.[195] Strasbourg was designated as seat of the EP, although its commissions continued to meet in Brussels and the secretariat remained located in Luxembourg.[196] The Council and Commission's seats were confirmed in Brussels and Luxembourg remained host of among others the Court of Justice, the European Investment Bank and the Court of Auditors.[197]

As mentioned above, a characteristic both ECSC seat application phases of the 1950s shared, was the uncertainty of who supported whom. One example presented the German stance towards Strasbourg as single seat mirrored in city administration documents. In July 1957, the German Foreign Minister replied to a letter, the city administration had sent to ask

---

189 Croisé-Schirtz, Croisé-Schirtz, Edmée, "La bataille des sièges (1950-1958)", in Trausch, Gilbert *et al.* (eds.), *Le Luxembourg face à la construction européenne – Luxemburg und die europäische Einigung*, Luxembourg, Centre d'Etudes et de Recherches Européennes Robert Schuman, 1996, p. 94; eluxemburgensia.lu, *d'Letzeburger Land 13/1958.*

190 AC, CM2/1958 0221, *Résultat du vote: Premier tour.*

191 AC, CM2/1958 0221, *Résultat du vote: Premier tour.*

192 AC, CM2/1958 0221, *Europäisches Parlament, Entschließung.*

193 E.g. AC, CM2/1960 0233ab-b, *Einleitende Aufzeichnung*, p. 2.

194 "Fusionsvertrag." <http://eur-lex.europa.eu/LexUriServ/LexUriServ.do?uri=OJ:P:1967:152:FULL:DE:PDF> (accessed 16.11.2013), *Anhang II.*

195 "Annex 6 to Part A, Decision taken by common agreement between the Representatives of the Governments of the member states on the location of the seat of the institutions and of certain bodies and departments of the European Communities, Edinburgh European Council 11 – 12 December 1992." <http://www.europarl.europa.eu/summits/edinburgh/a6_en.pdf> (accessed 27.06.2014), p. 51.

196 *Ibid.*

197 *Ibid.*, pp. 51-52.

for support for Strasbourg's candidature, in an extremely positive manner. He stated that Germany would always recognise the symbolic value of Strasbourg as the sign for reconciliation and would support the city.[198] Conflictingly, in December 1957, Pflimlin stated in a committee meeting to organise the city's application for the single seat that Adenauer apparently shared Luxembourg's negative opinion of Strasbourg's suitability, but without protesting openly against the Alsatian city.[199]

Moreover, symbolism remained another important factor, which had also been the decisive element of the siting of the CoE in Strasbourg. The European Communities had made the possession of a European mission or historic European influence of candidates a requirement which was evaluated by the expert committee.[200] Applicants other than Strasbourg generally focussed more on this latter aspect, and their promotion material contained references to local historical 'European' events to a lesser degree than in Strasbourg's publicity.

For instance, Luxembourg presented a brochure with information on lodgings, climate and other criteria that could later be found in the urbanism expert committee's report to them when they made their study visit to the Grand Duchy.[201] The publication contained a French and German version and although presenting the same facts, the introduction to the German one contained one page about Goethe and his visit to Luxembourg which was not included in the French variant.

> An Gemeinsamen Markt, an EURATOM und Montanunion hatte Goethe gewiß nicht gedacht. Doch ihm war die Schönheit der Landschaft nicht entgangen, als er, von der Höhe des Clausener Berges hinüberschaute genau nach jenem Ort, den die Stadt Luxemburg als Baugelände für die europäischen Institutionen zur Verfügung zu stellen bereit ist.[202]

Such references to cultural actors of European renown formed one strategy of applicants to present themselves as European, the other major manner was references to local historic events that could be constructed as significant for the entire continent.

---

198 AS, 208 MW 11, *Résumé des réponses; Allemagne.*

199 AS, 235 MW 273, *Minutes of the Bipartite Committee session, 27.12.1957*, p. 2.

200 AC, CM1/1958 0120, *Bericht der europäischen Fachkommission für Städteplanung.*

201 "Luxembourg siège des Institutions européennes, Considérations proposées à l'attention de la Commission européenne des Experts en matière d'Urbanisme, à l'occasion de leur visite à Luxembourg les 19 et 20 mars 1958." <http://www.ena.lu/luxembourg_seat_european_institutions_luxembourg_19_20_march_1958-2-14296.pdf> (accessed 15.02.2011).

202 *Ibid.*, p. 9.

All in all, attempts to find a permanent solution to the seat question in the 1950s were characterised by a confusing situation, conditioned by national interests of the single member states. Symbolism, next to political and infrastructural considerations, was a factor as well, especially during the second seat application round of the ECSC when it became an institutionalised prerequisite for a successful application. The key facts that were treated in this section, was a parallel strand of action to activity in Strasbourg during the time with a few mutual interlinkages. This issue will be returned to in chapter 2, where include more specific details will be included.

Chapter 2

Hosting Europe

Hosting efforts, the first theme of strategies to consolidate the position of Strasbourg as host of European institutions, encompassed various activities of the city administration and local private associations. These included offering receptions and leisure activities during session periods. In this book, this definition of 'hosting activities' will be extended to all kinds of promotional activities, such as municipal politicians campaigning in Strasbourg's favour at the national government or the European Communities. Responding to threats to Strasbourg capabilities as seat city is also included in the general term 'hosting activities'.

Such actions were observable over the entire period of study, but the bulk of activity occurred in connection with the second ECSC seat application round from 1957 to 1959. The central aim of these events constituted gaining the appreciation of their guests, also in view of the competition with other seats. City actors pursued this by attempting to impress parliamentarians and indirectly the European institutions with their hosting efforts and capabilities. The general motto of local actors' efforts was that delegates "soient accueillis dans les meilleures conditions possibles."[1] Another central theme included the construction of a European mission by municipal actors, which was likewise employed as an argument why Strasbourg would constitute an excellent host for European institutions. Through this conceptualisation, a continuity of a 'European' history was created in order to justify Strasbourg's seat status.

In this chapter, the activities of municipal actors in this area are separated into three distinct developmental phases. The first was characterised by unstructured measures, while the second phase contained the development of sophisticated specialised structures which were especially used during the second ECSC seat application round from 1957 onwards. The last phase shows a high level of sophistication following this attempt to determine a single seat. The division has been derived from documents of the city administration and mirrors activity

[1] AS, 236 MW 2/4, *Lettre du M. le Maire à Furler du 17.3.1961*, p. 1.

within Strasbourg, as opposed to external caesuras as the Treaties of Rome or the creation of the EC might have presented. The CoE was in the local actors' main focus until 1957. Even during the second hosting phase, when the city administration saw being a perfect host to support Strasbourg's candidature for the single seat as highly important, the CoE did not become an afterthought. As the municipality expressed, "l'idée du maintien du Conseil de l'Europe à Strasbourg et d'y concentrer même toutes les installations subsidiaires de caractère européen", was the goal of their hosting efforts.[2]

In the following subchapter, the analysis will concentrate on how local actors constructed Strasbourg's European mission, which was an important promotional strategy, both on its own or as part of other measures. Subsequently, the actor groups involved in hosting activities will be discussed, followed by the three periods of activity. Most of these measures were implemented by local actors in anticipation of European parliamentarians' demands. Delegates made specific requests, as well, which the city authorities were always quick to fulfil. The activities of local actors were conditioned by these two types of demands, to a larger degree what they thought parliamentarians would want and to a smaller degree what was concretely requested of them.

Section 1.07 Constructing Strasbourg's European mission

The European mission, or *vocation européenne* of Strasbourg was a central element to most strategies of local actors to consolidate their position as European institution host. Stating how and why Strasbourg possessed a European mission was a well-utilised strategy of municipal administration actors in this regard. Situating the headquarters of the CoE in Strasbourg in May 1949 commonly was the starting point of speeches and newspaper articles distributed by members of the city administration.

Throughout this sub-chapter, the actors' usage of *vocation européenne* as a strategy will form the main focus. Local actors employed it in order to bind the institutions to Strasbourg by constructing a history of devotion to European matters, which is a procedure isolated from archive documents. In city administration sources, the presence of the European mission in other plans was commonly expressed with terms such as *caractère*, *climat*, *prestige*, *atmosphère*, *mission*, *ville* or *capitale européenne*, which were employed to further prove the Europeanness of the city. This sub-chapter traces the local actors' interpretation and usage of Strasbourg's *vocation européenne*, as well as their conception of its evolution.

2 AS, 54 W 243, *Rapport des commissions principales du 3.10.1957*, p. 1.

The purpose was to present the city as highly suitable host for European institutions and to offset the city against other candidates. A characteristic example is the following quote from a newspaper article written by mayor Pierre Pflimlin, "s'il s'agit de faire vivre les institutions de l'Europe unie dans une atmosphère authentiquement européenne, je crois pouvoir affirmer qu'aucune ville ne peut invoquer des titres supérieurs à ceux de Strasbourg."[3] City actors commonly used this and similar argumentation, embellished by their interpretation of the term's origins, in resolutions, speeches and newspaper articles. There seems to have been a consensus which elements to employ in order to 'sell' it with the intention of presenting Strasbourg as a supporter of the European idea throughout history, since the examples from the municipal archive of Strasbourg were homogenous. The manner in which these aspects were employed as streamlined arguments to prove this also fell under the communality.

Especially during the second seat application round from 1957 onwards, the city administration frequently used a European mission to argue for the suitability of Strasbourg as seat. A reason for this emphasis on symbolism could be connected to the fact that Strasbourg's infrastructure was inferior to most other applicant cities.[4] Such stressing of a European mission could have been considered as the most viable strategy by the city administration in this context. Most speeches or articles about Strasbourg's European mission were made by Pflimlin as the representative of the city.

Such a strategy of ascribing a European mission to Strasbourg was not a tangible one like improvement of infrastructure for European institutions, but aimed at both creating a welcoming environment for them and to devise a European reputation for the city. Local actors, mainly the parts of the city administration involved in welcoming European institutions, produced a legend of European involvement of Strasbourg that could be used as justification for the siting of organisations on the city. Especially during the 1950s, such efforts of either creating a suitable climate for European institutions or employing symbolic considerations as strategic arguments for the presence of European institutions was common with most candidate cities for the ECSC seat. During the second seat application round, applicant cities were required to possess a European mission, but other candidate cities commonly heavily relied on their infrastructural capabilities as arguments, as well (cf. e.g. sub-chapter on the implementation phase: 1956-1959).

3 AS, 9 Z 192, *Revue Europa 3/1960*, p. 1.

4 Cf. chapter 3 for transport and chapter 4 for building infrastructure and how Strasbourg's local actors attempted to improve it and employ it strategically to remain comparable to other candidates or to gain an advantage.

Strasbourg's actors explicitly stated that this would have been a reason for the formation of the city's European mission with the presentation of historical facts which sometimes appeared constructed. In this context, which items local actors selected mattered. They chose events of which they thought they would support their assertion in order to use it as a strategy towards the continuing presence of the European institutions in the city.

Apart from the actor conception of the mission's development, evidence how it formed itself is not visible in the sources. Usually, actors inside and outside Strasbourg stated in letters, speeches and other publications from 1949 onwards that the city possessed a European mission, recognised by the placement of the CoE in the same year. Local actors involved in the creation of these texts appropriated historic events to use them strategically as arguments why Strasbourg was suited to host European institutions. The narrative strategy was to create a European mission which had long been rooted in the city's past.

The only instance alluding to the image's development, widely quoted in archive material by local actors themselves, was a speech by De Gaulle in October 1945. He stated his support of the reconciliation idea and added that "l'avenir de l'Europe occidentale passe ici, il passe à Strasbourg."[5] According to city actor statements, the universal assertion that Strasbourg had a *vocation européenne*, developed from the end of the conflict between France and Germany over Alsace and its slow transformation into reconciliation. For example, "Et puis, satisfaction suprême, Strasbourg, la veille encore pomme de discorde, était appelée à devenir un symbole de réconciliation et de paix."[6] One of the first instances the concept's usage was that Pflimlin stated in the newspaper *Nouvel Alsacien* in connections with the municipal elections in 1947 that Strasbourg had a *vocation européenne.*[7] It is plausible to assume that the mission's origins lay in post-war reconciliation and European integration as stated by actors, but sources from the municipal archive, such as letters, only indicate, that the strategy suddenly fell into widespread use with the placement of the CoE in 1949. The recognition of Strasbourg's European mission was apparently not just limited to Europe alone, as a demand for documentation from the Japanese embassy in Paris indicated.[8]

5 AS, 9 Z 192, *Allocution de M. Pflimlin du 21.11.1959*, p. 2.

6 AS, 9 Z 192, *Revue Europa 3/1960*, p. 3.

7 Baechler, Christian, "Les grandes mutations contemporaines et affirmation de la vocation européenne (1945-1986)", in Livet, Georges and Rapp, Francis (eds.), *Histoire de Strasbourg*, Toulouse, Privé/Dernières Nouvelles d'Alsace, 1987, p. 479.

8 ABR, 1130 W 894/1, *Note pour le Directeur.*

The usage of this concept as a city actor scheme to attract institutions strongly relied on a widespread acceptance of its existence. In this context, it is interesting that such a specific form of European mission had been apparently readily and universally accepted, while European ideas in general were diffuse with different organisations embodying a different form of it. Most communication pieces, often contained claims of its irrefutability as in the following, "Pour qui connaît l'histoire de l'Europe, la vocation européenne de Strasbourg ne saurait être mise en doute."[9] This acceptance could have aided the effectiveness of municipal actors constructing Strasbourg's European mission for promotion purposes.

These concrete examples of ascribing a European mission to a city in the sources were likely based on some form of general idea of Europe that were present in different form especially during the early years of European integration. For example, from the late 1940s, European movements such as the European federalists, who promoted the idea of the United States of Europe were especially active.[10] With European unity being a rather diffuse concept, it seems at first paradoxical that a city would claim to be the epitome of Europe. Applicant cities for the seat of the ECSC that created their own local European idea mainly seem to have been motivated by the candidature in order to appear as having a suitable mind-set. Such measures were purposive rather than general declarations of Europeanness. The fact that most publications on the *vocation européenne* of Strasbourg or similar texts for other cities only implied that it would make the respective location a suitable host, contributed to this. The fact that city history was portrayed as European by local actors in the environment of the European Communities' attempts to determine a definite seat contains these two elements, only implying the intended message, which was likely nevertheless understood by the intended audience due to the situation they were employed in.

The local actors' constructions of Strasbourg's history to create the tale of its *vocation européenne* can be separated into the three standard elements. Firstly, Ernest Bevin, the 'hero'; secondly, historic events of 'European' importance as proof for the existence of a *vocation européenne* in the city and its efforts to attain it, and thirdly, the conflict between France and Germany, especially from 1871-1945.

All three were employed in speeches and other publications. In this connection, the local actors appropriated isolated historical events to

9 AS, 9 Z 192, *Déclaration de M. Pflimlin (Parlement Européen), 12.2.1976.*

10 Dinan, Desmond, *Ever closer union, An Introduction to European Integration*, Basingstoke, Palgrave Macmillan, 2010, p. 11.

present them as European. Regarding the third point, the nineteenth and twentieth century history was used to construct causality for the reconciliation symbolism.

The British Secretary of State for Foreign Affairs Ernest Bevin was involved in the founding of the CoE and was regarded as the responsible for implanting this European institution in Strasbourg. Municipal actors commonly cited his speech on locating the CoE from the London conference and presented this event as the official recognition of the city's European mission.[11] Bevin's role was glorified by city actors, transforming him into a 'heroic' figure that acknowledged the figurative European presence of Strasbourg for everybody. The development of this narrative was subsequently employed as an argument for the importance of the *vocation européenne*, because an outsider had allegedly endorsed it. Citing his actions as the driving force behind the CoE's siting and his statements on the symbolic importance of Strasbourg was employed as evidence to substantiate their claim with his apparent endorsement.

In the same manner that Pflimlin's role for Strasbourg was mythicised, local actors did the same for Bevin in the context of their publications on the city's *vocation européenne*. In literature about Bevin, his involvement in the founding of the CoE and his insistence on Strasbourg as its seat, is commonly only briefly treated. For instance, in an over 850-page account on his tenure as foreign secretary from 1945 to 1951, his preference for the Alsatian city is indicated in one sentence without any further commentary, while another biography does not mention it at all.[12] Local actors employed an aspect which was otherwise treated as a side note and canonised Bevin's actions to construct a plausible validation of their statements. Repeatedly employing history to illustrate that Strasbourg was the symbol of Franco-German reconciliation might have been able to fulfil this role, as well, since it was widely accepted in European circles. Local actors seemed to have used a mythicised version of Bevin's decision for Strasbourg for this, since it almost exclusively was placed at the beginning of any speech or publication on the European mission. Subsequently, it was followed by the second element, the appropriation of history to prove the existence and longstanding tradition of the *vocation européenne*.

This part of the strategy drew on concrete historical facts and constructed them in a narrative of European significance which sets it

---

11 E.g. AS, 9 Z 192, *Strasbourg, ville européenne, 16.8.1973*, p. 273 and *Vocation, 15.12.1990*, p. 3.

12 Bullock, Allan, *Ernest Bevin, Foreign Secretary 1945-1951*, London, Heinemann, 1983, p. 658 and Weiler, Robert, *Ernest Bevin*, Manchester, Manchester University Press, 1993.

apart from the 'real' history partly outlined in chapter 1. Local actors imbued it with their normativity in the sense of how the city's history ought to have been and ought to be interpreted. Presenting a European tradition in this construction was employed to create a certain continuity of Strasbourg's European efforts which was also indicated in speeches and texts promoting Strasbourg's European mission. "Orientée résolument vers l'avenir Strasbourg reprend ainsi sa tradition la plus ancienne, que l'ère des nationalismes avait fait tomber en oubli. Souvent, en effet, au cours des siècles Strasbourg fut un de ces lieux d'élection où l'Europe s'efforçait d'attendre à l'unité."[13] Commonly, historic events spanning back to the eighth century were drawn upon to prove the city's *vocation européenne.* As the quote shows, actors attempted to construct a continuity of being dedicated to Europe throughout history.

One of the oldest occurrences that was recurrently employed to give evidence for the city's European mission was the foundation of *Notre-dâme de Strasbourg* by Charlemagne in 775. According to the municipal administration, this granted the city river navigation rights and subsequently constituted the *vocation rhénane de Strasbourg*, the oldest element of *vocation européenne.*[14] In this context, the Rhine was characterised as a river of European importance, as it connected the continent.[15] Arguing with geography comprised a supporting feature to citing historical events, which led city actors to the conclusion they had a "[...] mission assignée à notre ville par la géographie et par l'histoire."[16] Thus, the central argument was that historical occurrences and its geographic position had given the city its alleged European mission.

Other events that were commonly drawn upon were for example that in 842, Charles le Chauvre and Louis le Germanique met to exchange the *serments de Strasbourg*, which would present another instance of the European importance of Strasbourg.[17] Another indicator for the European mission of Strasbourg was in the interpretation of city administration actors that the Alsatian capital had been a spiritual centre during the Middle Ages, visible through its cathedral of European significance which had been constructed from 1459 onwards.[18] In the same vein, Strasbourg

---

13 AS, 9 Z 192, *Strasbourg, ville européenne, 16.8.1973*, p. 276.

14 AS, 9 Z 192, *Vocation européenne de Strasbourg, envoyé au Figaro, 5.9.1966*, p. 1.

15 E.g. AS, 9 Z 192, *Vocation européenne de Strasbourg, envoyé au Figaro, 5.9.1966*, p. 2.

16 AS, 9 Z 192, *Allocution de M. Pflimlin, 21.11.1959*, p. 3.

17 AS, 9 Z 192, *Conférence prononcée à l'Université des Annales à Paris le 9.11.1960 par Pierre Pflimlin*, p. 6.

18 AS, 9 Z 192, *Conférence prononcée à l'Université des Annales à Paris le 9.11.1960 par Pierre Pflimlin*, p. 6.

was characterised as an intellectual centre during the Renaissance.[19] Such constructions of local actors were supposed to give the city a historically provable significance for Europe.

Declaring Strasbourg as a European centre, geographical or otherwise, included a common element to construct its *vocation européenne*. Events or the visit of personalities, such as Johann Wolfgang Goethe, were described with a European bias by local actors, thereby constructing a past of supranational occurrences, where the city played an essential role. Subsequently, this argumentation was simultaneously employed to justify why Strasbourg became institution seat and why it should house more organisations.

This third element of the narrative construction employed history in the same manner as the second aspect to give basis to Strasbourg being the symbol for reconciliation. It nearly exclusively focussed on the conflict between France and Germany over Alsace in the nineteenth and twentieth century. According to local actors, this was the premise of *vocation européenne* after the Second World War. "C'est du souvenir de ces épreuves, essentiellement, qu'est née la vocation européenne de Strasbourg."[20] This citation, describing the events which led to the annexation of Alsace by Germany in 1871, formed the standard argument local actors employed to combine the reconciliation symbolism with the European mission.

The *vocation européenne* of Strasbourg was an important part of the entirety of city actors' Operation Welcome. In terms of employed historical events, especially recent Alsatian history and the resulting reconciliation symbolism formed the central element of local actors' constructions as stated in city communications with sentences like the following: "Telle est du moins la conviction sur laquelle se fonde l'esprit européenne de Strasbourg."[21] Using these facts, a story of a long-standing European tradition of the city of Strasbourg had been developed. Both the usage of local actors and the reception outside of the city had been in a form ritualised. Principally the municipality and other private organisations frequently stated it in speeches and other publications whose content followed an established pattern of constructing the European mission of Strasbourg, aided by other actions which will be analysed in the subsequent chapters. Its existence was not questioned by the outside and

19 AS, 9 Z 192, *Revue Europa Mars 1960, La vocation européenne de Strasbourg, par Pierre Pflimlin, Maire de Strasbourg*, p. 2.

20 AS, 9 Z 192, *Conférence prononcée à l'Université des Annales à Paris le 9.11.1960 par Pierre Pflimlin*, p. 15.

21 AS, 9 Z 192, *Strasbourg, ville européenne 16.8.1973*, p. 277.

the arguments of local actors were seemingly accepted. This aspect was important, because municipal actors relied on the fact that others outside Strasbourg regarded the existence of the city's *vocation européenne* as given.

Additionally, local historians followed the same argumentation as city administration actors to construct Strasbourg's *vocation européenne.*[22] The only difference included that they did not seem to be aimed at a specific audience or used as strategic devices to bind further institutions to the city. Even today the concept is still in use, for instance the *Centre d'Information sur les Institutions Européennes* describes the city's European mission on its homepage.[23]

Section 1.08 Central Actors

This sub-chapter contains the mapping of the different actors involved with hosting activities in the city of Strasbourg. This includes the formation and activities of structures within the municipal and the departmental administrations, as well as central private organisations. The information in this sub-chapter is based on minutes, as well as notes and letters and their senders and recipients from the municipal archive of Strasbourg and the departmental archive of Bas-Rhin. The analysis which kind of actors were involved in this constitutes a trace of the development from uncoordinated to sophisticated actions of local actors.

The city and departmental governments experienced the most encompassing changes. During the first period from 1949 to 1956, they were comparatively less active than private organisations. This changed with the second phase from 1956 to 1959, when special structures were implemented. Actors within the municipality, supported by the department, were the principal operators, although private and other associations remained active. Furthermore, the multitude of semi-independently operating actors, a characteristic of previous years, disappeared due to the development of centralised planning instances. From 1960 onwards, the city government accounted for most actions, supported by a small number of organisations outside their structures.

22 E.g. Stauffer, Charles, *Die europäische Berufung des Elsass (La vocation européenne de l'Alsace)*, Geispolsheim, Imp. Jung, 1978 or L'Huillier, Fernand, "Strasbourg, ville d'Europe", in *Extrait de l'Alsace contemporaine, Études politiques, économiques, sociales*, 1950, pp. 451-452.

23 "The European vocation of Strasbourg." <http://en.strasbourg-europe.eu/history,127, en.html> (accessed 05.06.2012).

(a) City/departmental administration

The terms city and departmental administration function as umbrella terms for the parts of them that participated in the effort to welcome European parliamentarians. Over the entire period of study, the city government of Strasbourg remained the central actor, while the department held more of a supporting role. Therefore, the city administration will be the focus of the analysis. The city administration was less involved in hosting activities from 1949 to 1956 if compared to the subsequent two hosting periods. Between the city and the *Département*, a division of labour was detectable that was more clearly visible in the first hosting period.

The documents from the departmental archive of Bas-Rhin and the municipal archive of Strasbourg indicated that in the early 1950s the department was occupied with the practical side of organising parliamentary sessions. This included security measures and reporting on session contents and the public's reaction to them. The city administration mainly stood for the organisation of leisure activities. Municipal administration documents on security during session periods are sparse in comparison to those archived in the departmental archive of Bas-Rhin. For example, in the municipal archive, documents on security during sessions mostly are collected in one single dossier, covering the period of 1951 to 1955. It includes security for buildings and the city and surveillance of accommodations, as well as which delegation was in which hotel.[24]

The city administration concentrated on offering receptions for European parliamentarians and institution personnel, but also assisted private local actors to plan their events and arranged excursions or accommodation for delegates on request. For instance, they provided the local tourism office with two translators and the services of the municipal *Office de Logement* (housing office) during the August 1949 session.[25] In terms of visibility, the mayor, the executive organ of the city, seems to have been regarded as the central organisation instance by institution staff, judging by the thank-you letters the municipal government received. In contrast to the *Département*, the city administration oversaw few security and other practical arrangements. One of these exceptions included compiling lists of which delegation was lodged in which hotel and which kind of rooms they occupied.[26]

---

24 AS, 235 MW 136, *Note de Service.*

25 AS, 235 MW 267, *Extrait de la Presse Libre du 9.7.1950.*

26 AS, 235 MW 136, *Liste.*

During the period of study, Strasbourg had three mayors; from 1945 (1935) to October 1955 Charles Frey, October 1955 to March 1959 Charles Altorffer and March 1959 to March 1983 Pierre Pflimlin.[27] Upon the death of Frey on 14 October 1955, his successor's actions, in office from 29 October 1955,[28] towards the European institutions did not change. In the early 1950s, the main actor was Frey, who if necessary instructed various appropriate municipal services to complete tasks. It has to be noted, that the post 'mayor' and not the person holding it constituted a central actor until Pflimlin's tenure.

(i) The formative years (1949-1956)

Before concentrating on the city administration, departmental activity will briefly be discussed. The *Préfet*, several members of the *Conseil Général* and parts of the *Préfecture* were involved. The central tasks, next to security arrangements, included the compiling of public opinion, usually in combination with a summary of session contents.[29] Otherwise, it was concerned with official proceedings during the first ECSC seat application round in 1952, and in contact with the national government.[30] In this case, the *Département* can be regarded as French state activity on the local level, since the *Préfet* was the direct representative of the national government.[31] Otherwise, according to the local documents of the administration, the national level was hardly involved in day-to-day activities regarding the presence of the European institutions in Strasbourg.

The President of the *Conseil Général* similarly held an executive position within the organisation An administrative reform in 1949 included a plan to transfer some of the competences of the *Préfet* to this office.[32] This post was held by Pflimlin during the first hosting phase. He also was the head of a delegation to lobby the French government for support of Strasbourg's candidature for the ECSC seat in 1952.[33] Therefore, the *Département's* central activity during the start-up phase concentrated on appraisal of

---

27 "Les Maires de Strasbourg." <http://archives.strasbourg.fr/site_maire/index.html> (accessed 20.03.2011). Frey was not in office during the German occupation from 1940-1944.

28 *Ibid.*

29 E.g. ABR, 544 D 205/1, *Note du 4.6.1952.*

30 E.g. ABR, 544 D 209/1, *Pool Charbon-Acier 1952.*

31 C., F, "Remarques sur le titre X de la Constitution et la réforme de l'Administration départementale", *Revue administrative* 2:8, p. 212.

32 *Ibid.*

33 AS, 198 MW 93, *Extrait des DNA, 26.6.1952.*

public opinion, the 'official' process of the first ECSC seat application with the national government, as well as the practical organisation of receiving European parliamentarians by assuring security. This matter will not be discussed further, since safety arrangements generally constituted an inherent feature of big events, rather than a specific strategy of Strasbourg's actors to host institutions during sessions.

This information gathering and security arrangements seemed to have ended by the mid-1950s, judging by the lack of archive sources. Activities concentrated on organising hosting activities together with the city administration in two specialised committees from 1957 onwards. They were chaired by the *Préfet*, Maurice Cuttoli, and counted several members of the *Conseil Général* among its members. Apart from them and *Sous-préfet* (deputy prefect) Georges Ridoux, the *Département* was not significantly involved in the majority of activities. Nevertheless, a permanent liaison between it and the city to coordinate and to unite their separate hosting efforts existed by 1958.[34] Dossiers in the municipal archive of Strasbourg on hosting activities often contained notes from Ridoux to the city administration, discussing certain measures, although the main exchange of ideas and opinions still occurred through one committee from the late 1950s.

From the early stages, some involved actors were presented as European, which also was the case on Frey's death in office. He was honoured as 'European' in eulogies, such as in a commemorative publication on his life.[35] His efforts to create a welcoming climate for parliamentarians and to promote the *vocation européenne* of Strasbourg were especially emphasised. "Il est une fâche par contre à laquelle il s'est consacré sans restriction: la défense de l'avenir européen de sa ville."[36] He was also the president of the most involved private organisation during the first hosting period. Therefore, some organisation processes overlapped, for instance, events conceptualised by the private association were also organised by city services and the mayor.[37] This circumstance added a further 'European' dimension to the actor Frey and to the hosting measures that were arranged.

34 AS, 236 MW 1/1, *Note de la Division VIII, 24.2.1958.*

35 Biedermann, Alfred, "Charles Frey l'Européen", in Robert Heitz and Casper, Paul and Knittel, Jean (eds.), *Un grand Strasbourgeois: Charles Frey*, Strasbourg, DNA, 1956, pp. 93-99.

36 *Ibid.*, p. 97.

37 E.g. AS, 14 MW 47, *Correspondances du Maire et le Comité de B.B. et SNS.*

(ii) Ordinary structures (1956-1979)

Frey's successor Charles Altorffer continued this type of politics and saw the implementation of specialised structures from summer 1956. That year marked the start of the second hosting phase, since a clear change from the at times uncoordinated organisation was visible. The processes of providing a session frame programme with distractions and leisure activities became more sophisticated. Although the mayor was not always involved in day-to-day processes, he held the formal decision power as the executive level in the city. Additionally, Pflimlin added his personal political network to these elements; before his tenure, the municipal archive of Strasbourg sources show that not the person holding the post constituted the important individual actor.

In contrast to the constant involvement of the mayor, the participation of ordinary city administration structures varied over time, both in terms of which organisations and how they participated in efforts to host Strasbourg's European institutions. During the initial years, city services were hardly involved with the exception of the *Office de Logement* which helped to arrange accommodation during sessions. This changed with the beginning of the second hosting phase and the institution of specialised structures. It translated into more activity of the municipality in general and the involvement of more of its divisions and services. These committees and other panels will be discussed in the subsequent section.

The promotion of Strasbourg as institution seat city by single actors, which constituted a secondary activity next to hosting activities, can be further subdivided into two elements: individual actors advertising its capabilities or responding to (perceived) threats to Strasbourg's seat status. These types of agency were just about the only occasions where Strasbourg's politicians, civil servants or private organisations, focussed on activities outside the city environs. The bulk of activity of the local level to consolidate Strasbourg's seat status ensued within city limits. Hosting events were almost exclusively geared towards the European institutions housed in the Alsatian capital and the parliamentarians attending European assembly sessions.

Ordinary structures that were centrally involved in the organisation of hosting measures were a small circle whose actors remained relatively stable over time. The *Division VIII* and its head Alphonse Heitz were most heavily involved in the organisation of European session frame programmes drafted by any of the specialised committees from the latter half of the 1950s until the 1970s. Formally, it was responsible for (traffic) circulation, as well as youth and sports.[38] According to signatures on notes and letters, the *(Service des) Relations Publiques* (Public Relations Service) created in the late 1960s which highly active in the following decade, was part of it. A. Heitz was very involved in it as well, also when he became *Secrétaire-Général Adjoint* (Deputy Secretary-General) during the 1960s. He shared this role with the head of the *Relations Publiques*, Pierre Schmidt. According to material in the municipal archive of Strasbourg, this service organised most of the events the local authorities offered to their European guests. The mayor was kept informed of the processes and asked to decide on aspects if necessary. Other members of the *Relations Publiques,* who often appeared in archive documents on the organisation of hosting events from the late 1960s onwards, were Alfred Feuerstein and Herbert Wehr. For example, in a letter to the Secretary-General of the EP in 1978, the municipality informed that he was among the civil servants who would be tasked with welcoming European parliamentarians.[39]

Next to this service, the city and *Département* each created a post *chargée des affaires européennes* (charged with European affairs) during the 1960s, which was assured by *Adjoint au Maire* Raymond Leissner and *Sous-préfet* Georges Ridoux respectively. Both were liaisons to the European institutions, while Ridoux also functioned as a link between the two administrations. Leissner was principally involved in infrastructure questions and will therefore not be covered further in this section. Through these actors, the city administration drew on questioning delegates to improve their activities, apart from anticipating demands and implementing complaints. Ridoux and A. Heitz cooperated in implementing most of the leisure activity programme offered by the local authorities. Additionally, the *Sous-préfet* communicated the session period dates to the *Relations Publiques* or the mayor and provided other, minor information from the European institutions conductive to the organisation of the hosting programme.

The *Division VIII*, the *Relations Publiques*, as well as Leissner's and Ridoux' posts were the centrally involved ordinary structures of the city administration. The two individual posts were mostly concerned with liaisons with the respectively other administration and the European institutions, while the two divisions were centrally implementing decisions made by specialised committees. Other structures were occasionally

38 Archives de la Ville et de la Communauté Urbaine, *Guide des Fonds 2006*, Strasbourg, Imp. Int. CU, 2006, p. 13.

39 AS, 97 W 39/1, *Note pour M. le Maire, 18.10.1978.*

involved in a very marginal role or just purely executing orders, such as being charged with installing decorations in the city.

(iii) Specialised structures (1956-1959)

In 1956, specialised committees were added as a new dimension. From 1956 to 1957, four committees were founded within the city, primarily to respond to the presence of the CoE. The EP joined this focus only after the candidature for the single ECSC seat had been submitted in July 1957. Sources are not clearly stating why the ECSC assembly was excluded at first, but it is probable that the reasons for this behaviour were that the CoE had its permanent seat in Strasbourg, while the placement of the Common Assembly was highly provisional during the 1950s and beyond.

By summer 1956, involved city administration actors were aware of the need to change their approach to dealing with the presence of European institutions, because they felt that relations between them should be improved. This can be seen in the statement regarding the creation of the first specialised committee. "Le Comité a été créé - comme on sait - en vue de rechercher des moyens et de proposer des mesures susceptibles de dissiper un certain "malaise" né parmi les délégués et les hauts fonctionnaires du Conseil de l'Europe vis-à-vis de la Municipalité."[40] This quote gives evidence that the hosting measures of the municipal actors were aimed at binding the institutions to the city. Such structures were specifically created to insure a welcoming environment for European organisations and to implement measures to address the competitive situation at the end of the 1950s.

They were the *Comité ayant pour tâche d'étudier les moyens susceptibles de resserrer les liens entre la Municipalité et le Conseil de l'Europe* or *Commission "ad hoc"* (Liaison Committee), the *Commission spéciale chargée des relations avec le Conseil de l'Europe* (Special Liaison Committee), the *(Commission d'Etude du) regroupement des Institutions Européennes à Strasbourg* (Placement Study Committee) and the *Commission Bipartite (Ville-Département) chargée d'étudier les problèmes soulevés par les institutions européennes,*[41] (Bipartite Committee). All of the four committees formed the central decision body for measures to welcome European parliamentarians and to promote the city as seat. Additionally, especially the Placement Study and Bipartite Committees

40 AS, 208 MW 267, *Minutes of the Liaison Committee, 24.9.1956*, p. 1.

41 Its title varied during the years, for instance during the 1970s, it was commonly described by *pour les affaires européennes*, or other similar appellations.

dealt with infrastructure matters. This aspect of their work will not be covered in this sub-chapter, but in the appropriate chapters on traffic and building infrastructures. Some politicians of the city administration were active in all four committees and continued in the Bipartite Committee until the 1970s. They were an 'inner circle' of centrally involved actors over nearly the entire period of study. They formed an elite of decision-holders who were responsible for presenting Strasbourg as a suitable host for European institutions, which will be covered later in this sub-chapter.

The Liaison Committee held its first meeting in August 1956. It is not possible to determine exact founding dates of the subsequent three committees. A note to mayor Altorffer on the history of these four committees, stated that each of them replaced its predecessor.[42] However, this was not mirrored by the minutes, where phases of operation overlapped. The documents in the municipal archive of Strasbourg and the departmental archive of Bas-Rhin showed that the Liaison Committee held meetings at least until mid-1957, the Special Liaison Committee and Placement Study Committee both operated between mid-1957 to the first half of 1958, while the Bipartite Committee was active from late 1957 into the 1980s. Only towards the end of the second hosting period, the Bipartite Committee remained the single committee in operation. It emerged as the sole planning and coordinating instance of the city and departmental administrations at the beginning of the 1960s and continued to operate well into the early 1980s. It is likely that the actual phases of operation overlapped due to the urgency of presenting a good image for the second ECSC seat application round. This hypothesis is supported by the fact that after the currency of the seat candidature declined due to the foreign ministers' repeated postponements of a decision, only one panel remained active. In this section, an overview of their composition, tasks, work and connections will be given, while concrete examples of their activities will be covered during the strategy section.

The decision to create the Liaison Committee was made in the *Conférence des Adjoints* meeting on 30 June 1956 in order to form personal contacts and to develop measures for a pleasant stay for European parliamentarians.[43] Additionally, the founding of the panel was deemed necessary because it was judged as dangerous not to act upon critique about the state of hosting, local actors had received.[44] The mayor asked

42 AS, 208 MW 287, *Note pour M. le Maire 4.5.1959.*

43 AS, 236 MW 23/1, *Compte-rendu de la Conférence des Adjoints du 30.6.1956.*

44 AS, 236 MW 23/1, *Compte-rendu de la Conférence des Adjoints du 30.6.1956*, p. 1.

Premier Adjoint au Maire Paul Wach to chair the Liaison Committee and to invite the other designated members, *Adjoint au Maire* René Radius, Marc Lucius, Georges Woehl and *Conseiller Municipal* Armand Kientzi, to the constitutive session.[45] The meeting minutes archived in the municipal archive of Strasbourg show that *Conseiller* Robert Heitz, the mayor,[46] and Léon Kien, the Secretary-General of the city, also participated regularly. All of the Liaison Committee's actors were members of private associations related to the European presence in Strasbourg, active in all three subsequent specialised committees and continued to serve in the Bipartite Committee beyond the 1950s.[47] Additionally, Pflimlin, at the time not yet a member of the city administration, occasionally attended sessions, but the minutes exhibit that he was sometimes also there 'in spirit', since he was often referred to.

The Special Liaison Committee had the same members as the Liaison Committee and followed the identical goals, which mainly included establishing stronger ties with the CoE. Both panels attempted to achieve this through providing ample and sophisticated leisure activities and comforts to delegates.[48] The Placement Study Committee was composed of the Liaison Committees' members and a number of General Councillors from the Department under the chairmanship of *Préfet* Maurice Cuttoli. It was the only specialised committee not occupied with hosting measures at all, but with studying infrastructure solutions to locate the ECSC institutions in Strasbourg in the case of a successful candidature. As evidence from the municipal archive suggests, it was the least important of these four committees, since the other three accounted for much more activity and decisions in the sources.

The Bipartite Committee was primarily occupied with hosting measures, but also with infrastructure issues, which will be discussed in the subsequent two chapters. Officially, it was composed of seven members from the city and the *Département* each, although the actual participation rate fluctuated from session to session and additional actors, as well as architecture experts, attended occasionally.[49] Furthermore, the full number of official members was never present, and by looking at the

---

45 AS, 236 MW 23/1, *Lettre du Maire à Wach 9.7.1956.*

46 Charles Altorffer until March 1959, from then on Pierre Pflimlin, who until his tenure as mayor began, sometimes participated in meetings as a guest.

47 Cf. appendix I.

48 AS, 208 MW 267, *Minutes of the Liaison Committee* and AS, 208 MW 11, *Minutes of the Special Liaison Committee.*

49 AS, 235 MW 273, *Bipartite Committeee.*

available session minutes, ten councillors each from the two councils were involved in this committee.[50]

The necessity of founding it had first been discussed between Pflimlin and Wach in April 1957. Later, Pflimlin charged Wach with facilitating its creation, since he did not have the necessary time to do it himself.[51] Although the name referred to was *Comité permanent de liaison avec le Conseil de l'Europe*, the Permanent Liaison Committee with the Council of Europe, it must have been the Bipartite Committee, since it also should include involvement of the *Conseil Général*.[52] The Placement Study Committee also included actors from the *Département*. However, the fact that it was more clearly aimed towards ECSC institutions and almost exclusively occupied itself with infrastructural issues, makes it unlikely that it was referenced in this context. The creation shows another instance of Pflimlin's strong involvement in the organisation of hosting the European institutions, although he was not yet part of the city administration.

During the second hosting phase, the four specialised committees can be viewed as a unit in regard to their members, where some of the most active belonged to all of them and their tasks were congruent. For example, the Liaison Committee created a list of measures that were repeated at every following session period until the 1980s with a few initial adjustments when aspects failed to meet the appreciation of the European parliamentarians. In the understanding of the Liaison Committee, events were regarded as suitable means to initiate a closer, personal contact with the CoE to strengthen their relationship.[53] The committees' work became especially important during the seat application round, when Strasbourg's candidature relied on hosting measures to support it. A significant number of their members were multipositioned actors who were involved in several public or private organisations to promote Strasbourg as European institution seat. Appendix I presents an overview of them.

The initiative of these measures came from a private organisation, the *Comité Strasbourgeois pour le Mouvement Européen (CSME)* that was highly involved in hosting issues from 1949 to 1953. It sent suggestions in a letter which were adopted by the Liaison Committee.[54] This is also an example for how closely different agents involved in welcoming European institutions cooperated for the best possible results. Shortly after the

50 AS, 235 MW 273, *Implantation* and AS, 208MW270, *Xe Anniversaire du Conseil de l'Europe.*

51 AS, 236 MW 23/1, *Lettre de Pflimlin à Wach 8.4.1957.*

52 AS, 236 MW 23/1, *Lettre de Pflimlin à Wach 8.4.1957.*

53 AS, 208 MW 267, *Minutes of the Liaison Committee, 24.9.1956*, p. 1.

54 AS, 208 MW 267, *Lettre de Biedermann au Maire 18.6.1956.*

initiation of this structured session frame programme, local actors must have come closer to their goal of creating the impression of a closer contact, since the number of thank-you letters remarking on this, such as the following, increased. "The town of Strasbourg is always so hospitable and generous. It makes our stay here so very happy."[55] These developments will be summarised in the sub-chapter on the second hosting period.

(iv) Specialised structures (1960-1979)

During the third hosting phase, the Bipartite Committee was the only remaining central organisational body which decided on measures and relegated tasks to the involved ordinary parts of the city administration. Following the end of the 1950s, it met irregularly until 1964, when a single annual planning session to draft all activities for the entire year became the norm. In the case of the Bipartite Committee, a random filing of material in the archives became especially apparent. From 1961 until 1964, no session minutes were archived, although some city administration documents of the time hinted that meetings must have been held. In the departmental archive of Bas-Rhin, meeting minutes from 1960, 1964, 1966 and 1968 to 1979 were present, while minutes for 1965, 1967 and some doublings from the departmental archive of Bas-Rhin were distributed in several dossiers of the municipal archive of Strasbourg. Although, meeting minutes from the beginning of the 1960s are sparse, the fact that the majority of the Bipartite Committee documents is available, will allow for a presentation of a comprehensive picture of its structure and work.

Officially, during the 1960s and 1970s, the committee had eleven members each from the city administration and the *Conseil Général*, but meeting minutes show that in practice, these numbers were a bit higher.[56] Regarding its members during the 1960s and 1970s, several had been involved in the hosting of European institutions in several capacities from the beginning. They can be characterised as an 'inner circle' among concerned city actors, since they usually started their 'European' activity during the first hosting phase in a private association and then held continuous memberships in the local administration's specialised committees from their foundations until the 1970s. The most active actors remained stable participants over time, while a certain fluctuation of members was observable from the minutes, where some only attended one or a few of the annual sessions. This could be due to extraneous factors like elections, but was not likely, since a continuous participation of a core group of members is observable.

55 AS, 236 MW 1/4, *Lettre de Hutchinson au Maire 12.10.1958.*

56 E.g. ABR, 1130 W 936/6, *Liste des membres 1976.*

From 1964 onwards, an annual meeting schedule had been established, with one meeting in January or February each year, when an evaluation of the previous year was made and a draft programme with all activities for the current year was created. Transport issues, such as shuttles within the city and air communications were covered extensively, as well, which will be presented in chapter 3. In comparison to the end of the 1950s, the number of offered events decreased from the middle of the 1960s onwards, when an average pattern of one excursion, reception, luncheon or dinner per session period became common. As will be analysed in the strategy section on the third hosting phase, their frequency was reduced due to the increasing number of sessions and for fear that the repetition of the same or similar events would induce boredom for the European parliamentarians.

From the 1960s, the Bipartite Committee could determine its budget for hosting activities and transport expenses by itself which was in even parts financed by the city and department.[57] It included a possibility of increasing it without any apparent administrative impediments should the spending exceed the sum fixed in the beginning of the year. For instance, the minutes of the 1977 Bipartite Committee meeting simply stated that the credit for 1976 had been raised by 50,000 Francs (28,000€) to cover all expenses.[58] Setting the annual budget for all activities related to the European institutions was a change from the 1950s. Then, expenses were covered by allotments from the ordinary budget, mainly grouped in a section entitled *institutions européennes*.

Thus, the matter of financing the hosting programme, as well as special transport for delegates, was fully moved into the bubble of city actors concerned with the European institutions. It has to be noted that the sources did not show any discussion about the budget for the European institutions before that. The Bipartite Committee seemed to have commanded a virtually unchecked spending power in regard to session frame programmes and transport. Restrictions did not seem to have been enforced. In the committee minutes on the subject of setting the credit for 1977, an increase was envisioned. A suggestion to fix a slightly smaller amount in the view of the ongoing requirement to limit general public spending, was hinted at in a hedging manner.[59]

The continuing nondecision in the seat question of the EC could have played a reason as well, since only the introduction of the direct voting procedure and the subsequent intensified discussion on the EP's location

57 ABR, 1130 W 936/5, *Compte "Europe"*, p. 1.

58 ABR, 1130 W 936/5, *Minutes of the Bipartite Committee session, 23.2.1977*, p. 5.

59 ABR, 1130 W 936/5, *Année 1976*, p. 6.

caused an increase in hosting activities as well. This suggests that the number of events for European institutions, as well as effort and money invested in them, were proportional to activity regarding the seat question. For example, in 1979, the Bipartite Committee met three times and significantly extended the budget for hosting activities. In the previous years, the budget and expenses had remained stable over time, with steady, minor increases due to inflation and other economic factors. During the second session in 1979 on 11 June, the budget was drastically raised from the 500,000 Francs (233,000€), granted at the beginning of the year, to two million Francs (931,500€), financed in equal parts by the city and *Département* in order to expand the hosting and promotion programme for the first session of the directly elected EP.[60]

(v) The inner circle of long-term decision makers

Most involved politicians and civil servants of the city administration, supported from selected counterparts from the department, were multipositioned actors, namely that they aided seat consolidation efforts in two or more capacities.[61] They essentially formed the bubble structure of those concerned with strengthening Strasbourg's position as European institution host. Actors, who only had one task over a brief time period, participated as well, but from the sources of the municipal archive, they seemed to have executed orders or were drawn upon for one specific assignment in a supporting role. One example would be *Adjoint au Maire* Georges Gilliot heading the *Division IX*, responsible for taxis, because he only participated in some meetings where measures to improve the taxi service in the city were discussed (see chapter 3).[62]

The majority of multipositioned actors was intensively involved over a shorter period or regarding a specific task. This included, for instance, the *Secrétaire-Général de la Ville* and director of the municipal construction firm *Habitation Moderne* Albert Fix in construction matters (see chapter 4).[63] A small number of these actors was, however, involved in various consolidation activities until the 1970s. Since hosting activities were the major focus of the 1950s, they were principally concerned with those activities, although they also made infrastructure improvement decisions in a minor capacity due to their membership in the Bipartite Committee, which also focussed on air links (see chapter 3). These actors give evidence for that consolidation activities were planned by a small concentrated circle

60 ABR, 1130 W 936/2, *Minutes of the Bipartite Committee session, 11.6.1979.*

61 Appendix I gives an overview of them, their positions and times of involvement.

62 E.g. AS, 114 W 206, *Compte-rendu du 9.3.1978.*

63 AS, 752 W 5, *Compte-rendu du 13.3.1970.*

of virtually the same actors that operated within a structure that was largely unaffected by elections or other personnel changes.

For this study, the selection criteria to constitute an inner circle member are the following: active involvement in all three of the hosting phases, member of at least one private organisation and each of the city administration's four specialised committees from 1956 to 1959, as well as a member of the Bipartite Committee from 1957 until the 1970s. The mandatory participation in the four committees assures that only the most active actors were included, as these organisations were the main decision makers during the second and third hosting periods. These 'inner-circle' actors belonged to the central decision-making bodies over time that developed measures which could be used strategically to consolidate Strasbourg's position as European institution seat.

1. The inner circle of actors[64]

Name	Main Position	Period	1st phase 1949-56	2nd phase 1956-9	3rd phase 1960-79
Heitz, Robert	Municipal Council	1949-1971	*CSME*	Four specialised committees	Bipartite Committee
Kientzi, Armand	Municipal Council	1949-1977	*CSME, Congrès du peuple euro-péen*		Bipartite Committee, *Cercle Européen*
Pflimlin,* Pierre	President General Council, Mayor	1952-1983	*Club Pan-européen de Strasbourg*		Bipartite Committee, *Cercle Européen*
Radius,* René	Deputy Mayor	1949-1977	*CSME*		Bipartite Committee, *Cercle Européen*
Schmitt, Antoine	Deputy Mayor	1956-1977	*Congrès du peuple euro-péen*		Bipartite Committee
Wach,* Paul	Deputy Mayor	1949-1974	*CSME, Club Pan-européen de Strasbourg*		Bipartite Committee, *Cercle Européen*
Woehl, Georges	Deputy Mayor	1953-1971	*CSME after dédoublement*		Bipartite Committee

*: member of PACE/EP *Italics:* Private association

[64] Cf. AS, 208 MW 267, *Minutes of the Liaison and Special Liaison Committee sessions* and 208 MW 11, *Minutes Placement Study Committee sessions* and 235 MW 273, *Minutes of the Bipartite Committee sessions* and ABR, 1130 W 936/2-16, *Minutes of the Bipartite Committee sessions* and ACE, 3279/27129, *Comité Strasbourgeois pour le Mouvement Européen* and ACE, 3358/2982, *Cercle européen de Strasbourg.*

Since a membership in all the four specialised committees is stipulated, departmental actors are excluded, because the two Liaison Committees were exclusive to the city administration. It has been chosen not to include regional politicians in the inner circle, as only one actor, General Councillor Marcel Gillmann, would qualify with these criteria. He not as actively participating as the others from the city administration meeting the same criteria were. From the 'technical' group, most actors were intensively involved over a shorter period. Examples were Georges Ridoux (*Sous-préfet chargé des affaires européennes*) in transport issues or Daniel Adam (*Secrétaire-Général de la Ville de Strasbourg* in the 1970s) in construction matters. An exception forms Alphonse Heitz (Head of *Division VIII*/ member of *Service des Relations Publiques*) who was highly active from the late 1950s to the late 1970s. Among these, the cases of Pflimlin, Radius, Wach and Kientzi can be characterised as family effort within hosting, since their wives were active in the private organisation *Cercle des Amitiès Européennes* (see below).[65] These 'inner-circle' actors also belonged to the central decision-making bodies over time that developed measures which could be used strategically to consolidate Strasbourg's position as European institution seat.

Three members of the four specialised committees were individually active, mostly in the form of lobbying the national government or the European Communities. Apart from Pflimlin, this concerned Radius and Wach. They employed their personal political contacts in order to promote Strasbourg or to respond to actions of other candidate cities they perceived as threats. The personal promotion aspect was especially important during the seat application round from 1957 onwards, when serious direct competition from other applicants needed to be responded to.

Albeit Wach's activities were mostly confined within city limits, he was an active actor regarding hosting activities to establish Strasbourg as an excellent host. In addition to his role in the hosting activities, he was the president of the *Foire Européenne*, an annual exhibition on various European topics until his death in 1974.[66] According to the municipal archive of Strasbourg documents, the city administration organised

---

65 Additionally, if the last names of the women involved in the committee of the Cercle des Amitiés are compared with the men participating in similar structures in another private association, the Cercle européen, many doublings occur, which possibly indicates that more couples were simultaneously involved in welcoming European institutions (cf. the structures of both associations in the relevant sub-sections of the next section).

66 ACE, 3068/2009, *Allocution de M. Pflimlin 5.9.1974.*

periodic activities around this event for European parliamentarians when it and session periods coincided.

All three actors were members of PACE, and in Pflimlin's case also the EP. In PACE, Radius held the longest membership of all three with 26 years, while Wach and Pflimlin joined for ten and eight years respectively.[67] This personal connection to the institution was also employed for city administration strategies.[68] In 1963, Radius became president of the French delegation and towards the end of the 1960s vice-president of PACE as well.[69] For instance, he participated in both the CoE and city/departmental committees to plan the 20th anniversary of the CoE.[70] Moreover, he published a journal article in 1976 on Strasbourg and the CoE where he concentrated on the European idea found within Strasbourg, which expressed parallels to the *vocation européenne* constructions analysed in the beginning of this chapter, for instance by employing the Bevin narrative.[71]

In the context of the official submission of the city's candidature in July 1957, Radius addressed missives to each of the foreign ministers of ECSC member states, asking them to support the endeavour due to Strasbourg being the symbol for reconciliation and European unity.[72] Next to this reference to the city's *vocation européenne*, he also capitalised on his PACE membership as credentials for his arguments. Incidentally, newspapers, such as *Le Monde*, reported on this event that only Pflimlin, who had contacted these officials at the same time, demanded acknowledgement of Strasbourg's role as the capital of Europe.[73] Other communications of individual local actors targeted the French national government, CoE

67 "PACE members, Paul Wach." <http://www.assembly.coe.int/nw/xml/AssemblyList/MP-Details-EN.asp?MemberID=816> (accessed 17.10.2013) and "PACE members, Pierre Pflimlin." <http://www.assembly.coe.int/nw/xml/AssemblyList/MP-Details-EN.asp?MemberID=781> (accessed 17.10.2013) and "PACE members, René Radius." <http://www.assembly.coe.int/nw/xml/AssemblyList/MP-Details-EN.asp?MemberID=391> (accessed 17.10.2013).

68 E.g. AS, 208 MW 11, *Lettre du Radius aux Ministres des Affaires Etrangères, 17.7.1957.*

69 AS, 236 MW 29/1, *Le Monde, 17.1.1963, Radius* and ACE, CB(68)19, *20th Anniversary of the Council of Europe*, p. 1.

70 ACE, CB(68)19, *20th Anniversary of the Council of Europe* and AS, 236 MW 32/1, *Note du 20.2.1969.*

71 Radius, René, "Strasbourg et le Conseil de l'Europe", *Saisons d'Alsace*, 60, 1976, pp. 110-112.

72 AS, 208 MW 11, *Lettre du Radius aux Ministres des Affaires Etrangères, 17.7.1957.*

73 AS, 208 MW 11, *Le Monde, 18.7.1957.*

officials or other ECSC organisations.[74] This included personally speaking on Strasbourg's behalf, such as Radius seeking an audience with Charles de Gaulle in June 1958 to promote the city as seat.[75]

The individual actors also had letter exchanges amongst themselves, such as Altorffer and Pflimlin informing each other about their activities before the latter became mayor.[76] Furthermore, such missives were sent between specialised committee members. A letter from Wach to the mayor on 20 July 1957 presented such an example, in which he advised Altorffer that the time to present all of the city's arguments had come and that they had to make an effort for a convincing seat application.[77]

Although these actions constituted a major part of city administration actors' individual agency, the success was questionable. A summary of received responses to Radius' letter to the foreign ministers showed for example that answers just pointed out that all candidatures would be considered.[78] In a letter to the mayor, the French foreign minister became more explicit and demanded that Strasbourg cease bothering others before the next foreign ministers conference, since the French government could not announce their position publicly beforehand.[79]

Additionally, Pflimlin, Wach and Radius had been active actors throughout the entire period of study, commencing primarily with engagements in private associations during the first hosting phase. During the second hosting period, it evolved into participation in all of the four specialised committees; Wach also assumed the chairmanship of the two liaison committees. From 1960 onwards, the trio remained active in the Bipartite Committee until the 1970s and early 1980s, which marked the ends of their careers. Their political life mirrored the fact that they were heavily engaged in securing European institution seats to Strasbourg. For example, in a brief biography from 1956, archived in the departmental archive of Bas-Rhin, Wach was described as "s'est intéressé vivement aux questions européennes."[80]

---

74 E.g. AS, 208 MW 11, *Lettre à Bourges-Manmory* and *lettre au Président de l'Assemblée Consultative du Conseil de l'Europe* and *lettre au Président de l'Haute Autorité de la Communauté du Charbon et de l'Acier, 7/1957.*

75 AS, 208 MW 9, *Lettre du Maire à De Gaulle, 12.6.1958.*

76 E.g. AS, 208 MW 11, *Lettre du Pflimlin au Maire, 19.7.1957.*

77 AS, 208 MW 11, *Lettre de Wach au Maire, 20.7.1957.*

78 AS, 208 MW 11, *Résumé des réponses.*

79 AS, 208 MW 11, *Lettre du Ministre des Affaires Etrangères au Maire, 7.10.1957.*

80 ABR, 544 D 85, *Paul Wach.*

This circumstance was extremely visible in Pflimlin's case, where not only the mythification of his role in the seat question contributed to constructing this image. During his political career, he was heavily involved in European politics, for example as French Minister of State for CoE Affairs in 1952.[81] His interest towards Europe even led him to quit De Gaulle's government in 1962 over differences in opinion regarding France's policies towards Europe.[82] The myth surrounding Pflimlin's activities in existing literature led to an overshadowing of the other actors like Wach and Radius, as well as the activity of the numerous actors within Strasbourg in those analyses.

This glorification of his role to the figurehead position as the visible actor of the city administration in scholarship was strongly based on the opinion of political levels. For instance, the Secretary-General of the CoE wrote him on the occasion of finishing his tenure as Mayor in 1983, stating that Pflimlin would have been the first magistrate of the city who welcomed the CoE since 1949.[83] While Pflimlin had constituted one of the most important local actors, which was mostly due to the fact that he was one of the only local politicians acknowledged outside of Strasbourg, he was not one of the most active local actors in day-to-day activities, especially before he became mayor.

(vi) Summary

All in all, the city administration covered the tasks of organising receptions, as well as other activities and the promotion of Strasbourg's seat status, which became highly important during the second ECSC seat application round. Most of the ordinary structures and all the four specialised committees were only present from the start of the second hosting phase from 1956 onwards. The city (and departmental) administration actors involved with hosting activities reflected the stages of development of each of the three phases activity regarding this strategy is grouped into. The character and involvement of actors developed from uncoordinated to specialised structures and the smooth running of organising a session frame programme within the 1950s. This also

---

81 ACE, COE001872, *Powers of Pierre Pflimlin.*

82 Pflimlin, Pierre, *Mémoires d'un Européen de la IVe à la Ve République*, Paris, Fayard, 1991, p. 210.

83 ACE, C1166/1/1-2, *Lettre du Secrétaire-Général du Conseil de l'Europe à Pflimlin, 21.3.1983.*

laid the foundation for activities of improving transport and building infrastructure which were the focus of the 1960s and 1970s respectively. The actors concerned with the presence of the European institutions were a form of local elite which used other relevant, usually high-standing positions within Strasbourg in their efforts to keep the CoE and EP in Strasbourg. Throughout the period of study, but especially during the initial phase until 1956, city administration activities were complemented and supported by private, purpose-founded organisations dealing with the European presence.

(b) Private organisations

In Strasbourg, several private organisations operated that had been founded in response to the presence of the European institutions in the city. They formed a separate category of actors from the city administration within the actor group of Strasbourg. Both structures did not remain separate, but interacted. Of the three most involved private associations, their principal period of operation lay in one different hosting phase each. The *Comité Strasbourgeois pour le Mouvement Européen (CSME)* was founded in 1949 and was highly active during the first half of the 1950s to welcome parliamentarians during PACE sessions. The *Cercle des Amitiés Européennes (CAE)* was created in 1957 and most involved during the end of the decade and early 1960s by providing a leisure programme for wives of parliamentarians and female assembly members. The last major private organisation was the *Cercle européen de Strasbourg (CES)* which was founded in 1962 and included local and European institution members. It was a club that primarily catered to the diplomatic corps of the city, principally during the 1960s.

(i) Comité Strasbourgeois pour le Mouvement Européen

The *CSME* was the first local organisation to be founded in relation to the presence of European institutions in Strasbourg and in the first years of their presence the only one. From its creation on 8 April 1949, the first of its two main objectives was the welcome and accommodation of CoE staff in support of the city administration.[84] The second task comprised the diffusion and promotion of a general European idea and the need for

84 AS, 208 MW 16, *Extrait du Journal d'Alsace, 8.4.1949.*

European unity among the population of Strasbourg and Alsace.[85] Despite its name, the association was not affiliated with the European Movement until late 1953.[86]

In this section, the structure of the organisation will be presented, as well as the changes leading to it becoming involved with the French European Movement. Subsequently, its goals and actions of welcoming parliamentarians and presenting Strasbourg as the perfect host will be outlined, which included the founding of a *Club Européen* for the recreational use of PACE members and promotion of Strasbourg as the European capital and seat of all European institutions in 1952. The general diffusion of the European idea will not be covered, as the welcoming of European parliamentarians is the main focus of this study.

The analysis of this association is based on material issued by the *CSME* itself, as well as its documents in the municipal and CoE archives. It has to be noted that hardly any sources are available after 1953, which mirrors the general decrease in concise actions visible in city administration sources. Therefore, most of the information about the *CSME* in this section is based on the period before it became formally involved with the European Movement. The member journal *Vers l'Europe* did offer the occasional glimpse of Strasbourg-promotion after 1953, but does not allow for a comprehensive picture of such activities, as it primarily provided information related to the European Movement and politics.

85 Comité Strasbourgeois pour le Mouvement Européen, "L'Assemblée générale extraordinaire du Comité Strasbourgeois pour le Mouvement Européen", in *Vers l'Europe*, 1:1, 1950, p. 6.

86 Comité Strasbourgeois pour le Mouvement Européen, "Réorganisation", in *Vers l'Europe*, 5:40, 1954, p. 8.

1. Structure

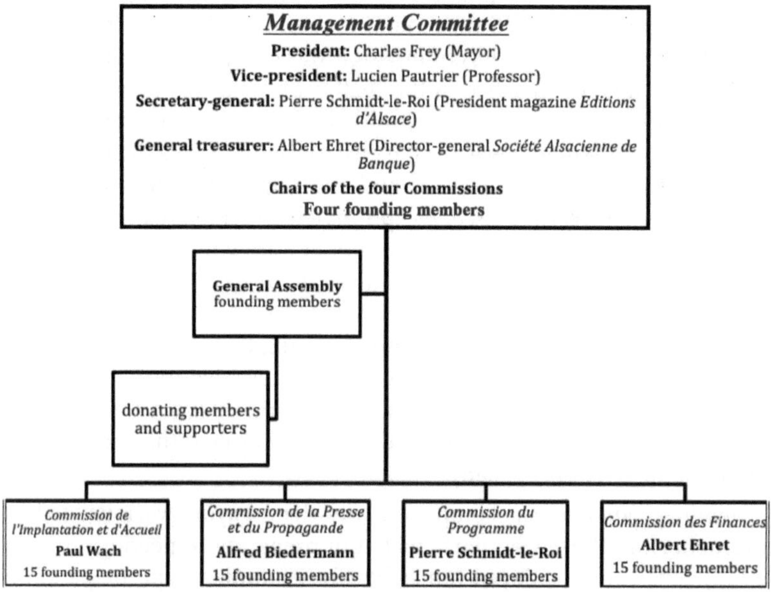

2. *Structure of the* Comité Strasbourgeois pour le Mouvement Européen[87]

The structure itself remained relatively unchanged during the period of study, although some personnel changes occurred due to deaths. For instance, Biedermann became first secretary-general and later president following the respective deceases of his predecessors.[88] After parts of the *CSME* became integrated into the European Movement in 1953, the administrative organisation did not change significantly either.[89]

87 Compiled from Comité Strasbourgeois pour le Mouvement Européen, "Les réunions de mars", in *Vers l'Europe*, 1:3, 1950, p. 8 and Comité Strasbourgeois pour le Mouvement Européen, "Composition du Comité Strasbourgeois pour le Mouvement Européen", in *Vers l'Europe*, 1:11, 1950, p. 2 and ACE, 3279/27129, *Statuts du Comité Strasbourgeois pour le Mouvement Européen*, pp. 2-4.

88 Comité Strasbourgeois pour le Mouvement Européen, "Au Comité Strasbourgeois pour le Mouvement Européen, Assemblée Générale", in *Vers l'Europe*, 5:43, 1954, p. 4 and AS, 209 MW 39, *Lettre de Biedermann au Maire, 18.7.1956.*

89 Comité Strasbourgeois pour le Mouvement Européen, "Réorganisation", in *Vers l'Europe*, 5:40, 1954, p. 8.

While the management committee (*comité-directeur*) and the financial committee (*commission des finances*) dealt with the functioning and general administration of the *CSME*, the other three commissions were responsible for reaching its aims.[90] Wach's commission was charged with receiving the CoE and its staff, for instance in the matter of assuring adequate (hotel) accommodation.[91] The tasks of Schmidt-le-Roi's formation were related to this aim, as it assured a welcoming environment and facilitated helpful relations between PACE delegates and the population during sessions. Furthermore, the organisation of receptions fell under its area of expertise.[92] This matter constituted an instance of cooperation with other actors, such as the tourism office *Syndicat d'Initiatives de la Ville de Strasbourg*, the city administration, or the CoE.[93] The press commission (*commission de la presse*) was largely responsible for implementing the *CSME*'s second aim, the diffusion of the European idea among the population.[94] The general assembly, attended by the founding members (*membres fondateurs*), convened thrice a year in ordinary sessions and elected the commissions and *comité-directeur* biannually.[95]

Membres fondateurs, comprised of the mayor, various federal movements and those who participated in preparation meetings prior to the *CSME's* creation, enjoyed full rights, for example the participation in the general assembly.[96] It would not be wrong to say that they belonged to the higher echelons of local society, including for example municipal/regional politicians such as René Radius; presidents of various local political, economic, or financial organisations like *Crédit Industriel d'Alsace et de Lorraine;* professors and teachers; as well as priests of all confessions.[97] Several members, especially Wach and Radius, continued to be prominently involved in various other organisations regarding the presence of European institutions in later years. The *CSME* actively

90 Comité Strasbourgeois pour le Mouvement Européen, "L'Assemblée générale extraordinaire du Comité Strasbourgeois pour le Mouvement Européen", in *Vers l'Europe*, 1:1, 1950, p. 6.

91 *Ibid.*

92 *Ibid.*

93 *Ibid.*

94 *Ibid.*

95 ACE, 3279/27129, *Statuts du Comité Strasbourgeois pour le Mouvement Européen*, pp. 2-4.

96 ACE, 3279/27129, *Statuts du Comité Strasbourgeois pour le Mouvement Européen*, p. 1.

97 AS, 198 MW 78, *Liste des membres fondateurs du Comité Strasbourgeois pour le Mouvement Européen.*

pursued this type of members, for instance by sending out individual letters to commerce and industry, inviting them to become members.[98]

The other two membership types comprised sympathisers of the association's aims. Donating members (*membres donateurs*) paid an annual membership fee of 10,000 (300€) instead of 1,000 Francs (30€) and supporters (*membres adherents*), composed of like-minded associations, 200 Francs (6€).[99] By own admission, the *CSME* had already gained 2,000 members in 1950.[100] Other forms of income included extraordinary donations, as well as subsidiaries from the *Département du Bas-Rhin.*[101]

2) Relations with the French European Movement

Although it could be concluded from the association's name that it was a local organisation of the European Movement, they were not formally affiliated until late 1953. Although the desire existed according to the *CSME,* it was impossible due to its statutes. It represented more political orientations than the European Movement and needed to show political neutrality when welcoming European parliamentarians.[102] In late 1952, however, the French European Movement began to form regional sub-organisations, and the *CSME* regarded itself to be predestined to become Bas-Rhin's.[103] In the *comité-directeur* meeting on 21 May 1953, it was decided to pursue the strategy of a *dédoublement* in this matter, namely forming two autonomous organisations according to the *CSME's* main tasks. The new *CSME,* self-styled as a para-municipal organisation, would continue to welcome the CoE. In addition, it would defend "des intérêts de Strasbourg, future capitale européenne", with the old *membres fondateurs* and *donateurs,* while the *membres adhérents* would form the new *Mouvement Européen du Bas-Rhin* and continue to diffuse the

---

98 Comité Strasbourgeois pour le Mouvement Européen, "L'Assemblée générale extraordinaire du Comité Strasbourgeois pour le Mouvement Européen", in *Vers l'Europe,* 1:1, 1950, p. 7.

99 Ehret, Albert, "Appel du Trésorier aux membres de notre association", in *Vers l'Europe,* 1:2, 1950, p. 8.

100 Biedermann, Alfred, "Zum Geleit", in *Vers l'Europe,* 1:1, 1950, p. 8.

101 AS, 198 MW 78, *Lettre du Comité Strasbourgeois pour le Mouvement Européen au Président du Conseil Général, 7/1949.*

102 Comité Strasbourgeois pour le Mouvement Européen, "Réunion du Comité directeur", in *Vers l'Europe,* 3:32, 1952, p. 7 and Comité Strasbourgeois pour le Mouvement Européen, "Réunion de notre Comité directeur", in *Vers l'Europe,* 4:36, 1953, p. 7.

103 Comité Strasbourgeois pour le Mouvement Européen, "Réunion de notre Comité directeur", in *Vers l'Europe,* 4:36, 1953, p. 7.

European idea among the population.[104] Both new associations held their constituent assemblies in December and November 1953 respectively.[105]

However, this did not mean that the *CSME* and the European Movement did not have any relations prior to that year. In May 1949, the European Movement described the *CSME* as a locally founded organisation which had accepted its patronage.[106] To which degree exactly both groupings were connected before the *dédoublement* is not entirely conclusive from the available sources in the local and the CoE archives. Generally, they point towards a loose association between two independent organisations. For example, the European Movement used the CoE as an intermediary to make demands to the local administration instead of asking the *CSME* as in the following occurrence. The secretary-general of the CoE was bidden to have the city administration promote the use of the European Movement's 'E' flag among the population during sessions to demonstrate the identification with the idea of European unity.[107] An instance showing the connection of both associations included that the *CSME* paid money in support of the European Movement.[108]

3) Activities

During the start-up phase, the *CSME* was, at least until the *dédoublement*, after which sources become scarce, a highly active actor in the matters of presenting Strasbourg as a perfect host. Areas of activity included offering events and accommodation to parliamentarians. It had also founded a club for this purpose. The *Club Européen* was founded as an informal meeting place for delegates who could also use it for their own receptions.[109] The *commission d'implantation* rented *Villa Schultzenberger* to accommodate the club and provided its furniture in 1949.[110]

Another central activity constituted the promotion of Strasbourg as European capital. A percentage occurred through their journal *Vers*

---

[104] *Ibid.* and Comité Strasbourgeois pour le Mouvement Européen, "Réorganisation", in *Vers l'Europe*, 5:40, 1954, p. 8.

[105] *Ibid.*

[106] ACE, 3262/27118/1, *Le Conseil de l'Europe à Strasbourg, 19.5.49*, p. 1.

[107] ACE, 3262/27118/1, *Lettre de Sandys à Paris, 15.6.49*.

[108] Comité Strasbourgeois pour le Mouvement Européen, "L'Assemblée générale extraordinaire du Comité Strasbourgeois pour le Mouvement Européen", in *Vers l'Europe*, 1:1, 1950, p. 7.

[109] ACE, 3262/27118/1, *Le Conseil de l'Europe à Strasbourg, 19.5.49*, p. 2.

[110] Comité Strasbourgeois pour le Mouvement Européen, "L'Assemblée générale extraordinaire du Comité Strasbourgeois pour le Mouvement Européen", in *Vers l'Europe*, 1:1, 1950, p. 7.

l'Europe, published under the direction of Biedermann and his commission from 1950-1964.[111] At first it was issued almost monthly, later the frequency slowly dropped to four publications per year. It informed not only about European politics, such as the proposed European Defence Community, but also about the CoE and Strasbourg as possible European capital. It was published in French, with the rare article appearing in German.

Texts in relation to Strasbourg and the institutions described for example the CoE or its headquarters, often in an enthusiastic and engaging manner.[112] Nevertheless, the tone of articles made it obvious that their intention remained the promotion of the general European idea, which included the main task of the *commission de la presse*. For example, in articles arguing for Strasbourg as the capital of Europe and/or seat of ECSC institutions, the general endorsement of the idea of European unity and a federal European government remained the (principal) underlying argument.[113] Still, these articles mirrored facets of what especially the city administration constructed as Strasbourg's *vocation européenne* and used as a promotion device. For instance, "le comité s'est trouvé d'accord pour estimer que notre association devait faire un effort pour défendre le prestige de Strasbourg, capitale européenne", was such an occurrence.[114]

Following the *dédoublement*, the journal became the organ of the *Mouvement Européen du Bas-Rhin*, which was also visible in the fact that the number of articles about Strasbourg and the seat question dropped significantly. For instance, while the first ECSC seat application round had been quite extensively covered with a poll in the journal and a *plaquette*,[115] the second application round from 1957-1959 received much less attention. In contrast, the city administration was highly active in this period.

---

111 Comité Strasbourgeois pour le Mouvement Européen, "Petites nouvelles du Secrétariat", in *Vers l'Europe*, 1:4, 1950, p. 8 and Comité Strasbourgeois pour le Mouvement Européen, "Les réunions de mars", in *Vers l'Europe*, 1:3, 1950, p. 8.

112 Cunin, Georges, "Le Palais du Conseil de l'Europe", in *Vers l'Europe*, 1:3, 1950, pp. 4-5 and Comité Strasbourgeois pour le Mouvement Européen, "Voici comment fonctionne le Conseil de l'Europe", in *Vers l'Europe*, 1:11, 1950, p. 7.

113 Biedermann, Alfred, "Autour de la querelle des capitales. Le véritable en jeu", in *Vers l'Europe*, 3:24, 1952, p. 1.

114 Comité Strasbourgeois pour le Mouvement Européen, "Nouvelles de notre association", in *Vers l'Europe*, 2:21, 1951, p. 2.

115 Comité Strasbourgeois pour le Mouvement Européen, *Strasbourg, capitale européenne, siège du Conseil de l'Europe, doit devenir le siège des autorités européennes*, Strasbourg, Impressions Strasbourg, 1952 and Comité Strasbourgeois pour le Mouvement Européen, "Notre enquête des personnalités européennes de tous pays et de toutes tendances se prononcent sur la concentration des autorités spéciales autour du Conseil de l'Europe", in *Vers l'Europe*, 3:26, 1952, pp. 1-8.

The highest phase of promotional activity occurred during the first application round of the ECSC in 1952. For this objective, the member journal *Vers l'Europe* was regularly used to circulate opinion pieces.[116] Most of these articles concentrated on presenting Strasbourg, the seat of the CoE, as the best option against other candidate cities which were considered as possible institution hosts and to promote it as the European capital. For example, in an article on the applicant cities, Alfred Biedermann outlined activities in a selection of possible candidate cities with Liège, Aachen, Luxembourg, Saarbrucken and Strasbourg and included grounds for objecting each of the options except the Alsatian city.[117] For each choice other than Strasbourg, he listed grounds for objection. For example, the fact that Liège as a mining area would not be suitable to host the federal European government.[118] Only for the French city, a weak, reasonably solvable disadvantage of not having enough facilities for accommodation was given, cushioned with the expression 'could object'.[119]

With this and similar articles, the *CSME* attempted to portray their city in a favourable light as the most suitable candidate for housing all European institutions. For instance, in regard to Aachen, Biedermann specified as argument against it hosting European organisms that it had been quite destroyed during the war.[120] As outlined in the previous chapter, Strasbourg had also suffered war substantial war damages which led to lack of space, among others, which had not fully been resolved in the early 1950s.

Apart from the promotion of Strasbourg in the member journal *Vers l'Europe*, the *CSME* published the book[121] *Strasbourg, capitale européenne, siège du Conseil de l'Europe, doit devenir le siège des autorités européennes* which reached a wider audience. It contained arguments why Strasbourg, as the capital of Europe, should become the seat of ECSC authorities.[122] The main argument was that the new European institutions should be installed at the chosen seat of the CoE, Strasbourg, for efficiency and concentration

---

116 Comité Strasbourgeois pour le Mouvement Européen, "Les réunions de mars", in *Vers l'Europe*, 1:3, 1950, p. 8.

117 Biedermann, Alfred, "Candidatures Européennes", in *Vers l'Europe*, 3:24, 1952, pp. 4-5.

118 *Ibid.*

119 *Ibid.*

120 *Ibid.*, p. 4.

121 This publication was referred to as *plaquette* in the original French description.

122 Comité Strasbourgeois pour le Mouvement Européen, *Strasbourg, capitale européenne, siège du Conseil de l'Europe, doit devenir le siège des autorités européennes*, Strasbourg, Impressions Strasbourg, 1952.

of all organisms in one place.[123] Prior to that, other options, such as each state receiving one institution had been presented in a negative light.[124] A second chapter entitled *témoignages* contained declarations from members of parliament and of the European Movement, such as Marinus van der Goes van Naters[125] or Salvador de Madariaga[126] and others from all CoE member states.[127]

The *CSME* had asked three questions regarding whether respondents felt that the creation of these institutions would foster a promotion of the European idea, whether a concentration of organisms with the CoE or a geographical dispersion of institutions was preferred, and whether it would be important for European integration that Strasbourg became the capital of Europe.[128] It is clearly visible that this questionnaire served the purpose of advertising the solution of grouping the institutions of the ECSC at the CoE's seat in Strasbourg. All of the selected respondents supported this goal and the fact that Strasbourg was the European capital, although some also indicated a preference for a polycentric capital system.[129] The same survey with only a slightly overlapping pool of respondents was published in *Vers l'Europe* in 1952. An entire issue was dedicated to presenting answers under the heading "notre enquête des personnalités européennes de tous pays et de toutes tendances se prononce sur la concentration des autorités spécialisées autour du Conseil de l'Europe à Strasbourg".[130]

The second query, "y-a-t-il intérêt à les [autorités spécialisées] grouper autour du Conseil de l'Europe, au sein duquel pourra se maintenir facilement la liaison entre les Etats-membres des différents pools et les autres pays européens; ou est-il préférable de les constituer en organismes autonomes, répartis dans les divers pays intéressés,"[131] contains elements of a leading question, as well. For the first option, the one in favour of Strasbourg, an advantageous result is given, while the second possibility

---

123 *Ibid.*, p. 12.

124 *Ibid.*, p. 8.

125 He was a member of PACE and member of the second chamber of the Netherlands.

126 He was the president of the Spanish National Council of the European Movement and a diplomat.

127 *Ibid.*, pp. 19-32.

128 *Ibid.*, p. 17.

129 *Ibid.*, pp. 19-32.

130 Comité Strasbourgeois pour le Mouvement Européen, "Notre enquête des personnalités européennes de tous pays et de toutes tendances se prononcent sur la concentration des autorités spéciales autour du Conseil de l'Europe", in *Vers l'Europe*, 3:26, 1952, pp. 1-8.

131 Comité Strasbourgeois pour le Mouvement Européen, *Strasbourg, capitale européenne, siège du Conseil de l'Europe, doit devenir le siège des autorités européennes*, Strasbourg, Impressions Strasbourg, 1952, p. 17.

lacks such an addendum. The rest of the *CSME's* book continues in the same vein, with a presentation of the city of Strasbourg's suitability and capability to house all European institutions, such as its European tradition[132] and its infrastructure.[133] All in all, this book, of which 1,000 copies were distributed constituted a promotional publication in order to advertise Strasbourg as seat for all European institutions. It was published at a time when the ECSC was still deliberating where and in which form to site its institutions, the High Authority, the Court and the Common Assembly. As outlined in the previous chapter, a (provisional) decision was only made in late July 1952, shortly before the organisation began its work.

(ii) Cercle des Amitiés Européennes

The second major private organisation, the *CAE*, primarily offered activities for the wives of parliamentarians. It was founded in 1957 by local high-society ladies, among them Pierre Pflimlin's wife Marie-Odile (henceforth referred to as O. Pflimlin).[134] It contributed to the hosting efforts of the city administration in the manner O. Pflimlin stated in 1963: "Il n'y a pas d'accueil possible dans une société sans l'acquiescement, la participation des femmes."[135] Thus, it aimed to add a personal and familiar touch to welcoming European parliamentarians in the city in order to gain favourable opinions on hosting capabilities in Strasbourg.

Another area, the *CAE* was active in from 1959 onwards, included finding host families for foreign young adults and welcoming international students to Strasbourg.[136] From 1960 onwards, the association's activity increasingly began to focus on welcoming international students and organising host families for young adults interested to live among French families. This was mirrored by the committee structure, which underwent changes during the 1960s, when more posts were created for these

---

[132] This European tradition, or *vocation européenne*, constructed by way of an appropiation of history was employed as a blanket strategy, predominantly by the city administration.

[133] *Ibid.*, pp. 33-52.

[134] AS, 208 MW 267, *Minutes Liaison of the Committee, 26.6.1957*, p. 1 and "Blog of the Cercle des Amitiés Européennes", <http://amitieseuropeennes.weebly.com> (accessed 15.12.2014).

[135] "Blog of the Cercle des Amitiés Européennes", <http://amitieseuropeennes.weebly.com> (accessed 15.12.2014).

[136] Pflimlin, Marie-Odile, "Amitiés Européennes", in Comité des Amitiés Européennes (ed.), *Amitiés Européennes*, Strasbourg, Dernières Nouvelles d'Alsace, 1977, p. 7.

activities than during the end of the 1950s.[137] This will not be covered further, since this study is about the efforts to welcome European parliamentarians to Strasbourg. Nevertheless, it is a part of the association's work that shows its general international mindedness. The *CAE* is still active in this area today.

This section is based on material issued by the *CAE* itself, a publication *(plaquette)* commemorating the association's tenth anniversary in 1967 and activity until 1977, as well as its and the city administration's documents archived in the municipal archive of Strasbourg. The *CAE's* work was supposed to complement the city administration's session frame programmes.[138] They addressed their events mainly to accompanying wives of delegates, although parliamentarians were welcome to attend some of them, as an information letter from the *CAE* to PACE delegates for the April 1958 session stated.[139] Furthermore, it was the only local organisation, which was composed of and driven by women. An analogy to the female role of the time of receiving people at home included the underlying philosophy of the *CAE.*

The association cooperated with the city in the same manner the *CSME* did during the first hosting period from 1949-1956. In this case, it included sharing information with the Liaison Committee.[140] Likewise, the *CAE* transmitted lists of its events to the city administration.[141] Both actors also coordinated their activities, for instance a letter from O. Pflimlin indicated that she asked the administration to reserve one evening for a *CAE* reception during the September 1959 session period, so that activities would not overlap.[142] Their work was characterised by concentrating on complementing areas, but also instances of collaboration, as will be analysed subsequently.

Both the *CAE* and the municipal administration aimed to promote closer ties between European institution personnel and the city, as well as its inhabitants and to provide an extensive leisure programme. Prior to 1956, the start of the second hosting phase, delegates had complained about the lack of activities, as a CoE-internal memorandum testified.[143] Local actors regarded this as especially important, since it constituted an

137 Comité des Amitiés Européennes (ed.), *Amitiés Européennes*, Strasbourg, DNA, 1977.

138 AS, 208 MW 267, *Minutes of the Liaison Committee, 26.6.1957*, p. 1.

139 AS, 236 MW 1/2, *Lettre du Cercle des Amitiés Européennes aux délégués des assemblées européennes, 18.4.1958.*

140 AS, 208 MW 267, *Minutes of the Liaison Committee, 26.6.1957*, p. 1.

141 AS, 236 MW 1/2, *Lettre d'O. Pflimlin à A. Heitz, 24.4.1958.*

142 AS, 236 MW 1/8, *Lettre d'O. Pflimlin, 22.8.1959.*

143 ACE, 121/0092, *Mémorandum du 24.7.1950.*

opportune way to bind the European organisations it hosted to the city. In the light of the approaching ECSC seat application round in 1957 and its highly competitive environment with several qualified cities vying to house institutions, counteracting criticism of Strasbourg's capabilities was highly important in order to be able to stay in the game.

During the seat application round, this climate of competition manifested itself in the effort, the city administration invested in its hosting activities. Special occasions, like the inaugural session of the EP in March 1958, were especially celebrated through such activities, as will be shown in the subsequent section. The *CAE* contributed to the municipal actors' efforts, as they asked their members in a letter to support this event of importance to the future of Strasbourg as seat and also to attend public sessions of the EP if possible.[144]

In the following, the founding, structure and activities of the *Cercle des Amitiés* will be discussed. Based on the available documents in the municipal archive of Strasbourg, four central aspects have been identified, which were unique to the *CAE* and not shared by any other local actor, private or municipal. It was the only association driven by women, placed a strong emphasis on including accompanying wives of delegates into the hosting effort, its events contained a private and cultural aspect and facilitated the active participation of members of the CoE's permanent staff or their wives.

1) Founding of the *Cercle des Amitiés*

The *CAE* was the only 'female element' in the hosting efforts of Strasbourg and was founded in early 1957 by local high society ladies, who also had private connections to the CoE permanent personnel. Others were wives of municipal politicians involved in presenting the city as attractive European institution host, most prominently among them O. Pflimlin. This could also be a minor aspect of the seat question, namely that women were prominently involved in hospitality issues, but not so much in other areas. A parallel can be drawn to the local organisation of the The Hague Congress in 1948. Then, a reception committee, also called 'Ladies Committee', composed of women existed that planned large parts of hosting efforts, among others accommodation of the delegates.[145]

---

[144] Cercle des Amitiés Européennes, "Lettre du Cercle des Amitiés Européennes à Madame, 4.3.1958", in Comité des Amitiés Européennes (ed.), *Amitiés Européennes*, Strasbourg, Dernières Nouvelles d'Alsace, 1977, p. 12.

[145] Beers, Marloes, "Hosting Europe. Local Organisation of the Congress of Europe", in Guieu, Jean-Michel and Le Dréau, Christophe (eds.), *Le "Congrès de l'Europe" à La Haye (1948-2009)*, The Hague, Brussels, Peter Lang, 2009, pp. 137-149.

As the newspaper *Dernières Nouvelles d'Alsace* (*DNA*) commented, the association was regarded in the same light, due to which the city administration had deemed the creation of its specialised committees necessary.

> Niemand wird sich über diese Initiative beklagen, denn wenn Strasbourg die "Hauptstadt Europas" bleiben will, ist es unerlässlich, die Atmosphäre der Langeweile zu "bereinigen", die schon zu lange hier geherrscht und dem guten Ruf einer Stadt geschadet hat, die doch über bedeutende Möglichkeiten verfügt.[146]

With their programme of excursions, luncheons, receptions and cultural activities, the *CAE* not only contributed to the events organised by other local actors, but also closed a gap in the hosting effort by concentrating on the wives of delegates who accompanied their husbands to Strasbourg. Therewith, the entirety of city actors' session frame programme focused on not just European parliamentarians, and constituted a holistic approach to being a good host with the inclusion of the families of their intended audience.

In the *plaquette*, the *CAE* had issued, O. Pflimlin recounted the foundation and early work of the association. According to this account, several of the permanent staff of the CoE, among them acting Secretary-General Dunstan Curtis, often met privately with one of the future founders of the *CAE*, Monique Grouvel and her husband, at the couple's mansion, the *Château d'Osthoffen*.[147] During one of these meetings in early 1957, their friends from the CoE complained they would feel isolated in Strasbourg and that a direct contact to the population would be necessary, also to help with accommodation problems.[148] Subsequently, Monique Grouvel contacted Altorffer who encouraged the idea and put her in contact with another future founder, Suzanne Schneegans.[149]

Since both women, as well as the other two principal founding members, Jeanne Graff and O. Pflimlin, were members of the *Club Europe-Amérique*, O. Pflimlin recounted that they recruited its members, as well as their personal friends for the endeavour of forming the *CAE*.[150] This club later figured prominently as co-organiser of various activities.

146 AS, 208 MW 267, *Extrait des DNA, 27.6.1957.*

147 Pflimlin, Marie-Odile, "Amitiés Européennes", in Comité des Amitiés Européennes (ed.), *Amitiés Européennes*, Strasbourg, Dernières Nouvelles d'Alsace, 1977, p. 3.

148 *Ibid.*

149 *Ibid.*

150 *Ibid.*, p. 5. Graff was president of the *Club Europe-Amérique* and Schneegans its treasurer.

On the constitutive meeting of the association in early May 1957, circa 70 people met to found the organisation and to propose a draft programme for the meeting of the common assembly of the ECSC in the end of June 1957.[151] The association defined its main goal as working in accord with the city administration to create an amendable environment and stay for delegates and their families.[152] In particular, it emphasised an approach to hosting on the basis of personal interaction.[153] This not only included the European parliamentarians, but also permanent staff living in Strasbourg.[154] Furthermore, the *CAE* strived to get to know the different languages and cultures of people.[155] The association's activities concentrated on mitigating the feeling of being closed off that some CoE staff had mentioned to Grouvel in a private setting, who then made the effort to create the association with other friends and acquaintances.

Following the June 1957 assembly meeting period, the *CAE* offered various events during each session period, visible in the monthly letters archived in the municipal archive of Strasbourg, they sent out to their members informing them about planned events.[156] The European parliamentarians and their wives were likewise informed about the current programme prior to each session period.[157] The association financed its running costs for the secretariat and rent through membership fees and also received regular subsidiaries from the *Département*, for instance 19,500 Francs (300€) for the April 1958 session.[158] Furthermore, members paid for their participation in *soirées*, luncheons or excursions and often covered costs for one or more of the invited European guests. They also contributed with preparing food for receptions or dinners in their own homes.[159]

151 *Ibid.*

152 AS, 236 MW 26/3, *Assemblée Générale du 1.12.1958*, p. 1.

153 AS, 236 MW 26/3, *Assemblée Générale du 1.12.1958*, p. 6.

154 AS, 236 MW 26/3, *Assemblée Générale du 1.12.1958*, p. 1.

155 AS, 236 MW 26/3, *Assemblée Générale du 1.12.1958*, p. 4.

156 AS, 236 MW 26/3, *Lettres du Cercle des Amitiés Européennes à Madame.*

157 AS, 236 MW 26/3, *Lettres aux représentatives.*

158 Pflimlin, Marie-Odile, "Amitiés Européennes", in Comité des Amitiés Européennes (ed.), *Amitiés Européennes*, Strasbourg, Dernières Nouvelles d'Alsace, 1977, p. 9 and AS, 236 MW 1/6, *Relève des factures payées par le Département du Bas-Rhin*, p. 3.

159 Pflimlin, Marie-Odile, "Amitiés Européennes", in Comité des Amitiés Européennes (ed.), *Amitiés Européennes*, Strasbourg, Dernières Nouvelles d'Alsace, 1977, p. 9.

2) Composition of the *Cercle des Amitiés*

After own admission, the *CAE* had about 350 members by the end of September 1957.[160] From the salutatory address of letters sent to members, *Madame*, one can conclude that the *CAE* was exclusively made up of female members, which was also visible in its executive administrational structure, which will be presented subsequently. This observation is in accord with the founding philosophy of the *CAE*, which emphasised the necessity of female involvement in Strasbourg's hosting effort, a sentiment comprised in the quote from O. Pflimlin cited in the beginning of the section. The house as the domain of the women was compared to the task the various local actors faced with receiving European parliamentarians. "Ouvrir sa maison suppose plus que des possibilités financières, plus que de la bonne volonté. Il faut une volonté de gentillesse, la compréhension des autres, du tact, de l'intuition."[161] The events, the *CAE* organised, mirrored these sentiments, since they commonly included a personal touch.

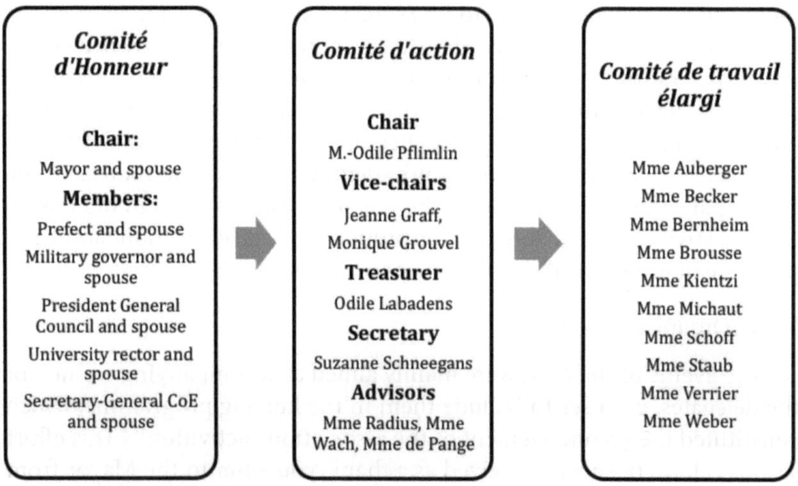

3. *Structure of the* Cercle des Amitiés Européennes[162]

---

160 *Ibid.*, p. 6.

161 *Ibid.*, p. 4.

162 AS, 236 MW 26/3, *Cercle des Amitiés Européennes de Strasbourg.*

The sources in the municipal archive of Strasbourg, mostly letters to members, programmes and a report on the general assembly of December 1958, showed that the *Comité d'Honneur* was not always participating in day-to-day business. One of the few instances, where a member of this committee was involved, included the infrequent hosting of an event.[163] According to the archived documents, the *Comité d'Action* constituted the most active part of the administration, from drafting the programme to its implementation. The *Comité de travail élargi* was composed of those members who were the most active since the founding of the association, such as by hosting an event at their home or putting their car at disposition for transportation during an excursion.[164]

Among the members of the three committees were also four wives of city administration actors involved in hosting activities, which included *Mesdames* Kientzi, Pflimlin, Radius and Wach. *Madame* de Pange, wife of Victor de Pange, Head of the Division of Cultural Affairs of the CoE, presented a liaison to that organisation. This seemed to have included a more active connection than to its Secretary-General as a member of the *Comité d'Honneur*, which, according to the sources, seems to have been more pro-forma, rather than constituting an active involvement in organisational processes. Next to the addition of structures to facilitate youth exchanges, Suzanne Schneegans became president of the *CAE*. Nevertheless, O. Pflimlin remained very active as honorary president, as mirrored by sources in the municipal archive of Strasbourg. She was primarily involved in organising leisure activities for the European institutions, as well as the foundation and planning of events for the *Cercle européen de Strasbourg*.

3) Organised events

The events of the *CAE* were mainly aimed at accompanying women of the delegates, in order to include them in the hosting programme, which constituted the second element of the association's activities.[165] This effort seems to have been well received as a thank-you letter to the Mayor from the wife of PACE member Charles Hale also made a reference to the *CAE*: "May I take this opportunity of thanking you and the Ladies of Strasbourg

[163] E.g. AS, 236 MW 26/3, *Sorties prévues, 4/1958.*

[164] AS, 236 MW 26/3, *Cercle des Amitiés Européennes de Strasbourg.*

[165] AS, 236 MW 1/2, *Lettres du Cercle des Amitiés Européennes aux délégués et époux 18.4.1958.*

to have always made us welcome."[166] The city administration also planned one event for wives, an excursion, to which they invited the Committee of the *CAE*, as well as the wives of the Special Liaison Committee members, to accompany the spouses on 30 April 1958.[167] Similarly, wives of specialised committee members were recruited, which included *Madame* Schwaab-Altorffer, mayor Altorffer's wife, and *Mesdames* Kientzi, Pflimlin and Radius, all *CAE* (honorary) committee members as well, to accompany an *excursion pour les dames* in May 1957.[168]

It is interesting to note that the husbands were generally only allowed to participate in luncheons, *soirées* or receptions, but usually not in activities during the day, such as excursions to places in Alsace or Germany, and other activities within Strasbourg. This was mirrored by the inscription forms, where delegates only were invited to these kinds of events, such as a reception following an excursion. The latter always carried the addendum *pour les dames*.[169] Events explicitly for both delegates and their spouses, were offered by the association as well, but not in the same frequency.

The organisational structure of the *CAE* itself further highlighted this emphasis, since it was assured by women, as mentioned above. The way of how events were hosted, mirrored this circumstance as well, for example, *Madame* Cuttoli, the wife of the *Préfet*, offered a reception in the *Préfecture* after an excursion as the only official host.[170] The events, the *CAE* organised, were characterised by either or both of the following two circumstances: a familiar atmosphere and culture. Arrangements falling into the first category included, for example, excursions to places close to Strasbourg, where private cars of members usually were used for transport.[171]

Another element of the familiar environment, the *CAE* attempted to offer was the way it was founded through one of the initial members having a personal contact to the CoE. Those likeminded people formed this organisation in order to counteract the feeling of essentially being in a bubble for the European parliamentarians. In the tradition of the private character of many of these events, the Grouvels received guests regularly in their home *Château d'Osthoffen*, such as on 24 October 1957, which also included

166 AS, 236 MW 1/4, *Lettre de Hale au Maire 18.10.1958.*

167 AS, 236 MW 1/2, *Note de la Division VIII, 21.4.1958*, pp. 2-3.

168 AS, 236 MW 19/1, *Lettres du Maire aux Mmes Schwaab-Altorffer, Pflimlin et Radius, 30.4.1957.*

169 E.g., Comité des Amitiés Européennes (ed.), *Amitiés Européennes*, Strasbourg, Dernières Nouvelles d'Alsace, 1977.

170 AS, 236 MW 26/3, *Sorties prévues, 4/1958.*

171 AS, 236 MW 26/3, *Assemblée Générale du 1.12.1958*, p. 2.

an *audition de musique.*[172] Nevertheless, luncheons or *soirées dansantes*, another staple of *CAE* events, took place outside of the frame of private homes. This and the final element of the association's activities, the participation of wives of CoE personnel and female delegates, fell into the categories of private and cultural as well. Events with their participation usually contained one or both of these elements. According to a speech by Schneegans on the occasion of the 20th anniversary, the city and *Département* had taken charge of all hosting activities by 1967, since the European sessions would be more and more frequent.[173] As will be analysed during the strategy section, the city actors reduced their activities for fear of being too repetitive in the face of the increased numbers of European assembly meetings. However, the *CAE* continued to offer a luncheon for female delegates and parliamentarians' wives for most EP or PACE sessions, as well as other events.[174] For instance, a letter to the members from October 1965 stated that there was already much organised during that month's parliamentary session and that there would not be planned anything before the luncheon in November.[175] Despite the reduced frequency of offered events, the work of the *CAE* to welcome parliamentarians remained an important factor on Strasbourg's hosting programme, for example in a letter from the 1970s, which thanked the Mayor for the welcome for the parliamentarian's wives and the luncheon offered by the *CAE.*[176]

In this manner, the *CAE* constituted a type of forum, in which cultural events and information could be consumed in a familiar environment. The latter type included, for example, a conference given by Prince Pierre of Greece on European topics, organised by Polys Modinos, who was affiliated with the CoE, and his wife.[177] Additionally, such presentations were occasionally held during the association's own events, such as a dinner-debate organised with the *Club Europe-Amérique* on 8 January 1959, during which Dunstan Curtis held a speech on English-French relations and the unification of Europe.[178]

---

172 AS, 236 MW 26/3, *Programme du Cercle des Amitiés Européennes 10/1957.*

173 Schneegans, Suzanne, "1957-1977. Allocution prononcée par Madame Schneegans, présidente des Amitiés Européennes, en présence de Madame Marie-Odile Pflimlin, présidente d'honneur", in Comité des Amitiés Européennes (ed.), *Amitiés Européennes*, Strasbourg, Dernières Nouvelles d'Alsace, 1977, p. 18.

174 *Ibid.*

175 AS, 236 MW 26/2, *Lettre du Cercle des Amitiés Européennes aux membres, 13.10.1965.*

176 AS, 236 MW 10/1, *Lettre de Boyden à Pflimlin, 3.5.1970.*

177 AS, 236 MW 26/3, *Lettre du Cercle des Amitiés Européennes à Madame, 5.11.1959.*

178 AS, 236 MW 26/3, *Assemblée Générale du 1.12.1958*, p. 1.

Next to the fact that the *CAE* was in contact with the city administration, O. Pflimlin was individually kept informed of organisational processes regarding events by A. Heitz, the head of *Division VIII*. He not only sent updates, when the *CAE* had been involved in organising events, but also because "je sais par ailleurs que vous êtes très intéressée par la façon dont nous organisons l'accueil."[179] During the third hosting phase, this information transmission intensified and O. Pflimlin was also frequently consulted on menu choices and asked to decide from 1959, which was intensified during the 1960s and 1970s as a type of 'unofficial consultant'.

To sum up, the *CAE* provided cultured activities for female delegates and parliamentarians' wives. From 1960 onwards, it was increasingly involved in welcoming international students, as well as participating in the European exchange programme for youths, *Mouvement "Experience in International Living."*[180] The *Cercle des Amitiés* primarily recruited its members to host young foreigners.[181] In its activities, it remained in close contact with the city administration to coordinate events and exchange information. Additionally, the *CAE* fulfilled a complimenting role in hosting effort, since it focused on the wives of parliamentarians.

(iii) Cercle Européen de Strasbourg

The last major private organisation, the *CES*, was founded in 1962 and still exists today. It held another special role within the array of actors concerned with hosting activities, because it constituted a 'bridge' between the two bubbles of local actors involved in hosting matters and the European institutions. It explicitly catered to permanent CoE civil servants, who were encouraged to become members. Additionally, all presidents were recruited from among high officials of or permanent representatives to the CoE.[182] According to archive documents, it was founded by actors from the city, the CoE, as well as O. Pflimlin, who was characterised as the initiator of the process.[183]

The main goal was to offer a discussion forum for European themes in a familiar atmosphere, as the following quote from the proposal to form

[179] AS, 236 MW 1/2, *Lettre d'A. Heitz à O. Pflimlin 30.4.1958.*

[180] AS, 236 MW 26/3, *Lettre du Cercle des Amitiés Européennes aux membres, 12.2.1960.*

[181] AS, 236 MW 26/2, *Lettre du Cercle des Amitiés Européennes aux membres, 25.2.1965.*

[182] "Les Anciens Présidents." http://cercleuropeen.eu/les_anciens_presidents.html (accessed 20.12.2012).

[183] "L'histoire du Cercle." <http://cercleuropeen.eu/lhistoire_du_cercle.html> (accessed 20.12.2012).

the *CES* by its future first President Polys Modinos, Deputy Secretary-General of the CoE, showed. "Depuis longtemps l'absence se fait sentir à Strasbourg d'un Cercle qui, à la manière des clubs anglais, serait le prolongement du domicile de chacun de ses membres."[184] The goal of the organisation also was to bind European personnel on a personal basis to Strasbourg and to provide a space where discussions on European topics could be encouraged.

In this section, the founding of the *CES*, its structure, as well as an overview of its activity will be presented. The analysis is based on letters, notes and minutes from the municipal archive of Strasbourg and the archive of the Council of Europe, as well as a *plaquette* issued by the *CES* on its 20th anniversary in 1982.

The lack of such a club as stated by Modinos and the fact that other major French cities such as Paris or Bordeaux had a *Maison de l'Europe* with a library and rooms where Europeans could meet was seen as ample reason by Ridoux in a letter to Pflimlin that Strasbourg also needed such an institution.[185] A mix of local administration actors, among them Ridoux, Schmidt and A. Heitz, together with Modinos and Dunstan Curtis, the acting Secretary-General of the CoE, as well as O. Pflimlin were involved in the founding process. The municipal government was primarily involved in acquiring a suitable building. O. Pflimlin and Modinos were occupied with drafting its aims, as A. Heitz stated in a letter to her, it would be her area of expertise.[186] At the end of October 1961, the involved actors had decided on a villa for the *CES*, which was bought by the city administration and subsequently rented by the association.[187] The constitutive meeting of the *CES* was held at the Chamber of Commerce on 24 November.[188]

184 AS, 236 MW 25/1, *Conseil de l'Europe, projet de création*, p. 1.

185 AS, 236 MW 25/1, *Note pour M. Pflimlin, 21.7.1961*, p. 1.

186 AS, 236 MW 25/1, *Lettre d'A. Heitz à O. Pflimlin.*

187 AS, 236 MW 25/1, *Lettre d'A. Heitz à Baillard, 28.11.1961.*

188 AS, 236 MW 25/1, *Note du 15.11.1961.*

1) Structure

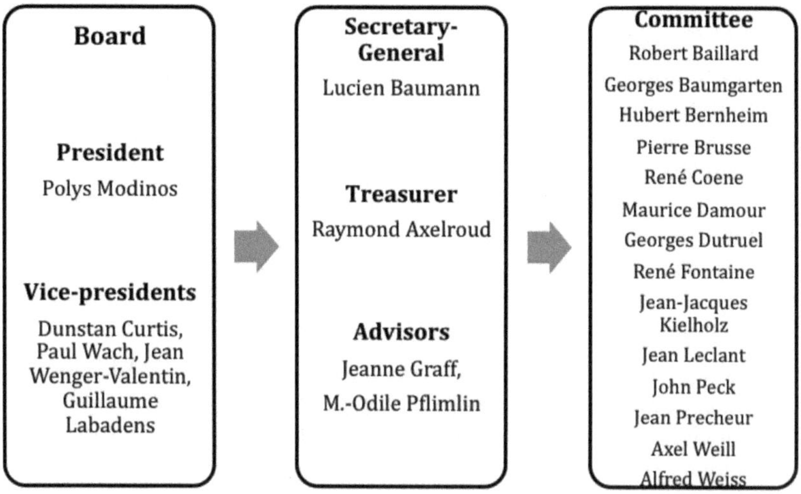

4. Structure of the Cercle Européen de Strasbourg.[189]

The entire committee was composed of the 23 members in the table above.[190] Members included a mix of local personalities, many of them from the local authorities, and personnel from the European institutions. For instance, Pflimlin, Wach and Radius, or Lodovico Benvenuti, Secretary-General of the CoE, and Curtis were admitted in March 1962.[191] Several members also had been in the *CSME* since 1949, like Wenger-Valentin. In April 1962, the *CES* had 224 members, this number remained rather stable over time, for instance, in 1975 the number was 246.[192] All in all, according to *CES* reports, 6,095 persons visited the association in 1963 or 7,216 in 1964.[193]

Four categories of members existed, *membres permanents, agrégés, temporaires* and *de droit*. Aggregated members were associations with a reciprocal accord with the *CES*, temporary members constituted foreigners who only stayed briefly in Strasbourg. They needed to be presented by two permanent members in order to get access. *Membres de droit* were comprised

---

[189] Cercle européen de Strasbourg, *Cercle européen de Strasbourg 1962-1982*, Strasbourg, Dernières Nouvelles d'Alsace, 1982, p. 6.

[190] ACE, 3358/2982, *Statuts du Cercle européen de Strasbourg*, p. 2.

[191] ACE, 3358/2982, *Cercle européen de Strasbourg, Liste, 15.3.1962.*

[192] AS, 236 MW 25/1, *Note pour M. Pflimlin*, p. 2 and 97 W 14/1, *Extrait des DNA, 24.4.1975.*

[193] AS, 236 MW 26/1, *Rapport moral du Cercle européen de Strasbourg, 24.4.1965.*

of the city administration, diplomats, consuls and other high-level civil servants of the European institutions. They did not possess an entry right, or the right to vote.[194]

In the beginning, the *CES* was conceptualised as a club for men in the tradition of English clubs, as hinted at by the quote in the beginning of this section. In November 1962, the committee addressed a letter to its members stating their wives would be allowed to accompany them in order to have the *CES* more frequented. In addition, the committee pointed out that they could organise bridge sessions.[195] In fact, O. Pflimlin was responsible for most social occasions according to archive sources and also chaired the *Commission des activités* during the 1980s, which was incidentally the only structure composed of women.[196]

The association's expenses were covered by annual fees.[197] Additionally, Modinos offered honorary membership to the local authorities, as well as high civil servants of the CoE and EP.[198] The administration also gave a subsidiary of 1,250 Francs (2,000€) for which they received five annual membership cards that civil servants of the local authorities interested in European questions could use, as A. Heitz, for instance.[199] The local authorities financed a number of membership cards for European assemblies as well. For instance, in 1970, the *Préfecture* paid the *CES* 4,000 Francs (5,000€) for 16 membership cards valid for a year, which they intended to offer to parliamentarians participating in functions in Strasbourg.[200] The CoE also made an initial financial contribution of 500 Francs (700€) in 1962.[201]

2) Activities

Next to this membership fee, the city or department gave further periodic subsidiaries to the *CES*, for instance 4,000 Francs in 1965.[202] The association also asked for support, in the reasoning that it would organise

194 ACE, 3358/2982, *Statuts du Cercle européen de Strasbourg*, pp. 1-2.

195 Cercle européen de Strasbourg, *Cercle européen de Strasbourg 1962-1982*, Strasbourg, Dernières Nouvelles d'Alsace, 1982, p. 8.

196 AS, 9 Z 497, *Annuaire 1985-1986.*

197 AS, 236 MW 25/1, *Projet de création*, p. 2.

198 AS, 236 MW 25/1, *Note pour M. Pflimlin, 3.4.1962.*

199 AS, 236 MW 25/1, *Note pour M. Pflimlin, 3.4.1962*, p. 2 and *Note pour le Secrétaire-Général Adjoint, 16.4.1962.*

200 AS, 236 MW 10/3, *Lettre du Cercle européen de Strasbourg à la Préfecture, 8.7.1970* and 236 MW 9/4, *Lettre du Cercle européen de Strasbourg à la Préfecture, 18.12.1969.*

201 ACE, 3358/2982, *Note pour la Division des Finances, 17.7.1962.*

202 AS, 236 MW 26/1, *Lettre de Modinos au Préfet, 6.3.1965.*

more and more receptions.[203] This was provided from the Bipartite Committee budget in exchange for membership cards for municipal administration civil servants. As Ridoux expressed in a note to Pflimlin, the local authorities saw the support as important, since the *CES* concentrated on the diplomatic corps.

> Il est certain que l'existence du Cercle européen est une nécessité et qu'il rend des services non négligeables aux personnalités diplomatiques et européennes qui résident ou séjournent à Strasbourg, il est également souvent utilisé pour inviter les experts qui participent aux réunions de travail organisées par le Conseil.[204]

It complimented the hosting programme of the city administration by concentrating on CoE civil servants and diplomatic corps, for which they gave support to the organisation. Further assistance included printing *CES* information material on demand of O. Pflimlin, and the *Service des Relations Publiques* also sent out the invitations for its events.[205]

CES activities had the following goal, "le Cercle s'était donné comme objectif 'de contribuer à l'accomplissement de la mission européenne de Strasbourg.'"[206] These events can be divided into three categories; dinners or receptions, presentations on general topics, or conferences on European history or issues. Receptions included periodically offered Monday luncheons with a member of the committee or dinners with European personalities.[207]

In summary, the *CES* was part of the hosting structure of local actors and covered the aspect of offering a forum for high civil servants of the European institutions, the CoE consular corps and local elites. As it was the case with the *CAE*, with which it also shared an address since its foundation, it was a high-society club. Likewise, it put a strong emphasis on actively including the European presence in its structure, most prominently visible in the fact that its president today still is recruited from among European institution staff. A major difference to the *CAE* was that it was addressed to men and basically only included the spouses of its members in the planning of social events. Especially O. Pflimlin, described

---

203 AS, 236 MW 26/1, *Lettre de Modinos au Préfet, 6.3.1965.*

204 AS, 236 MW 26/1, *Note pour M. Pflimlin, 9.3.1965*, p. 1.

205 AS, 97 W 14/1, *Note du 5.2.1975* and *Note pour M. Hoennige, 3.3.1975.*

206 Cercle européen de Strasbourg, *Cercle européen de Strasbourg 1962-1982*, Strasbourg, Dernières Nouvelles d'Alsace, 1982, p. 2.

207 AS, 97 W 14/1, *Invitation* and *Activités du Cercle européen de Strasbourg, 4e trimestre 1976.*

as the main force behind the constitution of the *CES*, was very active in this area.

(c) Other actors

Other actors involved in hosting activities were a relatively small group which was mostly involved in the early stages of hosting the presence of European institutions in Strasbourg. They were another sub-category of the local pool of actors that, as the private organisations-group, strongly interacted with the city administration actors concerned with consolidation activities. Over the entire period of study, various associations belonging to this category were rather concerned with the improvement of infrastructure, as will be analysed in chapters 4 and 5. One of the most involved other actors, *the Syndicat d'Initiative de la Ville de Strasbourg* (tourism office) will be presented and a small overview of associations will be given to which the city administration had outsourced some tasks to before it created specialised structures in 1956. Most actions of this type of actor organised accommodation for parliamentarians during sessions. They were actors who were involved in welcoming European institutions, because tasks related to that fell into their area of expertise and the city administration had not yet created appropriate instances to deal exclusively with European institutions.

The *Syndicat* was founded in 1922 and responsible for attracting tourism to Strasbourg, as well as providing information and accommodation for visitors.[208] Following the war, it resumed its work in August 1946.[209] During the first phase of hosting activities, it organised hotel rooms for parliamentarians during sessions and promoted the city, which constituted parts of its tasks as the local tourism agency. Apart from that, it was not concerned with other aspects concerning the CoE, as the *CSME* was, for example.

The tourism office mainly relied on subsidiaries from the city administration, the *Commissariat Général du Tourisme*, the *Conseil Général du Bas-Rhin*, the *Touring Club de France* and the Chamber of Commerce, which amounted to 992,000 Francs (34,000€) in 1948, for example. Other income included membership fees.[210] The *Syndicat* seems to have been in a bad financial situation as several applications for more funding to the main backer, the municipal administration, indicated between 1947 and

208 AS, 235 MW 266, *Bericht vom 29.6.1948*, p. 1.

209 AS, 235 MW 267, *Extrait du Journal d'Alsace 3.8.1946*.

210 AS, 235 MW 266, *Bericht vom 29.6.1948*, p. 1.

1949.[211] Therefore, city actors repeatedly demanded that the organisation reformed its spending, for instance with the closing of one of its offices.[212] Several members of the association's administrative board were also members of commercial associations or involved in the hotel business.[213] Its tasks included among others providing information about Strasbourg to tourists and commerce; the provision of visitor brochures, lists of hotels in the city and Bas-Rhin, timetables for trains and busses; the publication of information in the press; offering excursions, as well as providing a housing and congress service.[214]

During the sessions of European institutions, the *Syndicat* fulfilled two of these duties. It stood for the promotion of the city both as congress venue and as seat of the CoE, which seems to have been the secondary task, judging from the available archive material. Moreover, the local fraction of the party *Mouvement Républicain Populaire* deemed the efforts of advertising Strasbourg as insufficient for a 'European city'.[215]

The other task included one of its two central duties in connection to welcoming European parliamentarians from 1949 onwards. In this connection, the *Syndicat* asked the city for further funding, since the organisation argued that they required more subsidiaries with Strasbourg being the seat of the *Mouvement Européen*.[216] The tourist association organised lodgings for delegates during sessions as it likewise provided accommodation for congress participants.

In these endeavours, the organisation was supported by the municipal housing office and also recruited citizens willing to offer private rooms for lodging.[217] According to the *CSME*, which claimed itself responsible for organising hotel rooms for parliamentarians as well, it also cooperated with the *Syndicat* in these matters.[218] However, in municipal archive files on the tourism agency, only the abovementioned collaborators are mentioned, which gives evidence for the hypothesis that both organisations were semi-independently concerned with the same aspect of receiving parliamentarians. This circumstance also presents another instance of the

---

211 Cf. AS, 235 MW 266 *Subventions du Syndicat d'Initiative.*

212 AS, 235 MW 266, *Extrait du Procès-verbal, 5.7.1948.*

213 AS, 235 MW 267, *Extrait du Nouvel Alsacien, 2.7.1951.*

214 AS, 235 MW 266, *Revite du plan local.*

215 AS, 235 MW 267, *Extrait du Nouvel Alsacien, 16.4.1953.*

216 AS, 235 MW 266, *Note du 23.4.1949.*

217 AS, 235 MW 267, *Extrait de la Presse Libre 9.7.1950.*

218 Comité Strasbourgeois pour le Mouvement Européen, "L'Assemblée générale extraordinaire du Comité Strasbourgeois pour le Mouvement Européen", in *Vers l'Europe*, 1:1, 1950, p. 6.

uncoordinated manner of hosting institutions during the start-up phase, which was only alleviated with the founding of specialised organisation committees during the institutionalisation stage.

The *Syndicat* fulfilled an important practical role, since the organisation of congresses by assisting with accommodation, as well as the offering of touristic excursions already constituted some of its normal tasks. Therefore, its primary function was not the welcoming of European parliamentarians as opposed to organisations such as the *CSME* which were purpose-founded in relation to the European presence in Strasbourg. In the second and third phases of hosting activities, the association was still active, but not as a central actor. Usually its tasks were mandated by or delegated from the city administration. Its two main duties following the start-up phase included providing city guides for parliamentarians during sessions and the operation of a tourism office in the CoE building to assist delegates with practical matters or the purchase of tickets to various cultural events, for example.[219]

Other actors did not display much individual agency, because their tasks or actions were commonly mandated by one of the three actors covered in this section. For instance, the *Fédération des Hôteliers, Restaurateurs et Débitants d'Alsace et de Lorraine* occupied itself with providing an adequate amount of hotel rooms during sessions, commonly by reserving accommodation for delegates.[220] Furthermore, they attempted to counteract criticism of their dedication to presenting Strasbourg as the perfect host.[221]

Other actors were random and only offered an activity once or a few times. One example for this kind of actor presents the Bishop of Strasbourg Jean-Julien Weber, whose one-time invitation for a reception during the first PACE session in August 1949 was an example for minor actors during the first hosting period.[222] It also contributed to the welcoming atmosphere the central local actors attempted to construct, to which actors, who were otherwise not concerned with receiving parliamentarians, contributed. All these actions constituted the strategy of letting Strasbourg appear as the perfect seat city through the session frame programme. In the connection of this invitation, it has to be noted that Weber was a member

219 AS, 236 MW 5/6, *Invoice du Syndicat d'Initiative, hôtesse 31.1.1966* and AS, 460 W 1, *Convention*, p. 1.

220 AS, 235 MW 135, *Lettre du Président de la Fédération des Hôteliers, 19.5.1952.*

221 AS, 235 MW 135, *Lettre du Président de la Fédération des Hôteliers, 20.8.1952.*

222 AS, 198 MW 83, *Invitation de l'Evêque de Strasbourg.*

of the *CSME*.[223] It could be possible that a member of an organisation concerned with receiving parliamentarians during sessions, also used its own resources to contribute to this endeavour. Their activity partly overlapped with the *CSME* which was a characteristic of this phase that might have been due to the still developing coordination between actors and the routine of hosting European institutions that rapidly developed during the implementation phase.

Section 1.09 The start-up phase: 1949-1956

The first seven years of European institutions being located in Strasbourg was characterised by the gradual formation of strategies to consolidate Strasbourg's position as seat. These different measures were supposed to improve the city's position against the competition. It was an uncoordinated period of providing entertainment and leisure activities for European parliamentarians during sessions, with numerous actors involved without a central planning organisation. This was mainly due to the fact that organising structures first had to be created. The goal of such activities included from the start to appeal to the CoE and further possible European organisations.

It has to be noted that the general trend visible in city administration documents shows a lull concerning the organisation and effective implementation of hosting activities from circa 1954-1956. The principal reason for the local actors changing their approach to welcoming PACE delegates at the end of this period included the small number of leisure activities as well as the ineffectiveness of their organisation City actors acknowledged that they failed to reach the intended goal of securing the appreciation of European parliamentarians.[224] Thus, central planning and coordinating organisations were introduced starting from summer 1956, which constituted the beginning of the institutionalisation phase. These developments will be covered in the following sub-chapter.

Sources from the municipal and the departmental archives show that the efforts of local actors targeted the CoE, as well as Coudenhove-Kalergi's European Union to a smaller extent. The Common Assembly of the ECSC hardly became the focus of hosting activities. Two joint receptions with the CoE on 15 January and 22 June 1953 seemed to have been the only

223 AS, 198 MW 78, *Liste des membres fondateurs du Comité Strasbourgeois du Mouvement Européen*, p. 1.

224 AS, 208 MW 267, *Minutes of the Liaison Committee, 24.9.1956*, p. 1.

occasions when MEPs had been invited during the first hosting phase.[225] As evidence in the municipal archive suggests, local actors seemed to have concentrated on the permanently sited European institutions and hardly participated in the efforts to secure ECSC institutions from 1950-1952 as was analysed in chapter 1.

Although a number of receptions and other leisure activities were offered during the first years of the start-up phase, PACE delegates felt that Strasbourg organised an insufficient session frame programme. Reasons for these sentiments seem to have been caused by the fact that competences between the single local actors were not clearly assigned and that a general coordinating instance was missing. Nevertheless, it has to be kept in mind that these were the initial years of the European institutions' presence in Strasbourg and that local actors first had to develop strategies of receiving parliamentarians. The start-up phase contained this pre-formalised stage. Additionally, the political situation regarding the common assembly of the ECSC might have complicated that development, since the siting had been highly provisional and attempts to solve it had been without any result by the mid-1950s. It might have contributed to the initial concentration on the CoE by local actors.

Documents from the municipal archive of Strasbourg indicate that especially the *CSME*, followed by the city administration, attempted to bind the CoE to the city from the beginning with their hosting efforts. For instance, the *Conseil Municipal* voted in 1949 to authorise a credit of over 10 Million Francs (303,000€) for modifying the *Mairie* building to "accueillir dignement le Comité des Ministres et les Membres de l'Assemblée."[226] Before the CoE headquarter *Maison de l'Europe* was built in 1950, the city offered the town hall and university for the first PACE session in August 1949.[227]

Based on documents from the municipal archive of Strasbourg, the efforts of the various actors of the first hosting period can be separated into welcoming European parliamentarians with activities and accommodation, promoting the city as 'European,' and informing the public, as well as appraisal of their opinion. These three elements are ordered after the importance allocated to them by actors according to the frequency of occurrence in archive sources. They followed the goal of

225 AS, 235 MW 26, *Note du 12.1.1953* and AS, 235 MW 27, *Réception pour le Conseil de l'Europe et l'Assemblée Commune.*

226 AS, 198 MW 84, *Projet d'un exposé, 26.9.1949.*

227 AS, 198 MW 89, *Guides.*

binding the existing institutions to the city and to portray Strasbourg as an excellent host, in order to make it attractive to house further European organisations. This was the ultimate goal of local actors – gaining acclaim through these strategies in order to be able to compete with other seat cities or applicants. In this manner, welcoming parliamentarians received the most attention. These activities also included a promoting element, since the goal of such efforts was advertising the city as a perfect host. The second aspect included all other measures to advertise the city, such as the first ECSC seat application round or the dissemination of Strasbourg's European mission. Local actors believed that the third element, which should result in a favourable opinion towards the European institutions, was likewise an important part of a welcoming climate in the city.[228] Apart from this anticipation of events, demands of the CoE and the international organisation's own activities played a more minor role in shaping the manner in which hosting arrangements were offered.

(a) Events and accommodation

Regarding the first aspect of local actors' hosting strategies, the *CSME* was responsible for the majority of organised events, especially in the first years of the start-up phase. It also coordinated with the CoE by meeting with its Preparatory Commission on 13 June 1949 to discuss the welcoming of delegates, which included the topics accommodation, receptions arranged by the city and departmental administration, as well as leisure activities.[229] In several instances of such events, it was not quite clear from the sources, whether the city administration was involved in the drafting process. For example, for the planning of a sporting event, the mayor constituted the main coordinator.[230] Since Frey also held the office of president of the *CSME*, it cannot be clearly discerned in which capability he acted. Although communications on this event were only addressed to the Mayor and the *CSME*, several divisions of the city administration were involved. However, from the archive material, it can be assumed that the private association constituted the initiator for this hosting measure, although the organisation process itself ran via the municipal administration.

[228] E.g. ABR, 544 D 205/1, *Note du 30.9.1953*, pp. 1-2.

[229] ACE, 3279/27129, *Réunion avec le Comité Strasbourgeois pour le Mouvement Européen du 13.6.1949.*

[230] AS, 14 MW 47, *Note du 23.9.1949.*

Another marker for the high activity of the *CSME* in this phase was that the association organised numerous events or elements of hosting, which the city administration only implemented from the second hosting period onwards. For instance, in 1952, the association started planning to offer a free tram ticket to parliamentarians.[231] The fifth anniversary of the CoE in 1954 was a reason for a special celebration like all future jubilees of European institutions housed in Strasbourg. The *CSME* planned to hold a public conference on past and future work of the CoE, as well as a *soirée populaire européenne* for this occasion.[232]

Another measure the *CSME* implemented to provide a session frame programme were excursions to places in the region, such as a visit to the *Grande Foire des Vins Colmar* in August 1949.[233] Furthermore, the city administration offered such trips on request. For instance, the British PACE delegation asked the Secretary-General of Strasbourg whether the city could organise a visit to the wine caves in Colmar, while the parliamentarians travelled there on an unrelated invitation.[234] This shows that there was a certain willingness of the municipality to cater to any demand of their guests. An intended effect could have been to create an image of a good host as a tool to bind European parliamentarians and civil servants on a personal level.

Other than fulfilling wishes, the city administration mainly stood for receptions for parliamentarians and permanent staff during this first hosting phase, but also assisted in organising other activities. One example was a *Soirée Sérénade* during the second PACE session period on 21 August 1950, organised together with the *Société des Amis de la Musique*.[235] The CoE received 1,283 free tickets for parliamentarians, the national delegations and administrative personnel.[236] The *CSME* provided information to delegates regarding accommodation and leisure activities and published all receptions and manifestations, offered by both CoE personnel and various city actors, in a comprehensive list.[237] This kind of

231 Comité Strasbourgeois pour le Mouvement Européen, "Réunion du Comité directeur", in *Vers l'Europe*, 3:32, 1952, p. 7.

232 ACE, 3279/27129, *Lettre du Président du Comité Strasbourgeois pour le Mouvement Européen au Secrétaire-Général du 17.3.1954.*

233 AS, 235 MW 135, *ASTRA, Excursion 1.*

234 AS, 198 MW 90, *Lettre de la délégation britannique au Secrétaire-Général de la Ville de Strasbourg, 11.8.1949.*

235 AS, 235 MW 135, *Note du 3.11.1950.*

236 AS, 235 MW 135, *Invoice pour la Soirée du 22.8.1950.*

237 ACE, 3262/27118/1, *Le Conseil de l'Europe à Strasbourg, 19.5.49*, p. 2 and AS, 235 MW 135, *Liste des manifestations* and *ASTRA excursions.*

cooperation between actors to provide the European guests with leisure activities remained a common pattern throughout the entire period of study.

Apart from events, the city was decorated on the occasion of sessions. Usually, French flags were flown on buildings such as the *Préfecture*.[238] Additionally, several buildings such as the *Hôtel de Ville* were illuminated during session periods.[239] Despite these different kinds of leisure activities on offer, a CoE-internal note from 1951 reported that national delegations felt unhappy. In their opinion, session periods were only characterised by work and no fun and they wished for more events, such as a ball organised by the *Préfet*.[240] A previous memorandum stated that the city administration never announced their hosting arrangements in advance and that it was therefore difficult to compile a list of them. There was even a discussion about organising a programme themselves in order to keep parliamentarians entertained.[241]

The fact that PACE delegates felt a lack of leisure activities and communication of them could be attributed to the circumstance that several associations seemed to have been independently concerned with the same issues such as the *CSME* and the tourism office with accommodation. Judging by archive material, there had been offered a good amount of them, most of which were also centrally compiled in a list which was distributed by the *CSME*.[242] Furthermore, at least for the August 1950 session, Mayor Frey informed Jacques Camille Paris, the Secretary General of the CoE, on 26 July 1950 what was planned.[243] The uncoordinated manner, city actors attempted to implement a frame programme for session periods, could have played a role in this situation, as well.

Nevertheless, the perceived lack of distractions during session periods mirrored the apparent sub-par possibilities for leisure activities in Strasbourg in the immediate years after the founding of the CoE. As noted in chapter 1, a report to Schuman in 1949 describing leisure activities and infrastructure of Strasbourg, painted a bleak picture with emphasising that the only possibility for visitors in summer 1948 would

238 AS, 235 MW 135, *Note du 19.5.1952.*

239 AS, 235 MW 135, *Note du Directeur des Travaux Municipaux, 8/1950.*

240 ACE, 121/0092, *Entertainment for representatives 28.8.1951.*

241 ACE, 121/0092, *Memorandum, 24.7.1950.*

242 E.g. AS, 235 MW 135, *Comité Strasbourgeois pour le Mouvement Européen, liste des manifestations, 6.9.1949* and AS, 198 MW 89, *Guides.*

243 AS, 198 MW 84, *Lettre du Maire au Secrétaire-Général du Conseil de l'Europe, 26.7.1950* and *Réponse, 28.7.1950.*

have been cinemas.[244] The fact that the author of the note highlighted this circumstance by placing three dots before the word "cinema" to indicate negativity, an aposiopesis, further showed the lack of leisure activities adequate for a city housing an IO. It was an additional challenge local actors needed to overcome apart from developing a frame programme during PACE sessions and the structures to organise it.

Especially in the early years of the start-up phase an arbitrary division of labour occurred, as several different local actors were involved in handling housing requests. For example, in August 1949, in order to reserve a hotel room for a Canadian PACE observer, the European Movement transmitted the request to the *Syndicat*. Subsequently, further communication occurred between the High Commissioner for Canada in London and the city administration to solve additional questions regarding the reservation.[245] In another case, Frey asked the *Société Immobilière et Hôteliers de France* to organise lodging for Coudenhove-Kalergi and continued to forward resulting correspondence between both parties back and forth.[246] Despite the fact that one of the *Syndicat's* main tasks included the provision of accommodation, other actors were thus offering the same services independently without coordinating them.

Apart from temporary housing for delegates, city actors, especially the administration, offered assistance with finding permanent housing for CoE staff on request. An instance presented the case of Dutch representative Van Voorst tot Voorst in 1952. In this case, it was not only the municipal government which recognised that assisting institution personnel might reflect well on them. J. C. Paris, informed the Frey about the difficulties of the delegate to find an eight-room flat for him and his services and added:

> Il suffit en effet, que M. van Voorst fasse savoir à son Gouvernement qu'il ne peut trouver à se loger ici, et que, par conséquent, il est absurde de prétendre vouloir faire de votre ville le centre des communautés européennes, pour que la candidature de Strasbourg soit obstinément combattue par les Pays-Bas. Dans ce cas, il y a lieu de penser que Bruxelles aurait gain de cause.[247]

The *Service de Logement* of the city administration reacted immediately by providing a list of five apartments with the required specifics.[248] The city administration did not just anticipate demands from European

244 ACE, 044/00120, *Note pour M. Schuman*, p. 4.

245 AS, 198 MW 84, *Réponse de M. Schehr, 6.8.1949; Télégramme.*

246 AS, 235 MW 135, *Correspondance du Maire à la Société Immobilière et Hôteliers de France/Coudenhove-Kalergi et vice versa, 6/1950.*

247 AS, 198 MW 84, *Lettre du Secrétaire-Général du Conseil de l'Europe au Maire, 1.7.1952.*

248 AS, 198 MW 84, *Lettre du Maire au Secrétaire-Général du Conseil de l'Europe, 8.7.1952.*

parliamentarians, but also attempted to fulfil any requests they were informed of, in order to make an excellent expression as host. Such requests from European institution civil servants and delegates were frequently made to the city administration throughout the period of study.

The unconditional compliance with such demands was an indicator that local actors in the municipality employed hosting measures including offering housing assistance as strategies to consolidate indirectly their position as seat. They pursued that by showing that Strasbourg was capable of offering leisure activities and of providing for the needs of institution staff both to a general public and the CoE and Common Assembly personnel in the city. As hinted by J.C. Paris, the failure to provide adequately such aspects could be the incentive of a loss of the seat status. While the CoE was permanently sited in Strasbourg, the initial ECSC seat decision was still underway in 1952 with the first application round in the same year. This uncertainty of where the seat of the Common Assembly would be can be seen as the factor why local actors in Strasbourg attempted to fulfil even the smallest request.

(b) Promotion of Strasbourg as seat

Local actors, especially the *CSME*, implemented several measures to promote the city, which was the second element of their strategies. As already mentioned during the committee's description in the previous section, it strongly promoted Strasbourg during the first application round with a book and a special issue of their journal *Vers l'Europe*. These publications were the only instance of extensive local promotion. Municipal archive sources show that the city and departmental administrations concentrated on lobbying the French government for official support of Strasbourg. For instance, a delegation from the *Conseil Général*, including among others Mayor Frey under the leadership of the *Conseil's* President Pflimlin, lobbied the French government to propose the city as ECSC seat.[249] Special promotion activities by the authorities to support the seat application, did not occur from the evidence in the municipal archive of Strasbourg and the departmental archive of Bas-Rhin. During those years, they show that local actors concentrated on the CoE. It seems likely that the municipality did not see a need to make a special effort to gain this assembly before 1952, because it was not yet located in their city.

In the early years of the CoE's presence in Strasbourg, the *CSME* also summarised newspaper articles on Strasbourg and the CoE meeting from various countries in a *revue de presse*. During the first session of

249 AS, 198 MW 93, *Extrait des DNA, 26.6.1952.*

PACE in August 1949, articles from Scandinavia, Switzerland, the United States, France, England and Italy were summarised and evaluated in French.[250] In this document, the *CSME* analysed that the public opinion in Sweden was at the moment in favour of the CoE or that in Italy, people generally appreciated the European Movement, but also Richard Coudenhove-Kalergi's European Parliamentary Union.[251] In the United States press review, the association summarised that most articles would contain analyses why Great Britain and France would adhere to the European idea.[252] With this action, the impact of promotion of the city by its actors could potentially be monitored and the city or departmental administrations would be able to gain intelligence on negative portrayals and could develop actions to counter them.

The fact that organisations similar to European movements engaged in such promotion while the city administration did comparatively little in this regard, could imply that such organisations filled a vacuum in such promotion efforts. As mentioned before, the municipality of Strasbourg's activity for the first ECSC seat application round restricted itself to a resolution from the municipal council. The same case occurred during the second seat application round in Luxembourg in 1957. Its government had at first been reluctant to apply, because they did not want to become single seat, although they wanted to retain their position as host for the ECSC institutions sited in the city in 1952.[253] On the other, the *Comité Luxembourgeois pour les Etats-Unis de l'Europe* strongly supported the single seat.[254] For a similar aim, the local European movement of Luxembourg edited a book in 1957 to support and advertise Luxembourg as unitary location for all European Community institutions in lieu of government publications.[255]

---

250 AS, 198 MW 87, *Comité Strasbourgeois pour le Mouvement Européen, Revue de Presse, août 1949*.

251 AS, 198 MW 87, *Comité Strasbourgeois pour le Mouvement Européen, Revue de Presse, août 1949*, p. 1.

252 AS, 198 MW 87, *Comité Strasbourgeois pour le Mouvement Européen, Revue de Presse, août 1949*, p. 3.

253 Croisé-Schirtz, Edmée, "La bataille des sièges (1950-1958)", in Trausch, Gilbert *et al.* (eds.), *Le Luxembourg face à la construction européenne – Luxemburg und die europäische Einigung*, Luxembourg, Centre d'Etudes et de Recherches Européennes Robert Schuman, 1996, pp. 97; 100.

254 *Ibid.*, p. 99.

255 Conseil Luxembourgeois du Mouvement Européen (ed.), *Luxembourg, Ville Européenne*, Luxembourg, Imprimerie Hermann, 1957.

(c) Informing the public about European institutions

Informing the public about the CoE and gauging the opinion on the institution was the third element of strategies to bind European organisations to the city and to appear attractive to other IOs. This action was exclusive to the first hosting phase, from 1956, the local actors' efforts remained fully separate from ordinary activities. It could be said that this activity was a form of promotion as well, since it shed a 'favourable' light on the city. It was also yet another set of strategies to appeal as a host on a personal level. For example, a thank you-note from the CoE Committee of Ministers from 13 August 1949 highlighted that it had been a pleasure for the organisation to meet in Strasbourg, since its population would show attachment to the ideas it aimed to achieve.[256]

Local actors endeavoured to educate Strasbourg's population about Europe as well. A likely reason for that was the aim to create a welcoming environment for the European guests among the citizens of Strasbourg. For instance, for the first PACE session period in August 1949, the city and the *CSME* organised a meeting where the Mayor first introduced the CoE, followed by speeches of several PACE delegates to the greater public, since space at the university during sessions was limited.[257] In this manner, the early years of the CoE's presence were characterised by efforts to inform the population and to entice them to attend public PACE meetings. For the second session period in August 1950, the *CSME* organised a conference themed: "Que peut on – que doit on attendre de la 2e session du Conseil de l'Europe"?[258] The President of the *Union des Fédéralistes* presented reasons for attending to circa 330 participants, who also included local politicians or the Director of Information of the CoE, Paul Lévy, for instance.[259]

As a measure to gauge opinions in Strasbourg, the *Département* regularly compiled public attitudes towards the CoE and PACE session contents in notes. Most of these documents reported that despite the actors' efforts, the population largely remained unresponsive and hardly discussed the presence of European institutions. For instance, 90 percent would not be able to tell the difference between PACE and the Common Assembly.[260] Towards the end of the first hosting period, public opinion

256 AS, 198 MW 83, *Lettre du Président du Comité des Ministres du Conseil de l'Europe au Maire, 13.8.1949.*

257 AS, 198 MW 91, *Discours du Maire, 12.8.1949.*

258 ABR, 544 D 205/1, *Note du 9.8.1950.*

259 ABR, 544 D 205/1, *Note du 9.8.1950*, p. 1.

260 ABR, 544 D 205/1, *Note du 30.9.1953*, p. 1.

became even more indifferent. A newspaper article from 1956 stated that people thought the CoE would not be important, which was attributed to the circumstance that the short duration of PACE sessions did not facilitate close contact.[261]

Such reports support the hypothesis that the local actors concerned with the presence of European institutions were located in a bubble structure. Those organisations themselves were also contained in a similar construct and somewhat removed from daily life of the city. Additionally, the parliamentary sessions which only were of a limited duration might have contributed to this. The various activities to welcome the European institutions in the city essentially seemed to have occurred between two bubbles with concerned local actors on one side and the European organisations in the city on the other.

All in all, the first phase of hosting activities was characterised by pre-existing actors who added receiving European institutions to their general tasks, with the notable exception of the *CSME*. The lack of coordination between actors might have contributed to the fact that delegates felt that not enough leisure activities were on offer. By summer 1956, the city administration had recognised the ineffectiveness of the organisation of hosting activities vis-à-vis their intention of binding the CoE and other institutions to Strasbourg.[262] This marked the start of the second hosting period in the city. It was characterised by attempts to develop session frame programmes that would gain the appreciation of European guests and in turn make them identify with the city as the best possible host of European institutions.

Section 1.10 The implementation phase: 1956-1959

This phase was the most dominant of the three different periods of hosting activities, since it saw the introduction of special planning organisations, as well as more standardised and recurrent strategies to consolidate Strasbourg's position. Additionally, the second ECSC seat application round occurred during it, when hosting measures were the central way of local actors to support Strasbourg's candidature. The beginning of the implementation period is defined for summer 1956, because then the city administration saw the need to start a structured approach to receiving the European institutions with the formation of specialised committees. The chosen end date partly corresponds to extraneous factors. Following the official submission of Strasbourg's

[261] AS, 208 MW 267, *Extrait du Nouvel Alsacien, 20.6.1956.*

[262] AS, 208 MW 267, *Minutes of the Liaison Committee, 24.9.1956*, p. 1.

candidature for the second ECSC seat application round in summer 1957, the sources show that all hosting activities shared the goal of increasing the city's chances. This included a climate of constant crisis, since other qualified candidates presented a direct threat to Strasbourg's chances, which local actors had to counteract. As will be analysed in this sub-chapter, the activities city actors organised during European assembly session periods constituted the main strategy to achieve this and to become the single seat of ECSC institutions.

From 1960 onwards, the most intensive phase of the seat application round seemed to have passed, since the foreign ministers decided in spring 1959 not to change the status quo of the seat until 1962 (later 1963).[263] Decisions on the seat had been deferred by the Foreign Ministers Conferences between 1958 and 1959 several times. However, documents from the archive of the Council of the EU indicate that the effort of trying to find a solution decreased from 1960 onwards. Since the majority of the second hosting phase was dominated by the second application round this is a fitting end date. Another reason for choosing 1959 as the end date is that the nondecision of the ECSC was mirrored by the gradual decline of the frequency leisure activities were arranged during session periods. Furthermore, from 1960 onwards, the implementation of municipal structures to deal with European institutions had been terminated and the arrangements made in following years were characterised by a high level of sophistication.

The actor strategies from 1956 to 1959 can be further separated into two, albeit closely intertwined stages. During the first year, from August 1956 to July 1957, the city administration concentrated their efforts on establishing a structured approach to receiving parliamentarians. Following the submission of the candidature for the single seat on 25 July 1957, this development continued. However, the important concern was the competitive situation of the second ECSC seat application round. Municipal sources show a substantial increase of activities following the official submission of Strasbourg's seat candidature and similarly, a gradual decline of the frequency and amount of hosting activities during the 1960s. Supporting Strasbourg's candidature with various hosting activities during European assemblies' session periods was the main strategy of the municipality to outshine the competition. This will be discussed subsequently.

Although the second seat application round was intended to determine the headquarters of the institutions of the three European Communities,

263 AC, CM2 1960 0223ab-b, *Brève historique du siège*, p. 5.

the CoE did not lose any importance in the eyes of the local actors. After the application had been submitted in July 1957, a spill over of measures was detectable. Exactly the same session frame programme was instituted, regardless if it was for EP, PACE or other European assemblies' sessions. A reason for concentration of city actors on the CoE likely included that it had its permanent seat in Strasbourg since its founding in 1949. In contrast, the placement of the Common Assembly of the ECSC and later the EP was provisional and challenged.

Local actors regarded their hosting activity and presenting Strasbourg as a European symbol as the essential component of their efforts for a successful candidature. For example, Mayor Charles Altorffer wrote to the President of PACE in a letter to announce Strasbourg's application. "C'est ainsi que Strasbourg, en plus de la valeur symbolique, qui me parait essentielle pour l'idée européenne, réunit toutes les conditions souhaitables pour lui permettre de jouer pleinement le rôle que nous voudrions lui voir confier."[264] Possessing the adequate building infrastructure was described as secondary to the symbolic value.[265] The fixation on hosting matters might have been a reason why infrastructure was not a major city strategy, as opposed to the 1960s and 1970s.

After outlining measures for 'ordinary' meeting periods of the European assemblies, three special events will be analysed, for which the city administration made an extra effort. This will make visible how municipal actors employed them as a strategy during the critical phase of the seat application round between 1957 and 1959. They were the *Journées Européennes* in October 1957, the inaugural session of the EP in March 1958, as well as celebrations for the tenth anniversary of the CoE in April 1959. Prior to that, the intra- and international competition with the different seat city applicants will be discussed to illustrate the threat to the successfulness of Strasbourg's candidature. Through session frame programmes, local actors attempted to strengthen Strasbourg's position in comparison to other seat city candidates. To facilitate the binding of delegates and their institutions to Strasbourg in order to gain the parliamentarians' appreciation, events and arrangements for the occasion of a PACE, and later EP session were discussed and selected. If any problems occurred after the initial testing in practice, they were refined.

264 ACE, 3153/2409, *Lettre du Maire au Président de l'Assemblée Consultative du Conseil de l'Europe*, p. 2.

265 ACE, 3153/2409, *Lettre du Maire au Président de l'Assemblée Consultative du Conseil de l'Europe*, p. 2.

(a) Using session frame programmes to increase renown as a host

Based on the documents from the municipal archive of Strasbourg, the following arrangements were most common: welcoming gifts, such as Alsatian produce and flowers for parliamentarians' wives; receptions and dinners for all delegates, or single national groups and their spouses.[266] Other recurrent measures included European and French flags on principal buildings and on busses serving the line running by the *Maison de l'Europe.*[267] The city was further decorated through illumination of monuments and important buildings, decoration of streets with Christmas lights and other items.[268] As concessions for the European guests, the city financed free public transport and offered activities for delegates and/or their spouses (city tours, guided museum visits, free tickets to the theatre and the opera, or excursions).[269] Municipal archive sources show that expenses, down to the costs for stamps to mail invitations, were split evenly between the city and *Département.*

Most new measures had already been suggested in the inaugural session of the Liaison Committee on 24 September 1956, and only a few of them were altered or discarded after the first session period they had been used in. Their organisation and/or implementation processes also remained the same. For instance, city administration notes from the 1970s still contained the same organisational steps and commands as in the end of the 1950s. Another indicator was that notes instructing to illuminate certain buildings for session periods, already talked about *conditions habituelles* in 1957.[270] The aspect that experienced the highest number of alterations was the matter of providing various forms of transport for the delegates. This will be discussed during the next chapter where actions will be analysed that local actors took to improve traffic infrastructure to welcome European parliamentarians.

---

266 AS, 208 MW 267, *Minutes of the Liaison Committee, 24.9.1956.*

267 AS, 208 MW 267, *Minutes of the Liaison Committee, 24.9.1956.* Nowadays, trams are still decorated in national colours to honour the member state holding the presidency of the CoE *Committee* of Ministers. Examples include the UK presidency in 2011/12, the Armenian in 2013 or the Austrian in 2013/14 ("Le tram de Strasbourg prend à son tour une allure 'Sooo British!'" <http://www.strasbourg.eu/actus/actus?StartIndex=56&ItemID=2153110598> (accessed 12.03.2012, article no longer available online) and "L'Arménie préside. Strasbourg-Magazine Juillet-August 2013, p. 23." http://media.strasbourg.eu/alfresco/d/d/workspace/SpacesStore/530334e3-53cf-4494-aca7-dc35afc71550/201307_StrasMag_244.pdf (accessed 23.08.2013)).

268 AS, 208 MW 267, *Minutes of the Liaison Committee, 24.9.1956.*

269 AS, 208 MW 267, *Minutes of the Liaison Committee, 24.9.1956.*

270 E.g., 54 W 243, *Note pour la Division VIII, 4.10.1957.*

Paul Wach remarked after the first few European sessions in early 1957, "l'impression générale est que ces manifestations ont été bien accueillies et ont sans doute contribué à réchauffer le climat qui s'était quelque peu refroidi ces derniers temps."[271] This indicated that such events were also meant to introduce a better relationship between delegates and the city, which was one of the central reasons to institute a structured approach to hosting in 1956.

Parliamentarians voiced opinions, for instance, in a report of the French delegation to PACE commenting on arrangements, which had been written by Radius in his function as member of the assembly.[272] In this, the multi-positioning of Strasbourg's individual actors became visible again, since Radius was on the one hand an active participant in all of the four specialised committees and also a prolific individual actor. On the other, he was a member of the institution that constituted the recipient of the city administration's efforts. The Liaison Committee and the Mayor communicated with the CoE, so that sessions would not coincide with planned events.[273] Thus, the CoE did not only remain in the passive role, accepting the anticipated demand by the city administration, but also raised issues themselves.

Once an event had passed its initial test, it was repeated during the following sessions. Next to the decoration of the city and welcoming gifts, events included receptions, as well as leisure activities for delegates. Similar to the arrangements of the *CAE*, an emphasis on culture was inherent in most of them. For example, the city offered a reservation service for theatre tickets and would commonly assume the costs for them.[274]

Numerous thank-you letters of delegates or CoE personnel showed that the effort of local actors reached the European parliamentarians, as expressed in a letter from the clerk of PACE to Mayor Charles Altorffer in April 1957: "Je suis particulièrement sensible à votre désir d'agrémenter ainsi le séjour à Strasbourg des Représentants à l'Assemblée et des membres de leur famille, et je vous remercie beaucoup de cette charmante attention."[275] Similar notes, which deviated from generic expressions of appreciation, were references to specific aspects as well, such as thanks

---

271 AS, 208 MW 267, *Minutes of the Liaison Committee, 21.1.1957*, p. 1.

272 AS, 208 MW 267, *Rapport du 11.10.1956.*

273 AS, 208 MW 267, *Minutes of the Liaison Committee, 24.9.1956*, p. 2; *11.10.1956*, p. 3.

274 E.g. AS, 236 MW 1/5, *Paiements pour le Théâtre Municipal, 1/1959.*

275 AS, 236 MW 19/1, *Lettre du Greffier de la Assemblée Consultative du Conseil de l'Europe au Maire, 12.4.1957.*

for flowers, or the welcome gift of liqueur.[276] Binding European guests to Strasbourg on this personal level was local agents' main strategy that seemed to have gained the appreciation of the recipients.

Next to developing a standardised session frame programme designed to gain the European parliamentarians' appreciation of Strasbourg as a seat city, other, more general measures were taken. The Liaison Committee members saw the need to orchestrate a European climate, a term coined by them. This was the attempt to construct a physical incarnation of the European mission-rhetoric. One example is the postmark pictured below. Its existence was supposed to signal the identification of Strasbourg with the Council of Europe. Its creation was discussed between Mayor Altorffer and relevant services and spanned from September 1956 to April 1957. The fact that this was regarded as an important marketing device to show the European character of Strasbourg was clearly stated by the city administration.[277] The *Directeur des Musées*, who was involved in the design process of the drawing, proposed a different arrangement of the circle of stars due to artistic considerations, which would not correspond to the manner the stars were arranged on the CoE flag. This proposition was vetoed by the city, because the stamp should express the connection to the CoE more than it should meet artistic standards.[278] Thus, it was clearly intended to visualise the connection between the city and the European institution and to show that it identified with its status as seat.

5. Post-mark Strasbourg, Siège du Conseil de l'Europe (1957)[277]

[276] AS, 236 MW 1/7, *Lettre de Van der Ploeg au Maire, 25.6.1959* and 236 MW 1/1, *Lettre de Friedensburg au Maire, 20.3.1958.*

[277] AS, 209 MW 39, *Note pour M. le Maire, 2.4.1959.*

[278] AS, 209 MW 39, *Note récapitulative du 11.4.1957.*

Mayor Charles Altorffer intended to have this postmark on letters from the April 1957 PACE session onwards, which was, however, not possible to implement due to technical difficulties.[279] The following quote from the letter, Altorffer sent to the postal service after learning of this delay, showed that even such a small aspect as the opportune usage of a stamp in connection to a PACE session was regarded as essential to the effort of attracting European institutions to the city. "Or, j'ai l'honneur d'insister sur le fait qu'un tel contretemps pourrait avoir les conséquences les plus regrettables."[280] This postmark seemed to have had an element of cost-benefit to the city administration, to signpost the presence of Europe through this symbol.

Next to city administration activities, private organisations had developed their own hosting programmes. From the creation of the *Cercle des Amitiés Européennes (CAE)* in 1957, the association contributed with their arrangements aimed at the spouses of European parliamentarians who accompanied their husbands during sessions, as well as female delegates. The activities were characterised by a private, familiar atmosphere, which was attributed to a woman's influence on hosting, the core founding principle of the private organisation, as stated by O. Pflimlin.[281] Several of the *CAE's* members assisting with arrangements, were wives of city actors involved in hosting European institutions. For instance, *Madame* Wach, spouse of Paul Wach, the chair of the Liaison and Special Liaison Committees, hosted a tea party.[282] While most similar events were principally directed at the wives of the delegates and female parliamentarians, such private events were also offered for all European guests. For instance, *CAE* members hosted one foreign delegation each in their private homes for dinner or a *soirée*. One of such occasions presented the January 1958 PACE session, when eight members separately received either the complete Danish, Grecian, Belgian, German, Icelandic, Swedish, as well as parts of the Italian and British delegations and the permanent committee of the assembly in their own homes, before meeting at the restaurant *Aubette* later in the evening to finish the evening together.[283]

The personal character of *CAE* leisure programmes became visible in these types of activities which were intended to help form ties between the

---

279 AS, 209 MW 39, *Lettre du Directeur Régional des Services Postaux au Maire, 18.4.1957.*

280 AS, 209 MW 39, *Lettre du Maire au Directeur Régional des Services Postaux, 23.4.1957.*

281 Pflimlin, Marie-Odile, "Amitiés Européennes", in Comité des Amitiés Européennes (ed.), *Amitiés Européennes*, Strasbourg, Dernières Nouvelles d'Alsace, 1977, p. 4.

282 AS, 236 MW 1/3, *Programme du Cercle des Amitiés Européennes, 6/1958.*

283 AS, 236 MW 26/3, *Assemblée générale du 1.12.1958*, pp. 3-4.

city and institutions. All these activities constituted a private and familiar dimension of the session frame programme. Through the *CAE*, European institution personnel and their spouses had a forum to participate in activities which could have led to a closer binding to the host city. An examples included artistic renditions from members or wives of CoE personnel, such as *Madame* Baby, spouse of the President of the Personnel Association of the CoE exhibiting her paintings at a tea for the wives of delegates on 24 June 1959.[284]

These activities were almost exclusively aimed at PACE delegates and CoE civil servants from their first implementation in late 1956 to summer 1957. The same arrangements were employed for both this assembly and the EP, when the latter was more intensively focussed on by local actors during the seat application phase from mid-1957 to the end of 1959. These measures to build a reputation as an excellent host had the function of alleviating intra- and international competition, as well. This included threats to Strasbourg's capabilities as seat city. The city's status as CoE seat was not exempt either, since rumours of a possible move of the European organisation surfaced in 1957 and 1959. It presented an intensification of the threat situation during the ECSC seat application round, since the sources suggest that one widely accepted argument in favour of Strasbourg, was the concentration of ECSC authorities together at the CoE seat.

(b) Competition with other seat cities

Local strategies to present the city as a good host constituted the majority of activities regarding supporting Strasbourg and its candidature in the second ECSC attempt to determine a single seat from 1957-1959. Mayor Pflimlin stated in a newspaper interview in 1960 that the national government had not clearly supported Strasbourg's endeavours during the seat application.[285] The French government gave the majority of its support to Strasbourg and Paris, but also vouched for the countries other two applicants recognised by the Council of the European Communities, Département de l'Oise and Nice, and even officially submitted Lyon's proposal to house institutions. In fact, only from the 1970s onwards, when only Brussels, Luxembourg and Strasbourg remained viable candidates, the national government slowly began to intensify its support of the Alsatian city. This mainly included transport and building infrastructure and will be discussed in the subsequent two chapters.

284 AS, 236 MW 26/3, *Lettre du Cercle des Amitiés Européennes à Madame, 3.6.1959.*

285 AS, 9 Z 192, *Interview dans la Vie Française du 27.1.1960*, p. 6.

Hearsay and rumours of who supported whom conditioned city-internal discussions of which form the seat application should take. For example, in the Bipartite Committee meeting on 27 December 1957, the option of locating some institutions in Kehl was mentioned, but ultimately discarded due to the fear it might impede Strasbourg's chances.[286] Pflimlin asserted that he had heard that Adenauer was not interested in this and that a potential creation of a trans-border European city[287] across the river might produce problems in Franco-German relations.[288] Despite this, Croisé-Schirtz analyses that at least Luxembourg considered a combined application of Strasbourg and Kehl feasible, because in December 1957, the Grand Duchy's government feared this might endanger their position.[289] Thus, actors in the different candidate cities also responded to rumours or anticipated threats, apart from concrete challenges in order to retain a superior position against other applicant cities.

Apart from such diffuse hazards that arose from either the politics of the European Communities, its member states both on the national and intergovernmental levels, as well as local activity of competing cities, concrete threats from other sources arose. For example, Richard Coudenhove-Kalergi, the founder of the Pan-European Movement, promoted Paris as choice for the ECSC seat from December 1957 onwards (Strasbourg was to remain seat of the CoE). He published an article in the national newspaper *Le Monde*, which was also sent to national members of parliament (MPs) of ECSC member states when they were asked to indicate their preferred location in a poll conducted by the Pan-European Movement.[290] This and similar developments outside the city influenced the local actors' struggle to improve their position vis-à-vis other applicant cities, as well. Such statements as by the leader of the Pan-European Movement could have a negative effect on the value of the already negligible advantage city actors could draw from existing

286 AS, 235 MW 273, *Minutes of the Bipartite Committee session*, 27.12.1957, p. 2.

287 While this idea never came into fruition, a trans-border district, the *Eurodistrict Strasbourg-Ortenau*, for administrative cooperation was established between 2003 and 2005 (cf. Ries, Roland, "Vorwort", in de Grossouvre, Henri; Maulin, Eric and Forum Carolus (eds.), *L'Eurodistrict Strasbourg-Ortenau: la construction de l'Europe réelle = Der Eurodistrikt Strassburg-Ortenau: Konstruktion eines lebendigen Europa*, Vevey, Xenia, 2009, pp. 13-15).

288 AS, 235 MW 273, *Minutes of the Bipartite Committee session*, 27.12.1957, p. 2.

289 Croisé-Schirtz, Edmée, "La bataille des sièges (1950-1958)", in Trausch, Gilbert *et al.* (eds.), *Le Luxembourg face à la construction européenne – Luxemburg und die europäische Einigung*, Luxembourg, Centre d'Etudes et de Recherches Européennes Robert Schuman, 1996, p. 99.

290 AS, 9 Z 109, *Réalisation d'une enquête.*

infrastructure to use to improve their chances. Therefore, such threats were always addressed.

Pflimlin, a member of the movement's Central Council, was personally sent this article by Coudenhove-Kalergi and immediately started to oppose vehemently, also by resigning his post.[291] In the unfolding letter exchange, Coudenhove-Kalergi attempted to reason with Pflimlin by citing infrastructure deficiencies of Strasbourg as in the following: "A cause des avantages matériels de Bruxelles, Strasbourg n'a aucune chance d'être choisi."[292] He attempted to convince Pflimlin that Brussels' candidature would surely succeed. The French government was divided between Paris and Strasbourg, while the Belgian government was wholly backing its capital city. Furthermore, he claimed, Paris would be able to match Brussels in terms of facilities and be an all-around better choice than the Belgian capital as headquarters for the ECSC.[293]

In the report on the poll, Coudenhove-Kalergi interpreted the results with a strong bias for Paris and stated that choosing Strasbourg would encourage Alsatian autonomist tendencies.[294] In response, Pflimlin addressed a letter to him, writing that he was appalled at this insinuation, before stating: "Je romps désormais toutes relations avec vous."[295] The fact that Pflimlin's salutatory address changed from *M. le Président et cher ami* to *Monsieur* in the space of three months,[296] was another indicator how serious some local actors pursued to negate challenges to Strasbourg's image and capabilities as seat city.

René Radius was involved in his own letter exchange with Coudenhove-Kalergi on the same issue as well.[297] Both he and Pflimlin kept Mayor Charles Altorffer informed of their steps.[298] These countermeasures of local actors led him to address a letter to Altorffer in May 1958, asking for an intervention and a stop of the campaign against him, as it would be based on a misunderstanding, accompanied by a lengthy explanation of why he made this proposal in favour of Paris.[299] Apparently, the Mayor

---

291 AS, 9 Z 109, *Lettre de Pflimlin à Coudenhove-Kalergi, 3.1.1958.*

292 AS, 9 Z 109, *Lettre de Coudenhove-Kalergi à Pflimlin, 23.1.1958.*

293 AS, 9 Z 109, *Lettre de Coudenhove-Kalergi à Pflimlin, 23.1.1958.*

294 AS, 9 Z 109, *Europe à la recherche.*

295 AS, 9 Z 109, *Lettre de Pflimlin à Coudenhove-Kalergi, 23.4.1958* and *L'Europe à la Recherche.*

296 AS, 9 Z 109, *Lettre de Pflimlin à Coudenhove-Kalergi, 3.1.1958* and *23.4.1958.*

297 AS, 208 MW 9, *Lettre de Coudenhove-Kalergi à Radius, 11.2.1958.*

298 AS, 208 MW 9, *Lettre de Radius au Maire, 14.2.1958* and *Lettre de Pflimlin au Maire, 23.4.1958.*

299 AS, 208 MW 9, *Lettre de Coudenhove-Kalergi au Maire, 3.5.1958.*

ignored this missive, as Coudenhove-Kalergi re-sent the letter in June 1958, because he hadn't yet received an answer, to which Altorffer curtly replied, he wouldn't intervene.[300]

Coudenhove-Kalergi advocating Paris was part of the crisis local actors faced in early 1958 during the seat application round. At that time, it was at its peak with the committee of urbanism experts in the process of examining each of the ten official candidates. The newspaper *Voix d'Alsace* reported in April 1958 that the French government had seemed to move away from fully supporting Strasbourg's candidature and that Pflimlin and others, among them Radius, would have established the city's application for the single ECSC seat against the opposition of Altorffer.[301] The article continued with the following statement, which was symptomatic to the manner, the various local actors attempted to address threats to the successfulness of their application to house ECSC institutions: "Die Strassburger Bürgerschaft hat Anspruch darauf, zu wissen, wer im Gemeinderat hinter dem Oppositionsmacher Altorffer steht, wer sich zum Totengräber der Zukunftsinteressen der Stadt Strassburg machen will."[302]

The municipal administration documents in the municipal archive of Strasbourg, however, do not give such a clear picture that the mayor was against the candidature of Strasbourg, although Pflimlin, at the time still president of the *Conseil Général*, seemed to have been strongly involved in the application process. It is interesting to note that the population was cited in this circumstance, which occasionally also occurred in city administration documents archived in the municipal archive of Strasbourg. However, in the process of the actual organisation of the hosting programme as a strategy to appear attractive as seat, the citizens of Strasbourg were hardly included. They were sometimes employed as an argument, but the important actions all occurred within the bubble of actors involved in hosting measures.

In response to multi-level threat situations, three special occasions were celebrated to announce Strasbourg's seat candidature, next to the general session frame programme. They were the festive announcement of the application in 1957, the inaugural EP session in 1958, as well as the tenth anniversary of the CoE in 1959.

---

300 AS, 208 MW 9, *Lettre de Coudenhove-Kalergi au Maire, 5.6.1958* and *réponse 10.6.1958.*

301 AS, 208 MW 9, *Extrait de la Voix d'Alsace, 1.4.1958.*

302 AS, 208 MW 9, *Extrait de la Voix d'Alsace, 1.4.1958.*

(i) Journées Européennes

The *Journées Européennes* from 19 to 20 October 1957 introduced Strasbourg's plans for the candidature of the ECSC single seat. They reflected the central strategy of local actors to support it with symbolic measures as they were supposed to "[…] montrer leur attachement à l'idée européenne."[303] Among the invited were, for example, French ministers, representatives from the economy and finances, as well as journalists.[304]

The festivities were also aimed at including the public in this process, since an internal note of the municipality stated that the population approved of the implemented procedures.[305] As already mentioned, the alleged full support of the population was recurrently cited by local actors as validation for why Strasbourg should become seat of further European institutions. The sources, however, suggest no evidence that the citizens of Strasbourg changed their generally disinterested opinion towards the presence of the European organisations as during the first hosting phase.

Similar to events organised during session periods, a luncheon, two evening galas and various touristic activities were planned during the two days.[306] The PACE session, which took place close to these festivities, featured the usual hosting arrangements as well. In extension, Mayor Altorffer asked the association of retail businesses to decorate shop windows in European themes and to illuminate them at least until 23:00 hours to contribute to the city administration's efforts to welcome the delegates.[307]

Another central part was the publication of the resolution to re-announce the city's candidature, not only within the city, but also to the outside. It was drafted by a joint meeting of the *Elus de la Ville et du Département* on 19 October 1957.[308] It essentially contained the rhetoric employed to construct Strasbourg as European city, by employing a reference to the city being the symbol for Franco-German reconciliation. This was expressed by an explicit reference to the European mission of Strasbourg – "[…] proclament solemnellement la vocation européenne de Strasbourg."[309] Thus, apart from attempting to appeal to European

303 AS, 208 MW 15, *Lettres du Maire et Pflimlin au Président de l'Assemblée Consultative du Conseil de l'Europe, 30.9.1957*, p. 1.

304 AS, 208 MW 15, *Personnalités invitées.*

305 AS, 208 MW 15, *Note (ville).*

306 AS, 208 MW 15, *Programme des Journées Européennes.*

307 AS, 54 W 243, *Lettre de l'Association des Commerçants au Maire, 12.10.1957.*

308 AS, 208 MW 15, *Discours du 19.10.1957.*

309 AS, 235 MW 268, *Résolution.*

parliamentarians on a personal level to increase chances in the application round, the alleged European history of the city was emphasised.

Additionally, the resolution argued that situating European institutions in one place would be the only possible solution.[310] Strasbourg, the chosen seat of the CoE and the assemblies of the ECSC and Western European Union (WEU), would constitute the ideal candidate.[311] Only the last sentence contained a vague and noncommittal reference to infrastructure. The *Elus* stated they would do their utmost to assure the housing of the European institutions under the best possible conditions so that the organisations could find everything in Strasbourg they needed to function.[312]

This was a contrast to city administration resolutions of other candidate cities, which concentrated on emphasising their infrastructural advantages. For example, Brussels' application highlighted its infrastructure and willingness to reserve the Plateau Heysel, bar the *Grand Palais*, for the European Communities to redevelop after their requirements, or its accessibility and capacity to accommodate the institution personnel.[313] It only included a small reference to symbolism, which could not be compared to the degree Strasbourg's actors constructed a symbolic image of their city. The Mayor of Brussels stated that politically, his city would be especially suitable, since it was the capital of a nation with a tradition for diversity without any imperialistic involvement.[314] In the latter aspect, a tendency to construct history to suit specific needs is detectable, as it completely omits historical occurrences such as the Belgian involvement in the Congo.

Like Brussels, the proposal of the Département de l'Oise only contained a small reference to the historic significance of the region. Its city administration concentrated on infrastructural advantages, such as a possibility to develop infrastructure freely and the close proximity to the national capital Paris, the central railway and air hub of France.[315] Incidentally, Strasbourg's resolution for the first ECSC seat application round in 1952 was also much more factual with its main argument to

---

310 AS, 235 MW 268, *Résolution*.

311 AS, 235 MW 268, *Résolution*.

312 AS, 235 MW 268, *Résolution*.

313 ACE, 3153/2409, *Lettre du Maire de la Ville de Bruxelles au Président de l'Assemblée Consultative du Conseil de l'Europe, 12.11.1957*.

314 ACE, 3153/2409, *Lettre du Maire de la Ville de Bruxelles au Président de l'Assemblée Consultative du Conseil de l'Europe, 12.11.1957*, p. 2.

315 ACE, 3153/2409, *Candidature du Département de l'Oise, 12.11.1957*.

group all institutions at the CoE seat for efficiency.[316] While the 1957 resolution also pursued this argument, the symbolism of Strasbourg was highly emphasised, which constituted one of the central strategies of the municipality to support the city's candidature. Regarding the other candidate cities, publications in which its European mission was highlighted tended to be promoted by other actors than the municipalities. An example was Luxembourg's European Movement's *plaquette* from 1957.

The book, *Strasbourg invite l'Europe*, the city administration had published, was also used to announce the city's application. A *Complément* was added in 1960, containing descriptions of further projects of the city.[317] It contained information about the infrastructural plans the municipality had made in the case of a successful candidature. Therewith, it fulfilled the requirements of the European Communities. In the late 1950s and at the turn of the decade, a European district included their favourite solution to housing European institutions.[318] Nevertheless, it contained the usual symbolic reasoning as well.

The *Strasbourg invite l'Europe* contained plans of how to accommodate the European institutions should Strasbourg become single seat. Other cities did not offer a fully completed infrastructure either, such as Brussels which only had reserved the Plateau Heysel for European institution use.[319] Nevertheless, the rest of Brussels' proposal pointed to a capable general infrastructure, while *Strasbourg invite l'Europe* contained the only significant mention of infrastructural plans from Strasbourg's actors during the application phase from 1957 to 1959.

Although the *Journées Européennes*' aim was presenting the candidature for the single seat, it became apparent how much emphasis was placed on the presence of the CoE by city administration actors. It had been generally asked to assist city actors with the festivities and PACE delegates were invited to receptions and meetings; the president of PACE had been invited to preside over a luncheon as well, which could, however, not be realised due to other obligations.[320] On the one hand, the inclusion

316 ACE, 3153/2409, *Résolution du 25.2.1952.*

317 Ville de Strasbourg and Conseil Général du Bas-Rhin, *Strasbourg invite l'Europe*, Strasbourg, Editions de la Calanque, 1957 and Ville de Strasbourg and Conseil Général du Bas-Rhin, *Strasbourg invite l'Europe. Complément 1960*, Strasbourg, Editions de la Calanque, 1960.

318 AC, CM2 1960 0233ab-b, *Einleitende Aufzeichnung vom 5.5.1960*, p. 3.

319 ACE, 3153/2409, *Lettre du Maire de la Ville de Bruxelles au Président de l'Assemblée Consultative du Conseil de l'Europe, 12.11.1957*, p. 1.

320 AS, 208 MW 15, *Lettres du Maire/Pflimlin à Dehousse, 30.9.1957*, p. 2.

of the CoE was supposed to signal that local actors welcomed a placement of European institutions next to that organisation and on the other to alleviate general threats to Strasbourg as already established seat of some European organisations. This goal was also shared by the second special event, the inaugural session of the EP.

(ii) The first EP session

The *Journées Européennes* were the main vehicle to announce Strasbourg's application for the single seat. The celebration of the inaugural EP session fell in the period where the process of deciding a seat went into a decisive phase. By showing appreciation to MEPs, this event was supposed to boost Strasbourg's candidature at this critical point. The session frame programme for the session from 19 to 23 March 1958 had been meticulously planned down to the last minute detail by the city administration. The visit of the Urbanism Expert Committee which evaluated all candidates coincided with this event.

In an eleven pages long note and further documents, the *Division VIII* had summarised all details which needed to be organised, which constituted a more elaborate programme than the ordinary leisure arrangements for other session periods.[321] The programme had been created by the Special Liaison Committee as an extra effort to support the seat candidature.[322] The application round was entering its most important phase with the approaching submission deadline of 31 March. This city actor approach gives further evidence to the fact that hosting measures were the main strategy for a successful candidature, also because it encompassed the threat situation arising from the competition. "Mais la concurrence avec d'autres villes est sérieuse et nous ne devions négliger aucun des moyens qui pourraient militer en notre faveur. Dans cet ordre d'idée, il est essentiel que les délégués des six Nations qui viendront siéger à Strasbourg aient la meilleure impression."[323] Thus, the central strategy of local actors was to best their competition by gaining the personal favour of European parliamentarians.

In addition to the recurrent measures of every European assembly session, the programme for the first EP meeting contained more cultural events. These included concerts in selected restaurants, or flowers not only for accompanying wives, but also for MEPs and journalists.[324] A table with

321 AS, 236 MW 1/1, *Note pour la Division VIII, 3.3.1958.*

322 AS, 208 MW 267, *Minutes of the Special Liaison Committee session, 24.2.1958*, p. 2.

323 AS, 236 MW 1/1, *Note pour la Division VIII, 3.3.1958*, p. 5.

324 AS, 236 MW 1/1, *Note pour la Division VIII, 3.3.1958*, p. 3.

all offers and activities and costs is listed in appendix II, which amounted to 5,473,729 Francs (94,800€).[325] 'Ordinary' session periods during the turn of the decade rarely drew expenses of more than 20,000€ in today's value (see appendix II for an example). Another indicator for the importance of this session period was the attention to minute detail. For instance, the city administration wrote to the hotels, where delegates commonly stayed in, and asked them to make a special effort in the reasoning that their image of a good host would also depend on accommodation.[326] Likewise, restaurants were asked to contribute by offering good quality meals at reduced prices and so-called *menus de propagande*.[327] Furthermore, the local government decided to suspend all road works to after the session period.[328]

In the eyes of the municipality, the visit of the expert committee to study their application merited another special effort. This included a chaperone from the city administration, flowers, and information material on Strasbourg.[329] The municipality also appealed to the population, but as already mentioned before, this circumstance has to be seen as an argument and not a strategy proper to appear attractive as seat. Apart from statements full of pathos and radio appeals, asking citizens to install flags on their properties, the local actors' efforts concentrated on the bubble of the European institutions.[330]

On the visit of the Urbanism Expert Committee to study the candidates, the city made the following press release to highlight the importance of this event. "Le succès de la candidature de Strasbourg pour devenir le siège des Institutions européennes se joue actuellement. C'est l'avenir de notre ville qui est enjeu et toute la population est priée de s'associer à l'effort entrepris."[331] In an appeal to the population this visit and the inaugural EP session was additionally described as *semaine historique*.[332] Apart from the festivities of the convening of the parliament, the three-day visit of the Urbanism Expert Committee from 17-19 March, the city administration did not spare any effort either to host them. Each of the committee members was provided with a car and a driver, there were two

325 AS, 236 MW 1/1, *Factures*.

326 AS, 236 MW 1/1, *Note pour la Division VIII, 5.3.1958*, p. 6.

327 AS, 236 MW 1/1, *Note pour la Division VIII, 24.2.1958*, p. 4.

328 AS, 236 MW 1/1, *Note pour la Division VIII, 24.2.1958*, p. 4.

329 AS, 236 MW 1/1, *Note du 12.3.1958* and *Note du 13.3.1958*.

330 AS, 236 MW 1/1, *Appel*.

331 AS, 236 MW 1/1, *Note pour la Division VIII, 5.3.1958*, p. 1.

332 AS, 236 MW 1/1, *Appel*.

organised dinners, a visit to the opera, a presentation and guided visit of the proposed sites where to implant European institution buildings and possibly the European district by the responsible architects Jean-Henri Calsat and Charles-Gustave Stoskopf.[333] This engagement of the city could be regarded in the light of making the members of the committee feel especially welcome and to leave positive impression for a good review in the panel's report. This behaviour did not differentiate much from the approach of other candidate cities. For example, in Nice, two dinners were held; one hosted by the city administration and the other by the *Préfet* and the city organised the accommodation of the committee members in hotels.[334] Planning events for the urbanism committee was common for candidate cities, but in Strasbourg, these arrangements were included with special activities for MEPs which did have the explicit intention of furthering the seat candidature.

The city administration ascribed a high importance to the inaugural session period. This can be seen in their statement that the success of their application would strongly depend on this first EP meeting.[335] The competitive environment strongly manifested itself, caused by the concrete effort of the Council of the three European Communities to find a solution. It was especially visible in the increased hosting activities of the phase which included more symbols to indicate Strasbourg's attachment to Europe.

(iii) The 10th anniversary of the Council of Europe

The third high profile event was the tenth anniversary of the CoE. As mentioned before, this organisation had been the initial focal point for local actors' hosting activities, and did not become redundant during the second ECSC seat application round. Since it was employed as an argument for Strasbourg becoming the ECSC single seat as well, the festivities for its jubilee were used as an instrument by municipal actors. A more minor goal was the reaction to hearsay that the CoE might move, to which city actors reacted, regardless of their tenability. Even though the organisation had its permanent seat in Strasbourg, local actors often included it in their efforts during the seat application round for the ECSC. It is possible that the CoE was used as a form of testimony through its presence and apparent endorsement of Strasbourg as host for European institutions.

---

333 AC, CM2 1958 210, *Programme*.

334 AC, CM2 1958 210, *Lettre de Pierre Tampon-Lajarriette (Sous-préfet/Directeur de Cabinet de la Préfecture des Alpes-Maritimes) à M. Calmes (Secrétaire Général du Conseil de la Communauté Economique Européenne), 2.4.1958.*

335 AS, 236 MW 1/1, *Note pour la Division VIII, 5.3.1958*, p. 3.

One of these rumours in 1957 was that the institution might move to Paris. Pflimlin informed Altorffer by letter on 20 March that, while he did not think it substantial, he had mobilised resources to counteract it.[336] Pflimlin contacted CoE officials who assured him that there were no plans to move.[337] Nevertheless, upon learning that the next PACE session was to be held in Paris, which he thought as an indicator for a possible move, Pflimlin wrote to the French Foreign Minister to protest and encouraged Altorffer to do the same and publish a resolution.[338] The *Conférence des Adjoints* subsequently drafted a document that the CoE should remain in Strasbourg, which was approved by the *Conseil Municipal* and transmitted to the national government by a delegation composed of the Liaison Committee members and Pflimlin.[339] These actions were another example of how local actors immediately reacted to even the smallest probabilities of danger to their status as institution seat, as well as Pflimlin's high-profile involvement in campaigning to the outside.

Another rumour, which was similarly responded to, occurred in 1959. That year, the consolidation of European institutions was under discussion, when the CoE studied the possibilities of merging with the Organisation for European Economic Co-operation (OEEC), as well as forming a general European parliament with the EP, PACE and the WEU assembly. The Commission for Political Affairs of PACE, under the chairmanship of Fernand Dehousse, stated that the headquarters of the combined institutions should be either Strasbourg or Paris. In a ballot in July, the commission voted in favour of choosing the latter option with 15 for and three abstentions, arguing that only a national capital could offer the required facilities.[340]

Regarding this decision, Pflimlin remarked in a letter to architect Jean-Henri Calsat who had composed the studies contained in the *plaquette Strasbourg invite l'Europe* that the rapport would have been adopted on 11 July 1959 without his attendance.[341] This statement implies that Pflimlin would have taken some kind of action against this had he been present. It hinted both at strategies of local actors, as well as at the efforts of individual

336 AS, 208 MW 21, *Lettre de Pflimlin au Maire, 20.3.1957.*

337 AS, 208 MW 21, *Lettre de Pflimlin au Maire, 20.3.1957.*

338 AS, 208 MW 21, *Lettre de Pflimlin au Maire, 20.3.1957.*

339 AS, 208 MW 21, *Compte-rendu de la Conférence des Adjoints du 23.3.1957* and *lettre du Maire au Préfet, 27.3.1957.*

340 Dehousse, Fernand. "Rationalisation of European Institutions other than those of the Six 1959." <http://www.assembly.coe.int/nw/xml/XRef/X2H-Xref-ViewPDF.asp?FileID=1347&lang=en> (accessed 08.10.2013), pp. 8-9.

341 AS, 236 MW 31/1, *Lettre de Pflimlin à Calsat, 17.7.1959.*

actors. Additionally, the newspaper *Nouvel Alsacien* reported the following in June 1959, "Fernand Dehousse, der ausscheidende Präsident des Europarates, erklärte gestern vor dem Rotary-Club in Brüssel, Strasbourg sei kein Sitz für den Europarat, sondern eine 'Beerdigung'."[342] However, the Political Commission abandoned its stance in December when the decision was made not to give a recommendation for the seat location.[343] Pflimlin in particular, who due to his multiple posts on different political levels was in the position to employ them for Strasbourg's benefit, was engaged in this. In the context of the ongoing seat application round of the three European Communities, the CoE played an important role in the strategies of the city administration to promote the city's candidature.

In the matter of forming a single European Parliament, Strasbourg's status as seat was similarly threatened. The British PACE delegation specified in their proposal that the city would not be a suitable location and that they preferred Paris or Versailles to house the new assembly.[344] It was likely that in the event of the CoE and the OEEC forming a single organisation, or a consolidation of the three European assemblies, Strasbourg would lose its seat status. Only the WEU proposal for a single parliament stated it should remain in Strasbourg, since it was geographically better located than Paris.[345] The municipal actors saw this as a concrete threat situation and reacted with arguments why their city should remain seat in such an event, but also with measures, as, for example, the intensive celebration of the CoE's jubilee. Such a strategy of indirectly influencing the European institutions by providing a lavish session frame programme and festivities for its delegates and civil servants was a common mode of operation, especially during the 1950s.

Festivities were planned by various city administration entities to celebrate the tenth anniversary of the CoE in 1959 in addition to the reception and luncheon offered by the European organisation itself.[346] The commemoration of the jubilee in Strasbourg took already place during the April PACE session, from 18 to 20 April 1959.[347] The plans of the municipality included a reception, dinner, a theatre gala and a *soirée des ballets*.[348] The offered events seem to have been well received by CoE

342 AS, 236 MW 28/1, *Extrait du Nouvel Alsacien, 3.6.1959.*

343 AS, 236 MW 28/1, *Extrait du Nouvel Alsacien, 10.12.1959.*

344 ACE, 3153/24010/1-2, *Scheme for a general parliamentary assembly*, p. 3.

345 ACE, 3153/24010/1-2, *WEU, Unification of the European Assemblies*, p. 5.

346 AS, 235 MW 273, *Minutes of the Bipartite Committee session, 13.2.1959*, p. 24.

347 AS, 236 MW 21/1, *Minutes of the Sous-commission session, 16.3.1959.*

348 AS, 235 MW 273, *Minutes of the Bipartite Committee session, 13.2.1959*, p. 25.

staff. For example, John Edwards, the President of PACE, wrote, "May I take this opportunity to say how much I personally appreciate the diverse arrangements that you, your City and the Department of the Lower Rhine are making as a contribution to the tenth anniversary of the Council of Europe."[349] It contributed to increasing the renown of Strasbourg as host.

It could have played a role in increasing the city's chances in the seat application round, as well. Local agents explicitly referred to increasing a personal connection to delegates during the drafting process of the programme. Wach said during the discussion of which kind of plays to offer in the theatre, "Il faut le faire d'une façon telle que nous séduisions les membres de l'Assemblée Consultative, afin qu'ils viennent déjà avant."[350] Therefore, the goal of celebrating the CoE's jubilee was to bind personally PACE delegates to the city which in the context of the application round of the European Communities could also contribute to increasing their chances.

The effort, local actors put in the organisation was also visible from the incurred costs. As with all session periods, it is difficult to determine the exact amount, since invoices are distributed over several dossiers. Since the city and *Département* split the costs as usual, them sending invoices and overview tables back and forth, contributed to that circumstance. However, a note from October 1959 stated that the sum, the city had to pay amounted to 5,566,573 Francs (96,000€).[351] As the *Département* was responsible for the other 50 percent of the costs, the total expenditure for this anniversary celebration must have been a sum corresponding to circa 190,000€ for three days of festivities. A *Conseiller Municipal* outside the bubble of those concerned with European institutions raised the question about the financing. In the answer, Mayor Pflimlin first gave several arguments how important these festivities were for the image of the city and the binding of the CoE and EP to it, before answering the actual query. It would all be covered by current credits and there would not be the question of how to finance it.[352] The fact that such questions from local actors outside this bubble were virtually brushed aside gives evidence for the separate nature of ordinary structures.

This intention of improving Strasbourg's reputation as ideal host city seemed to have worked in some ways as the following excerpt from

349 AS, 236 MW 21/2, *Edwards au Maire 23.3.1959.*

350 AS, 235 MW 273, *Minutes of the Bipartite Committee session, 13.2.1959*, p. 28.

351 AS, 236 MW 21/1, *Note du 22.10.1959.*

352 AS, 236 MW 21/1, *Conseil Municipal, 4.5.1959*, pp. 18-20.

a thank-you letter Italy's permanent representative to the CoE wrote, showed.

> Ces manifestations solennelles seront un nouveau témoignage de l'esprit sincèrement européen qui anime la population de votre ville, dont le nom est devenu un symbole d'unité pour tous ceux qui – comme moi – sont profondément attachés à l'idéal de la collaboration toujours plus étroite entre les Pays Libres et démocratiques de notre continent.[353]

The tenth anniversary of the CoE improved the standing of Strasbourg as institution host. In the light of the ECSC seat application round, this was especially important in order to match the competition, although the most active phase had passed by 1959. For example, the Foreign Minister Conference of 16 March 1959 decided to postpone a decision until 1963.[354] However, the city did not cease its high level of activity which had begun with the submission of their seat candidature in 1957, until 1960/1961, when the amount of events slowly began to decline.

To summarise, the first year of the implementation phase was characterised by the creation of coordinating organisations for planning events during sessions and a sophistication of the offered events. From summer 1957 onwards, local actors fully concentrated on the candidature for the ECSC single seat, during which various hosting measures, among them the promotion of Strasbourg, were the central strategy to gain credentials as seat and to consolidate the city's position. Additionally, it was employed to be superior to other applicant cities. The entire period from 1957 to 1959 was a time of constant acute crisis, when not only the competition had to be addressed, but where other threats to Strasbourg's position occurred as well.

Section 1.11 The business-as-usual phase: 1960-1979

The final phase of hosting activities, which spanned the 1960s and 1970s, was a relatively stable phase. Activities tended to follow the standardised norm developed during the end of the 1950s. Additionally, the theme of hosting was replaced first by transport and later by building infrastructure improvements as primary focus. As already stated in the introduction to the second hosting phase, 1960 is set as the beginning of another period of receiving parliamentarians, since the intensive period of the second seat application round seemed to be over with the EC decision to postpone a decision until 1963. This caused the reaction on the local

353 AS, 236 MW 21/2, *Lettre du représentant permanent d'Italie auprès le Conseil de l'Europe à Pflimlin, 23.3.1959.*

354 AC, CM2/1960 0233ab-b, *Einleitende Aufzeichnung*, p. 2.

level that the Bipartite Committee emerged as the only central planning organisation. In the beginning of the 1960s, its meetings were sporadic as well, until an annual meeting structure established itself from the middle of the decade, when all events for the year were drafted. While the amount of events was still on a comparable level to the end of the 1950s in the early 1960s, the number began to decrease steadily.

The year 1979 marks the end of the timeframe, since most of the actors involved from the early stages reached the age of retirement in this decade, which can also be seen in the fact that several new actors became concerned with tasks. It would have been possible to choose already 1969 as a caesura, because in that year the Bipartite Committee changed its approach to hosting activities by reducing the number due to costs and to avoid boring their guests with repetitive arrangements.[355] However, a continuity in the organisation and type of events was visible; therefore, it will not be used as a marker. The ends of the previous two phases were marked by distinct changes in the approach of local actors to providing a session frame programme for parliamentarians.

The business-as-usual phase presented a very stable time, during which only minor peaks in activity were detectable in response to the European Communities' actions regarding the seat question. One of these occasions was the discussion whether institutions should be moved with the foundation of the EC. Likewise, the decision to introduce the direct voting procedure in 1976 caused an increase of hosting activities which culminated in 1979 with the meeting of the first directly elected EP. While all organisation processes of activities exhibited the high level of sophistication developed during the late 1950s, the following decades had two major differences. Firstly, the amount of hosting activities had been reduced gradually by city actors to only one reception or dinner per session period. For some assembly meetings no arrangements except decorations were made, as during the EP session of 10 to 14 March 1975.[356] The increasing number of EP meetings was one reason for that, as stated by Pflimlin in 1961.[357] This showed that hosting measures were used strategically to consolidate the city's status, since they were more intense when a decision on the seat seemed feasible.

Secondly, the contents of the hosting programme mirrored the fact that infrastructure became an increasingly more important aspect for city actors. Concerns about improving long distance travel for the

355 ABR, 1130 W 936/12, *Activités de l'année 1968.*

356 ABR, 1130 W 936/7, *Projet des manifestations, 1975.*

357 AS, 236 MW 2/4, *Note pour A. Heitz, 9.3.1961*, p. 2.

parliamentarians gained more and more relevance, as well as offering easily accessible transport structures within the city. Hosting activities with session frame programmes and promotion already had attained an established and tested standard. At the end of the 1970s, few changes had been made to the hosting regime. Nevertheless, while traffic and building infrastructure became more and more the focus of local actors as strategies in the face of the increased direct competition with Brussels and Luxembourg, hosting activities remained an important set of measures to consolidate the city's seat status.

The threat situation to Strasbourg's position was not as acute as during the second seat application round from 1957 to 1959. Nevertheless, hosting and infrastructure activities during the third hosting phase followed the same goal of securing European institutions through gaining the personnel's and parliamentarians' appreciation. This can also be traced through thank-you letters, the Mayor received, as, for instance, from the permanent representative of the UK to the CoE on occasion of a dinner for the British PACE delegation on 10 July 1975. "Comme toujours vous avez apporté à une historique occasion, réalisée dans un milieu splendide, votre humeur caractéristique et un élément de Gemütlichkeit qui nous a fait beaucoup de plaisir."[358]

Gaining the appreciation of the delegates remained the principal goal of the events, local actors organised, which was a continuation of the desire of the prior two phases of the 1950s. The hosting programme was strongly curtailed towards the parliamentarians' wishes, since even the smallest requests were adapted to immediately and the entire organisation intended to gain the delegates' appreciation. Subsequently, this was employed to attain a higher position than the competition. In addition, it shows that European parliamentarians could feel entitled that they expected that all their wishes would be granted. Then, the city administration fulfilling these demands would be needed in order to remain in the race as seat candidate.

The primary competitors, Luxembourg and Brussels, mainly relied on infrastructure to advertise themselves as ideal seat city. Since they possessed superior prerequisites in this area due to being national capitals, for example, Strasbourg's hosting programme and the resulting appreciation from European guests has to be regarded as a strategy to compensate for infrastructural deficits, as well. The promoting of Strasbourg's seat capabilities to primarily the EC complemented this,

[358] AS, 97 W 17/2, *Lettre de Foster au Maire, 10.7.1975.*

in order to convince the stakeholders that the city's features would be superior to the competition.

For the third hosting phase during the 1960s and 1970s, the following important elements from material of the municipal archive of Strasbourg material have been identified, supplemented by documents from the departmental archive of Bas-Rhin. They were offering a session frame programme in order to bind European parliamentarians to the city, the competition with Brussels and Luxembourg and reacting to EC activities on the seat question and resulting crises.

(a) Session frame programmes

For the organisation of the session frame programme, the bubble of city administration actors was composed of two levels, which partook in a two-step organisation process. The Bipartite Committee, which organised the leisure activities, was one of them. The other was composed of the city services and divisions' members who implemented the drafted plans. There was a clear distinction between both levels, for example, members of services occupied with the hosting programme hardly participated in Bipartite Committee meetings. Additionally, measures such as flag decorations or flowers for women were excluded from these discussions, as they remained unchanged from their first implementation in 1956. These elements remained important parts of local actors' hosting arrangements.

An example for a single event organised by the city outside the Bipartite Committee was hunting for European parliamentarians in 1962 and 1963. It also presented an instance for the city administration's habit of attempting to fulfil even the most minuscule demand and to provide a varied session frame programme, even if only a handful of parliamentarians were interested. In 1960, the *Conseil Supérieur de Chasse* had invited all interested delegates to such an excursion on 10 January.[359] Since then, however, this had not been offered, although the President of the *Fédération des Chasseurs du Bas-Rhin*, Guillmot, had separately invited one or two delegates at a time to hunt. The local authorities raised the question whether they had the intention to do so again.[360] The president of the federation answered that they could not continue to offer this due to hunting ground holders, who usually invited a small number of European parliamentarians, could not pay their lease. Ridoux and A. Heitz attempted to find a solution, also because some delegates specifically asked for

[359] AS, 236 MW 2/1, *Invitation pour la chasse, 10.1.1960.*

[360] AS, 236 MW 19/6, *Note pour Ridoux, 16.11.1962.*

this.[361] They decided to contact hunting ground leaseholders personally in order to convince them to invite European guests, which was handled by Wach.[362] At the same time, Ridoux contacted each national delegation to ask them which of their members would be interested in hunting during session periods.[363]

Despite the city administration's efforts, a large-scale organisation for all parliamentarians was not possible due to the decreased number of Strasbourgese renting hunting grounds. Therefore, they used personal contacts to organise such an event for a small number of interested parliamentarians. For instance, A. Heitz approached the mayor of Ostwald, a town close to Strasbourg, if it would be possible to include three or four European parliamentarians in hunting events he organised.[364] Ridoux was involved in the planning of this as well, in his function as the contact person for delegates.[365] To mirror this organisational model, the city administration cancelled its annual insurance fee for hunting on advice of Guillmot, since taking out a daily insurance when needed seemed more suitable.[366] While archive documents show that it were never more than four parliamentarians who participated, it serves as an example that municipal actors tried to meet even the smallest demand made by their guests, as well as offering a diverse leisure programme as possible.

Additionally, with this issue the demand-side to hosting became apparent again, not only because delegates asked to be taken hunting, but also because some organised their own hunts. For example, Per Federspiel, the President of PACE, had a personal contact to Guillmot and Federspiel was always invited by him during session periods.[367] Apart from anticipating broad demands of European parliamentarians, the city administration actors in the strategies of pleasing their guests attempted to please everybody, even if the concrete request just encompassed a few people.

Regarding recurrent events, a common feature of receptions, luncheons and dinners organised by the city administration was offering good food. O. Pflimlin played an important role in the selection of menus, especially from 1960 onwards. From the sources in the municipal archive of

---

361 AS, 236 MW 19/6, *Note pour Pflimlin, 23.11.1962.*

362 AS, 236 MW 19/6, *Note pour A. Heitz, 12.3.1963; Note, 21.3.1963.*

363 E.g. AS, 236 MW 19/6, *Lettre de la délégation d'Allemagne à Ridoux, 26.3.1963.*

364 AS, 236 MW 19/6, *Note pour Ridoux, 26.9.1963.*

365 AS, 236 MW 19/6, *Note pour Ridoux, 26.9.1963.*

366 AS, 236 MW 19/6, *Note pour Pflimlin, 3.7.1963.*

367 AS, 236 MW 19/6, *Note pour Pflimlin, 3.7.1963.*

Strasbourg, it became apparent that A. Heitz or Schmidt from the *Service des Relations Publiques* sent her the restaurant's menu proposals for nearly every reception, luncheon or dinner at the behest of Mayor Pflimlin and asked her to decide.[368] In this process, the communication went through official channels, as the Mayor charged A. Heitz to ask 'Madame Pflimlin' to select the menu.[369] Subsequently, the *Relations Publiques* sent a letter to O. Pflimlin, stating that the Mayor wanted her to decide what kind of food to serve. Her answer was then transmitted via A. Heitz or another member of the *Relations Publiques* to the Mayor for information. Less frequently, the same procedure was observed for the guest list.[370] O. Pflimlin was also occasionally asked to participate in meetings to implement a reception or dinner, for which the Bipartite Committee had set the date.[371]

This procedure was standard for most events that it could be said that O. Pflimlin was an unofficial consultant in this area. For example, during the organisation process of a *soirée* hosted by the city and the *CAE* in 1961 in the hotel *Maison Rouge*, when Ridoux gave the following advice to A. Heitz. "Je pense que comme d'habitude votre service soumettra pour avis et décision à Madame Pflimlin les propositions de la Maison Rouge en ce qui concerne la nature et la quantité des plats devant constituer le dîner de la soirée du 25 Avril."[372] O. Pflimlin was proactively involved in the organisation as well, for instance, for a reception on 11 April 1960, she phoned Schmidt to tell him that the wives of European parliamentarians and civil servants should also be invited. Furthermore, she said she found the food selection of wine, champagne, sandwiches, as well as *feuilletés salés* boring and demanded to add *canapés* and *petits fours glacés et secs* to the buffet, which was accepted by the Mayor.[373] This arrangement also gives evidence for the close attention to detail the city administration payed in planning events. A reason could be the fact that such activities were intended to be strategies to increase the reputation of Strasbourg as European institution seat and were planned to achieve the highest possible result.

Thus, O. Pflimlin was an important actor within the local bubble in two roles. As president and later honorary president of the *CAE*, she facilitated the inclusion of especially the wives of European parliamentarians in the

368 E.g. AS, 236 MW 19/2, *Lettre d'A. Heitz à O. Pflimlin, 13.10.1960.*

369 E.g. AS, 236 MW 12/3, *Lettre d'A. Heitz à O. Pflimlin, 13.9.1966.*

370 E.g. AS, 236 MW 12/3, *Lettre d'A. Heitz à O. Pflimlin, 13.9.1966.*

371 AS, 236 MW 19/4, *Lettre d'A. Heitz à O. Pflimlin.*

372 AS, 236 MW 19/3, *Note pour A. Heitz, 13.4.1961.*

373 AS, 236 MW 12/2, *Note pour M. le Maire, 8.4.1960* and *Formules de Réception.*

hosting programme and participated in the providing of good food at city administration events. This role was also acknowledged by the European institutions, not only in thank-you letters mentioning *CAE* activities, but also by the Danish PACE delegation in May 1963. Per Federspiel, PACE's president from 1960 to 1963, awarded her and Germain Muller, active in the Bipartite Committee, the *Dannebrog orden* for their efforts in cultural affairs and the unity between the peoples of Europe.[374]

Despite the continuous organisation of events, a concern was raised within the Bipartite Committee that they might be losing their effect of pleasing European guests. In the presentation of the summary report for 1968 during the Bipartite Committee meeting on 15 January 1969, the point was raised that due to the recurrent activities, they would not be seen as spectacular anymore by parliamentarians.[375] "De la Préfecture à la Mairie, de l'Aubette à la Maison Rouge, du Village viticole à la manifestation folklorique, tout a été montré, exploité, visité."[376] Since the hosting activities were supposed to be something exceptional for the delegates, they tried to rectify the situation. Another factor constituted that the French state had ordered less public spending which meant that the overall budgets of the city and department were characterised by austerity in 1969.[377]

In the reasoning that the presence of the European institutions was not only an economic gain, but also was a matter of prestige for the region, they attempted to diversify their programme to avoid routine and to counteract complaints of parliamentarians.[378] Additionally, they decided not to organise the same for EP sessions and to stop the traditional excursion for joint EP and PACE sessions. They only planned five events for 1969 compared to nine in 1968 in order to alleviate the dullness.[379] While documents in the departmental archive of Bas-Rhin and the municipal archive of Strasbourg show that the content of leisure programmes was not significantly altered during the 1970s as compared to the 1960s, the events were arranged in a manner that alternating ones were offered for consecutive session periods. The same was done for PACE

374 AS, 236 MW 29/1, *Extrait du Nouvel Alsacien, 7.5.1963.*

375 ABR, 1130 W 936/13, *Activités 1968*, p. 3.

376 ABR, 1130 W 936/13, *Activités 1968*, p. 3.

377 ABR, 1130 W 936/13, *Activités 1968*, p. 2.

378 ABR, 1130 W 936/13, *Activités 1968*, p. 3.

379 ABR, 1130 W 936/13, *Activités 1968*, p. 4.

sessions, although the local actors meant it was harder to diversify their actions when the assembly only held three annual sessions.[380]

Archive documents show that averagely 11 European sessions per year were held in Strasbourg during the 1970s, which included both assemblies, joint sessions and meetings of the Congress of Local and Regional Authorities. This measure can be regarded as an adaption of the city's hosting programme to a long-term implementation, so that it could remain an effective strategy to gain the appreciation of their guests and therewith consolidate their position as seat. Judging by the numerous thank-you letters archived in the municipal archive of Strasbourg, local actors managed to achieve this goal to some degree. "The hospitality of the Maire and of the Président du Conseil is truly something special."[381] Expressions such as this one written by the wife of a PACE member in 1975 can be used as marker how well the local actors' efforts were received by the intended audience.

Another important aspect that was a hybrid of hosting and infrastructure was housing and transport for delegates during sessions. This will be covered further in the subsequent two chapters, but complaints of delegates were taken serious in order to be a perfect host. An example was Italian MEPs criticising their hotel accommodation in 1961.

> L'avenir européen de Strasbourg dépend dans une large mesure des impressions qu'emportent de notre Ville nos hôtes européens et à cet égard il faut attacher une particulière importance aux réactions italiennes, car les Italiens sont nombreux à l'Assemblée Parlementaire Européenne. Beaucoup d'entre eux étaient hostiles à Strasbourg.[382]

Such cases, where municipal actors reacted to specific demands or grievances of European parliamentarians to uphold the image of an excellent host, showed the demand side from the European institutions towards the local actors. During the 1960s and 1970s, they were nearly exclusively about transport or accommodation. Like demands regarding leisure events, the quick solution of any issues can also be regarded as a strategy to increase the reputation of Strasbourg as host and to remain ahead in the competition with other seat cities.

---

380 ABR, 1130 W 936/13, *Activités 1968*, p. 4.

381 AS, 97 W 2/2, *Lettre de Scott-Hopkins au Maire, 21.5.1975.*

382 AS, 236 MW 23/2, *Note pour A. Heitz, 9.3.1961.*

(b) Developments threatening Strasbourg's position 1960–1979

Apart from organising a diverse number of events, local actors also addressed the competition and attempted to solve crises through promotional activity. The actors' efforts differed in comparison to the end of the 1950s. Due to the development that Brussels, Luxembourg and Strasbourg remained the only viable seat candidates and the more direct competition resulting from it, infrastructure became much more important. The city administration attempted to employ the improvement of traffic connections, as well as constructing new office buildings to match the other two competitors. Especially the inferior air communications of Strasbourg became a major point of critique from European parliamentarians during the 1960s.

In the period from 1960 to 1979, three major threats occurred to Strasbourg's status as seat city. They were caused by the EC attempting to solve the nondecision in the issue where to site its institutions. Local actors reacted with either hosting strategies or individual action/ promotion to these cases. They were a possible move of the EP in 1964, an ever-increasing number of part-time sessions of the EP held in Luxembourg from 1967 onwards, as well as the first meeting of a directly elected parliament in 1979.

The foundation process of the EC incurred rumours that the EP would move away from Strasbourg. In 1963 and 1964, the EP intensified debates on the seat question and planned to present a special draft resolution on the need for a rational seat selection in spring 1964.[383] Moreover, the EEC Committee of Ministers discussed to move the High Authority from Luxembourg to Brussels, in which case Luxembourg demanded the EP as compensation.[384] The Bipartite Committee session on 26 February 1964 occupied itself with this crisis among others and tried to formulate strategies.

Separately, Pflimlin already had several meetings with the French Foreign Minister and received the assurance that the French government would not 'sacrifice' Strasbourg.[385] At the same time, local actors identified other problems, such as an EP report on the seat status being unfavourable to Strasbourg and positive about Brussels.[386] They decided that an important course of action was convincing MEPs to vote in favour of their

---

383 Archive of the EP - Centre Archivistique et Documentaire (CARDOC), PE0 AP RP/ POLI.1961 A0-0064/640040, *Aperçu chronologique de la question du siège*, pp. 21-22.

384 ABR, 1130 W 936/16, *Minutes of the Bipartite Committee session, 26.2.1964*, p. 2.

385 ABR, 1130 W 936/16, *Minutes of the Bipartite Committee session, 26.2.1964*, p. 2.

386 ABR, 1130 W 936/16, *Minutes of the Bipartite Committee session, 26.2.1964*, p. 2.

city should it come to a ballot on the seat in the assembly.[387] This included, for instance, improving the air communications, a frequent complaint of parliamentarians.[388] Two other issues where action needed to be taken were identified as counteracting the demands of Luxembourg, as well as organising an event that would grip the MEP's attention.[389] Additionally, the Bipartite Committee estimated, it would be preferable to switch from defensive to offensive by demanding the transfer of the EP General Secretariat to Strasbourg.[390] To this effect, they published a resolution, coupled with an affirmation of the *vocation européenne*.[391] The response of the Bipartite Committee to the threat of the EP moving away is another indicator for the use of promotion and events for parliamentarians as strategies to consolidate Strasbourg's seat status.

Apart from these actions, the city administration prepared another measure targeted to MEPs in order to convince them to decide in favour of Strasbourg. At the end of September 1964, the city had prepared the post card pictured on the next page bearing the image of the sad-looking girl with the traditional Alsatian headdress and the inscription "do not leave me" in all four official EC languages. It was supposed to be sent to the delegates, since they would probably deliberate on the seat during the following EP session. It is, however, unclear from the sources, whether the card was sent, since a note from the city administration only stated, that while all had been prepared, the expedition should wait until the Bureau of the EP announced that the discussion definitely would take place.[392]

This card belonged to the more blatant attempts, bordering on emotional blackmail, to persuade the intended audience that the Alsatian city was the best possible seat, by presenting Strasbourg in the personification of a sad-looking girl with the traditional Alsatian headdress. In the Merger Treaty, signed on 8 April 1965, Brussels, Luxembourg and Strasbourg were confirmed as provisional seats of the EC.[393]

387 ABR, 1130 W 936/16, *Minutes of the Bipartite Committee session, 26.2.1964*, p. 2.

388 ABR, 1130 W 936/16, *Minutes of the Bipartite Committee session, 26.2.1964*, p. 2.

389 ABR, 1130 W 936/16, *Minutes of the Bipartite Committee session, 26.2.1964*, p. 3.

390 ABR, 1130 W 936/16, *Minutes of the Bipartite Committee session, 26.2.1964*, p. 4.

391 ABR, 1130 W 936/16, *Resolution.*

392 AS, 236 MW 26/4, *Note du 21.9.1964.*

393 "Fusionsvertrag." <http://eur-lex.europa.eu/LexUriServ/LexUriServ.do?uri=OJ:P:1967:152:FULL:DE:PDF> (accessed 16.11.2013), *Anhang II.*

6. *"Do not leave me"-post card (1964)*[394]

The EP voted on the seat question during their November 1964 session, with the result of not changing the provisional distribution of institutions made during the Foreign Minister Conference in January 1958.[395] Nevertheless, the existence of this postcard showed that the local actors hosting strategies could have aimed at consolidating the city's status as seat. All of them were located on the personal level, since they were aimed at European parliamentarians staying in Strasbourg, usually with subtle persuasion implied, like in the organisation of events. It is likely that the result of this vote was due to the city's hosting programme. The *Préfet* reported that a MEP had told him privately that in contrast to Strasbourg, the municipality of Luxembourg would be indifferent to the presence of the delegates. Therefore, he was convinced it constituted the reason why the ballot had been in favour of the French city.[396]

The second threat situation was an apparent slow erosion of Strasbourg's status as host of the EP. Since 1967, an ever-increasing number of part-time sessions were held in Luxembourg, starting with one in that year and three in 1970, as well as five in 1971.[397] This threat to Strasbourg's status as seat of the EP was an example for individual promotional action to mitigate it in the form of Pflimlin lobbying both the French government and the executives of the EP. Pflimlin addressed a lengthy letter to the President of the EP on 31 December 1970 stating what the city had done to improve conditions for MEPs and using it as an argument why Strasbourg should be the only meeting place of the assembly. He especially criticised that five of the eleven planned sessions were to be held in Luxembourg in 1971.[398]

394 AS, 236 MW 26/4, *Carte postale.*

395 CARDOC, PE0 AP PV/POLI.1961 POLI-197601190040, *Opinion for an enlarged Bureau*, p. 23.

396 AS, 236 MW 4/2, *Minutes of the Bipartite Committee session, 9.2.1965*, p. 2.

397 CARDOC, PE0 AP PV/POLI.1961 POLI-197601190040, *Opinion for an enlarged Bureau*, pp. 13-14.

398 CARDOC, PE1 P1 243/EXEM SIEG-1962-0100120, *Lettre de Pflimlin au Président du Parlement Européen, 31.12.1970.*

The Bureau of the EP occupied itself with the missive on 27 January 1971. In the preparation material for this meeting, it was pointed out that the decision to sojourn in Luxembourg for five sessions no longer than two days had been taken while considering the political situation and that it was just based on technical and financial advantages.[399]

In fact, in an EP memo from 1975, which traced the history of the seat question, the assembly defended this practice by using a loophole. Since the French government had only protested against regular part-time sessions in Luxembourg, the Bureau was of the opinion that nobody could protest against them holding individual part-sessions in the city.[400] The EC argued that since the EP secretariat moved exceptionally for the meetings held in Strasbourg, the vice versa should be permissible as well.[401] The practice to meet partly in Luxembourg continued during the 1970s, which the city administration of Strasbourg attempted to counteract with infrastructural optimisation, rather than hosting activities.

Similar action was taken in the case of the direct election. Additionally, building infrastructure constituted a large part of actions in order to remain seat of the directly elected EP (see chapter 4). The city administration employed hosting strategies in order to bind the MEPs further to the city on the first directly elected parliament meeting. This was regarded as an important element to the city's strategies in compliment of infrastructure improvements "car il aura la possibilité de décider d'aller siéger ailleurs si le séjour strasbourgeois ne lui convient pas ou ne lui est pas agréable."[402] Special measures included the publishing of a book in all official languages of the EC, the exposition *Strasbourg et l'Europe* that traced the European history of Strasbourg, a TV emission and a commemorative medal.[403]

Next to a general threat that the EP could move away and remove a prestigious institution from Strasbourg, which gained more attention with the introduction of the direct voting procedure, a concrete crisis developed. In September 1979, its president, Simone Veil, made disparaging statements on Strasbourg's capabilities in an interview, since infrastructure, such as offices, would not even be permanently available for the EP.[404] In response, Pflimlin addressed a five-page letter to her on the same day, wondering

399 CARDOC, PE1 P1 243/EXEM SIEG-1962-0100120, *Examen d'un lettre.*

400 CARDOC, PE0 AP PV/POLI.1961 POLI-197601190040, *Opinion for an enlarged Bureau*, p. 28.

401 CARDOC, PE0 AP PV/POLI.1961 POLI-197601190040, *Opinion for an enlarged Bureau*, p. 27.

402 ABR, 1130 W 936/2, *Minutes of the Bipartite Committee session, 11.6.1979*, p. 2.

403 ABR, 1130 W 936/2, *Minutes of the Bipartite Committee session, 11.6.1979*, p. 2.

404 AS, 752 W 114, *Extrait des DNA, 21.9.1979.*

why she made these allegations, before launching into a description of his opinion on the distribution of seats between Brussels, Luxembourg and Strasbourg. He added that he had long campaigned for Strasbourg to become seat of the EP secretariat as well.[405] Pflimlin also requested a meeting to talk further about the issue, since the letter would only provide a brief summary.[406]

This action presented yet another example for individual action, mostly by Pflimlin, in order to offset any negative opinions or publications on Strasbourg's capabilities as seat. During the third hosting phase, this was not as acute as during the end of the 1950s, when not only the EP was affected, but also the dispelling of rumours of a possible move of the CoE was seen as necessary by local actors. The 1960s and 1970s showed a concentration on the bubble of European institutions and to keep the leisure activities from being boring. However, individual promotion or addressing of issues was still employed to resolve crises, of which the three largest were discussed in this section.

In summary, the third period of hosting activities covering the 1960s and 1970s was less intense than the preceding phase. Threats to Strasbourg's position caused by EC activity within the seat question were less constant and severe. In response, the frequency of events had been reduced, but without sacrificing the quality achieved in 1956. The fear of local actors that their events might become too unspectacular through excess repetition contributed to this as well. Additionally, the city administration began to focus more on traffic infrastructure, a common complaint of delegates, in order to match the remaining competition Brussels and Luxembourg. While hosting activities remained important strands of action, they were not the only principle strategy anymore to attract European institutions.

Section 1.12 Concluding Remarks

The three hosting phases conceptualised in this chapter mirrored a development from an uncoordinated to a sophisticated long-term organisational structure of offering events. They did not correspond to the periods of EC activities regarding the seat question. They trace responses of local actors to important events in the seat decision process as they perceived it. In an EP Political Affairs Committee memo on the EC's decision processes from 1975, three different time spans were identified. The first stage from 1952 to 1957 was in their opinion characterised by

405 AS, 114 W 283, *Lettre de Pflimlin à Veil, 21.9.1979.*

406 AS, 114 W 283, *Lettre de Pflimlin à Veil, 21.9.1979*, p. 5.

difficulties in reaching anything but a provisional decision, the second from 1958 to 1964 by attempts to make a final decision, and the third from 1965 to 1973 by inactivity.[407] The hosting activities in Strasbourg primarily focused on the bubble of the European institutions located within the city, as a strategy to support Strasbourg's status as seat through gaining the appreciation of the parliamentarians through a spectacular hosting programme.

Numerous thank-you notes archived in the municipal archive of Strasbourg show that these events gained the appreciation of European parliamentarians, as for example expressed in a letter from the retiring EP president Gaetano Martino in 1961. "Tous les membres du Parlement ont beaucoup apprécié l'infatigable hospitalité de la Ville de Strasbourg et je ne veux pas quitter la Présidence du Parlement Européen sans vous exprimer en leur nom et au mien un très sincère merci."[408] Such letters provide an indication that a number of parliamentarians appreciated these efforts which might have translated into an increased support for Strasbourg as definitive seat.

The various actors slowly and comprehensively expanded across the three phases of activities. It was an accumulative process with several developmental stages where activity spread to new areas, especially in the city administration. They contained a multitude of interests to keep the European institutions in the city which overlapped and/or complimented each other. One overarching example would be the fact that different actor groups covered the entire spectrum of European institutions; the city administration was mostly responsible for the parliamentarians and civil servants who arrived for the session periods, the *Cercle des Amitiés Européennes* was responsible for the accompanying spouses and the *Cercle Européen* for the permanent, diplomatic corps and other dignitaries.

A central group of actors largely remained the same over the entire period of study, while actors were more commonly replaced on the fringes of activity. A feature, this 'inner circle' had in common, was that they contributed to the hosting programme in several public and/or private organisations simultaneously or consecutively starting from 1949 until the 1970s, which was the usual retirement age for this generation. They were most actively concerned with receiving European parliamentarians over the entire period of study.[409]

---

407 CARDOC, PE0 AP PV/POLI.1961 POLI-197601190040, *Opinion for an enlarged Bureau*, pp. 21; 22; 24.

408 AS, 236 MW 16/1, *Lettre de Martino à Pflimlin, 21.4.1961.*

409 Compiled from meeting minutes and member lists archived in the municipal archive of Strasbourg and the departmental archive of Bas-Rhin.

An inherent feature of all hosting and promotion measures included expressing Strasbourg's European mission. It was mainly employed in speeches or resolutions as argument why Strasbourg should be seat of European institutions and was based on the city's long 'European' history. To validate their construction, local actors employed Bevin and his involvement in the founding of the CoE as validation and endorsement from an outside source. In this manner, Bevin and his statement were used as a banal symbol to indicate the city's European mission.

The measures of the hosting programme itself were intended to accumulate reputation and renown as the seat of the CoE and EP and possibly to attract further institutions. They were an indirect strategy, through gaining the appreciation of European parliamentarians of Strasbourg as host city, this good opinion might influence the decision holders on the intergovernmental level. The message of the European mission of Strasbourg which was often at the forefront concealed this intention of consolidating the seat status and the further development of the city through such measures.

It has to be noted that the apparent successfulness of this approach to rely on hosting activities in the 1950s was strongly conditioned by the manner in which the European Communities attempted to determine a definitive seat. Until the mid-1960s when the three provisional hosts Brussels, Luxembourg and Strasbourg emerged as the only viable candidates, both the number of official candidate cities strongly fluctuated and the competitive situation between them was undefined. The number of applications which were not officially recognised by the European institutions contributed to this. With the two clear competitors Brussels and Luxembourg from the mid-1960s onwards, this strategy became difficult to pursue. Hard infrastructure facts were easier to compare and the rivalry grew stronger, since the number of viable applicants was drastically reduced. This was a likely reason that the municipality of Strasbourg began to focus on the improvement of infrastructure from the 1960s and began to use it as the principal strategy to eclipse Brussels and Luxembourg's efforts.

In this chapter, only the bubble of local actors occupied with offering the most spectacular hosting programme possible has been analysed. While this constellation presented a harmonious endeavour without any dissent, the only instance of criticism from the outside in the sources was ignored or marginalised.[410] These principles also characterised transport and building infrastructure improvements which will be discussed in the subsequent two chapters.

[410] E.g. AS, 208 MW 7, *Interpellation de M. Boosz, 30.12.1957.*

Chapter 3

L'Europe vient à Strasbourg

Traffic infrastructure was the second theme of strategies to consolidate Strasbourg's position as seat. The heading of this chapter, *l'Europe vient à Strasbourg*, was the title of a brochure containing timetables for all air links with which to reach the city, the municipal government distributed to European parliamentarians from the mid-1960s onwards.[1] It is a well-suited slogan for the efforts of local actors in this area. This had long been a concern for improvement, not only of city actors, but also in the CoE. In a PACE resolution from 2004, a need for improved air and train links still is assessed in order to fully honour its potential as seat city.[2] This assessment is congruent with a statement the CoE made in 1957: "If Strasbourg wishes to retain, let alone develop, its status as a European centre, a considerable effort, probably with state assistance will be required to remedy the present situation."[3] Prior to that year, Strasbourg had had no air traffic of note. During the 1960s, the nearest major airports Frankfurt and Zurich that offered connections to other European countries, both slightly more than 200 kilometres away, remained important transport hubs for access to the city.

Improvements had the goal of consolidating the city's status as seat city, similar to the area of hosting measures. As with hosting activities, further developments of traffic infrastructure were conditioned by anticipated and concrete demands of European parliamentarians. They strongly influenced the activities of local actors. These strategies intended to offset competing cities through quality infrastructure, but also portray the city as European. The latter seemed to have occurred especially with extraordinary transport measures, on which the city administration concentrated from 1960 onwards. This is also substantiated in a publication on the history of Strasbourg, where the analysis is made that air links were created due to political motivations and in the light of the

1 E.g. AS, 236 MW 27/2, *Horaires 6/1964.*

2 "Resolution 1357 (2004) 1: Realising Strasbourg's potential as a European capital." <http://assembly.coe.int/Documents/AdoptedText/ta04/ERES1357.htm (accessed 27.08.2012).

3 ACE, 1007/0765, *Air/rail connections 1957*, p. 4.

European mission of Strasbourg, rather than economic reasons.[4] The central set of strategies seemed to have been motivated by presenting the city as European, improvements within infrastructure seemed to have been caused by the need to keep up with the competing cities Brussels and Luxembourg.

Based on the documents from the municipal archive of Strasbourg and the departmental archive of Bas-Rhin, transport only became a major concern from 1960 onwards, while the 1950s were dominated by hosting efforts. For instance, in Bipartite Committee minutes, infrastructure issues only gained prominence from 1960 onwards. Nevertheless, committee members acknowledged the importance of a well-functioning transport infrastructure for the parliamentarians. "L'amélioration des liaisons avec Strasbourg constitue un problème essentiel pour les parlementaires qui participent aux sessions des institutions européennes, aussi rien ne doit-il être négligé à cet égard."[5] It can be speculated that since hosting affairs had been fully institutionalised in the phase from 1956-1959, local actors could concentrate on other issues. However, especially air links, which according to archive sources constituted the centrepiece of efforts to improve transport, had been impeded during the 1950s due to inadequate facilities. For example, a proper airport terminal had only been built in 1957.[6]

Nevertheless, Strasbourg's actors promoted the image of a centrally located and well-connected seat city to the outside as signal that they were able to house institutions. It was supposed to demonstrate that the city could compete with its rivals, especially Brussels and Luxembourg which had of a superior transport network. For instance, the book *Strasbourg, capitale européenne*, the *CSME* had published in 1952 contained a map entitled "Strasbourg nœud ferroviaire européen", depicting available railway connections to ECSC and CoE member states.[7] It is interesting to note that the *CSME* would present Strasbourg as central transport hub by employing the railway system, since this mode of transportation

---

4 Nonn, Henri and Livet, Georges and Fuchs, René, "Livre VII. Les grandes mutations contemporaines (1945-1980)", Livet, Georges and Rapp, Francis (eds.), *Histoire de Strasbourg des origines à nos jours. Tome 4: Strasbourg de 1815 à nos jours, XIX*e *et XX*e *siècles*, Strasbourg, Éditions des Dernières Nouvelles d'Alsace, 1982, p. 517.

5 AS, 236 MW 2/6, *Minutes of the Bipartite Committee session, 21.12.1960*, p. 6.

6 "Depuis 1935, l'aéroport de Strasbourg et la CCI, Le Point éco, No. 224, 2003." <http://www.strasbourg.cci.fr/web/pointeco/pe_dossiers/pe_dos_t7/aeroport_strasbourg1138.php> (accessed 04.02.2014).

7 Comité Strasbourgeois pour le Mouvement Européen, *Strasbourg, capitale européenne, siège du Conseil de l'Europe, doit devenir le siège des autorités européennes*, Strasbourg, Impressions Strasbourg, 1952, p. 49.

hardly figured in local archive sources. However, in the early 1950s, this seemed to have been the only way to ascribe accessibility to Strasbourg. In that decade, the city hardly possessed any possibilities for air travel. Such images to prove the centrality and accessibility of Strasbourg for European parliamentarians could have been a way to improve the city's position against other candidate cities to house European institutions.

Likewise, the city included maps in their book *Strasbourg invite l'Europe*, published in 1957, to illustrate the alleged centrality and accessibility of Strasbourg.[8] There, no concrete modes of transportation and routes were given, but arrows superimposed on the map of Europe, converging from all directions towards the Alsatian city, were employed.[9] These examples should likely give it an image of centrality. To portray competence in the area of infrastructure was important, since it was often employed by actors outside the city to point out Strasbourg's disadvantages. An example included the aforementioned altercation between Pflimlin and Coudenhove-Kalergi in 1958, when the latter argued that compared to Brussels the French city would not have any chances due to its lacking infrastructure.[10]

Similar to hosting activities, the local level was responsible for improving infrastructure. Only from the 1970s onwards, the French state began to assist financially which led to the creation of several air links to major European cities.[11] Before, the improvement of transport infrastructure for European parliamentarians had been slow to develop, and was one of the major deficiencies of Strasbourg as seat. This pattern is observable over the entire period of study. In 1979, some of the same issues that initially became apparent in the early 1950s were still present despite municipal actors' efforts as will be shown subsequently.

The local engagement of the city to improve conditions also seems to have been acknowledged by the European parliamentarians and civil servants, as some missives show. An example was the letter British MEP Neil Balfour sent to Pflimlin in November 1979 following a meeting where members of the assembly had criticised the traffic infrastructure. "I hope you will not interpret this morning's outburst on transportation problems as a slur on your own or your city's outstanding efforts to welcome us & make our lives comfortable & pleasant. […] We realise you are doing your best.

8 Ville de Strasbourg and Conseil Général du Bas-Rhin, *Strasbourg invite l'Europe*, Strasbourg, Editions de la Calanque, 1957.

9 *Ibid.*

10 AS, 9 Z 109, *Lettre de Coudenhove-Kalergi à Pflimlin, 23.1.1958.*

11 AS, 9 Z 109, *Desserte aérienne.*

Good luck to you."[12] While this hints at the fact that MEPs are dissatisfied with the possibilities, they acknowledge that the local administration has given their best efforts. Only in 1980, a structured support was instituted with a three-year contract between the state, department and city which included next to the improvement of air and railway connections mostly building infrastructure.[13] In the following, the most central actors involved will be discussed, before analysing major efforts to improve both long distance and inner-city traffic for parliamentarians and the modalities of its functioning.

Section 1.13 Central Actors

In the following, the most involved local actors concerned with strategic improvement of the city's transport system will be investigated. The information is based on the content of city administration sources, authors and recipients of documents from the municipal archive of Strasbourg and the departmental archive of Bas-Rhin. In the first section, the concerned city and departmental entities will be presented and in which capacity they acted, before likewise portraying involved other actors. In the last sub-section, instances and modalities of cooperation between the two groups will be outlined. Other than with hosting efforts, relevant local actors had to communicate with organisations outside their group, such as taxi associations, to enforce measures. Nevertheless, the group of actors occupied with consolidating Strasbourg's status remained separate from ordinary structures of the municipality and other associations.

Administration actors were simultaneously responsible for hosting measures, as well as traffic and building infrastructure. With transport, a slight shift towards a more technically-oriented group was observable, which fully manifested in the realm of building infrastructure (see chapter 4). For instance, while the Bipartite Committee retained a central role, actors like Georges Ridoux or Alphonse Heitz, who were more concerned with the implementation of hosting arrangements than the conception of them, were more strongly involved in infrastructure than in hosting measures.

(a) City/departmental administration

As with hosting activities, principally specialised actors, supported by certain ordinary structures of the two administrations, were active in the matter of improving transport for European delegates to remain

12 AS, 9 Z 110, *Lettre de Balfour à Pflimlin, 5.11.1979.*

13 AS, 114 W 284/1, *Contrat.*

attractive as seat city. City administration personnel accounted for most of the activity and contact with the European institutions in Strasbourg. Therefore, this sub-chapter will concentrate on the municipality, since its involved actors were responsible for most processes and decisions. The Bipartite Committee was responsible for developing measures. The rest of the centrally involved administration actors are separated into two parts; the ordinary services involved with welcoming European institutions and more recurrent single actors acting in a special role.

(i) Ordinary structures

One of the centrally involved ordinary city services during the 1960s was the *Division VIII*, responsible for traffic among others.[14] Parts of the division served as one of the principal organisational instances with the implementation of measures. Its tasks seem to have been overtaken by the *Service des Relations Publiques* towards the end of the 1960s, because several key members were identical, such as A. Heitz. During the 1970s, it functioned as a liaison to the European guests, as well. For instance, Herbert Wehr, one of the principal actors of the service, was regularly present at the airport to welcome parliamentarians.[15] Thus, transport measures included a hosting dimension, as well. It also indicates that the city administration obligingly welcomed parliamentarians.

Most of the more engaged single actors belonged to one of these two services. They were occupied with aspects of traffic infrastructure, mostly in the execution of measures, but also in the day-to-day running, for example with air links. The *Préfet* stated in a letter to one of the charter companies charged with the execution of special links during the 1960s that Alfred Feuerstein of the *Relations Publiques* would be their contact person in matters of flight execution under the supervision of A. Heitz, while invoices should be addressed to the *Cabinet du Préfet* or Ridoux.[16] This division of labour also illustrates that sometimes different administration instances were charged with aspects of the same process which will be further expanded on in the following.

The *Division II* was responsible for among others commerce, industry, and traffic infrastructure.[17] It was concerned with the optimisation of the

---

14 Archives de la Ville et de la Communauté Urbaine, *Guide des Fonds 2006*, Strasbourg, Imp. Int. CU, 2006, p. 13.

15 AS, 114 W 207, *Lettre de Pflimlin à Simmons.*

16 AS, 236 MW 32/2, *Lettre du Préfet au Balair, 9.12.1964.*

17 Archives de la Ville et de la Communauté Urbaine, *Guide des Fonds 2006*, Strasbourg, Imp. Int. CU, 2006, p. 12.

public transport system. Likewise, the *Division IX* was involved with the second major inner city traffic feature; taxis, which was included in its tasks during the 1970s. The *Adjoint au Maire* in charge of this service, Georges Gilliot, was together with Leissner and members of the *Relations Publiques* involved with coordination meetings between the administration, European institutions and taxi associations.[18] His agency constituted a rare exception that someone from outside the 'bubble' of local actors concerned with welcoming the European guests actively participated.

(ii) Specialised structures

As with hosting matters from 1956 onwards, the two Liaison Committees and the Bipartite Committee were the centrepieces of developing measures to improve traffic infrastructure. From 1960, only the latter remained active. From its meeting minutes and annual activity summaries from the 1960s and 1970s, it becomes apparent that the improvement of air links was its main task next to hosting activities. Public transport and building infrastructure included minor concerns.[19] Only the matter of taxis was never mentioned in the minutes. It was the only area of transport improvement organised wholly outside this body. For the other areas, the committee largely determined the course of action which was subsequently implemented by the competent services.

Globally, the Bipartite Committee, the mayor, the *Adjoint* and *Sous-préfet chargée des affaires européennes*, Leissner and Ridoux, as well as select members of the *Relations Publiques* constituted the most active entities and simultaneously the executive decision holders. Mayor Pflimlin was hardly involved in processes and mostly only informed about actions taken.[20] Nevertheless, he retained the final decision power. Additionally, he was the addressee of most complaints or notes of gratitude from European institutions and delegates. In the matter of air links, however, he filled a role as chief-lobbyist for the institution of connections that could be of use to delegates. Pflimlin was also involved in this area before he became Mayor in 1959 and was President of the *Conseil Général du Bas-Rhin*. One example constituted the creation of a stopover in Strasbourg on the link Paris-Frankfurt-Berlin at the end of the 1950s which existence was ascribed to him in a newspaper article.[21] He had a dual role as figure head

18 E.g. AS, 114 W 206, *Compte-rendu du 9.3.1978.*

19 ABR, 1130 W 936/1-16, *Minutes of the Bipartite Committee session, 1964-1979.*

20 Charles Frey held the post from 1935 to 1955, Charles Altorffer from 1955 to 1959 and Pierre Pflimlin from 1959 to 1983.

21 AS, 54 W 144, *Extrait du Nouvel Alsacien, 6.10.1959.*

to the outside and as executive inside the city administration, while the drafting of tasks was relegated to certain subordinates of the municipality.

Both Leissner's and Ridoux's posts had been created in the 1960s and they were generally responsible for the contact with the European institutions and the effective running of selected aspects. Ridoux was also tasked with the coordination of the city and *Département* in European affairs.[22] In this matter, he mostly communicated with A. Heitz, but also Pflimlin according to various notes archived in the municipal archive of Strasbourg.[23] Interestingly, Ridoux was only active during the 1960s, when his central tasks next to this general liaison concentrated on air links, while in the 1970s, he or his position hardly figured in the sources. Inversely, Leissner only became a major actor during the 1970s, when he was centrally involved in the improvement of inner-city traffic and communication with the European institutions.

During the 1970s, the *Relations Publiques* was the most actively involved city service. Next to A. Heitz, who had also been included in his function as head of *Division VIII* and *Secrétaire-Général Adjoint* during the 1960s, Wehr, Feuerstein, and S. Jantkowiak counted among the names that occurred most often in administration documents. A. Heitz was mainly involved with air links, as was Feuerstein, while the other two, but also Feuerstein were generally active during the 1970s. Their tasks included being contact persons to European institutions and parliamentarians, as well as participation in coordination meetings with them and other actors. Apart from these services of the two administrations, the executive positions of the Secretary-General, during the 1970s Daniel Adam and his deputy Roger Hannsler were occasionally involved in implementation processes.

Next to the inter-administration coordination with Ridoux, A. Heitz also communicated with the companies, as did Pflimlin and occasionally the *Préfet*. Feuerstein was the official recipient for invoices next to Ridoux and received timetables and letters about technical issues from the charter plane companies as well.[24] Hence, although the involved central instances from the two administrations exhibited traces of certain actors being exclusively tasked with particular aspects, they often worked on the same area with different entities effectuating nearly identical tasks. These processes were extended by the coordination with other actors occupied with Strasbourg's traffic system for European institutions.

---

22 AS, 236 MW 32/2, *Lettre du Préfet au Directeur du Balair, 9.12.1964.*

23 E.g. AS, 236 MW 27/10, *Lettre de Ridoux à A. Heitz, 16.4.1962.*

24 Cf. AS, 236 MW 27/1 and 236 MW 27/10, *Liaisons aériennes.*

(b) Other actors

The three most important other actor groups involved in the improvement of Strasbourg's traffic infrastructure were the chamber of commerce – *Chambre de Commerce et d'Industrie de Strasbourg et Bas-Rhin* (*CCI*), the public transport of the city *Compagnie des Tramways/ Transports Strasbourgeois* (*CTS*), as well as several local and regional taxi associations. According to the sources, they were partners of the relevant city administration entities, since certain areas of transport infrastructure constituted their responsibility. Nevertheless, they also showed elements of active agency, for instance in the form of suggestions to measures administration actors wanted to implement. Thereby, the *CCI* constituted the biggest contributor of the three groups. Other than with hosting affairs, none of these entities had been purposely founded in response to the European institutions like the *Comité Strasbourgeois pour le Mouvement Européen (CSME)* or the *Cercle des Amitiés Européennes (CAE)*, but their activity rather involved areas they were generally responsible for.

(i) Chamber of Commerce

The *CCI*, representation of the local enterprises, was mostly active regarding the improving of air links, since it was the concessionary of the airport.[25] Its *Commission Consultative Economique de l'Aéroport d'Entzheim* stood for the operation of the airport and occasionally was involved with organisation of air routes for parliamentarians.[26] The city was invited to participate in the meetings with one representative from their technical services, since they would have interest in the airport and its development, as well as asked whether they had any input.[27] Its tasks included economy, passengers, and airport buildings.[28] This commission also produced flight statistics which local city actors subsequently used to evaluate the state of their efforts.[29] The *CCI*'s biggest involvement

25 "Arrêté du 27 décembre 1966: Aménagement et exploitation commerciale de l'aérodrome de Strasbourg-Entzheim (zone civile) par la Chambre de Commerce et d'Industrie de Strasbourg." <http://www.legifrance.gouv.fr/affichTexte.do?cidTexte=JORFTEXT000000489410&fastPos=1&fastReqId=1714940285&categorieLien=id&oldAction=rechTexte> (accessed 04.02.2014) and "Chambre de Commerce et d'Industrie de Strasbourg et de Bas-Rhin. Présentation Générale." <http://www.strasbourg.cci.fr/cci-pratique/presentation-generale> (accessed 06.02.2014).

26 AS, 68 MW 88, *Commission Consultative* and 68 MW 89, *Minutes de la commission.*

27 AS, 68 MW 88, *Commission Consultative* and 68 MW 89, *Minutes de la commission.*

28 AS, 68 MW 89, *Commission.*

29 E.g., AS, 68 MW 88, *Trafic 1965.*

constituted financial assistance by covering one fifth of the costs special flight connections incurred.[30]

Additionally, next to the city administration, it played a part in promoting Strasbourg's air links and was it usually informed by airlines about schedule changes.[31] This also included minor lobbying, for instance, in 1964 René Uhrich, Secretary-General of the *CCI* informed Pflimlin of his talks with *Air France* on the subject of more frequent departures on the link to Frankfurt.[32] In these two aspects it constituted a major partner to the local administration which will be outlined in the subsequent section.

(ii) Public transport

The *CTS* was, compared to the *CCI*, slightly more passively involved. The *CTS* had been founded in 1877 and was the local transport company.[33] In the majority of cases, it just executed measures concerning public transport, the administration had mandated, but occasionally made suggestions or raised concerns. For instance, with the initial institution of special offers for parliamentarians in 1956, it made the final proposal after rejecting the one created by the city administration actors.[34] As an example for the latter action, it broached the issue of profitability of special services in 1977.[35] The *CTS* was included in hosting affairs, as well, since the Liaison Committee decided to decorate the regular trolleybus line running by the CoE with French and European flags and to issue booths decorated with flags to the *CTS* for further embellishment.[36] Today, the company itself contributes to such measures by, for example, having decorated trams with a 'welcome' to the capital of Europe in all official EU languages.[37]

(iii) Taxi associations

A good number of local, departmental and regional taxi associations and syndicates existed and were equally involved by the local administrations regarding their input or execution of measures. Since no particular of

---

30 E.g. ABR, 1130 W 936/4, *Activités de l'année 1977*, p. 4.

31 E.g. AS, 236 MW 27/5, *Note pour A. Heitz, 27.3.1963* and 236 MW 27/6, *Lettre de Uhrich à Pflimlin, 24.7.1964.*

32 AS, 236 MW 27/2, *Lettre d'Uhrich à Pflimlin, 24.7.1964.*

33 "C'était en 1877." <http://www.cts-strasbourg.eu/fr/la-cts/c-etait-en-1877/> (accessed 06.02.2014).

34 AS, 208 MW 267, *Lettre de la CTS au Maire 12.10.1956.*

35 ABR, 1130 W 936/5, *Lettre de la CTS au Maire 10.1.1977.*

36 AS, 208 MW 267, *Minutes of the Liaison Committee session, 24.9.1956.*

37 "Notre démarche patrimoniale." <http://www.cts-strasbourg.eu/fr/la-cts/notre-demarche-patrimoniale/> (accessed 06.02.2014).

these was singled out by the administration, but all were approached equally according to sources from the municipal archive of Strasbourg, several examples of the form of their involvement will be given rather than presenting each association mentioned. One central mode of participation, which will be expanded on in the subsequent section, constituted working groups with representatives of taxi organisations, city actors and the European institutions to discuss issues regarding the cab service and to draft solutions.

The most frequent topic during such meetings or in general directives from the city administration was the mitigation of the shortage of taxis during session periods. It was a controversial issue, since the legitimate interests of the associations and syndicates clashed with those of the city. In a meeting in 1963, the administration placed the blame on these organisations, since they would refuse raising the number of cabs and threaten with strikes should the municipality press the issue.[38] According to the archive documents, this area presented a central concern over the entire period of study.

Additionally, taxi associations directly corresponded with the European institutions, mostly regarding modalities of reservations. For example, the President of the *Association Centrale des Autos-Taxis de Strasbourg* informed the CoE in 1977 that a direct phone line between the dispatch and the *Palais de l'Europe* had been created.[39] Moreover, cab associations also placed demands about the functioning of the taxi service to the *Division IX*, for instance the *Association Centrale des Artisans du Taxi de Strasbourg* asked for a telephone line from the CoE to the taxi rank outside the building. Another example was that all cab organisations in general wanted to be informed beforehand about how many taxis would be needed at the airport as in 1979.[40]

(c) Cooperation between actors

Cooperation between the groups analysed in the two sections above concerned all other actors to different degrees and occurred during the drafting, but especially the execution of measures to implement improvements to Strasbourg's transport infrastructure. It was of a slightly different nature than the occasional partnerships between private organisations and the city administration for certain hosting activities. In transport matters, the collaboration occurred more often and in a

38 AS, 68 MW 40, *Procès-verbal, 13.2.1963*, p. 3.

39 AS, 114 W 206, *Lettre de Clamer à Matter, 14.3.1977.*

40 AS, 114 W 207, *Note pour Leissner, 9.5.1979.*

more structured manner. While the *CTS*, apart from occasionally voicing suggestions and concerns, did not provide further input regarding the improvement of transport structures, the *CCI* and various taxi associations were more actively involved, although parts of their agency also included fulfilling tasks of the administrations. Therefore, the *CTS* will not be covered further, since it only cooperated in a minor capacity with the city, but present central instances of collaboration between the *CCI* and taxi organisations with the city and department.

The most central element regarding the *CCI* was sharing the financial burden of special air links to European capitals or centres for convenience of European parliamentarians with the local and regional administrations. In this connection, the three partners were referred to as the *collectivités locales*. The municipal and departmental share of the monetary contribution remained higher; the portion the *collectivités locales* assured was separated with two fifths each for the two administrations and one fifth for the *CCI*.[41] Additionally, multipositioned actors were active, for example the President of the *CCI* in the beginning of the 1970s, Jean Precheur, sat as *Conseiller Général* in the Bipartite Committee which was chiefly responsible for the improvement of air links in the 1970s. Additionally, he was a member of the *CES*. He also lobbied *Air France* to draft convenient timetables in his role as *CCI* representative.[42] Such an accumulation of tasks was quite common for the more active actors.

Collaboration of the city and departmental administrations and the various taxi associations generally concentrated itself on meetings between them and European institution representatives. In these meetings, actions were coordinated. For instance, in 1979 the agenda of one meeting included the connection of the *Palais de l'Europe* and Entzheim airport with cabs, reservation of taxis, as well as the demand of taxi associations to be guaranteed proceeds during EP sessions.[43] Next to such concrete demands, meetings often contained the attempt to resolve issues which more often than not regarded the number of taxis in the city. Some minutes of these occasions only contained declarations that more actions needed to be taken in lieu of concrete results. For example, in 1978, during a reunion demanded by Hans Nord of the EP, where among others the poor availability of taxis at the airport was discussed, taxi organisations maintained that complaints could not be serious, since passengers would often be picked up by chauffeurs. As a possible solution, the protocol specified that Feuerstein would contact the

41 E.g. ABR, 1130 W 936/4, *Activités de l'année 1977*, p. 4.

42 ABR, 1130 W 936/9, *Minutes of the Bipartite Committee session, 1972*, p. 5.

43 AS, 114 W 209, *Agenda du 27.9.1979.*

delegation secretaries about the issue of taxi reservations.[44] All in all, these meetings constituted a central forum to discuss and attempt to consolidate the at times diverging interests of the three parties involved in them, as becomes apparent from municipal archive documents.

Section 1.14 Long-distance transport

Long distance transport infrastructure and especially the improvement of air links was a set of central strategies to improve Strasbourg's seat status by exhibiting the capability to cater to the presence of European institutions. In supplement, the city offered a chauffeuring service, where parliamentarians were driven to major air hubs in the vicinity such as Frankfurt in cars.

Railway transport only constituted a minor concern during the period of study. Connections to Brussels and Luxembourg existed, but sources only seemed to appear more frequently from the beginning of the 1980s in the municipal archive of Strasbourg. They generally alluded to that trains as transport were not very well used by parliamentarians travelling to Strasbourg. For instance, from June 1981, the link to the other two provisional seat cities had to be stopped, since the French railway operator *SNCF* incurred too many losses.[45] Improvements to the railway system were apparently slow to be instituted, for instance, a connection with the high-speed train *TGV* to Brussels had first been proposed in 1982, but extensive *TGV* connections linking Strasbourg to the European high-speed train network only occurred in the 2000s.[46]

Regarding the matter of air links which local actors chiefly developed to improve transport infrastructure, an underlying desire seemed to be present to be able to provide at minimum comparable facilities to the other two provisional EC seats. Such needs manifested themselves in lobbying efforts, among others. Multiple reports and notes from the city administration stressed that good air connections were essential to assure the parliamentarians' satisfaction and therewith chances for Strasbourg to remain seat. For example, in 1965, a study stated that air connections should be a priority for being able to provide well-functioning services as institution host.[47] This mode of employing infrastructure improvements

---

44 AS, 114 W 206, *Compte-rendu du 29.3.1978*, p. 1.

45 AS, 752 W 99, *Lettre du Ministre des Affaires Etrangères à Pflimlin, 6.4.1981.*

46 AS, 752 W 99, *Extrait du Nouvel Alsacien, 5.11.1982* and "Resolution 1357 (2004) 1: Realising Strasbourg's potential as a European capital." <http://assembly.coe.int/Documents/AdoptedText/ta04/ERES1357.htm> (accessed 27.08.2012).

47 AS, 209 MW 52, *Note, liaisons aériennes*, p. 1.

to offset competing cities became increasingly common during the 1960s and the following decade. The competition with Brussels and Luxembourg became more concrete during these times.

In this context, the historic development of air links gives evidence that the placement of European institutions also sparked a modernisation story. The clearest instance presents the leap from the 1960s to the 1970s when state assistance markedly accelerated the at times cumbersome, locally-driven process of expanding flight connections.

(a) Air links

The creation of new air links that could be of use for European parliamentarians travelling to the city for assembly sessions was the centrepiece of the local actors' efforts to improve the city's transport infrastructure. Based on sources from the municipal, regional and the Council of Europe archive, which detail the efforts of the *collectivités locales* (city, *Département*, chamber of commerce), the historic development of Strasbourg's air links relevant to European institution personnel will be analysed.

The city administration informed delegates prior to each PACE or EP session by sending the brochure *L'Europe vient à Strasbourg* with flight timetables of all connections from the 1960s onwards.[48] Two different approaches were employed in order to create a functioning route network for those travelling to Strasbourg for sessions of the European assemblies. They were lobbying airlines to create links useful to transport of institution personnel, and organising suitable air links. Local actors stood for introducing air links on their own until the 1970s, when the French state began to support them financially. Regarding the entire period of study, the self-organisation of air routes constituted the most important and elaborate activity in the matter of long-distance transport infrastructure improvement.

However, these efforts only started during the 1960s, when traffic infrastructure replaced hosting activities as forefront concern. During the 1950s, attempts to improve Strasbourg's connections concentrated on lobbying airlines to establish links to the city which could be used by European parliamentarians, but were hampered by the lack of developed facilities, among others. In the subsequent two decades these actions slowly became a background issue to purposive, self-organised connections. Nevertheless, lobbying activities will be discussed first, since the lack of suitable commercial connections constituted the premise of the local actors'

48 AS, 236 MW 27/7, *Note du 1.9.1961.*

efforts to organise air links themselves as evidence from the municipal archive of Strasbourg suggests. The central strategy behind these measures constituted creating a route network useful for European parliamentarians. Another goal was to be able to remain seat of the European institutions and to provide at minimum similar infrastructure to the closest competition of the 1960s and 1970s, Luxembourg and Brussels. Prior to analysing these two elements, key facts on the airport Strasbourg-Entzheim will be outlined.

Entzheim airport, located to the West of Strasbourg, had been created through a cooperation of the *CCI* and the city administration in 1935. Operations started with a connection to Paris which was interrupted during the war and only continued in the early 1950s.[49] From 1945, it also served as a military air base, while the *CCI* had only been accorded the concession to operate the airport from the French state in May 1955.[50] However, the license for commercial exploitation was apparently only given from 1967.[51] Regarding the capabilities of the airport, it became an *aéroport de première classe* in August 1960, meaning its lighting system was suited for intense traffic.[52] Entzheim was a smaller airport, ranging from 15,000 travellers in 1957 to 500,000 in 1972.[53] Proper operations only seemed to have started in 1957, when a terminal for civilian air traffic was constructed.[54] In that year, documents from the municipal archive of Strasbourg set the inauguration of the international airport.[55] It might explain why the sources on the first approach of local actors, the lobbying

49 "Depuis 1935, l'aéroport de Strasbourg et la CCI, Le Point éco, No. 224, 2003." <http://www.strasbourg.cci.fr/web/pointeco/pe_dossiers/pe_dos_t7/aeroport_strasbourg1138.php> (accessed 04.02.2014).

50 "Décret du 6 mai 1955 portant approbation du cahier des charges type applicable aux concessions d'outillage public d'aéroport aux Chambres de Commerce." <http://www.legifrance.gouv.fr/affichTexte.do?cidTexte=JORFTEXT000000850699&fastPos=14&fastReqId=871802162&categorieLien=id&oldAction=rechTexte> (accessed 04.02.2014).

51 "Arrêté du 27 décembre 1966: Aménagement et exploitation commerciale de l'aérodrome de Strasbourg-Entzheim (zone civile) par la Chambre de Commerce et d'Industrie de Strasbourg." <http://www.legifrance.gouv.fr/affichTexte.do?cidTexte=JORFTEXT000000489410&fastPos=1&fastReqId=1714940285&categorieLien=id&oldAction=rechTexte> (accessed 04.02.2014).

52 "Décision du 24 août 1960 relative au classement de l'aéroport de Strasbourg-Entzheim en ce qui concerne le balisage lumineux." <http://www.legifrance.gouv.fr/affichTexte.do?cidTexte=JORFTEXT000000320039&fastPos=51&fastReqId=700958906&categorieLien=id&oldAction=rechTexte> (accessed 04.02.2014).

53 AS, 697 W 118, *Airport International.*

54 "Depuis 1935, l'aéroport de Strasbourg et la CCI, Le Point éco, No. 224, 2003." <http://www.strasbourg.cci.fr/web/pointeco/pe_dossiers/pe_dos_t7/aeroport_strasbourg1138.php> (accessed 04.02.2014).

55 AS, 697 W 118, *Airport International.*

for commercial air links, leave the impression that prior to that year, Strasbourg did not offer any possibilities for air travel.

(i) Commercial links 1949-1957

However, in the archive of the Council of Europe, a dossier details that the CoE was very actively lobbying for flight connections before that date, while city or departmental administration documents hardly contained evidence for early efforts to create regular air links. The period until 1957 was characterised by attempts of the local administration and the CoE to improve infrastructure which were impeded by legal hassles, lacking economic incentive or usage. As a note from July 1949 from the French Foreign Ministry to the Secretary-General of the CoE, Jacques Camille Paris, suggested, a connection to Paris had been instituted by the state to be effective during PACE sessions. However, J.C. Paris was asked to take steps to assure a satisfactory capacity utilisation, since the airline would demand eight million Francs (244,000€) for six days of service with two return journeys per day.[56] This connection seemed not to have existed long, since a *Vers l'Europe* article from 1952 asked, "a quand notre escale aérienne", when *Air France* created a connection from Paris to Luxembourg in order to 'support the European integration'.[57] Despite the obvious need for a flight connection as evidenced by the efforts of the CoE, economic concerns from the airlines were a factor. In later years, economic concerns did not always take precedence over the maintenance of routes which will be discussed later in this chapter.

Early efforts to institute air links were not fruitful, for instance, a connection between Brussels, Luxembourg and Strasbourg, established from June 1953 by the Belgian *Sabena* airline, was already in deficit little more than a year later with daily losses of circa 30,000 Francs (650€).[58] It was discontinued despite the fact that the CoE had expressed strong interest in this connection to transport PACE delegates and members of the Common Assembly of the ECSC, as well.[59] The local actors saw the need for air links for the use of European institutions, but efforts seemed to have been inadequate because they seemed to be lacking the necessary resources or competences to institute them.

56 ACE, 1007/0765, *Note pour Paris, 20.7.1949.*

57 Comité Strasbourgeois pour le Mouvement Européen, "A quand notre escale aérienne?", in *Vers l'Europe*, 3:31, 1952, p. 8.

58 ACE, 1007/0765, *Note du 4.6.1953* and *Note du 7.10.1954.*

59 ACE, 1007/0765, *Note du 4.6.1953* and *Note du 7.10.1954.*

(ii) Commercial links 1957-1970

From 1957, judging by documents from the municipal archive of Strasbourg, Strasbourg finally gained continuous, albeit still not stable connections with the combined inaugurations of the new airport terminal and a link to Paris. From that date the local actors intensified their lobbying for commercial air routes. The CoE seemed to have pursued a less active role as compared to the early 1950s, restricting itself mainly to reports and communication with the local administrations, although the organisation was initially consulted by the city on their needs with the planning of connections in 1957.[60] As in the previous developmental phase, this had a minor impact, but was supported by the creation of specialised links for the European parliamentarians from the early 1960s.

This study will only concentrate on commercial connections that local actors deemed useful for European parliamentarians. These included Paris, Frankfurt and Brussels.[61] Additionally, links to, for instance, Lyon, Nice-Alger, and Lydd (Southern England) existed.[62] The route Paris-Strasbourg was the only long lasting, albeit frequently discontinued and re-established travel possibility parliamentarians could use. It was operated by *Air Inter*, France's domestic airline. It had been founded in 1954 and offered links between many French cities from 1957 onwards, although 86 percent of its routes were connections to Paris.[63] During the 1960s, sources from the municipal archive of Strasbourg suggest that lobbying airlines for connections was a parallel activity to self-organised charter flights. It ceased to be a forefront concern during the 1970s, since financial assistance of the state made it possible to introduce purposive, but commercial links. They were operated by *Air France*. Commonly, small aircrafts were used which had between 10 and 40 seats on average.[64]

The link to Paris was one of the more prominent examples, local actors cited when presenting available air routes of use to parliamentarians. For instance, a note from 1965 claimed that with a renewed institution of

60 AS, 54 W 144, *Note du 28.6.1957.*

61 AS, 68 MW 88, *Trafic commercial 1965.*

62 AS, 68 MW 88, *Trafic commercial 1965.*

63 Thibault, Philippe-Michel, *Air Inter la révolution intérieure*, Paris, Le cherche midi, 2005, p. 271 and François-Poncet, Jean, and Jean-François Le Grand. "Sénat session ordinaire de 2000-2001, Rapport d'Information No. 327 fait au nom de la commission des Affaires économiques et du Plan par le groupe de travail sur l'avenir des dessertes aériennes régionales, ainsi que sur le fonctionnement du fonds d'investissement des aéroports et du transport aérien (FIATA)." <http://senat.fr/rap/r00-327/r00-3271.pdf> (accessed 31.07.2014).

64 E.g. ABR, 1130 W 936/1-16, *Minutes of Bipartite Committee sessions 1964-1979.*

this connection, the route network would again be satisfactory.[65] By own admission, they did not know whether it was used by European delegates at all.[66] A likely reason they promoted this route despite this uncertainty could be that flying to Paris was one of the few stable connections. Local actors made an effort to promote this route, for instance by asking the *Chambre de Commerce* to organise publicity, since many inhabitants would ignore its existence.[67] Furthermore, the city advertised this possibility intensively to delegates, hoping to cut charter expenses by parliamentarians deciding to travel via Paris with the commercial link rather than Frankfurt via an extraordinary connection paid for by the local administrations.[68]

This circumstance could be due to the centralised system in France that Paris was the natural point of referral. *Air France*, although not responsible for domestic links, which were the realm of *Air Inter*, participated in the coverage of the deficit by paying half of it during the winter of 1961 and 1962.[69] The official reasoning was that the link would hold an international importance due to the *caractère européen* of Strasbourg.[70]

In practice, local actors gave regular subsidiaries. For example, in 1966, 50 percent of the incurred annual deficit of the airline was paid by the city and *Département* with two fifths each and the *Chambre de Commerce* with one fifth of that sum.[71] From circa 1963 to 1968, the French state covered 47.5 percent and the airline 2.5 percent of the loss.[72] This action can only partly be ascribed to the desire of local actors to keep this connection. *Air Inter* received subsidiaries from the state and all *collectivités locales* of the cities it connected.[73]

Despite these costs, local actors were keen to keep the air link to Paris running. It gives evidence for the fact that they saw it as important that Strasbourg was in possession of good transport infrastructure in order

65 AS, 209 MW 52, *Extrait de la note du 5.2.1965*, p. 2.

66 AS, 209 MW 52, *Note pour le Secrétaire-Général Adjoint, 20.5.1965.*

67 AS, 236 MW 27/5, *Note pour A. Heitz, 27.3.1963.*

68 AS, 236 MW 27/6, *Note pour M. le Maire, 14.1.1963.*

69 AS, 236 MW 27/6, *Air Inter* and 59 MW 110, *Lettre du Ministre des Travaux Publiques à Pflimlin, 9.10.1961.*

70 AS, 236 MW 27/6, *Air Inter* and 59 MW 110, *Lettre du Ministre des Travaux Publiques à Pflimlin, 9.10.1961.*

71 AS, 68 MW 98, *Décompte provisoire 1966.*

72 AS, 68 MW 98, *Décompte provisoire 1966.*

73 Fainsilber, Denis. "L'adieu à Air Inter. Une saga qui résume trente-sept ans d'histoire de France, No. 17367." <http://www.lesechos.fr/imprimer.php?chemin=/archives/1997/LesEchos/17367-129-ECH.xml> (accessed 09.12.2013, article no longer available online).

to remain in the competition with other seat cities. The municipality reacted accordingly whenever *Air Inter* planned to reduce the running frequency or discontinue it in order to retain favourable conditions for the parliamentarians' travel. For example, in July 1964, the President of the *Chambre de Commerce*, René Uhrich, told Pflimlin that the airline had informed him that they would offer less flights during the winter, since previous years had shown a low number of passengers.[74] In a note, reporting on a meeting between Radius and Pflimlin on the issue, the necessity to continue this link was emphasised, while stressing that it was essential not to discontinue the morning flight to Strasbourg and the evening flight to Paris for the delegates.[75] Next to the *Chambre de Commerce*, Pflimlin charged A. Heitz to intervene with *Air Inter* and offered to talk to them personally should A. Heitz consider it opportune.[76]

Other regular connections of the 1960s showed that low usage and financial losses were factors local actors had to combat while attempting to create flight routes for the use of European parliamentarians. Most other commercial routes were short-lived, as the link to Frankfurt, inaugurated on 8 May 1964. It had already been suspended during the following winter and after a resumption of service in March 1965 definitely terminated from October due to inadequate usage with only 412 passengers in 1964 and 769 in 1965.[77] As replacement, a connection to Brussels was established from April 1966, which was seen as essential to connect the European institutions by the city administration.[78] For this thrice weekly connection, the *collectivités locales* paid *Air France* 70,000 Francs (90,000€) a month (two fifths city/department each, one fifth *CCI*).[79] This also shows a willingness of local authorities to support endeavours financially to establish transport routes.

The second lobby activity, asking for stopovers on existing lines, was another strategy to introduce air links for the travel of European parliamentarians. Comparatively, it was a smaller measure to improve Strasbourg's air route network and likely was an effort to avoid economic concerns of airlines regarding new routes. In a note from 1965, the municipal administration drafted several possibilities to improve Strasbourg's air links with an evaluation of probability regarding the links Brussels-Rome to create

74 AS, 236 MW 27/6, *Lettre d'Uhrich à Pflimlin, 24.7.1964.*

75 AS, 236 MW 27/6, *Note du 7.8.1964.*

76 AS, 236 MW 27/6, *Note pour A. Heitz, 22.10.1964.*

77 AS, 68 MW 88, *Trafic 1965*, p. 2 and 236 MW 27/2, *Lettre de Roos à Pflimlin, 12.10.1964.*

78 AS, 68 MW 88, *Trafic 1965*, p. 2.

79 AS, 69 MW 24, *Note pour le Secrétariat Général, 18.2.1965*, p. 1.

a stopover, Frankfurt-Rome to include a detour, Brussels-Luxembourg to prolong the connection, and Strasbourg-Nice to use the possibility of a connecting flight Nice-Rome.[80]

The first option was prioritised, while the second would include longer travel time and the third would be useful for delegates, but the airline demanded a minimum amount of passengers. The last suggestion was deemed as the least attractive solution.[81] Such endeavours sometimes also failed due to practical hurdles, for instance in 1967, Pflimlin reported that during his repeated talks with *Lux Air*, the airline had finally approved of the suggestion to prolong their Brussels-Luxembourg link to Strasbourg, but that the *Aviation Civile* had not given its accord yet, which was necessary, since a foreign company was involved.[82] This was another example that the local government of Strasbourg had to rely on its own means in this matter and that state assistance, if it was present, was not substantial.

Municipal actors seemed to have a sense of entitlement regarding receiving corporate assistance for their position as European institution host. "M. le Président Pflimlin estime que la politique d'Air France devrait s'aligner sur celle du Gouvernement français qui a pris position pour le maintien de Strasbourg comme siège des institutions européennes."[83] It is interesting that Pflimlin used such a formulation, since the French state regulated the route selection of the airline until 1983.[84] This issue will be returned to during the analysis of the special air links of the 1970s. The citation provides evidence of the local actors' desire to implement strategically a route network to assist them in remaining institution seat.

(iii) Special air links

The second approach of the *collectivités locales* consisted of self-organised, purposive connections. This activity can be further separated into two phases – locally organised charter flights during the beginning and end of each session period in the 1960s, and purposive, but commercial connections during the 1970s. For the latter, the French state gave

80 AS, 69 MW 24, *Note pour le Secrétariat Général, 18.2.1965*, p. 3.

81 AS, 69 MW 24, *Note pour le Secrétariat Général, 18.2.1965*, p. 3.

82 AS, 236 MW 24/1, *Minutes of the Bipartite Committee session, 1967*, p. 2.

83 ABR, 1130 W 936/11, *Minutes of the Bipartite Committee session, 29.1.1971*, p. 3.

84 Golder, Matthew, "The Changing Nature of French Dirigisme. A Case Study of Air France", Thesis submitted in partial fulfillment of the requirements for the degree of M. Phil. in European Politics and Society in the Faculty of Social Studies at the University of Oxford, 1997, p. 25. No page numbers were given, page number is from the electronic document.

considerable (financial) assistance. During the 1960s, the charter flights connected Zurich and until 1969 Frankfurt to Strasbourg as a convenient possibility for connection flights from the closest air hubs. Flight times amounted to one hour to the Swiss and one hour and 15 minutes to the German city.[85] Different sources from the municipal archive of Strasbourg indicate that administration actors regarded the connection to Zurich as important to provide Italian delegates with an easy way to travel to Strasbourg, while especially the Nordic PACE delegates arrived via Frankfurt.

With the supplement of lacking air links from the major airports in the area, the local authorities aimed to make Strasbourg easily and comfortably accessible during session periods. The institution of these special services addressed competing seat cities Luxembourg and Brussels. Both national capitals possessed a superior long-distance travel infrastructure than Strasbourg. The French city had one reasonably continuous commercial link the city administration deemed to be of relevance to travelling European parliamentarians during the early 1960s, Paris-Strasbourg; while connections to central airports abroad were slower to be established.

In contrast, Luxembourg had links to all ECSC member states, as well as London and New York with three to five weekly departures in 1957, as the book showed, the *Conseil Luxembourgeois du Mouvement Européen* had edited to present and support the city's seat candidature.[86] A comparative level was only reached by Entzheim airport approximately 20 years later. Offering special flights during session periods included a method to mitigate the lack of extensive connections. Through such activities, Strasbourg's position in the struggle to consolidate its position could be improved. Another contributing factor might have been the economy, because newly created commercial routes, such as the *Air France* service Strasbourg-Frankfurt from 1964 to 1965, were short-lived due to inadequate usage.

(iv) Charter air links of the 1960s

In the following, the three charter companies the city and *Département* successively charged with the execution of the special air links to Frankfurt and Zurich will be discussed. This will include the modalities of the services for the parliamentarians. The three subsequent charters operated

---

85 AS, 236 MW 27/2, *Lettre d'A. Heitz à Südflug, 22.4.1964.*

86 Bodson, Victor, "Le Luxembourg et les Communications internationales", in Conseil Luxembourgeois du Mouvement Européen (ed.), *Luxembourg, Ville Européenne*, Luxembourg, Imprimerie Hermann, 1957, p. 42.

the connections: from 1960-1962 *Deutsche Taxiflug*, 1962-1964 *Südflug*, and 1965 to 1973 *Balair*. *Deutsche Taxiflug* was founded in 1959 and based in Mannheim in Southwest Germany.[87] It facilitated regular short distance connections such as Hamburg to various North Sea islands or any form of charter travel.[88] In December 1962, it fused with the *Deutsche Nah-Luftverkehr*,[89] a similar company, to *Air Lloyd Deutsche Nah-Luftverkehrs AG*.[90] *Südflug* (Stuttgart) was another German charter company founded in the 1950s. In December 1967, it was bought by *Lufthansa* due to financial troubles.[91] *Balair*, based in Basel, was a charter and tour operator founded in 1957, where both *Swissair* and the Swiss government held shares.[92]

The charter service was commonly executed by relatively small aircraft with fewer than ten seats, although *Südflug* also possessed a plane with room for 14 passengers.[93] They were generally not designed to fly during severe weather, which led to cars being used as replacements. For instance, in October 1969, the service could not depart to Zurich because of a storm, when passengers took either the train or a car to Basel and were reimbursed their ticket costs.[94] From September 1960 to April 1961, both charter links had even been entirely suspended citing bad atmospheric conditions and replaced by cars.[95] This will be discussed further during the sub-chapter on the chauffeuring service. The following winter, this measure was not necessary anymore, since *Deutsche Taxiflug* had acquired a twin motor aircraft in the meantime, which had two, instead of one pilot, and was capable of flying during the night, as well as without visibility due to its radio equipment.[96] The two subsequent charter companies

87 Kurzok, Jan. "Luftsprünge nach Nordseeinseln", in *Die ZEIT*, 14, 1966, <http://www.zeit.de/1966/14luftspruenge-nach-nordseeinseln/komplettansicht> (accessed 28 Nov 2013).

88 "Im Lufttaxi zum Baden", in *Die ZEIT*, 26, 1961, <http://www.zeit.de/1961/26/im-lufttaxi-zum-baden/komplettansicht> (accessed 28 Nov 2013).

89 This company approached the city administration in 1960/1961 with offers to execute regular flights for European parliamentarians without resulting in any concrete plans (AS, 236 MW 27/8, *Pourparlers avec le Deutsche Nah-Luftverkehr*).

90 AS, 236 MW 27/10, *Lettre du Taxiflug à la Mairie, 25.1.1962.*

91 "Südflug unter dem Kranich", *Die ZEIT*, 51, 1967, <http://www.zeit.de/1967/51/suedflug-unter-dem-kranich/komplettansicht> (accessed 28 Nov 2013) and "Dünne Luft", *Der Spiegel*, 35, 1967, <http://www.spiegel.de/spiegel/print/d-46211731.html> (accessed 29 Nov 2013).

92 "Balair Ltd. 1967." <http://www.flightglobal.com/pdfarchive/view/1967/1967-0574.html> (accessed 29.11.2013), p. 560.

93 AS, 236 MW 27/9, *Lettre du Südflug au Maire, 5.3.1962.*

94 AS, 236 MW 32/3, *Note du 10.10.1969.*

95 AS, 236 MW 27/3, *Note pour Pflimlin, 2.11.1961*, p. 1.

96 AS, 236 MW 27/3, *Note pour Pflimlin, 2.11.1961*, p. 1.

possessed similar planes. The information booklet on flight schedules or its accompanying letter contained instructions on how to book a ticket, costing circa 100 Francs (100-130€) for a charter flight, which could be purchased via any airline for the outward, and from the tourism office information desk in the CoE building for the return journey.[97]

As Ridoux stated in a note in 1964, the local administrations deemed the existence of the charter flights essential in order to offer delegates a convenient manner of reaching the city.[98] The aim of the city and department was to provide easy access to Strasbourg to maintain their position as provisional seat. Charter air links to Frankfurt and Zurich operated from 1960 and were initially assured by *Deutsche Taxiflug*.[99] Its flights in many cases only had one or two passengers each, for instance eight passengers on five connections during the April 1961 PACE session period, or five sold tickets for four air links during the October 1961 EP meeting.[100] In the available sources, the EP and PACE sessions in June/July 1960 saw the biggest utilisation of the two routes with a total of 19 passengers on nine flights.[101] Nevertheless, the local authorities deemed the existence of this traffic infrastructure important, since it seemed to mitigate an obvious lack. They claimed that their initiative had gained the parliamentarians' appreciation, which some thank-you letters mirrored.[102] It seemed as if the existence of these links was more important than their cost-effectiveness. They showed that the city was willing to improve their transport infrastructure for parliamentarians.

There seemed to have been a concern regarding financial matters, even if the mere existence still seemed to be higher valued than any economic concerns. The impending fusion of *Deutsche Taxiflug* and *Deutsche Nah-Luftverkehr* to *Air Lloyd* caused Ridoux and A. Heitz, as well as others involved in dealing with the charter flights, to solicit offers from other companies to choose the best possibility.[103] Next to *Air Lloyd*, Ridoux also

---

97 E.g. AS, 236 MW 27/2, *Horaires, 6/1964*.

98 AS, 236 MW 32/2, *Note pour Pflimlin, 25.6.1964*, p. 2.

99 The company offered A. Heitz in October 1961 to execute a regular connection to Frankfurt, with commencement in May 1962. This remained a plan since the *Aviation Civile* stipulated that such a contract with a foreign company had to include special legal modalities which the local administrations were not able to assure (cf. AS, 236 MW 27/9, *Lettre du Taxiflug à A. Heitz, 8.10.1961* and *Note du 13.12.1960* and *Note du 19.5.1961*).

100 AS, 236 MW 2/3, *Taxiflug invoice 1699* and 236 MW 2/7, *Taxiflug invoice 2144P.*

101 AS, 236 MW 2/2, *Taxiflug invoice 1151.*

102 AS, 236 MW 27/9, *Note pour la Division II, 13.10.1960* and 236 MW 27/7, *Lettre de Hallstein au Maire, 3.10.1961.*

103 AS, 236 MW 27/10, *Note pour A. Heitz, 12.2.1962.*

suggested *Südflug* and the *Groupement aérien du Haut-Rhin, Colmar* as possible candidates to operate air links to Zurich and Frankfurt in a note to Pflimlin in April 1962.[104] Even though the existing contract would not have changed with the new *Air Lloyd*, the local authorities decided to switch to *Südflug*, since it would be most similar to commercial airlines and also possess more comfortable aircraft.[105] Although this company was slightly more expensive, the city administration hoped that its features would translate into a higher utilisation to mitigate the extra expenses.[106]

The city administration's institution of such specialised air links carried connotations of prestige, as Strasbourg's actors would be seen as implementing something just for the parliamentarians. Next to the practical reason of providing delegates with ready access, the organisation of special flights in comfortable conditions aimed at gathering prestige. Another instance mirroring this included an event from the March 1964 EP session period, when a note to the mayor criticised *Südflug* for using a small plane which could only transport four to five passengers for a service where five MEPs had purchased a ticket. Although the report stated, there had not been any complaints, the author characterised it as unnecessarily uncomfortable.[107] Similarly to the predecessor company, *Südflug's* flights averagely had one or two passengers per journey, with few diversions from that pattern. One of these included the May 1963 EP session, when 13 passengers were distributed on four flights.[108] The norm was two connections with a total of three passengers during the June 1963 EP session period or two air links with four passengers during the September 1964 meeting of the assembly.[109]

The switch from *Südflug* to *Balair* in 1964 for liaisons to Zurich and Frankfurt, effective from 1965, was due to practical and financial reasons. The German company had sold its bigger, 14-seat plane and was only left with a seven-seat aircraft. In a note to Pflimlin, Ridoux regarded this as a problem, because *Südflug* would not be able to honour the contract should more parliamentarians than the plane had capacity book a ticket. After contacting *Balair*, he determined that the company was slightly cheaper and would not charge cancellation fees up to 24 hours before the scheduled flight as opposed to *Südflug*. Since the city regularly had to annul

---

104 AS, 236 MW 27/10, *Note pour Pflimlin, 14.4.1962.*

105 AS, 236 MW 27/10, *Lettre de l'Air Lloyd à la Mairie, 5.3.1962; Note pour M. le Maire, 18.4.1962.*

106 AS, 236 MW 27/10, *Note pour M. le Maire, 18.4.1962.*

107 AS, 236 MW 27/2, *Note pour Pflimlin, 10.4.1964.*

108 AS, 236 MW 3/6, *Südflug invoice 30.5.1963.*

109 AS, 236 MW 3/8, *Südflug invoice 29.6.1963* and 236 MW 27/2, *Südflug invoice 8.10.1964.*

air links because no seat was booked, Ridoux saw this as an advantage.[110] The financial concern contributed to the switch in flight operators, as Ridoux stated that from January to June 1964, 10,468 Francs (14,000€) had been spent on cancellations alone.[111] A. Heitz feared in a note to Ridoux that *Südflug* selling the bigger plane could mean that European parliamentarians regarded the offered connections as unattractive.[112] This and the resulting danger of *Südflug* not being able to fulfil their part of the contract were cited by the administration in the termination letter as well.[113] As mentioned before, the presence of these air links seemed more important as a signal that the city tried to improve its facilities to the advantage of the European institutions they hosted.

According to the lists, the city administration kept on the number of parliamentarians using the charter connections for each session period, the usage of *Balair* flights remained comparable to the previous years. Nevertheless, occasions when it was booked in larger numbers, occurred more frequently than with the other two companies. For instance, for the May 1965 EP session, a total of 28 tickets were sold for six flights.[114] It is unclear from dossiers from the municipal archive of Strasbourg, how long the local authorities used the company's services. A note from 1972 stated that *Swissair's* takeover of *Balair* would not affect the contract.[115] It was likely discontinued soon after, since the service to Zurich had been stopped in 1972 due to a new link to Milan; the Bipartite Committee also stated in 1974 that no one had used it in 1973.[116]

Similar to hosting activities, the charter flights were offered in anticipation of demand from the side of European parliamentarians and strongly curtailed to their wishes by the local administrations. For example, the Bipartite Committee, among others, planned to terminate the *Balair* link to Frankfurt in 1969, since it would hardly be used due to cars being preferred on this leg. In June, it was decided to stop this route, which could be done without inconvenience, as nobody had used it in May.[117] It had only been maintained during that month due to "psychological reasons" – namely

---

110 AS, 236 MW 32/2, *Note pour Pflimlin, 25.6.1964*, pp. 2-3.

111 AS, 236 MW 32/2, *Note pour Pflimlin, 25.6.1964*, p. 4.

112 AS, 236 MW 27/2, *Note pour Ridoux, 28.4.1964*, p. 2.

113 AS, 236 MW 32/2, *Lettre du Préfet à Südflug, 9.12.1964.*

114 AS, 236 MW 5/3, *Balair invoice 14.6.1965.*

115 AS, 236 MW 32/2, *Note du 13.3.1972.*

116 ABR, 1130 W 936/10, *Balair* and 1130 W 936/8, *Minutes of the Bipartite Committee session, 1974*, p. 6.

117 AS, 236 MW 32/3, *Note pour M. le Maire, 9.6.1969.*

the 20th anniversary of the CoE.[118] Administration actors curtailed their actions to infrastructure demands of European parliamentarians in order to remain easily accessible in compliance with their wishes and gain their appreciation through this. Nevertheless, they were conscious of not sending a wrong signal, like with discontinuing a measure during a special occasion, when special scrutiny from the outside might be possible.

By looking at passenger numbers of the Strasbourg-Zurich connection, which was deemed as important by city actors, it was more frequented, for instance with the high number of nine arriving and ten departing passengers in May 1969.[119] Objectively, the organisational effort and running costs were undertaken for a relatively small number of parliamentarians. According to the invoices in the city archive, expenses for one EP or PACE session averaged between 2,500 and 4,000 Francs (3,500-5,600€).[120] Passenger numbers per session commonly did not reach double digits and even the rare instances of high usages hovered around 20.[121] With approximately 11 meeting periods per year (both EP and PACE), this was a significant special local/departmental subsidiary of transport for parliamentarians. The extraordinary charter links should be seen as a principally psychological feature to create the image of a city administration that improved access options. This provision of special air links also included a strong notion of pleasing parliamentarians. A strategy to consolidate Strasbourg's connection could have been that local actors wanted to be seen as making an effort to mitigate infrastructural problems in order to improve their position.

(v) Special commercial air links of the 1970s

The second phase of purposive connections was characterised by a new development; a strong involvement of the French state, primarily in financial, but also organisational matters. This served as an impetus for an accelerated modernisation of air links. Prior to the 1970s, the improvement of air routes had only been pursued by the local level, assisted by the *Département*. A document detailing the progress of these actions from the state's point of view archived in Pflimlin's private collection in the municipal archive of Strasbourg leaves the impression that before 1972, when the first two connections of this kind to Brussels-London and Milan

118 AS, 236 MW 32/3, *Note pour M. le Maire, 9.6.1969.*

119 AS, 236 MW 32/3, *Note pour M. le Maire, 9.6.1969.*

120 E.g. AS, 236 MW 2/2 and 236 MW 2/7 and 236 MW 27/2 and 236 MW 27/10 and 236 MW 5/3 and 236 MW 5/7 *Invoices of charter flight companies.*

121 The bulk of invoices is archived in AS, 236 MW 1 – 236 MW 10.

were inaugurated, Strasbourg had not been in possession of any air links of note. "Pour consolider la position de Strasbourg en tant que siège et lieu de réunion d'institutions européennes le gouvernement français a créé un certain nombre de liaisons aériennes reliant Strasbourg aux capitales et autres villes importantes de pays de la Communauté Européenne."[122] In 1974, the Brussels-London link was split into two separate connections and Rome was added as a destination, while Amsterdam (1976), Cologne (1977) and its replacement Frankfurt (1979) completed the route network of regular, purposive connections.[123] The entirety of it was referred to as *lignes européennes*. Relatively small aircraft types were used for these connections, for instance, with a capacity of 12 passengers.[124]

This reasoning was also propagated by *Air France* which operated the new connections.[125] The airline was not a separate actor, but was an extension of state influence. Until 1983, the French state mandated which routes the company could offer.[126] As mirrored by the quote, this type of air links constituted an increase led by actors outside of Strasbourg of the continuous effort of local actors to improve the city's accessibility and to update infrastructure to suit the organisation's needs. The intervention of the French state was not a singular case. It also mandated *Air France* to institute certain air links due to public interest or to improve France's prestige, such as connections to the (former) colonies.[127] It can be hypothesised that the national government had similar motives of increasing the reputation of the country by providing a route network from European centres to the host city of the EP, especially when competition between the three provisional EC seats began to intensify during the 1970s.

As with the charter airlines, financial losses occurred. It is another evidence for the fact that these connections were primarily regarded as improving the reputation of Strasbourg as a good seat choice. Through it, it could be shown that the city was in the possession of the necessary infrastructure to house European institutions. The financial loss of these connections, was in its majority covered by the state, while the rest was

---

[122] AS, 9 Z 109, *Desserte aérienne*, p. 1.

[123] ABR, 1130 W 936/2-9, *Minutes of the Bipartite Committee session, 1972-1979.*

[124] ABR, 1130 W 936/1-16, *Minutes of Bipartite Committee sessions.*

[125] ACE, 1007/0765, *Lettre du Président de l'Air France au Secrétaire-Général du Conseil de l'Europe, 7.4.1972.*

[126] Golder, Matthew, "The Changing Nature of French Dirigisme. A Case Study of Air France", Thesis submitted in partial fulfillment of the requirements for the degree of M. Phil in European Politics and Society in the Faculty of Social Studies at the University of Oxford, 1997, p. 25.

[127] *Ibid.*, p. 26.

paid for by the *collectivités locales*. From 1972-1977, the distribution was 75 and 25 percent (city/department $^{2}/_{5}$ each, *CCI* $^{1}/_{5}$), and from 1977, 66 and 34 percent respectively.[128] The global deficit amounted to 7.8 million Francs (4.4 million €) in 1977 and 6.5 million Francs (4 million €) in 1976, for example.[129]

The *Délégation interministérielle à l'aménagement du territoire et à l'attractivité régionale* (*DATAR*) covered the state portion.[130] Created in February 1963, it was a service directly reporting to the Prime Minister to prepare, instigate and coordinate politics of regional development mandated by the state.[131] Its central tasks included the development and improvement of infrastructure and economy within regions, as well as the coordination of local regional development policies instituted by the prefects.[132] Interestingly, the part of the deficit, the city was responsible for, was not covered by the special budget *institutions européennes*, but by the regular one, under the *chapitre interventions économiques*.[133] According to the annual reports in the Bipartite Committee meetings, the coefficient of the air links lay between 60 and 80 percent in the late 1970s, although just introduced links commonly started below 50 percent capacity utilisation, going even as low as 18 percent for the connection to Cologne in 1977.[134]

Local actors still were the main force in creating and maintaining these air links as a strategy to prove their suitability as host. The Bipartite Committee was the main actor in the drafting and optimising of these links, additionally Pflimlin filled the role of the chief negotiator with *Air France*, *DATAR* or the Ministry of Transport. For instance, in the committee minutes from June 1979, just after the direct EP election, he proposed to talk to the airline on the subjects of bigger planes for the Rome connection.[135] The creation of new routes by instituting stopovers on links between Copenhagen-Madrid or Amsterdam-Rome was another concern.[136] Moreover, the Mayor communicated with the Secretary-

---

128 ABR, 1130 W 936/4, *Activités de l'année 1977*, p. 4.

129 ABR, 1130 W 936/4, *Minutes of the Bipartite Committee session, 1978*, p. 3.

130 Until 1975, money came from its fund *FIAT*, *Fonds d'intervention pour l'aménagement du territoire* (ABR, 1130 W 936/6, *Activités de l'année 1975*, p. 3).

131 "Qui sommes-nous?" <http://www.datar.gouv.fr/qui-sommes-nous> (accessed 26.11.2013).

132 "Les missions de la Datar." <http://www.datar.gouv.fr/les-missions-de-la-datar> (accessed 26.11.2013).

133 AS, 752 W 90, *Minutes of the Bipartite Committee session, 20.12.1979*, p. 5.

134 ABR, 1130 W 936/4, *Activités de l'année 1977*, p. 4.

135 ABR, 1130 W 936/2, *Minutes of the Bipartite Committee session, 11.6.1979*, p. 3.

136 ABR, 1130 W 936/2, *Minutes of the Bipartite Committee session, 11.6.1979*, p. 3.

General of the CoE on the air links. For example Pflimlin sent him the timetables of the newly established links to Brussels-London and Milan in 1972, asking whether he found the proposed departures inconvenient as well.[137]

Apart from trying to anticipate from which cities parliamentarians would most need connections, the Bipartite Committee implemented measures to make the journey as comfortable as possible, which manifested itself in repeated aircraft type changes. As further incentive for parliamentarians, Pflimlin envisioned the aircraft type switch to improve travel conditions which *Air France* occasionally, as in 1977, did not approve of.[138] This measure was for example used in 1974, when the committee hoped to inspire a higher usage for the Milan link, since the coefficient for 1973 had been 18.5 percent.[139] Similarly, in June 1979, just before the first session of a directly elected EP, the aircraft type of most routes was changed to a newer and bigger type.[140] These actions were only partly in anticipation of demands, since a CoE internal report on the initial connections in 1972 remarked, "On pourrait imaginer, surtout si un avion de plus grande classe était mis en service, que celui-ci arbore le drapeau de l'Europe, et que la liaison porte un nom évoquant sa vocation européenne."[141] Thus, there also seemed to have been a certain expectation of symbols and comfort on the side of European institutions which could be one of the reasons why local actors pursued these kind of strategies to gain their appreciation.

Based on the objective of providing delegates with attractive air links, Pflimlin remarked in 1977 that new interventions needed to be made, since *Air France* just seemed to be oriented towards profitability.[142] In the quest for improving connections for Italian MEPs in 1971, which the city deemed essential, the Bipartite Committee criticised the airline's refusal to allow plans involving a foreign company, since *Air France* did not want it using French airports.[143] Although the French state and the air carrier became more involved in the improvement of infrastructure for the intention of European parliamentarians, the city administration could not rely on unconditional support, seeing the refusal to allow foreign companies to use Entzheim airport, which was only changed in

137 ACE, 1007/0765, *Lettre du Maire au Secrétaire-Général du Conseil de l'Europe, 12.1.1972.*

138 ABR, 1130 W 936/5, *Minutes of the Bipartite Committee session, 1977*, p. 3.

139 ABR, 1130 W 936/8, *Activités de l'année 1973*, p. 3.

140 AS, 752 W 90, *Liaisons aériennes, 12/1979.*

141 ACE, 1007/0765, *Liaison avec Londres.*

142 ABR, 1130 W 936/5, *Minutes of the Bipartite Committee session, 1977*, p. 3.

143 ABR, 1130 W 936/11, *Minutes of the Bipartite Committee session, 1971*, p. 3.

1980. Additionally, the city and department assured a comfortable travel experience in other ways. For example, on 9 October 1978 they financed an additional link from London, since not all British delegates were able to purchase a ticket for the regular connection due to overbooking.[144] Thus, the element of independent local agency remained.

(vi) Summary

All in all, the improvement of air traffic infrastructure was a constant area of concern during the entire period of study which was mainly attempted through self-organised, purposive links. The 1950s were characterised by a distinct lack of airport infrastructure and a concentration of local actors on hosting measures. The improvement of infrastructure strongly increased during the 1960s, when the local level created goal oriented connections to air hubs nearby, via which a majority of parliamentarians were likely to travel. This development was intensified during the 1970s, when financial aid by the state contributed to the establishment of commercial, but useful routes. Nevertheless, Bipartite Committee minutes allow for the assumption that this organisation was chiefly responsible for the drafting and running of connections.

The fact that these special, but commercial connections were also referred to as *lignes de prestige*,[145] infers a considerable amount of importance of them as a strategy to remain institution seat. This objective manifested itself mainly in employing comfortable planes and attempts to organise links of use to parliamentarians, even though they were not profitable. A prominent example includes the connection to Frankfurt in different forms, via which many delegates, especially Nordics, travelled. The charter connection of the 1960s often carried fewer passengers than the number of parliamentarians who chose to be chauffeured to the same airport by cars. The commercial link from 1964, which the local authorities had lobbied for on top of the charter connection had been terminated due to low usage only a year later, and the *Balair* link ceased its operation due to the same reason in 1969. After negotiations, Frankfurt had been included in the special connections in 1979, but had been terminated shortly after, only to be re-established in 1981 with other special connections during session periods.

With such measures, actors attempted to incorporate the improvement of air traffic infrastructure as a strategy to remain institution seat in the face of the competition. A psychological factor could also have played a role by assuring parliamentarians that the city and departmental administrations

144 ABR, 1130 W 936/3, *Activités de l'année 1978*, p. 5.

145 ABR, 1130 W 936/10, *Activités de l'année 1972*, p. 3.

worked to improve access options to welcome them to Strasbourg. After the first direct EP election, this strategy became especially apparent, since it was employed to mitigate possible repercussions when the assembly seemed to favour a move to Brussels which possessed a superior transport infrastructure.[146] This time, it was not the local level acting, but the French state, which decided to cover the entire costs of establishing special flights that were operated by *Air France* during session periods to European centres such as London, Dublin and Copenhagen.[147] This involvement had been motivated by a concrete demand, as well. The president of the republic wrote to Pflimlin that several MEPs had voiced the desire for improved air links to Strasbourg.[148] Until the 1990s, these special links, similar to the city's charter planes in the 1960s, had been extended to Athens or Lisbon, among others.[149] In conclusion, most air links from Strasbourg to other European cities were not economically viable on their on which necessitated a high amount of subsidiaries. It was necessary to give financial assistance, because the suitability of the city as seat of European institution was among others dependent on parliamentarians being able to travel there easily. Thus, it was an investment to remain in the competition of the seat cities and another set of strategies, next to the efforts to raise the symbolic value of Strasbourg through hosting arrangements and promotion of the city.

(b) Chauffeuring service

The chauffeuring service of the *Mairie* and *Préfecture* served as a shuttle for European parliamentarians to bigger airports near Strasbourg from the 1960s onwards as a supplement to the air links. It was supposed to send the message that local actors tried to do their utmost to provide easy access to Strasbourg. "En outre, pour contrebalancer les critiques faites à la desserte aérienne de Strasbourg, les deux collectivités se sont engagées à transporter gratuitement par la route les parlementaires arrivant ou partant des aérodromes de Frankfort, Zurich, Bâle etc."[150] Hence, this offer constituted another measure of local actors to improve transport conditions to be able to strengthen their position as institution host.

The city administration kept a list for each session period, where they detailed which delegate made use of the service to which destination

146 AS, 9 Z 109, *Desserte aérienne*, p. 1.

147 AS, 9 Z 109, *Desserte aérienne*, p. 2.

148 AS, 752 W 115, *Lettre du Président de la République à Pflimlin, 25.3.1981.*

149 AS, 114 W 223, *Horaire.*

150 ABR, 1130 W 936/5, *Compte "Europe"*, p. 1.

and whether the *Mairie* or *Préfecture* provided the car. These lists also mentioned trips to Entzheim airport, but they are not included in this analysis, since they were in the realm of local transport. Numbers of passengers fluctuated from year to year, but a clear tendency for an increase from the 1960s to the 1970s was visible.[151] From 1974, well over 100 parliamentarians demanded this service of the local administrations per session period. It was mostly used by Turkish or Nordic delegates, especially Danes, since their preferred airport was Frankfurt.[152] The Bipartite Committee determined that the EC enlargement of 1973 had certainly played a role, since the demand would have increased with Denmark sitting in both major European assemblies.[153] From the city administration lists, Italian parliamentarians primarily used this offer to Zurich or Basel.

The Bipartite Committee activity summary of 1976 specified that the committee was not happy with the increased demand and that they attempted to counter this trend with the improvement of air links which, however, did not have the desired effect.[154] The reason administration actors gave constituted that the combined vehicle fleet of the *Préfecture* and *Mairie* proved to be too small to satisfy the demand and that taxis had to be ordered on account of the city to transport all delegates. The budget for the welcoming of European institutions for 1976 had to be increased, since a taxi from Strasbourg to Frankfurt cost around 450 Francs (300€).[155]

Destinations deviating from the common three cities included Stuttgart and Offenburg. Any limitations in terms of routes did not seem to exist. During the May 1963 PACE session, French substitute Michel de Grailly was chauffeured on a return trip to Bonn in a *Préfecture* car.[156] The above example was just noted in the overview lists, but such special requests were likely fulfilled without complaint as the following event supports. French MEP Roger Carcassonne wrote to Pflimlin in December 1961 explaining that it would be the easiest for him to fly into Mulhouse, but that it would involve a long wait until he could reach the train station of the town to continue his trip to Strasbourg. He wondered whether it was possible that a car could pick him up and drive him from the airport to the

151 ABR, 1130 W 936/2-16, *Minutes of the Bipartite Committee session, 1964-1979.*

152 ABR, 1130 W 936/5, *Activités de l'année 1976*, p. 4.

153 ABR, 1130 W 936/5, *Compte "Europe"*, p. 3.

154 ABR, 1130 W 936/5, *Activités de l'année 1976*, p. 4.

155 ABR, 1130 W 936/5, *Activités de l'année 1976*, p. 4.

156 AS, 236 MW 3/6, *Liaisons voitures, 5/1963.*

train station.[157] Ridoux arranged with the *Sous-préfecture de Mulhouse* to send a chauffeur without any questions asked.[158]

This common and universal practice of the city administration to fulfil demands of European parliamentarians without hesitation hinted at an asymmetrical relationship between the two groups where no request seemed to be too outlandish to be met. Keeping the European guests happy by acquiescing to such demands and anticipating them constituted a central strategy to consolidate indirectly the seat position through gaining the appreciation of European institution personnel.

Moreover, during the 1960s, the chauffeuring offer served as a replacement for charter flights that had to be suspended during severe weather. This mainly concerned the winter of 1961 and 1962, the only longer period of interruption, which otherwise only occurred on rare, single days. It again provides evidence for the strategy of the local authorities to offer parliamentarians an as well functioning and easily accessible transport system as possible to consolidate Strasbourg's position. Delegates had to order a car by letter, telegram or telephone prior to their departure and were then picked up at the information desk of the airline they had used.[159] This substitute service likewise included deviations from the common destinations Frankfurt and Zurich, for instance, at the end of the January 1962 PACE session, two Icelandic politicians were chauffeured to Stuttgart airport.[160] It is interesting to note that comparatively more European parliamentarians used the car replacements during the suspension than normally made use of the charter links. For instance, in January 1962, 19 vehicles transported 46 passengers to Frankfurt, Zurich, but also Stuttgart and Offenburg during the PACE session period.[161] In comparison, *Deutsche Taxiflug* had transported five delegates on four flights during the October 1961 EP session.[162]

It can be concluded that the chauffeuring service, which was intended as a supplement to air links, and in the case of winter 1961/1962 as a temporary replacement, proved to be more popular with parliamentarians than the flights local actors intended for them to primarily use. Beyond that, during the normal running of the air links, the figure of delegates using cars was often similar or higher than those flying to reach bigger

157 AS, 236 MW 27/3, *Lettre de Carcassonne à Pflimlin, 29.12.1962.*

158 AS, 236 MW 27/3, *Rapport pour le Maire, 19.1.1962.*

159 E.g. AS, 236 MW 27/3, *Macmillan, 1/1962.*

160 AS, 236 MW 27/3, *Liaisons routières, 1/1962.*

161 AS, 236 MW 27/3, *Liaisons, 1/1962.*

162 AS, 236 MW 2/6, *Invoice 2144P.*

air hubs. For instance, during the September 1963 PACE and EP session periods, the number of cars and passengers tripled the corresponding flight statistics.[163] All in all, the chauffeuring service constituted an important element in Strasbourg's long-distance transport improvements due to its apparent popularity, although it had originally just been devised as a supplement.

Section 1.15 Local transport

The improvement of inner-city transport conditions was especially intended for European parliamentarians to provide excellent transport facilities within the city for them. These efforts concentrated mainly on the public transport system assured by the *CTS* and the availability of taxis in the city and at the airport Entzheim. The goal of these measures was similar to the aim of long distance transport; being able to please the European institution personnel with convenient and comfortable solutions. Simultaneously, these actions were supposed to signal that Strasbourg was capable of housing IOs, which could be employed to improve the city's position against other candidates.

According to the sources in the municipal archive of Strasbourg, improvements to the taxi and public transport systems began with the second hosting phase in 1956, when the Liaison Committee implemented first steps. During the 1960s and 1970s this trend was continued and intensified by the various actors involved in dealing with the *CTS* and the taxi associations. In contrast to long-distance transport, local traffic was not subject to modernisation triggered by the presence of European institutions in the city on the scale observable with air links. While the trolleybus running by the CoE headquarters *Maison de l'Europe* was completely revamped during the 1950s, this action cannot necessarily be attributed to the presence of the organisation. A note stated that the equipment used dated from 1905/10 and that therefore an update was required.[164]

Similarly, a notorious shortage of taxis during sessions, about which European institutions repeatedly complained, could only partly be attributed to their presence. Sources in the municipal archive of Strasbourg suggest that, while the local administrations implemented improvements in response, these neither reached the same dimension as the improvement of air links, nor did the French assist state in any capacity. As a letter to the editor in the newspaper *Dernières Nouvelles*

163 AS, 236 MW 3/9, *Invoice Südflug, 26.9.1963* and *Liaisons voiture, 9/1963.*

164 AS, 61 MW 4, *CTS-Ligne 3/13.*

d'Alsace specified in 1970, the lack of taxis constituted a general problem which was only slightly exacerbated during meeting periods or any kind of events. Furthermore, an included statement of a taxi association did not see this as sufficient reason to increase the number of cabs.[165] Thus, practical issues also influenced the efforts of local actors to improve infrastructure for European parliamentarians.

(a) Public transport

The issue of public transport constituted one of the two central elements of local actors' strategies to remain attractive as institution seat by improving Strasbourg's local traffic infrastructure. The regular (trolley-) bus line 3/13 (later 3/13/23) ran from the central railway station to Robertsau via the *Maison de l'Europe*. It was the only regular connection to the CoE. As mentioned during the previous chapter, the 3/13 was decorated with French and European flags during sessions and belonged to the hosting regimen of the city.

Next to the city's medium-term goal of providing a satisfactory transport system, the improvements had the same underlying objective as hosting arrangements; signalling the competition that Strasbourg was coping well with the task of housing European institutions. In the sources this became especially apparent during the second ECSC seat application round from 1957-1959, when the rivalry between applicants was most intense. For example, in a note from October 1957 to the *Division II*, Mayor Charles Altorffer indignantly complained about the *CTS*'s refusal to move the zone boundary *Orangerie* to the bus stop closest to the CoE and concluded,

> La direction [*CTS*] devrait en effet, se rendre compte que son obstination place la Ville de Strasbourg dans une position des plus difficile à une époque où elle se voit souvent reprocher un manque de dynamisme à l'égard du Conseil de l'Europe et où la Municipalité ne saurait ménager aucun effort pour s'opposer avec succès à certaines tendances envisageant la possibilité d'un transfert des institutions européennes dans une autre ville.[166]

Such minor aspects of optimising the regular traffic system were seen as important by administration actors to support the bigger picture of attempting to suit the available infrastructure to the delegates' needs. During the first meeting of the Liaison Committee the statement was made that the *CTS* needed to move the bus stop closer to the CoE building.[167]

---

165 AS, 68 MW 37, *Extrait des DNA, 5.9.1970.*

166 AS, 62 MW 99, *Note pour la Division II, 4.10.1957.*

167 AS, 208 MW 267, *Minutes of the Liaison Committee session, 24.9.1956*, p. 2.

Although the city instituted specialised offers for local transport, parliamentarians seemed to regard the regular bus as important as well. In 1972, the *CTS* had changed the route of 3/13/23 so that the CoE did not possess a direct link to the railway station anymore. A multinational group of seven PACE delegates led by British MP George Darling drafted a declaration indicating the inconvenience caused and demanded that the Secretary-General intervene with the city to re-establish the old route.[168] This did not come into fruition, but the city organised another service that could constitute as a replacement which will be covered in this sub-chapter.

On behest of the local administrations, the *CTS* was involved in improving inner-city transport in four ways by providing free transport for parliamentarians, two extra busses between 20 and 21 hours for the 3/13, a shuttle from the railway station to the CoE during session periods, and busses after night sessions.

The areas of involvement are ordered thematically in the manner that the two special additions to regular public transport are followed by the two extraordinary measures. These measures were enforced over nearly the entire period of study, although changes were made based on delegates' wishes and behaviour. All these efforts of the involved local actors aimed at providing a free and functioning public transport system in order to facilitate fast and easy journeys within Strasbourg. As with the hosting measures investigated in chapter 2, the arrangements city actors made with the *CTS* had the purpose of presenting themselves as good hosts, as well.

(i) Free transport

The idea of free transport for delegates counted among the first hosting measures for European parliamentarians introduced by the Liaison Committee in 1956.[169] It was supposed to bind parliamentarians on a personal level as with hosting activities. Through its strategic use, the renown of Strasbourg as institution host was supposed to be increased.

Paul Wach and René Radius were responsible for negotiations with the *CTS* which culminated in the following result proposed by the transport company, in force from the October 1956 session.[170] The transport company would accept the different CoE identity cards as ticket, note down the numbers and invoice the city for the total amount after each

---

168 ABR, 1130 W 936/9, *Déclaration écrite No. 12 (1972).*

169 AS, 208 MW 267, *Minutes of the Liaison Committee, 24.9.1956.*

170 AS, 208 MW 267, *Minutes of the Liaison Committee, 24.9.1956.*

session period, since they refused to allow parliamentarians to travel for free.[171] As a concession to the city, it only billed the fare from the central Place Kléber to the CoE, even if delegates travelled elsewhere.[172] The costs of this measure varied, for instance, transport during the January 1957 PACE session cost 2,450 Francs (50€), while the 1960s generally saw an increased expenditure as during the March 1967 EP session with 146.40 Francs (200€).[173]

Regarding the 1970s, an EP communication gave evidence that the free transport not only applied to parliamentarians, but also expert committees, CoE security employees, delegation secretaries and accredited journalists, among others.[174] However, in 1974, the city discontinued the practice to offer the European institution personnel free transport for the entire public transport network due to increased misuse. For a consultation between Alfred Feuerstein and representatives of the EP, CoE and *CTS*, the European institutions had determined that the offer was not abused by delegates or civil servants, but by support staff such as ushers or temporary stenographers.[175] The meeting participants proposed to cancel the free transport for everything but the special shuttle bus for all who could present one of the official ID-cards which was approved by the Mayor.[176]

(ii) Increasing services

The second measure, the extension of the regular bus line in the evening by two busses, sparked little controversy and counted among the recurrent arrangements for each session period. This service was instituted in 1959 to provide delegates with a departure every ten minutes from 20:00-21:00 as during the daytime. On request of the *Préfecture*, the *CTS* informed that three extra busses during the hour would cost the city and department 3,300 Francs (55€); the local administrations decided to pay for two extra busses from April 1959.[177]

It was another strategy to strengthen the position of Strasbourg through gaining the appreciation of parliamentarians. As with the specialised services (see below), the symbolic value of their presence seems to have

171 AS, 208 MW 267, *Lettre de la CTS au Maire, 12.10.1956*, p. 1.

172 AS, 208 MW 267, *Lettre de la CTS au Maire, 12.10.1956*, p. 1.

173 AS, 1 W 167, *Avis de règlement, 14.2.1957* and 236 MW 6/3, *Invoice de la CTS.*

174 AS, 97 W 42/1, *European Parliament communication, 74/18.*

175 AS, 97 W 42/1, *Note pour M. le Maire, 14.6.1974*, p. 1.

176 AS, 97 W 42/1, *Note pour M. le Maire, 14.6.1974*, p. 2. Also cf. the section on the shuttle service.

177 AS, 1 W 1599, *Lettre de la CTS à la Préfecture, 13.2.1959*, p. 2.

been held in higher esteem than their actual capacity utilisation. The *CTS* computed the passenger numbers, which was not only restricted to parliamentarians, as they still were regular busses, and came to the conclusion that during the initial time of operation, an average of 2.57 and 2.89 passengers used the first and second bus respectively. Only when the ends of meetings coincided with departure times a higher number of 11 passengers was reached.[178] In 1959, costs of around 7,290 Francs (120€) were incurred as during the May PACE session.[179] In 1960, the execution of this service was changed, since many of the supplementary busses did not carry any passengers at all. The *Préfet* asked the *CTS* whether it was possible that it could be transformed into an on-demand service.[180] After discussions, it was decided that the CoE itself should call the *CTS* for an extra bus for the regular line should the need arise.[181]

This measure met a concrete demand side of the European institutions. For example, Bent Paludan-Müller, Director of Finance at the EP, wrote to Raymond Leissner in January 1978 that many civil servants working late could not benefit from free transport, since the special offers would terminate at 18:30 and the EP would only reimburse taxi fares from 22:00. Therefore, he asked whether the city could provide an additional bus at 19:30, as the EP would consider paying for taxis from 20:00 onwards in the future.[182] In his reply, Leissner referred to the improved timetable, but also wrote that the EP should call the *CTS* if need arose which would consequently provide a supplementary bus immediately.[183] The acquiescence of demands from the EP was a common strategy of local actors to improve the reputation of Strasbourg as host.

(iii) Shuttle service

Regarding the extraordinary arrangements, the shuttle, a service that still exists today, constituted an exclusive offer for delegates. Like the other measures, it was supposed to increase Strasbourg's chances for remaining institution seat through the appreciation of parliamentarians. The idea of such a service was mentioned in initial talks with the *CTS* in 1956,[184] but seemed to have operated only from 1974 according to the sources. Before,

178 AS, 1 W 1599, *Lettre de la CTS au Préfet, 5.5.1959.*

179 AS, 1 W 1599, *Lettre de la CTS au Préfet, 21.5.1959.*

180 AS, 1 W 1599, *Lettre du Préfet à la CTS, 11.3.1960.*

181 AS, 1 W 1599, *Lettre du Préfet à la CTS, 24.3.1960.*

182 AS, 97 W 42/1, *Lettre de Paludan-Müller à Leissner, 11.1.1978.*

183 AS, 97 W 42/1, *Lettre de Leissner à Paludan-Müller, 19.1.1978.*

184 AS, 1 W 167, *Lettre du Maire à la CTS, 10.10.1956.*

such an offer was neither mentioned in Bipartite Committee files nor in city notes detailing all the measures to take for each session period.[185] However, when the shuttle became central to the city's efforts to improve the transport system in 1974, it was expressed in a manner that hinted at that it must have existed longer. That year, its route from the railway station to the CoE was changed to include stops in the city centre to serve as an alternative because the practice of free transport for parliamentarians was stopped.[186] The shuttle and the night bus were hardly frequented towards the end of the 1970s. Bipartite Committee files detailed that in 1977, the *CTS* asked the Mayor to discontinue both the shuttle and the supplementary night bus service, since the former was hardly used and the latter not at all and incurred a major deficit.[187]

Due to the financial burden, the *Cabinet du Préfet chargé des affaires européennes* recommended following the *CTS* suggestion of terminating the shuttle, as the department would pay most of the costs. Since the Bipartite Committee was reluctant to stop this service on which hinged also connotations of them being a capable host, they convinced the *CTS* after *pourparlers laborieux* to instead improve the timetable by offering less departures during off-peak hours, while the financial question was adjourned to the following year.[188] This action also took wishes of delegates into account, as they had complained of the interruption of the service in the morning.[189]

The behaviour of the city administration to forego economic considerations again gives evidence for a message to parliamentarians and ultimately the competition that Strasbourg was able to offer convenient transport possibilities. Running costs remained high, for example, they were approximated at more than 2,000 Francs (1,100€) per day and for 1978 the *CTS* estimated an expenditure at 122,983.39 Francs (65,000€).[190] In the 1980s, the European institutions were even more included, since the timetable was drafted by the Protocol Service of the EP.[191] In this case, the

185 E.g. AS, 68 MW 37 for examples of city notes from 1970/1971 and ABR, 1130 W 936/7-8, the shuttle is mentioned in activity report for 1974 in the 1975 meeting, but not in proposals for the year in the 1974 meeting.

186 AS, 97 W 42/1, *Note pour M. le Maire, 16.4.1974*, p. 2.

187 ABR, 1130 W 936/5, *Lettre de la CTS au Maire, 10.1.1977.*

188 ABR, 1130 W 936/4, *Note pour M. le Maire, 15.12.1977*, p. 2.

189 AS, 752 W 98, *Note pour M. le Maire, 15.12.1977*, p. 3.

190 ABR, 1130 W 936/4, *Note pour M. le Maire, 15.12.1977*, p. 2 and AS, 752 W 98, *Lettre de la CTS au Maire, 30.1.1978.*

191 AS, 114 W 216, *Note du 15.1.1981.*

message of capabilities to house institutions again took precedence over expenditures.

Similar to the air links, the city administration and delegates apparently valued comfortable transport conditions. In September 1978, Wehr admonished the *CTS* for using old busses, since parliamentarians had complained.[192] Additionally, this letter exchange gave evidence for the symbolic character of these measures to be used strategically in the competitive situation with other seat cities. Wehr stressed that it would be essential that MEPs received a good impression during the November session, since all spring 1979 EP meetings would be held in Luxembourg and the directly elected assembly would meet for the first time in July in Strasbourg.[193] Thus, even the provision of cosy busses constituted an element, together with hosting arrangements and building infrastructure improvements (see next chapter) of local actors' efforts to present themselves as best seat choice possible in the light of the prestigious event of the EP session after the first direct election.

(iv) Supplementary night-time busses

The last measure, providing two busses after night sessions, was a relatively minor aspect. It was instituted in 1958 after the previous solution did not function well.[194] Before, from 1956, the city had asked a taxi syndicate to send a number of cars to the CoE after night sessions (see taxi sub-chapter).[195] One bus served all the hotels where parliamentarians commonly stayed, while the other took a route through the quarters in which permanent staff and civil servants lived.[196] The city and department paid for this service which amounted to 3,000 Francs (50€) per bus.[197] This system was curtailed to the demand of the European institutions, since they could if necessary order from the *CTS* directly.[198] The night bus still operated in 1979 and was not subjected to any reforms, counting among the permanent measures for each session period. During the late 1970s, the *CTS* reported the night busses as absolutely unoccupied, but they were,

192 AS, 97 W 42/1, *Lettre de Wehr à la CTS, 13.9.1978.*

193 AS, 97 W 42/1, *Lettre de Wehr à la CTS, 9.10.1978.*

194 AS, 236 MW 23/1, *Note pour la Division Centrale, 29.11.1958.*

195 AS, 236 MW 23/1, *Lettre du Maire au Secrétaire-Général du Conseil de l'Europe, 15.10.1956.*

196 AS, 236 MW 23/1, *Lettre du Maire au Secrétaire-Général du Conseil de l'Europe, 19.1.1959.*

197 AS, 236 MW 23/1, *Note pour la Division II, 19.1.1959.*

198 AS, 236 MW 21/1, *Lettre du Maire à la CTS, 31.3.1959.*

as the shuttle service, not stopped,[199] elevating the city's intention to please strategically parliamentarians over economic considerations.

All in all, the four different special services, the *CTS* had been charged with, were the central inner-city transport infrastructure together with taxis. In this manner, their presence as a signal that Strasbourg was capable of providing a satisfactory and convenient traffic system for the institutions it housed was more important than any financial issues. Other than the economic concerns in 1977/1978 which raised questions of the necessity of the special services, but were ultimately turned down, Bipartite Committee or other city administration documents did not mention any controversy. These transport measures were commonly listed as part of the permanent arrangements for each session period without comment. This circumstance further illustrates that the message of a capable transport infrastructure was more important to local actors than any economic considerations. It was also evident in the manner the arguments of the *CTS* and the *Cabinet du Préfet* were discarded by the decision holders in the committee.[200] The elements of special services continued to be extended and improved, for example, from 1980 a shuttle linked several hotels with the CoE.[201]

(b) Taxis

Efforts of local actors regarding the taxi system in Strasbourg were the second central inner-city transport mode for European parliamentarians and civil servants, as well as the main connection to the airport. It was another important strategy of appearing as a competent institution host by providing effective local transport options. Over the entire period of study, a need for improvement was present, as can be seen through administration documents. In them, largely the same issues were raised in the 1970s as in the 1950s. The department was formally responsible for taxis.[202] However, most of the organisation and fielding of complaints was arranged by the city as municipal archive documents suggest. Those frequent letters of complaints contained in the dossiers further illustrated a continuous need for improvements. In fact, judging by the missives, the area of taxis was to delegates the most unsatisfactory aspect of Strasbourg's hosting or infrastructure measures.

199 ABR, 1130 W 936/5, *Lettre de la CTS au Maire, 10.1.1977.*

200 Cf. ABR, 1130 W 936/4.

201 AS, 114 W 217, *Note du 20.1.1983.*

202 AS, 68 MW 40, *Note pour M. le Maire, 24.5.1963*, p. 2.

For example, in 1979, British MEP Richard Cottrell distinctly reproached the manner in which taxis functioned in a letter to Pflimlin after the cab he had ordered from a restaurant never arrived. "Ce service, d'après mon expérience, est le pire en Europe: inadapté, inefficace et trop coûteux."[203] The city administration saw it as important to counteract these negative opinions, since its main strategies to remain seat of European institutions aimed at gaining their European guests' appreciation. Some letters of complaints also stated that the taxi problems constituted one of the reasons why parliamentarians were reluctant to come to Strasbourg.[204] In order to present a positive image of the city as host, administration actors endeavoured to improve the system to be able to stay in the competition with especially Brussels and Luxembourg. One of the reasons issues still remained in 1979 and beyond can partly be attributed to conflicts of interest between local actors attempting to consolidate Strasbourg's position and other, local actors unrelated to efforts to consolidate the city's position.

As will be shown below, the actors working to welcome European institutions attempted to solve the overarching problem of an at times poor functioning repeatedly, but were met with opposition by primarily the taxi associations or other administrative services. In this regard, taxis were one of the few instances where actors outside of the 'in-group' concerned with the European presence managed partly to obstruct efforts. Local actors were involved in two kinds of struggles in different areas. On the one hand, they had to offer at least comparable transport options to competing cities, on the other, they had to deal with local opposition to achieve it.

While local actors concerned with European institutions were prone to overriding objections, similar action was not pursued in the area of taxis. It can be speculated that especially the threat of strikes, which would cause the taxi system to stop functioning completely, halted such behaviour of simply ignoring opposition and instead encouraged a more hesitant conduct. From the archive documents in the municipal archive of Strasbourg and the departmental archive of Bas-Rhin, local actors concentrated on three central aspects in order to attempt to improve facilities. They were increasing of the number of taxis, special measures, and reservations for taxis. All these elements were informed by complaints on one part and coordination meetings with taxi associations and/or European institutions on the other.

203 AS, 114 W 208, *Lettre de Cottrell à Pflimlin, 7.11.1979.*

204 AS, 223 W 121, *Lettre de Douro à Pflimlin, 12.12.1979.*

(i) Increasing the number of available taxis

The first aspect, the need to increase the numbers of taxis in the city, was the central concern and was subject to the majority of complaints of European guests over the entire period of study. Occasionally, documents from the municipal archive of Strasbourg characterised the situation as adequate. For instance, in 1979, a document stated that the number of taxis would be satisfactory, that the waiting time at the railway station would average between 10 and 15 minutes, and that only a high number of arrivals simultaneously would pose a problem.[205] However, sources describing areas which needed improvement remained more common, usually spurred on by complaints of European institutions or parliamentarians. The main topics were the concrete availability of taxis in certain situations and the general need to raise the number of cabdrivers in Strasbourg.

Slow increases of the number of licenced taxis were made over the period of study, demanded both by city actors and the European guests. In 1952, a decree of the *Préfet* had fixed the number of cabs in Strasbourg with a population of over 200,000 at 85.[206] Mayor Frey argued that this number was insufficient seeing that in 1939, 140 taxis had operated in a Strasbourg with 180,000 inhabitants.[207] In 1957, the *Mairie* urged the *Préfecture de Police* to increase the number to all in all 125, citing the lack of taxis during sessions.[208] Newspaper articles gave evidence that cabdrivers generally opposed such measures because of feared competition and threatened a strike, arguing that being the seat of the CoE would not constitute an adequate reason.[209] Next to the struggle between candidate cities, an inner-city conflict was thus visible which limited on the process of using taxis as a strategy to improve Strasbourg's position against the competition.

Since 1972, 165 taxi licences existed which was still regarded as an inferior number, as there were not enough taxis when trains arrived or events finished.[210] Hans Nord, Secretary-General of the EP, also raised these points in 1978 when he asked for immediate improvement, because the EP would otherwise have to rent cars from Luxembourg or Kehl.[211] He added that they habitually rented 23 taxis, which was also done in

205 AS, 114 W 206, *Table ronde, 18.4.1979*, p. 2.

206 AS, 68 MW 39, *Lettre du Maire au Préfet, 27.6.1953.*

207 AS, 68 MW 39, *Lettre du Maire au Préfet, 27.6.1953.*

208 AS, 68 MW 38, *Note du 23.11.1957.*

209 AS, 68 MW 38, *Extrait du Nouvel Alsacien, 18.12.1957* and *Extrait des DNA, 28.1.1958.*

210 AS, 114 W 206, *Note du 25.1.1978.*

211 AS, 114 W 206, *Lettre de Nord à Pflimlin, 9.3.1978.*

Brussels, to increase the number of vehicles at disposition.[212] In his response to Nord's critique, Leissner indicated the improvements made, which included raising the number of taxis to 200 in 1977, direct access to the CoE's main entrance, as well as easier access to taxi ranks in the city centre.[213] This representative example of complaints showed that local actors strived to accommodate the demand side of the European guests as usual. However, other actors with stakes in the issue that did not concern the institutions hampered efforts to raise the number of taxis.

The number of taxis in Strasbourg remained insufficient in the eyes of the European institutions even in the end of the 1970s, although the city and department had continuously attempted to raise the number from the end of the 1950s. This situation gives evidence for the fact that in the matter of taxis, municipal actors had to fight opposition of other local actors who were not involved in consolidating Strasbourg's position as seat.

(ii) Special measures

The second category, special measures, contained two main elements: the attempt of the city to found their own taxi company in the early 1960s and a special service after night sessions from 1956-1958. In 1963, at a meeting of local actors including A. Heitz, Ridoux and Feuerstein, the question was raised whether to found a taxi company.[214] It was seen as a solution to the fear of instigating strikes with raising the number of cabs to mitigate the issues of long waiting times and insufficiency of cars.[215] The *Division VIII* endeavoured together with the *Société de Surveillance et Rondes de Nuit*[216] to study this proposal. Practically, the service of the *Préfecture* concerned with taxis confirmed that both independent taxis[217] and a company, where drivers were salaried, could exist in the same city, the *Société* was in favour of the idea as well.[218] Thus, it was an attempt to circumvent the issue of taxi association opposing the increase of the number of taxis and to satisfy the parliamentarians' demands.

This was the only time in all the different strategies of the local actors to remain seat city, where they bowed to outside demands. A reason for

212 AS, 114 W 206, *Lettre de Nord à Pflimlin, 9.3.1978.*

213 AS, 114 W 206, *Lettre de Leissner à Nord, 15.3.1978.*

214 AS, 68 MW 40, *Procès-verbal du 13.2.1963*, p. 3.

215 AS, 68 MW 40, *Procès-verbal du 13.2.1963*, p. 3.

216 It operated parking lots subject to fees, among others.

217 Author's translation, the original French term is *artisans du taxi.*

218 AS, 68 MW 40, *Note pour M. le Maire, 24.5.1963*, p. 2.

that could be that the repercussions of a taxi strike would be an even more negative opinion on Strasbourg by European parliamentarians. For example, in the planning, it became apparent that local actors were careful not to agitate taxi associations they had to cooperate with in the process of improving the transport system for European parliamentarians. Asked by A. Heitz which position the city should take in regard to the prospective creation of a taxi company, Pflimlin hedged that events needed to be cautiously watched and that the *Syndicat des Chauffeurs du Taxi* needed to be contacted before any decision.[219] The *Préfet* was equally tentative in giving his approval. He stated in a letter to the Mayor that while he was prepared to give his consent, the recent increase of the number of cabs from 95 to 110 had already caused dissent among drivers and that such a company would mean even more competition.[220] Finally, it was separately concluded by the *Division VIII* and the *Conférence des Adjoints* to shelve this idea until the opinion of cabdrivers was more positive.[221]

The second special measure, the night taxis were introduced as one of the first measures of the Liaison Committee in 1956. It was another offer exclusively for delegates. In October, the Mayor, Charles Altorffer, informed the Secretary-General of the CoE that he had talked with the *Syndicat Départmental des Artisans du Taxi* to station three cabs close to the CoE after night sessions.[222] The syndicate soon raised concerns of effectiveness, because only two of the three taxis were taken after the first night session.[223] In January 1957, the Liaison Committee characterised it as a disaster, while the syndicate claimed they could not provide such a service.[224] From 1958, the *CTS* night busses served as a replacement for this offer.

(iii) Reservation of taxis

One attempt to solve the availability problem, especially regarding connections to the airport, constituted an effort related to the last aspect, the improvement of taxi reservations. In 1979, the *Service des Relations Publics* wrote to the commander of the airbase in Entzheim, Colonel Alegria, asking for permission that pilots could transmit how many of their

---

219 AS, 68 MW 40, *Note pour la Division VIII, 29.5.1963.*

220 AS, 68 MW 40, *Lettre du Préfet au Maire, 17.6.1963.*

221 AS, 68 MW 40, *Note du 30.7.1963* and *note du 25.10.1963.*

222 AS, 236 MW 23/1, *Lettre du Maire au Secrétaire-Général du Conseil de l'Europe, 15.10.1956.*

223 AS, 236 MW 23/1, *Lettre du Syndicat au Préfet, 11.12.1956.*

224 AS, 208 MW 267, *Minutes of the Liaison Committee session, 21.1.1957*, p. 1.

passengers needed a taxi to air traffic control which could then inform the taxi dispatch.[225] After Alegria gave his consent, Wehr proceeded to inform *Air France*, *Air Inter* and *Dan Air* which operated the links concerning European parliamentarians.[226] However, only *Dan Air* gave a favourable answer, the other two airlines refused and raised identical concerns which included the uniqueness of the proposal, the danger that ordered taxis might not be used, as well as other practical issues.[227]

A solution to this was only found in 1980 after *Air France* proposed to Leissner that the airport of origin could accept taxi reservations, fax them to the *Chambre de Commerce*, where staff could order the cabs.[228] This procedure was in operation from February 1980 but soon proved not to be completely effective, as the *Chambre de Commerce* stated in September that some airports did not transmit the reservations or that some were not honoured by delegates.[229] Additionally, parliamentarians complained and one example shows how solicitous local actors were in solving these specific issues in order to please their European guests. After British MEP Richard Simmons had written that his reserved taxi had not arrived, the Mayor replied that for the next session he should call Robert Witt or Herbert Wehr of the *Service des Relations Publiques* with his arrival time who would make sure a cabdriver waited for him at Entzheim airport.[230] The reaction from Simmons gave evidence that such extra efforts served to raise the reputation of Strasbourg as welcoming host. "I would like to place on record how much I appreciate everything you have done to make the lives of Members of the Parliament easier."[231] Such assiduous dealing with complaints gives evidence that transport infrastructure also followed the dual intention as hosting measures; pleasing the European guests and proving that Strasbourg was capable of accommodating the European institutions it hosted.

All in all, local actors were aware of the issues with the functioning of taxis and attempted to implement solutions, but were often hampered by conflicting interests of their cooperation partners. These were situated outside the immediate group of actors concerned with consolidating Strasbourg's position. It was a unique situation, since concerns in other

---

225 AS, 114 W 207, *Lettre de Jantkowiak à Alegria, 7.6.1979.*

226 AS, 114 W 207, *Lettre de Wehr à l'Air Inter, 23.6.1979.*

227 AS, 114 W 207, *Lettres du Air Inter/Air France/Dan Air à Leissner, 27./28.6.1979/31.10.1979.*

228 AS, 114 W 207, *Lettre de l'Air France à Leissner, 18.1.1980.*

229 AS, 114 W 207, *Note du 26.9.1980.*

230 AS, 114 W 207, *Lettre de Simmons à Pflimlin, 31.3.1981; réponse.*

231 AS, 114 W 207, *Lettre de Simmons à Pflimlin, 20.4.1981.*

measures were often disregarded. Despite this, the manner in which the city responded to complaints shows that they were aware of the importance of presenting a good image of their capabilities as institution host.

Section 1.16 Concluding Remarks

In this chapter, the most important actors and their activities regarding transport infrastructure have been analysed. The set of strategies to improve air links for the use of parliamentarians was the biggest factor. Although not as elitist as before the Second World War, frequent and cheap flying was not entirely common until the 1970s, although developments for this trend already began in the 1950s.[232] Based on the emphasis of local actors on this mode of transport and the attempt to provide comfortable modalities still indicated that the city administration saw it as a prestigious way for European parliamentarians to travel to Strasbourg.

A difference to hosting affairs was that, while still somewhat self-contained, external actors participated. They were responsible for other tasks than the welcoming of European institutions with leisure activities. Still, the main agency remained with the administration members especially concerned with the European guests. In this, strategies regarding the improvement of the taxi service formed an exception. In no other area did the local actors concerned with consolidating the position of Strasbourg as seat face profound opposition. It also was the only instance where they took this disagreement into account. Usually, activities seemed to occur within a bubble of European institutions and concerned actors. The reasons that concessions were made to taxi associations could have been that strikes would be disruptive and impact negatively on the attitude of European parliamentarians towards Strasbourg.

Improvements were based on both anticipations of demands and concrete wishes from the European institutions, although the former seemed to be more common. One central example were the charter air links of the 1960s, when the connection to Frankfurt was deemed as advantageous for PACE sessions by the city administration.[233] Many Nordic delegates used the connection to Frankfurt, while the link to Zurich was only used by Italian parliamentarians.[234] The existence of these routes was a concession to them for easy access and aimed to bind delegates to Strasbourg. For this, the city administration made an effort of creating a special service for easy

232 Hudson, Kenneth and Pettifer, Julian, *Diamonds in the Sky. A Social History of Air Travel*, London, The Bodley Head, 1979, pp. 130; 132; 160; 199.

233 AS, 236 MW 27/3, *Note pour Pflimlin, 2.11.1961*, p. 1.

234 AS, 236 MW 27/3, *Note pour Pflimlin, 2.11.1961*, p. 2.

access. Although sources in the municipal archive of Strasbourg show that for a good number of flights, one or two passengers were not uncommon, charter air links to Zurich and Frankfurt remained an important aspect of local actors' attempts to improve Strasbourg's traffic infrastructure. Since the city administration had determined that these two airports were used by a good number of parliamentarians, the city strategically improved their transport connections to them.

Air links, in contrast to the other transport infrastructure subject to improvement, experienced a visible modernisation caused by the presence of the European institutions. Especially from the 1970s with the special state assistance, the major improvement to the route network was visible. Otherwise, it might not have developed this rapidly, judging by the improvements achieved during the two previous decades, when the city and department only had their own resources available. Concrete demands always seemed to take precedence as could be seen with the chauffeuring service, which most parliamentarians preferred for travelling to nearby air hubs. Originally, local actors had only intended it to be a fill-in and not a major mode of transport as specified by Bipartite Committee documents. The fact that they kept offering it in the same amount shows that local actors kept acquiescing to demands in order to gain the appreciation of parliamentarians.

Rather than cancelling this offer, the committee accepted to increase the budget for 1976 to 350,000 Francs (220,000€) to accommodate the use of taxis to satisfy demands among others.[235] Generally, the total costs of infrastructure improvements are hard to determine, as only expenditure for some special measures are archived in the municipal archive of Strasbourg. However, the examples given in this chapter, as well as the Bipartite Committee annual expenditure for transport listed in appendix II, gives evidence for the comportment of the local actors to accommodate demands to the best of their ability regardless of financial considerations.

Next to these practical elements, symbolic considerations, reminiscent of the goal of hosting activities, seem to have been an inherent feature. The decoration of *CTS* busses with European flags, was such an example.

All in all, traffic infrastructure was the second of the three major themes of local actors' strategies to present Strasbourg as a capable and attractive seat. The importance of this sometimes became visible in opinions of delegates as in 1980 when the city had sent a questionnaire on the state of transport options to parliamentarians. In the answer of the Marquis of Douro, the MEP emphatically stated that he would always choose

[235] ABR, 1130 W 936/5, *Activités de l'année 1976*, p. 4.

Brussels as seat, since travelling to Strasbourg would be a struggle and the air links needed serious improvement.[236] Traffic infrastructure was an important element of the city's efforts, both to assure a favourable opinion of parliamentarians and to remain at least comparable to the competition. These efforts were also supported by building infrastructure improvement which will be investigated in the next chapter. A difference between these two aspects was that involved actors seemed to have had a general perception that their building infrastructure was lacking in comparison to the other seat contenders, especially Brussels. In the transport sector, this did not become as apparent, but is visible especially during the 1970s when the competition between the three provisional EC seats intensified. Air links experienced a corresponding growth which was supposed to maintain the image of the centrality of Strasbourg as an easily accessible place.

[236] AS, 114 W 283, *Lettre de Douro à Leissner, 11.7.1980.*

Chapter 4

Building Capacity to Cope

Building infrastructure for the European institutions was the third major theme of strategies of the various local actors to bind the EP and CoE to the city and to strengthen its position in the EC seat question. Especially during the 1970s, this became an important strategy, since the closet competition Brussels and Luxembourg executed similar large-scale projects in what could be described as a 'building race'. While air links also were a main activity during the decade, a concentration on buildings within Strasbourg was apparent. This was especially the case for the *Immeuble Parlementaire Européenne (IPE)* in the context of the competition with Brussels and Luxembourg. During the 1950s and 1960s, hosting measures and the improvement of transportation systems took precedence over construction activities as the central focus of local actors.

Nevertheless, the creation of a building infrastructure was also employed as a strategy in these two decades, however, only in a lesser quantity. For example, in order to finalise the official decision to construct the C block, an office building for the EP in 1959, the following statement of Mayor Pflimlin was recorded in the minutes. "M. le Maire estime qu'il convient d'attacher une importance particulière à ce projet: son exécution rapide et conforme aux desiderata est peut-être la seule chance pour Strasbourg que la situation provisoire se consolide."[1] It indicated that local actors regarded the fulfilling of concrete wishes as essential to remain a seat contender. The element of fulfilling any explicit and implicit requirements of the European institutions in order to gain their appreciation as host city activities became visible again. It was a pattern that all three themes of local strategies had in common, be it hosting, transport or building infrastructure.

From 1970, providing sufficient real estate was the principal concern of the city administration which peaked in the years leading up to the first direct election of the EP in 1979. Due to this event, the rivalry between the three provisional seats became especially visible in an increase in construction projects for the EP in each of the three cities. In

1 AS, 209 MW 18, *Compte-rendu de la Conférence des Adjoints du 4.4.1959*, p. 3.

vying for the housing rights of the assembly, Brussels and Luxembourg executed building projects or procured office space, as well. Apart from this competition aspect, anticipated and concrete demands of European parliamentarians who participated in sessions in Strasbourg conditioned activities. In this, the main focus will be on the construction process on paper rather than the physical one. This is an analysis of how buildings and the planning of them were strategically used by local actors to consolidate the seat position against the other two provisional seats.

The direct election played a role in the latter half of the 1970s, since the seat question re-attained a currency after the decision to hold it was made. It had originally been planned for 1978, but in 1977, the European Council decided to postpone it for a year, since the organisation of it had been slow to develop.[2] While the EP had regularly formulated resolutions demanding to determine a definite seat over the period of study according to sources in the archive of the European Parliament, before and after the direct election in 1979, more efforts were made. Most of these documents referenced the financial burden of three seats, the amount of working hours that could be saved with a reduction of meeting places and allusions to the lack of political decision over time.[3] A second element influenced by the direct election was the renewed construction activity in Brussels, Luxembourg and Strasbourg to prepare for the larger directly elected parliament which led to this aforementioned increased competition between the three provisional seats for the premier choice as host.

Thirdly, local actors in Strasbourg attempted to capitalise on a general symbolic dimension. In the speeches and newspaper articles on the city's European mission, the direct election was covered as well. In an article from May 1979, intended for a German audience, Pflimlin stated in connection to his belief that the EP would likely remain in the city following the direct election, "[…] weil es einsieht, dass unsere Stadt würdig ist, auch weiterhin seine europäische Mission zu erfüllen, als Garant der deutsch-französischen Freundschaft, diesem unersetzlichen Fundament der europäischen Einigung."[4] Next to the necessity of providing adequate physical working conditions and the symbolism inherent in the presence of facilities for the European institutions, strategies which derived from Strasbourg's alleged European reputation were employed. This also comprised hosting measures, when a greater effort was made for the first session of the directly elected parliament as with all 'special' occasions

2 Dinan, Desmond, *Europe Recast*, Basingstoke, Palgrave, 2004, p. 169.

3 CARDOC, PE1 AP PR B1-0493/79 0010, *Motion for a resolution, 13.11.1979.*

4 AS, 9 Z 192, *Europastadt Strassburg, 28.5.1979*, p. 3.

such as the inaugural meeting of the EP in 1958. During an extraordinary session of the Bipartite Committee on 11 June 1979, its budget was drastically increased from 500,000 Francs (230,000€) to two million Francs (930,000€) to 'celebrate' this occasion.[5] As with other special occasions, no expense was spared to present the city in a favourable light.

The investment in building infrastructure for the European institutions in Strasbourg was of a different nature than hosting activities and remained a background issue to them until the 1970s, when it became a central concern of local actors. It also addressed the competition Brussels and Luxembourg in regard to the need to offer at minimum facilities on the same level as them. In literature on the housing of IOs, mainly situated in the field of urban planning, an emphasis is placed on which infrastructure is needed as a prerequisite. This research is relevant to the seat question of the EC, because next to the competitive situation between the three provisional EP locations to offer the best facilities, the organisation itself deliberated on which features its physical placement should possess. For instance, in the 1960s, the idea of a European district was popular, judging by documents in the archive of the Council of the EU which covered how it should look like and what its status should be. Furthermore, such concerns were the central parts of IO seat agreements (as the UN), which chiefly the Council of Ministers and COREPER employed as inspiration in developing a draft agreement for a European district.[6]

In general, scholarship on buildings of IOs characterises it as a symbol for the values and goals of the organisation which need to be planned in a way that takes these into account.[7] In connection with the United Nations Educational, Scientific and Cultural Organisation (UNESCO) headquarters in Paris, Iris Schröder analyses that the building was conceptualised as a symbol for the importance of the organisation.[8] Additionally, the general significance a city might ascribe to the organisation it houses was visible in this case, as well. Schröder describes that the first plan of the architect the UNESCO had charged was refused by the city administration of Paris, because it would clash with the townscape.[9] Only when the IO threatened to move to another city did the municipality relent and withdrew all

5 ABR, 1130 W 936/2, *Minutes of the Bipartite Committee session, 11.6.1979.*

6 AC, CM2/1962 0246, *Problèmes "district européen."*

7 Hein, Carola, *The Capital of Europe. Architecture and Urban Planning for the European Union*, Westport, Praeger, 2004, pp. 1; 37.

8 Schröder, Iris, "Der Beton, die Stadt, die Kunst und die Welt. Der Streit um die Pariser UNESCO-Gebäude", in *Zeithistorische Forschungen (Online-Ausgabe)*, 7, 2010, Abschnitt 1-13. p. 11.

9 *Ibid.*, p. 4.

objections except regarding the height of the building.[10] While this exact conflict was not present in Strasbourg, its city administration was intent on satisfying or anticipating any request on building infrastructure the EP and also the CoE might pose. Through this approach, the institutions in Strasbourg could become appreciative of their host and from improving facilities; local actors could possibly generate appreciation of the European guests to use in view of consolidating its status.

The provisional nature of the EC assembly's presence was another factor. For example, in 1958, during the second application round for the single seat, the Bipartite Committee characterised the accommodation of the European Communities' wishes on working facilities and housing for its civil servants and MEPs as an issue, since it was uncertain when they would permanently designate the parliament's host city.[11] The municipality had reserved lodgings, for the eventuality of a successful candidature. Since this was too expensive over time, some reservations were cancelled.[12] The Bipartite Committee decided to keep flats *de grand standing* and rather rescind reservations for cheaper accommodation, since its members were concerned that the EC otherwise would regard their application as insufficient.[13] Second-guessing European institutions' preferences and attempting to make their stay in Strasbourg as comfortable as possible played a role in building infrastructure, as well. Judging by archived complaints, it seemed as if the European guests were expecting such kinds of privileges. This added the dimension that demands such as comfortable flats or transport conditions had to be catered to, not only to create an impression, but also to meet expected standards to remain at a contending position regarding the seat question.

In the first sub-chapter following the introduction of involved actors, the major construction efforts from 1950 to 1970 will be covered. The other two parts will be devoted to each of the two major projects of the 1970s; in the first half of the decade the *Palais de l'Europe*, the permanent CoE headquarters, as well as from 1977 the *Immeuble Parlementaire Européen (IPE)*. The focus of this chapter is not on the architectural concepts or construction processes, but rather on the symbolism, the buildings

10 *Ibid.*, p. 5.

11 AS, 235 MW 273, *Minutes of the Bipartite Committee session, 14.1.1958*, p. 2.

12 AS, 235 MW 273, *Minutes of the Bipartite Committee session, 14.1.1958*, p. 3.

13 AS, 235 MW 273, *Minutes of the Bipartite Committee session, 12.6.1958*, p. 3.

possessed for the status of Strasbourg as host of European institutions, and how local actors employed them strategically to consolidate the city's position. The bulk of sources on these processes stems from the municipal archive of Strasbourg, while information on the CoE properties is also supplemented from the archive of the Council of Europe.

Section 1.17 Central Actors

In this sub-chapter, the city/departmental administration and other actors that were involved in building infrastructure for European institutions will be mapped. In the matter of building infrastructure, the trend for a shift in the nature of actors intensified that had already been observable with transport. Thus, city administration civil servants accounted for the central agency regarding the consolidation of Strasbourg's status through building infrastructure. The most common administrators participating in the improvements included the Secretary-General of Strasbourg or architects rather than those who conceptualised hosting arrangements. This development also became visible in the participation other actors, such as construction businesses.

(a) City/Departmental Administration

Due to the shift in actor types from hosting to infrastructure activities, most of the involved administration actors did not seem to possess another 'European' agenda. They were not a member of a local European organisation as the *Comité Strasbourgeois pour le Mouvement Européen* or the *Cercle Européen de Strasbourg* outside their work. They were the 'technical' category within the group of local actors working to welcome European institutions to Strasbourg. Although they participated in this effort due to the fact that these tasks were related to the post they held within the municipality, they nevertheless formed part of the 'in-group' within the city and departmental administrations. Most of them were involved in several construction projects, also in multiple capacities to consolidate Strasbourg's seat status.

As with hosting measures and transport infrastructure, ordinary city administration politics did not influence decision makers occupied with constructions for the European institutions. This is also visible in the fact that reforms which introduced the *Communauté Urbaine de Strasbourg*

(CUS) in 1967[14] and the *Région Alsace* in 1973[15] were only marginally visible in the sources. Judging by these documents, they did not play a significant role as the old structures before that had done.

The majority of activity originated from city administration actors, the *Département* was only marginally involved, as with the construction process of the *Palais*, for example. The *Préfet* was mainly kept informed of the projects progress by its architect Henri Bernard.[16] During the construction of the office building for the EP at the end of the 1970s, the bulk of official communication with the national government for information purposes functioned via the *Préfet* as the local representative of the state.[17]

(i) Ordinary structures

Mayor Pierre Pflimlin as the highest representative of the city administration not only served as coordinator for the involved local actors, but also was the addressee of most communication from the European institutions on the subject of building infrastructure. For instance, the EP Secretary-General Hans Nord communicated the assembly's opinions on a building Strasbourg had constructed for it in 1963.[18] The *Secrétaire-Général de la Ville de Strasbourg* was the most involved official after the mayor. In the early 1960s, Léon Kien held this position and was succeeded by Albert Fix in the latter part of the decade, while Daniel Adam held the function during the 1970s. These three actors principally held the contact with involved parties, such as European institutions, architects and construction agencies. For example, in June 1960, Kien chaired a working party with architects regarding future projects for European institutions.[19] Thus, the *secrétaire-général* of the city held a key position in the organisation and coordination of building infrastructure improvements.

Additionally, Fix counted among the multi-positioned actors, as he was the director of the municipal construction agency *Habitation Moderne* which was responsible for most projects until the 1970s.[20] Next to the fact that the actor circle remained small due to one person holding several

14 The *CUS* was created by a law from 31.12.1966 and generally an area of administration for big agglomerations (Moreau, Jacques, *Administration régionale, locale et municipale*, Paris, Editions Dalloz, 1972, p. 53).

15 Regions as administrative entities were introduced in 1973 (*Ibid.*, p. 91).

16 ABR, 709 D 1, *Lettre de Bernard au Préfet, 15.6.1972.*

17 E.g. ABR, 1130 W 894/1, *Lettre du Préfet au Premier Ministre, 12.1.1979.*

18 AS, 752 W 1, *Lettre de Nord à Pflimlin, 8.2.1963.*

19 AS, 481 W 75, *Compte-rendu du 9.6.1960.*

20 AS, 752 W 80, *Lettre de Monnet à Fix, 28.11.1963.*

different posts, it could also have functioned as a deterrent for random actors to enter this bubble structure.

During the various construction processes, several divisions of the city administration were recurrently involved, as is visible from city administration documents. Most prominently among them was the *Division III* (architecture), the *Division I* (city properties) and the *Division CF* (finances).[21] During the 1960s, the *Division VIII* and/or its head Alphonse Heitz often participated in activities, as well. Examples include working parties set up to resolve a particular issue. In March 1963 one of these panels, where A. Heitz was a member, met to discuss possibilities how to apply the CoE's fiscal immunity to the construction of the Human Rights Court building.[22] Other recurrent actors included in this meeting were *Premier Adjoint au Maire* Robert Baillard, who was also prominently involved in the construction of the *IPE* in this position and as president of a local planning agency. In the 1960s, Fix, A. Heitz and Adam, who at that time was a member of the *Service des Contentieux*, were also participating in meetings to organise construction activities.[23]

(ii) Specialised structures

Apart from the recurrent ordinary structures of the city administration that were involved in creating most strategies to bind the European institutions closer to the city, especially created committees existed as well. They were mostly used to discuss, plan and coordinate building projects. Especially during the construction of the *IPE*, multiple working groups on different aspects surrounding this operation existed. Some of these were internal to the city administration, but the majority of them were common fora for different construction and urban planning agencies, architects, the city and the European institutions. These will be presented during the cooperation-section.

One of the municipality-only panels was the *Groupe de travail concernant les initiatives à prendre pour défendre la mission européenne de Strasbourg* which met several times in 1977. It belonged to the pre-planning phase of the *IPE*, where next to concerned divisions, Daniel Adam (its chairman), Alfred Feuerstein and Raymond Leissner participated.[24] Such working parties had the purpose of discussing ideas and finding solutions

---

[21] Archives de la Ville et de la Communauté Urbaine, *Guide des Fonds 2006*, Strasbourg, Imp. Int. CU, 2006, pp. 12; 13.

[22] AS, 752 W 1, *Compte-rendu du 1.3.1963.*

[23] AS, 752 W 1, *Compte-rendu du 1.3.1963.*

[24] AS, 752 W 12, *Compte-rendu du 26.10.1977.*

regarding the office situation of the EP and CoE among the most involved local actors. In all of these working parties, both internal and external, Adam was a member; this frequency of participation was followed by Leissner and Baillard, according to the various session minutes archived in the municipal archive of Strasbourg.

In contrast to hosting and traffic infrastructure, the Liaison, Special Liaison, Placement Study and Bipartite Committees were not regularly involved in the efforts to develop a building infrastructure for the European institutions in Strasbourg. Only at the end of the 1950s, the Placement Study and Bipartite Committees occupied themselves with such issues. The Placement Study Committee seemed to have been centrally responsible to conceptualise possible future sitings should Strasbourg become the single seat of the institutions of the European Communities.[25]

All in all, mostly city administration actors were involved in the improvement of building infrastructure. They almost exclusively belonged to a second group of 'European' local actors, since they were included because of their position and/or technical expertise, rather than in specialised committees like most actors occupied with hosting arrangements. Nevertheless, they likewise formed their own group within the city administration, since most of them participated in several building projects and some of them in multiple positions, as well.

(b) Other actors

Other actors involved in creating a building infrastructure were mainly urban planning, financing and construction agencies, as well as architects. Some of these also had ties to the city administration, such as the municipal construction agency. They are grouped in here, because they did not belong to the immediate decision structures of the city government as the actors that were described in the previous section. They were mostly concerned with the construction process proper which will only be marginally covered in the subsequent analysis. This study analyses how local actors endeavoured to strategically employ buildings for the CoE and EP; namely to strengthen their position as host by providing both adequate working conditions and superior facilities to those of competing cities. The brief presentation of this type of actors mainly serves as background information to outline construction processes. Nevertheless, these other actors especially participated in the *IPE* construction in various working parties with city and/or European institution civil servants to discuss

25 AS, 208 MW 7 and 208 MW 11, *Placement Study Committee.*

elements, such as the installation of the heating system.[26] A short overview of them will be presented in the following section.

Two construction/urban planning organisations were principally involved in the building activities for European institutions. The *Habitation Moderne* executed most of the projects until the 1970s. It was the municipal construction agency and was created on 26 November 1951.[27] The founders included the city administration, chamber of commerce, *Chambre des Métiers d'Alsace*, *Fédération des Entrepreneurs du Bâtiment et des Travaux Publics d'Alsace*, *Caisse d'Epargne de Strasbourg*, *Port Autonome*, and *Association d'Aide à la Construction*.[28] As capital, the city gave 180,000 Francs (4,000€) and the others 20,000 Francs (500€) each.[29] During the late 1950s and early 1960s, Fix, simultaneously the Secretary-General of Strasbourg, was its director.[30] He was a multipositioned actor, since he was also tasked with planning the city's involvement in the building project in his function as civil servant.

The *IPE*-project was mainly planned and executed under the direction of the *Société d'Aménagement et d'Equipement de la Région de Strasbourg* (*SERS*). It had been founded by the city and *Département* on 4 June 1957 to organise all types of equipment regarding real estate.[31] Next to the two administrations, the *Habitation Moderne*, chamber of commerce (*CCI*) and banks, among others, contributed to its capital.[32] During the 1970s, its director Robert Adjedj was majorly involved in working parties to discuss construction aspects. For example, he participated in a working group with the city and representatives of local construction and planning agencies to discuss and organise aspects of the project.[33] Additionally, Robert Baillard, *Adjoint au Maire*, held the post of president of its *Conseil d'Administration*.[34] Thus, he principally participated in two functions in the edification of the *IPE*. Hence, local actors involved in consolidating

26 E.g. AS, 752 W 27, *Compte-rendu du 18.1.1979*, p. 4.

27 AS, 16 MW 93, *Statuts de l'Habitation Moderne*, p. 1.

28 AS, 16 MW 93, *Statuts de l'Habitation Moderne*, p. 1.

29 AS, 16 MW 93, *Statuts de l'Habitation Moderne*, p. 2.

30 AS, 752 W 5, *Compte-rendu du 13.3.1970.*

31 "La SERS d'hier à aujourd'hui." <http://www.sers.eu/content/la-sers-dhier-a-aujourdhui> (accessed 14.04.2014).

32 "Répartition du Capital de la SEM." <http://www.sers.eu/content/gouvernance> (accessed 14.04.2014).

33 E.g. AS, 752 W 17, *Compte-rendu du 12.9.1978.*

34 AS, 752 W 13, *Lettre de Baillard à Pflimlin, 5.3.1980* and 752 W 18, *SERS, construction*, p. 8.

Strasbourg's position as seat held executive positions among the organisations and firms concerned with building activities.

While sources show that funding was either assured by the European institutions, their member states, local/national French banks or the city, the financial backer of the *IPE* was more involved, since it was an investor, not a creditor whose representatives participated in meetings on the project. The Dutch pension fund *Stichting Bedrijfspensioensfonds voor de Bouwnijverheid* (*SFB*) provided a maximum amount of 125 million Francs (65 million €) for which they expected an annual return of 6.5 percent of the invested sum.[35] The constructor and proprietor of the *IPE* was a purpose-founded organisation between *SERS* and *SFB* on 29 September 1978, called the *Société Civile Immobilière Etudes et Réalisations de l'Aménagement des Structures et Moyens Européens* (*SCI ERASME*).[36] Its capital of one million Francs (520,000€) was financed by the *SFB* by 90 percent, while *SERS* assured the remaining share.[37] According to its statutes, the Dutch fund was the principal manager, but in practice, Adjedj, the director of SERS, corresponded with the city.[38]

Over the period of study, several architects were involved in constructions or plans for a European district. Bertrand Monnet, *Architecte des Bâtiments du France* (all subsequent references to 'Monnet' will regard him), was responsible for the European institution buildings until the 1970s.[39] Architect Henri Bernard, who was employed by the French state, as well, had planned the Palais.[40] The *IPE* was the only building planned by a municipal architect, François Sauer.[41] Additionally, to explore the possible implantation of a European district in or near Strasbourg, Pflimlin had commissioned architects Jean-Henri Calsat and Charles-Gustave Stoskopf to produce studies in 1957 and 1959.[42] As analysed in chapter 2, these were published in *Strasbourg invite l'Europe* and distributed among European officials.[43]

---

35 AS, 752 W 16, *Note pour le Président, 19.12.1978* and 752 W 12, *Procès-verbal du 31.7.1978*, p. 9.

36 AS, 752 W 16, *Extrait du Procès-verbal du 31.10.1978*, p. 7.

37 AS, 752 W 14, *Statuts*, p. 3.

38 AS, 752 W 14, *Statuts*, p. 13 and *Lettre d'Adjedj à Pflimlin, 18.10.1978.*

39 AS, 55 W 86, *Note du 10.10.1958.*

40 AS, 752 W 37, *Lettre de Baillard à Pflimlin, 1.10.1978.*

41 AS, 752 W 13, *Note du 8.10.1979.*

42 236 MW 32/1, *Lettre de Pflimlin à Calsat, 17.7.1959.*

43 Ville de Strasbourg and Conseil Général du Bas-Rhin, *Strasbourg invite l'Europe*, Strasbourg, Editions de la Calanque, 1957.

In summary, the main task of these most central other actors was the practical realisation of building projects, but they also communicated with the city or European institutions during this process of which an overview will be presented subsequently.

(c) Cooperation between actors

Cooperation or coordination between actors mainly occurred during the construction of the *IPE* in various working parties. Such partnerships were more institutionalised with continuous close collaboration than was the case with previous activities. Prior to that, a more informal correspondence was established between construction agencies, the European institutions and the city administration. The inclusion of the CoE and the EP allowed for their input during planning phases, which could have been of strategic importance in terms of the local actors' efforts to consolidate their seat status. This participation could have ensured that the European organisations fully approved of the city's activities. Thus, they might not be as susceptible to the idea of leaving Strasbourg.

Prior to the *IPE* working groups, examples of cooperation included meetings between Kien, Monnet, other architects and town-planners of the city on possibilities of a European district.[44] Next to the city administration, Monnet also communicated with Fix (in his position as Director of the *Habitation Moderne*), for instance on changes the EP wished to make.[45] The biggest part of cooperation of the two local actor groups, the administrations and urban planning agencies and construction enterprises occurred during the late 1970s for the construction of the EP office building. They met in different fora to discuss and plan its construction. Most of these were concerned with deliberating on specific aspects of the architectural process or questions of engineering features.

From the city, Adam, B. Grandjean, a civil servant with the Secretariat-General, Baillard and/or Leissner commonly participated as representatives of the municipality, according to the different minutes archived in the municipal archive of Strasbourg. This type of panels also included meetings with European institution representatives, such as a round table with the city, CoE and EP from late 1977 to discuss the office needs of the EP, which also regarded the CoE, since the EC assembly used the plenary hall and offices in the *Palais*.[46]

44 AS, 481 W 75, *Compte-rendu du 9.6.1960.*

45 AS, 752 W 80, *Lettre de Monnet à Fix, 28.11.1963.*

46 AS, 752 W 12, *Procès-verbal du 8.12.1977*, p. 1.

Another working party between the city and *SERS* occupied itself with discussing the funding proposals to determine the best option. This *Groupe de travail chargé d'examiner les modalités de financement de l'immeuble destiné aux institutions européennes* submitted their recommendation for the SFB following their last meeting on 4 September 1978 to the *Conférence de la Municipalité* for the official decision.[47] An example for a panel from 1979 to 1980 which discussed specific aspects of the construction project included the *Groupe de travail concernant la construction à Strasbourg d'un bâtiment pour le Parlement Européen.*[48] It was comprised of Adam and Sauer as city representatives, as well as intermediaries from *SERS*, *ERASME*, involved town-planning and engineering companies, as well as observers from the EP administration.[49] Another major forum was the working party *Bureaux du Parlement Européen*, where city civil servants, *SERS* and representatives from the various enterprises occupied with the drafting and effectuation of the *IPE* met during the construction phase to discuss progresses, modalities and issues with single aspects of the project.[50]

The fact that representatives from the European institutions actively participated in several of the working panels, pointed to a slightly different dynamic than with hosting and transport measures. For these, the local actors principally decided what needed to be improved with the European institutions making demands regarding lacking aspects after such decisions. In construction matters, especially with the *IPE*, this was much more embedded and the European institutions rather were partners than addressees of measures.

Section 1.18 Creating a European infrastructure: 1949-1964

While hosting activities and transport infrastructure were in the main focus of local actors in the 1950s and 1960s respectively, the construction projects of these two decades still were important strategic devices to consolidate the seat position. Until the 1970s, building infrastructure was just comparatively less discussed by local actors than hosting measures. The only major projects included the initial implantation of the CoE from 1949 to 1950, different activity around the second seat application phase from 1957 to 1959 which included the construction of an office building for the EP, as well as the Human Rights Court from 1962 to 1964. The

47 AS, 752 W 12, *Compte-rendu du 4.9.1978.*

48 E.g. AS, 752 W 19, *Compte-rendu du 9.7.1979.*

49 E.g. AS, 752 W 19, *Compte-rendu du 9.7.1979.*

50 E.g. AS, 752 W 16, *Compte-rendu du 19.12.1978.*

intention of causing the European institutions to appreciate the facilities the city provided to strengthen its position as host remained the same as with hosting activities.

Additionally, the competitive situation between Brussels, Luxembourg and Strasbourg manifested itself in these matters, especially concerning the available number of offices and lodgings. It became apparent from documents in the municipal archive of Strasbourg and the archive of the Council of Europe that the CoE and EP, which shared facilities, sometimes struggled to accommodate all their departments. The city administration worked to ease this shortage and constantly monitored whether Brussels or Luxembourg provided any new offices or housing for the European institutions. Therefore, they had a twofold overarching strategy, namely improvements of infrastructure within the city and reacting to any building projects in Brussels and Luxembourg in order to remain on an at least comparable level. From the sources, three areas where local actors sought to improve building infrastructure with different approaches can be identified, of which the most central ones will be investigated in this sub-chapter. They were construction for the IOs, as well as accommodation for delegates and civil servants. A more minor activity was, for example, a study for a possible European district in relation to Strasbourg's candidature in the second seat application round of the European Communities. The final plan was published in the book *Strasbourg invite l'Europe*.[51]

(a) Constructions

The first category accounted for most activity. The construction of the *Maison de l'Europe* was one of the bigger pre-1970s projects and was completed in the short period of five months, from March to August 1950. It was built just before the second PACE session. This preceded a long decision process about the features and location of the headquarter building in Strasbourg, spanning from the formation of the CoE on 5 May 1949 to January 1950. A large part of agency in this matter originated from the European organisation. Since the focus is on the municipal actors operating in Strasbourg itself, not every aspect described in CoE archive documents will be included here to the smallest detail. In this sub-chapter, the focus will be placed on this process than the construction or architectural features of the building itself, since connotations about the symbolism of the CoE for Strasbourg and other actors can be better inferred from this.

---

[51] Ville de Strasbourg and Conseil Général du Bas-Rhin, *Strasbourg invite l'Europe*, Strasbourg, Editions de la Calanque, 1957.

In general, the city administration had a vested interest that the CoE found a place in the city in order to honour its position as seat. A note from the end of 1949 stated that during the recent Committee of Ministers' meeting of the CoE, some doubts about Strasbourg's status were raised.[52] The events leading to the construction of the *Maison* were decided without state involvement, the only participation of the French government was it granting permissions, among others in the Committee of Ministers of the CoE.[53] Apart from the practical need to have a well-functioning building infrastructure for the European organisation, in this early phase a lack of involvement of the French state was visible in municipal and departmental documents of the time. Even in the departmental archive, not much information on the matter was present, the main agency seemed to have come from the city administration.

For the inaugural PACE session, which took place in August 1949, the assembly had been temporarily housed in the university. The necessity to adapt the venue to the CoE's needs which cost 25 million Francs (760,000€) had already shown in the organisation's opinion that the modification of an existing building to suit them was hardly possible.[54] These changes had been executed by Bertrand Monnet and were charged to the institution.[55] The Committee of Ministers was housed in the *Mairie* and the city covered the costs of 12.5 million Francs (380,000€) for changes to the building made to welcome them in a "dignified" manner, even though the *Conseil Municipal* had only granted a credit of 10 million Francs (300,000€).[56] This circumstance again provides evidence that local actors spared no expense to make the European institutions feel welcome even for one single parliamentary session. In the report for the authorisation to increase the above sum, the reasoning was used that these changes had been appreciated by delegates. Several thank-you letters were cited as evidence.[57] Since the beginnings of the European institutions in Strasbourg, the city administration seems to have placed the satisfaction of delegates with hosting activities and facilities above any financial concerns.

---

52 AS, 198 MW 82, *Note, 12/1949.*

53 AS, 782 W 343, *Lettre de Paris au Maire, 20.3.1950.*

54 ACE, 3358/2981, *Place Lenôtre, 17.7.1950*, p. 1.

55 ACE, 126/0106, *Lettre du Recteur Académie à Paris, 28.6.1949.*

56 AS, 198 MW 84, *Exposé du 26.9.1949*, p. 1.

57 AS, 198 MW 84, *Exposé du 26.9.1949*, p. 1.

(i) Construction of the Maison de l'Europe

The matter of finding or providing the CoE with adequate premises was a necessity, the institution identified itself. Its Preparatory Commission concluded that, since the university was only empty and usable during the summer holidays, another, more permanent solution needed be found.[58] Apart from finding a building suitable or easily adaptable to housing an assembly, the process was complicated by the fact that the definitive requirements for space, offices and other factors were not yet known.[59]

The commission drafted several proposals where to house the CoE which were later also transmitted to the city administration. The preparatory committee's first of three proposals was the exposition ground in Wacken, where they asked the city to allow them to use three halls. Henri Weber, the President of the *Foire Européenne*, responsible for the management, gave a tentative accord to this request, although he also raised organisational issues.[60] The second proposal was the semi-permanent installation of the CoE in the *Château de la Robertsau*, while the last was the construction of a building on the sports areal on Place Lenôtre as the most expensive solution.[61] An expert committee appointed by the Committee of Ministers decided to choose the last proposal on 23 November 1949 in the understanding that the municipality would only charge a symbolic rent of 1 Franc (0.03€).[62] This was accepted by the city; the CoE only had to pay this amount annually for the ground the *Maison* was built on.[63] It can be inferred that the city was very interested in welcoming the organisation that they acquiesced to charging virtually no rent for the site, an action which repeated itself with several subsequent building projects.

The CoE accepted the expert committee's decision and Monnet, the director of works, presented a draft project in collaboration with architects Lucien Cromback, Fernand Guri and V. Schirer.[64] The latter three also published an article in the journal *L'architecture d'aujourd'hui*, in which

58 AS, 235 MW 137, *Lettre du Commission Préparatoire du Conseil de l'Europe au Maire, 23.9.1949.*

59 AS, 198 MW 82, *Rapport du 2.12.1949*, p. 1.

60 AS, 235 MW 137, *Lettre de Weber au Maire, 30.9.1949.*

61 AS, 198 MW 82, *Rapport du 2.12.1949*, p. 2.

62 ACE, 3358/2981, *Place Lenôtre, 17.7.1950*, p. 3 and AS, 198 MW 82, *Rapport du 2.12.1949*, p. 3.

63 ACE, 3358/2981, *Place Lenôtre, 17.7.1950*, p. 4.

64 ACE, 3358/2981, *Place Lenôtre, 17.7.1950*, p. 3.

they described the building features and the construction process.[65] The CoE approved their plans in January 1950 and construction was set to commence on 6 March 1950, to be completed by 31 July 1950.[66] A group of local enterprises, coordinated by the Société Alsacienne de Travaux Publics, executed the construction.[67] A contributing factor to the rapid completion might also have been that the *Maison* constituted a rather functional building, judging by the emphasising leather wall coverings in the debating chamber as a special measure and by stating that decoration would otherwise be minimal.[68] The construction costs were covered by the member states which each provided a sum in proportion to their population size. With various other factors, such as that the European organisation was exempt from paying taxes on business deals,[69] the costs were evaluated at 207 million FF (5.7 million €) and 95 million FF (2.6 million €) for equipment.[70] The demolition and moving of the sport facilities on the building site costs were projected at an additional 15-20 million FF (460-610,000€).[71] From the start, this building was regarded as a temporary solution, pending a definitive decision when all needs for housing were known.

The building was the first purpose-built construction for the European institutions, among others with a plenary hall, which gave Strasbourg an important argument for acquiring further IOs. As has been outlined in chapter 1, the Common Assembly only was provisionally located in Strasbourg due to the CoE's facilities. The Secretariat-General of the CoE initially proposed to the Committee of Ministers a duration of eight to ten years for this building.[72] In reality, the *Maison* was used for over 20 years until it was replaced by the permanent headquarters *Palais de l'Europe* in the 1970s (see next sub-chapter). Until that building was completed,

---

65 Cromback, Lucien and Guri, Fernand and Schirrer, V., "Les bâtiments semi-permanents du Conseil de l'Europe à Strasbourg", in *L'architecture d'aujourd'hui*, 22, 1951, pp. 86-89.

66 ACE, 3358/2981, *Place Lenôtre, 17.7.1950*, p. 3 and *Place Lenôtre, 21.7.1950*, p. 1 and *Construction, 13.2.1950*, p. 6.

67 ACE, 3358/2981, *Place Lenôtre 13.4.1950*, p. 2.

68 ACE, 3358/2981, *Place Lenôtre 17.7.1950*, p. 1.

69 "General Agreement on Privileges and Immunities of the Council of Europe 2.IX.1949." <http://conventions.coe.int/Treaty/en/Treaties/Html/002.htm> (accessed 17.03.2014), *Art. 7*.

70 ACE, 126/0106, *CM/Adj (50)/1, proposal accommodation*, p. 3 and 3358/2981, *Place Lenôtre 17.7.1950*, p. 3 and *Construction 13.2.1950*, p. 4.

71 AS, 198 MW 82, *Rapport 2.12.1949*, p. 3.

72 ACE, 3358/2981, *Place Lenôtre, 21.7.1950*, p. 2.

the European organisation rented office space in different locations throughout the city.[73]

(ii) C block

The second project for the European institutions, the B block in 1953, designed by Monnet as well, sparked little discussion. It was commissioned because more office space was needed due to among others the accession of Iceland and Germany in 1950.[74] Therefore, the C block, comprised of offices for the EP, will be analysed in this chapter, since it was the second biggest project of the 1950s. As with all other activities of local actors towards the European institutions, this building was a strategy to bind the parliament closer to the city by offering the amenities it expected without any reservations. It also offers the opportunity to study relationships both between the local and supranational levels in the city and the CoE and EP. A common theme through not only infrastructure improvements was a certain uneven relationship, since the European institutions often demanded events or facilities which local actors were quick to meet. One likely reason for that was that municipal actors might have feared that the institutions might have moved elsewhere – especially in the case of the Common Assembly.

After the creation of the EP in 1958, which entailed that the assembly met more frequently in Strasbourg, they needed more space in the European institution buildings. The WEU also used up some capacity, since the CoE overtook some of its tasks.[75] The distribution of offices between the CoE and EP remained an area of discussion between the two institutions with frequent studies and meetings. For example, the CoE *Chef du Service du Bâtiment et des Installations* Georges Cunin and CoE *Chef de la Division du Matériel/du Service* Roger Clamer met with EP Secretary-General Frits de Nerée tot Babberich in Luxembourg on his demand in March 1959 to determine the distribution of offices in the new C block.[76] Among others, the CoE would occupy the ground floor.[77] Next to the administrative process of sharing facilities, the CoE charged the EP rent for its use of offices in the *Maison*, for instance about 4.3 million Francs

[73] ACE, 126/0106, *Note du 6.12.1951* and *Lettre du Préfet au Secrétaire-Général, 4.12.1951* and *Lettre de Marchal au Préfet, 12.3.1954* and *Renting, 27.9.1971* and *Memorandum, 24.3.1972* and AS, 752 W 7, *Note pour M. le Maire, 23.4.1980.*

[74] "Bâtiment B du Conseil de l'Europe." <http://www.strasbourg-europe.eu/batiment-b-du-conseil-de-l-europe,41441,fr.html> (accessed 24.03.2014).

[75] ACE, 127/01011, *Note pour Curtis, 28.12.1959*, p. 1.

[76] ACE, 127/01011, *Note du 17.3.1959*, p. 1.

[77] ACE, 127/01011, *Note pour Curtis, 28.12.1959*, p. 1.

(75,000€) from June to October 1958.[78] As material in the CoE archive shows, this issue was decided without the input of the city administration or other local actors.

Nevertheless, the municipality supplied office space if it was needed in its own buildings. This extra effort also was a strategy to gain the appreciation of European institutions through these actions, although it shows that building infrastructure for the CoE and EP was an issue in Strasbourg that could only be mitigated by temporary solutions. The existence of the C block eased the tight office situation, because before, the CoE had to ask the local authorities to house some of its services in the *Mairie* and other local administration buildings, when the European organisation had to allocate offices to the EP and High Authority during their sessions.[79] The *Préfet* had also given offices to the European institutions during sessions, in order to show that Strasbourg was the *capitale européenne*.[80] This practice was continued until 1961; the local administrations always provided office space on demand, even if they temporarily had to move some of their own services.[81] Thus, it was an example for the strategy of strengthening the city's position through gaining the appreciation of the European institutions.

City administration actors were aware that keeping especially the EP satisfied was paramount to remaining seat. They reasoned that they needed to offer adequate space to the executives of the European Communities and the EP in Strasbourg to avoid them moving to Brussels.[82] Local actors were aware of the fact that the seat of the EP was only provisional and that erecting a new office building would strengthen the city's position.[83] This was also emphasised by the finding the city made that Brussels had already provided large offices for the European institutions.[84] For these reasons, they decided to construct the building, since the EP was not prepared to do so.[85] Additionally, demands of the EP regarding the facilities of the future building were accommodated. The Bipartite Committee discussed and implemented the wish of the assembly to have conference halls in the

78 ACE, 3203/2431, *Lettre de Loth au Secrétaire-Général du Parlement Européen.*

79 ACE, 127/01011, *Note du 20.10.1959*, p. 3.

80 AS, 209 MW 5, *Lettre du Préfet au Maire, 2.12.1958.*

81 AS, 209 MW 5, *Note pour M. le Maire, 13.6.1961.*

82 AS, 55 W 86, *Lettre du Préfet au Maire, 7.10.1958*, p. 1.

83 AS, 209 MW 76, *Procès-verbal du 21.9.1959*, p. 2.

84 AS, 16 MW 11, *61e séance 17.11.1958*, p. 311.

85 AS, 208 MW 270, *Minutes of the Bipartite Committee session, 7.10.1958*, p. 3.

new block.[86] During the discussion, the point was made that if the MEPs did not find fault with the features of the new building, it could be an advantage for the city.[87]

In contrast to the other buildings projects, the Bipartite Committee was involved in the early planning phase. An extraordinary meeting on 14 October 1958 was dedicated to the initial planning process. The committee decided that the best course of action was to construct the building between the city and department and that they should retain ownership of the site.[88] Based on this accord, the *Conférence des Adjoints* decided on a location close to the *Maison de l'Europe* where sport facilities were located on.[89] The investment sum of the city was 100 million Francs (1.7 million €).[90] In this meeting, especially the *Adjoints au Maire* sitting in the Bipartite Committee pushed for an adoption of the proposal. Both Wach and Radius insisted that the plan should be approved due to the advantage it could give the city in the seat application round that was underway and that it should not be hampered by administrative obstructions.[91]

Next to placing specific demands, the EP was involved in the general construction process. For instance, on the request of Pflimlin, Monnet contacted the deputy secretary-general of the EP, Walter Hummelsheim, for input on the project.[92] He was also part of coordination meetings between the different instances. For example, in November 1959, Monnet met with him and civil servants from the European institutions, among them Cunin as CoE observer, Ridoux and Fix to talk about the facilities of the new building.[93] The EP also placed other demands than just sufficient office space for their services. For instance, Hummelsheim stressed that in Sicily, every MP had a private bathroom.[94] Such demands visualise that the European institutions also expected a certain standard which influenced the efforts of local actors.

Already in 1962, the office space in the C block was not sufficient anymore and the EP and city decided that an additional fourth floor

86 AS, 235 MW 273, *Minutes of the Bipartite Committee session, 12.6.1958.*

87 AS, 235 MW 273, *Minutes of the Bipartite Committee session, 13.2.1959*, p. 5.

88 AS, 208 MW 270, *Minutes of the Bipartite Committee session, 14.10.1958.*

89 AS, 55 W 86, *Extrait du compte-rendu, 18.10.1958*, p. 1.

90 AS, 55 W 86, *Extrait du compte-rendu, 18.10.1958*, p. 1.

91 AS, 55 W 86, *Extrait du compte-rendu, 18.10.1958*, p. 1.

92 AS, 236 MW 31/1, *Lettre de Monnet à Pflimlin, 27.4.1960.*

93 AS, 236 MW 31/1, *Note pour Pflimlin, 7.11.1959.*

94 AS, 236 MW 31/1, *Note pour Pflimlin, 7.11.1959*, p. 2.

needed to be built on top of it. The EP offered the city to assist with the costs, by paying the interest of the loan that would be necessary for the new construction which could in turn function as rent for the entire building.[95] Since the seat was not permanently determined, the secretariat-general of the EP was not allowed to invest directly.[96] Monnet was again the responsible architect and estimated the costs at circa 500,000 Francs (700,000€).[97] In this, the city actors' strategy of satisfying their guests' needs became visible again. From the sources on the C block, no state support of their endeavours was visible.

The fact that the building space soon became insufficient also shows for the patchwork manner, the city administration attempted to alleviate the building shortage. In municipal archive sources, no involvement or cooperation with the state is visible. The same situation was present in the departmental archive. Therefore, it is reasonable to assume that judging by the lack of any correspondence, the French state was not significantly involved in the improvement of infrastructure during the 1950s and early 1960s.

(iii) Human Rights Court

The planning phase and construction of the Human Rights Court from 1961 to 1964 presented another instance that costs did not necessarily constitute the primary concern of local actors, but that the aim was to consolidate Strasbourg's position as seat. For example, Pflimlin stated in the beginning of the building phase in a note to Fix, "Je défendrai donc devant la Municipalité et devant le Conseil Municipal la solution qui me paraîtra la plus valable du point de vue de l'intérêt moral de la ville."[98] These two actors, especially the Secretary-General, were responsible for the city's side of the organisational process. Additionally, Fix was involved in his position as Director of the *Habitation Moderne* which executed the project. In this role, he was mostly informed by Monnet about changes demanded by the CoE and how much this would cost.[99]

The building project lay in the responsibility of the city administration, although actions were coordinated with the CoE. The ministers' deputies of the CoE made the decision in March 1961 to contact the city regarding

---

95 AS, 752 W 1, *Note pour Pflimlin, 24.11.1962*, p. 2.

96 AS, 752 W 1, *Note pour Pflimlin, 28.12.1962*, p. 1.

97 AS, 752 W 1, *Lettre de Monnet à Pflimlin, 21.12.1962.*

98 AS, 752 W 80, *Note pour Fix, 6.9.1962*, p. 2.

99 E.g. AS, 752 W 80, *Lettre de Monnet à Fix, 28.11.1963.*

the construction.[100] The municipality considered two different building sites, in Contades and in Robertsau, adjacent to the *Maison de l'Europe*.[101] The decision fell to the latter option. The demolition and relocation of inhabitants from existing buildings was easier there, as the area, called *Cité de la Redoute*, consisted of temporary barracks.[102] Furthermore, the city offered the European organisation to cover the costs.[103] This might also hint at the economic impact of the European institutions on Strasbourg, since the city regularly financed construction projects at least partly, presumably to keep them in the city.

Monnet was again charged with the construction by the city administration in April 1962.[104] The first draft project was endorsed by the CoE. However, Pflimlin regarded the costs of over 3.2 million Francs (4.7 million €) too high for the city. The amended project, Monnet presented subsequently, which cost around 2 million Francs (2.8 million €) met the approval of the city, but was deemed as too modest by Armand Daussin, the Director-General of Administration and Finances of the CoE.[105] The third proposal of the architect, submitted in October 1962, costing around 2.4 million Francs (3.5 million €) finally met with both parties' consent.[106] Although the city administration normally spared no expense in regard to the European institutions, occasionally they did try to save costs in the execution of measures. Thus, the municipality did not necessarily try to limit funds for the CoE and EP's amenities, but if possible actors attempted to find a cheaper way which, however, did not impinge on the strategies to gain the European delegates' appreciation as a host.

The city also looked for further ways to save money, while providing the Human Rights Court with good working conditions. The city noted that the taxes amounted to 593,880 Francs (860,000€), which could be saved if the CoE was the official constructor.[107] Officially, the organisation was exempt from paying taxes on business deals.[108] In order to achieve

100 AS, 752 W 80, *Note du 2.3.1961.*

101 AS, 752 W 80, *Note pour M. le Maire, 15.11.1961.*

102 AS, 752 W 80, *Lettre du Maire à Jesel, 25.11.1961.*

103 AS, 752 W 80, *Lettre de Daussin à Pflimlin, 24.11.1961.*

104 AS, 752 W 80, *Lettre de Monnet au Maire, 26.4.1962.*

105 AS, 752 W 80, *Lettre de Monnet à Fix, 26.10.1962.*

106 AS, 752 W 80, *Lettre de Monnet à Fix, 26.10.1962* and *Lettre de Daussin à Pflimlin, 28.12.1962.*

107 AS, 752 W 80, *Rapport au Maire, 21.2.1963.*

108 "General Agreement on Privileges and Immunities of the Council of Europe 2.IX.1949." <http://conventions.coe.int/Treaty/en/Treaties/Html/002.htm> (accessed 17.03.2014), *Art. 7.*

this, Fix informed Daussin that the city would give the CoE a subsidiary of 3 million Francs (4.1 million €), the CoE would in turn charge the *Habitation Moderne* with the construction after the plans established by Monnet against the lump-sum payment of this amount.[109] In order to avoid the fiscal payments, the city additionally suggested that the CoE should own the building for 20 years and just pay rent for the site, while the city still would pay for the building's upkeep.[110] This was another instance of an effort to save money, while still fulfilling wishes and needs of the European institutions.

(b) Accommodation

The second aspect of building infrastructure from 1950-1964 were temporal and permanent accommodations for the European guests. They were another important area where local actors planned improvements as strategies to gain the appreciation of European parliamentarians and civil servants. Regarding the issue of hotel accommodation, local actors mainly concentrated on the improvements of room rates and facilities, except the deliberation on a hotel construction in 1957. This discussion was about whether it should exclusively suit the needs of European Institution personnel or not. The deliberation in the Placement Study Committee mainly spanned attempting to second-guess preferences and which solution would be eligible for outside funding.[111] The matter of improving existing hotel operations, however, remained forefront in the subsequent years. Permanent housing mostly regarded civil servants and diplomats affiliated with the CoE.

Temporal accommodation mainly comprised the improvement of hotels for the use of European parliamentarians. For example, in 1959, Mayor Pierre Pflimlin, Albert Fix, Alphonse Heitz, and specialised committee members Robert Baillard, André Bord, Robert Heitz, Germain Muller, René Radius, Antoine Schmitt, Paul Wach and Georges Woehl met to deliberate on improvements for the measures to welcome European parliamentarians.[112] Among others, the hotel situation was discussed and next to discounts in restaurants, the idea to offer European parliamentarians lower room rates was evaluated, especially because Brussels seemed to reduce the expenses by 20 percent for them.[113] In the meeting it was also decided to present

109 AS, 752 W 80, *Notice du 3.10.1963*, p. 2.

110 AS, 752 W 80, *Notice du 3.10.1963*, p. 1.

111 AS, 208 MW 11, *Minutes of the Placement Study Committee session, 23.7.1957*, pp. 6-7.

112 AS, 54 W 412, *Note du 1.10.1959.*

113 AS, 54 W 412, *Note du 1.10.1959*, p. 1.

all hotels which agreed to this in a brochure for the European guests.[114] To this effect, the Mayor sent a questionnaire to all directors of the major hotels in Strasbourg, asking about facilities and whether they granted any concessions to delegates.[115] This brochure was distributed to all European parliamentarians and civil servants in April 1960 and exclusively intended for them.[116] The reduction of room rates for European parliamentarians later met with opposition from hotel associations, like the *Fédération des Hoteliers* which from 1963 refused to apply it.[117] Additionally, Ridoux noted in 1962 that the discount was rarely given.[118]

Despite such efforts, frequent letters of complaint showed that some parliamentarians found the hotel service lacking. For instance, Italian MEP Antonio Carcaterra complained in 1961 that his and others reservations had been mismanaged.[119] The city always reacted promptly to such grievances and talked with the hotel about the issue. In this case, the city effected a reimbursement of the room rate.[120] In these matters, the city always seemed to have pursued a strategy of keeping their guests happy and of mitigating criticism. Unsatisfied parliamentarians might have diminished the impact of the local actors' strategies.

Long-term housing mainly was an issue for European civil servants that became current in the early 1960s. Before, the Bipartite Committee had already attempted to improve the situation, but large-scale efforts only commenced in that decade. Otherwise, in the Bipartite Committee session of 14 January 1958, the cost involved in the reservation of living space for European institution civil servants was under discussion, and it was decided rather to maintain reservations for the housing *de grand standing* than more modest flats or houses.[121] The concern was voiced that stopping to reserve particular housing should not leave the impression that Strasbourg would withdraw the seat candidature or see it as failed.[122]

In this manner, the competition between seat city candidates manifested itself. From sources from the municipal archive of Strasbourg, it became apparent that local actors regarded Brussels and Paris as closest rivals

---

114 AS, 54 W 412, *Note du 1.10.1959*, p. 2.

115 AS, 54 W 412, *Lettres du Maire aux hôtels, 30.10.1959.*

116 AS, 54 W 412, *Note du 20.4.1960.*

117 AS, 68 MW 40, *Procès-verbal du 13.2.1963*, p. 6.

118 AS, 54 W 413, *Note pour Pflimlin, 25.10.1962.*

119 AS, 236 MW 23/2, *Lettre de Carcaterra à Pflimlin, 7.3.1961.*

120 AS, 236 MW 23/2, *Lettre de Pflimlin à Carcaterra, 13.8.1961.*

121 AS, 235 MW 273, *Minutes of the Bipartite Committee session.*

122 AS, 235 MW 273, *Minutes of the Bipartite Committee session, 12.6.1958.*

around the end of the 1950s, while Luxembourg had replaced the French capital by the 1970s. For instance, studies by the French government showed that Paris possessed better infrastructure, and Strasbourg's city administration saw it as essential to be the successful French applicant.[123] Additionally, they were convinced that the French government favoured Paris, because no government plans existed to improve the infrastructure in Strasbourg.[124]

This assessment presented another example that Strasbourg also was in an intra-national struggle with the French capital to be the country's chief choice and not just in the competitive situation with the other two provisional seats. This generally remained current until the Merger Treaty which was signed in 1965, from when on the only meaningful competition occurred between the three provisional EP seat cities. Therefore, the city administration regarded providing accommodation not only as essential to welcome parliamentarians adequately, but also to convince the French government of their suitability.[125] Additionally, to remain comparable to their closest competition, city administration actors monitored how many lodgings Brussels provided and increased their holdings accordingly.[126]

Following the seat application phase from 1957 to 1959, the housing issue continued to be discussed and improved by local actors, also due to demands by the European institutions. For example, Lodovico Benvenuti, the Secretary-General of the CoE, asked Ridoux in 1962 if it was possible to construct small apartments that could be rented by secretariat members.[127] They had to stay in Strasbourg 50 to 60 days in hotels which were expensive and difficult to find reservations for.[128] The common approach of the city administration to such requests was to place ads in newspapers, which they renewed repeatedly if necessary and transmitted the resulting offers to the European institutions.[129] This situation both shows the demand side of the European institutions and that the city administration was willing to make an effort to fulfil even small wishes and make the stay of institution personnel easy.

In order to be able to offer permanent or regularly visiting civil servants with adequate lodgings, meetings with Bipartite Committee actors, city

---

123 AS, 208 MW 11, *Minutes of the Placement Study Committee session, 23.9.1957*, p. 3.

124 AS, 208 MW 11, *Minutes of the Placement Study Committee session, 23.9.1957*, p. 6.

125 AS, 208 MW 11, *Minutes of the Placement Study Committee session, 23.9.1957*, pp. 4-12.

126 AS, 235 MW 273, *Minutes of the Bipartite Committee session, 27.12.1957*, p. 2.

127 AS, 236 MW 23/6, *Lettre de Ridoux à Fix, 24.10.1962.*

128 AS, 236 MW 23/6, *Lettre de Ridoux à Fix, 24.10.1962.*

129 AS, 236 MW 23/6, *Note pour A. Heitz, 26.11.1962.*

service and housing associations were held. For instance, on 7 March 1961, under the chairmanship of Pierre Pflimlin, René Radius, Robert Heitz, Robert Baillard, Michel Kistler, Léon Kien, Georges Ridoux, Albert Fix, representatives from the *Divisions I* and *CF* and Cesari, president of *SERS* during the 1960s, met to find solutions to this issue.[130] Globally, it was decided to construct lodgings, but special solutions for specific persons were also made.[131] For example, already in 1961 Benvenuti had had difficulties finding adequate housing and therefore, the Mayor suggested for the city to buy the villa he currently lived in and to offer it to him at a favourable rent.[132] This sense of entitlement of European institution civil servants and parliamentarians became visible, since similar requests occurred with regularity. This could have been fostered by the local actors who either simply fulfilled them or found ways to ease the situation as in Benvenuti's case. It is likely that the city administration saw it as yet another strategy to consolidate indirectly Strasbourg's position by proving themselves as capable hosts. Additionally, Pflimlin's involvement in the above case gives evidence how much he steered this agenda of the municipality.

It was not uncommon for the local authorities to accommodate European civil servants in this manner. As mentioned in chapter 2, already in the first hosting phase, the local authorities acted as de facto real estate agents by finding lodgings for them after their specific demands. For example, during the 1960s, Ridoux frequently charged the city's *Service des Logements* to find adequate housing on behalf of European staff.[133] The European institutions placed concrete demands in this matter, as the case of Irish permanent representative to the CoE Thomas Woods in 1961 presented. He asked for a comfortable furnished flat with three bedrooms and a living room with an adjacent dining room large enough to hold receptions.[134]

Since the system with placing ads in newspapers to solicit offers for single demands did not always prove fruitful, the city administration actors attempted to find a general solution to the lodging problem.[135] One suggestion was to create a housing agency to accommodate temporary occupancies of apartments which had been practiced in Geneva with

---

130 AS, 236 MW 23/2, *Réunion du 7.3.1961*.

131 AS, 236 MW 23/2, *Réunion du 7.3.1961*, p. 2.

132 AS, 236 MW 23/2, *Réunion du 7.3.1961*, p. 2.

133 AS, 236 MW 23/2, *Note pour A. Heitz*.

134 AS, 236 MW 23/2, *Note pour la Division I, 21.3.1961*.

135 AS, 236 MW 23/3, *Note pour Pflimlin, 26.1.1963*, p. 3.

the League of Nations and was also the case with the UN in New York.[136] From 1962, *SERS* constructed apartment blocks on the former military site Esplanade where the city envisioned reserving 450 flats with four or more rooms for civil servants from 1963 and 1964.[137]

City administration actors also attempted to procure flats for European institution personnel through their personal networks. For instance, when Hans Nord asked in October 1962 on his and others' behalves to rent studio apartments, as they often came to Strasbourg, the municipality was not able to find any vacant ones.[138] Fix noted that private landlords would offer such housing and A. Heitz gave Ridoux the name of a notary who agreed to reserve housing for institution staff.[139] Since these studio apartments were still under construction and would only be finished in 1964, the municipality placed ads in newspapers, but was not able to find any through this method.[140] Finally, Ridoux suggested that the city should buy luxurious lodgings to improve the chances of Strasbourg's seat candidature and to solve the accommodation problem anytime a new European institution civil servant was appointed.[141] This proposal was implemented and in February 1963, the city decided to reserve two to three furnished apartments as a temporary solution for newly-appointed institution officials.[142] All these efforts provide an indicator that the fulfilment of single, but recurrent demands, became institutionalised, meaning that meeting these demands became the norm.

Local actors seemed to be aware of the fact that insufficient housing for European civil servants reflected on their capabilities to house European institutions, especially in comparison to their competition. In the book *Strasbourg invite l'Europe*, intended to present the city's seat candidature in 1957, the city among others presented itself as being active in this area.[143] In the *Complément* published in 1960, they claimed that the housing problem would have been resolved.[144] They stressed that since 1957, 6,000 lodgings had been constructed and that their rate would double the average French

136 AS, 236 MW 23/3, *Note du 30.1.1963*, p. 2.

137 AS, 236 MW 23/4, *Note pour Cesari, 5.11.1962.*

138 AS, 68 MW 40, *Note pour Pflimlin, 26.1.1963*, p. 2.

139 AS, 68 MW 40, *Note pour Pflimlin, 26.1.1963*, p. 2.

140 AS, 68 MW 40, *Note pour Pflimlin, 26.1.1963*, p. 2.

141 AS, 68 MW 40, *Note pour Pflimlin, 26.1.1963*, p. 3.

142 AS, 68 MW 40, *Procès-verbal du 13.2.1963*, p. 8.

143 Ville de Strasbourg and Conseil Général du Bas-Rhin, *Strasbourg invite l'Europe*, Strasbourg, Editions de la Calanque, 1957.

144 Ville de Strasbourg and Conseil Général du Bas-Rhin, *Strasbourg invite l'Europe. Complément 1960*, Strasbourg, Editions de la Calanque, 1960.

one.[145] Thus, they attempted to project a favourable picture of the situation to convince the European Communities of their capabilities.

All in all, the improvement of building infrastructure for the institutions and their personnel served the goal of remaining an attractive seat choice. For instance, during the second seat application round, city actors judged it as essential to fulfil housing and office requirements, lest the EP would move elsewhere.[146] To pursue this goal, the practical value for the European institutions often took precedence over general city politics. One example presents the Human Rights Court.[147] Furthermore, the city made other financial concessions by mostly only charging symbolic rents. From EC documents, the different institutions generally paid non-nominal amounts for the buildings they leased. In Luxembourg, the EC paid 7,554,272 Luxembourg Francs (190,000€)[148] in 1957 for 20 buildings their institutions occupied.[149] Another list of paid rents for all the EC institutions in Brussels, Luxembourg and Strasbourg amounted to annually 92,279,000 Belgian Francs (2.3 million €)[150] in 1961.[151] Although the city administration claimed it primarily was a matter for them, economic consideration in the form of revenue for a seat city must at least have played an implicit role.

Section 1.19 The Palais de l'Europe

The *Palais de l'Europe* was the permanent headquarter of the CoE and the first of two grand construction projects of the 1970s. With the exception of the Human Rights Court, all prior construction for the European institutions had only been provisional like the *Maison*, or were supplementary buildings like the B and C blocks in order to meet the growing needs of the CoE, as well as the EP. The process was mainly driven by the European organisation itself, while the city played a more minor role compared to the construction projects analysed in the previous chapter. Since this study is about the local efforts of consolidating Strasbourg's

145 Ville de Strasbourg and Conseil Général du Bas-Rhin, *Strasbourg invite l'Europe. Complément 1960*, Strasbourg, Editions de la Calanque, 1960.

146 AS, 208 MW 270, *Minutes of the Bipartite Committee session, 7.10.1958.*

147 AS, 752 W 1, *Extrait du compte-rendu de la Conférence des Adjoints du 4.1.1963.*

148 Since a currency converter that includes the inflation is not available for Luxembourg Francs, the conversion rate from 2002 to Euros has been chosen in order to give a point of reference.

149 AC, CM1/1958 123, *Locaux loués, 16.1.1958.*

150 Since a currency converter that includes the inflation is not available for Belgian Francs, the conversion rate from 2002 to Euros has been chosen in order to give a point of reference.

151 AC, CM1 1961 57.1, *Annexe I, Loyers.*

position, local actors will be concentrated on and the CoE's agency will only be summarised.

The plan was made by the French architect Bernard, after a proposal of Monnet was judged by the CoE as using the site poorly after aesthetic considerations.[152] Additionally, the *Palais* was the first instance of significant French state involvement, since the national government in 1969 granted a loan of 70 million Francs (78 million €) for the project.[153] The *Palais* had a relatively long planning process from 1966 to 1972, when works began. On the other, the construction proper from 1972 to 1977, when the building was opened, seemed to have generated significantly less material, judging by available documents in the archive of the Council of Europe and the municipal archive of Strasbourg. The drafting of the project will be the primary focus of this sub-chapter, since most of the symbolic considerations for Strasbourg's image and capabilities as host were discussed in this phase.

Next to the practical implication of finally constructing a permanent, representative building for the European organisation, capable to house all its services, a symbolic dimension was present as well. This was the area to which local actors dedicated most of their activity. Frequent strategic mentions of the importance Strasbourg attached to the presence of the European institutions and the unequivocal support of them were made to serve as a strategic device to strengthen the city's position as seat. One example from when the construction was already underway was a statement made by Pflimlin during his exposé on the city's budget in the *Conseil Municipal* on 3 February 1975 which he also sent to CoE Secretary-General Lujo Toncic-Sorinj for information.

> Le nouveau Palais de l'Europe, achevé lui aussi, accueillera dans un cadre digne de la grande ambition européenne les hommes de gouvernement, les parlementaires, les diplomates qui dans notre ville s'attacheront à poursuivre malgré les vents contraires, l'œuvre de paix et d'unité dont Strasbourg, pour d'innombrables Européens, demeure le symbole.[154]

In this manner, the new building was stylised as the concrete symbol expressing the values of European ideas which can be likened to the flying of the European flag. Hence, this project was a strategic way of the city to express their alleged Europeanness to construct a positive image of themselves as institution host.

---

152 ACE, C156 2/2, *Working party meeting, 24.10.1966.*

153 ACE, 122/0103/2-3, *Lettre de Ehrhard au Secrétaire-Général, 16.12.1969.*

154 ACE, 3358/2981, *Exposé de Pflimlin, 3.2.1975*, p. 14.

Additionally, in practical terms, the city's involvement in the planning and building process concentrated itself on the cessation of the site, the moving or demolition of existing structures on it, as well as the general support of the European institutions' wishes. The city especially endeavoured to highlight the importance they ascribed to the presence of the European institutions, also to one that had its permanent seat in the city and where there was no concrete threat of it leaving. For example, in 1972 a note to the Secretary-General of the city stated, Strasbourg needed to show that they favoured and prioritised the construction of the *Palais*.[155]

It is important to note that the EP remained a central factor in the process of erecting the CoE building. Since both European institutions shared certain facilities during sessions, the *Palais* constituted an important aspect for strengthening Strasbourg as EP seat, as well which was emphasised on different occasions in the sources. The EC assembly paid the CoE rent for the usage of its premises, for instance 1,000 Francs (1,200€) for the use of the plenary hall per day during the 1960s.[156] Supporting the construction of the *Palais* could also be employed as an argument against EP sessions moving permanently to its other two seats, since the assembly would continue to use the new building's plenary hall.

(a) Planning

The CoE started the process of drafting a project for a permanent building in 1966 with a "working party to study the problem of CoE buildings", because of the poor state of the *Maison de l'Europe* and lack of office space. In 1958, the roof of the *Maison* had collapsed during a storm and in 1966 and 1967 room partitions had shifted during similar weather conditions.[157] The building was also overcrowded and not representative anymore.[158] Additionally, the local population in the Alsatian dialect referred to it as *Bruchbütik*,[159] a dilapidated building.[160] All in all, the CoE evaluated that the poor state of the *Maison* would affect the European organisation's prestige, next to providing inadequate space.[161]

155 AS, 752 W 3, *Note du 21.2.1972.*

156 ACE, 121/0103/1, *CM(66)15, Conditions*, p. 22.

157 ACE, 121/0103/1, *Working party draft report*, p. 6.

158 ACE, C156 2/2, *Ways in which 5.3.1970*, p. 1.

159 In the CoE document, *Bruchbütik* is translated as "the shacks" (cf. ACE, C156 2/2, *Ways in which 5.3.1970*, p. 1).

160 ACE, C156 2/2, *Ways in which the Council of Europe's work is obstructed by inadequate premises, 5.3.1970*, p. 1.

161 ACE, C156 2/2, *Ways in which the Council of Europe's work is obstructed by inadequate premises, 5.3.1970*, p. 1.

The working party also heard involved parties such as PACE, the EP or the city. During the sixth working party meeting on 27 February 1967, Pflimlin made a statement on the city's preparedness to aid in the construction process. In his speech, he focussed on symbolic aspects, but also political decisions of the EC seat question during the second round to find a permanent siting from 1957-1959.[162] The Mayor prefaced his talk with stressing that Strasbourg had always been supportive of being institution seat.[163] This sentiment was mirrored by the Secretary-General of the CoE as well. "He [Secretary-General] was also anxious to emphasise that the Council had most friendly relations with the Strasbourg authorities and had always received support and assistance from them."[164]

Pflimlin continued with including the EP by stating which building projects, namely the C block, the city had built for it.[165] The importance of the EP was repeatedly stressed during this meeting, for instance, by Pflimlin emphasising that the city's "only wish" was that both European institutions were satisfied with a solution, or the deputy secretary-general of the CoE noted that members of the EEC Commission had expressed the buildings were unsuitable.[166] It again gives evidence for the local actors' unconditional concessions towards the European institutions, which constituted central strategies to consolidate the city's seat status by being an excellent host.

Likewise, PACE in the form of its President Geoffrey de Freitas, as well as Vice-President René Radius and member Albert Voilquin who respectively represented the city administration's and the Budget Committee's interests, communicated the requirements of the assembly to the working party during its third meeting in December 1966.[167] In this aspect, the common multi-positioning among certain local actors manifested itself anew. Next to being one of the central individual actors in the city administration, Radius also used his position as PACE representative and from the end of the 1960s Vice-president to further support city interests in regard to the European institutions. The EP was asked about their demands by the working party, as well.[168]

---

162 ACE, 121/0103/1, *Working party minutes, 27.2.1967*, p. 2.

163 ACE, 121/0103/1, *Working party minutes, 27.2.1967*, p. 2.

164 ACE, 121/0103/1, *Working party minutes, 27.2.1967*, p. 3.

165 ACE, 121/0103/1, *Working party minutes, 27.2.1967*, p. 2.

166 ACE, 121/0103/1, *Working party minutes, 27.2.1967*, p. 3.

167 ACE, 121/0103/1, *Working party minutes, 11.12.1966.*

168 ACE, 121/0103/1, *Working party draft report.*

The working party came to the conclusion that the Human Rights Court was the only satisfactory building, while the A block (*Maison de l'Europe*) would present the biggest problem.[169] The B block was characterised as a utility-type, second-rate construction with an inadequate distribution of offices, the C block was also included in the considerations, since the EP wanted use of the ground floor which was occupied by the CoE.[170] The shabby and old-fashioned appearance of the buildings was also cited, as well as a demand from the EP and PACE for "premises worthy of European assemblies."[171] In the report, the working party recommended constructing a new building in place of the *Maison*, while the exteriors of the B and C blocks should be renovated.[172] The committee added that the B block should only be kept due to pragmatic considerations.[173]

For the period from 1967 to 1970, less archive material exists on the planning progress, but it is likely that a project for the Palais was further specified during the period. For example, in 1969, the French permanent representative to the CoE, François Ehrhard, wrote to Lujo Toncic-Sorinj that his government had decided to accord a long-term loan of 70 million FF via the *Caisse des Dépôts et Consignations* with an interest rate of 6.25 percent.[174] In 1970, the working party was re-convened to present a concrete plan for the construction of the new building.[175] After the precision of a building project, the city sold an additional site at Place Lenôtre, which housed parts of a tennis club, to the CoE. The sale agreement, specifying the symbolic price of 10,000 Francs (10,000€) was signed on 11 June 1971 by the Mayor and the Secretary-General of the CoE and approved by the *Préfet*.[176] The process to reach a consensus for the features of the area between the two parties already began in the previous year, for instance, a note to the *Division I* from May 1970 stated that the negotiations needed to be accelerated.[177] Therefore, the main involvement of the city administration was providing the building site and demolish pre-existing constructions on it which they did readily.

169 ACE, 121/0103/1, *Working party draft report*, pp. 5-6.

170 ACE, 121/0103/1, *Working party draft report*, p. 6.

171 ACE, 121/0103/1, *Working party draft report*, p. 6.

172 ACE, 121/0103/1, *Working party draft report*, pp. 21-26.

173 ACE, 121/0103/1, *Working party draft report*, p. 20.

174 ACE, 122/0103/2-3, *Lettre de Ehrhard à Toncic-Sorinj 16.12.1969.*

175 ACE C156 1/1, *Report 17.12.1971*, p. 3.

176 AS, 752 W 3, *Contrat du 11.6.1971*, pp. 1; 5.

177 AS, 203 MW 24, *Note pour la Division I, 4.5.1970.*

The working party was also tasked with considering a counter-proposal made by Germany. It included severely limiting the expenditure by only constructing a new building for the Secretariat-General and retaining and renovating the other buildings.[178] The working party rejected this, since it involved keeping the *Maison*.[179] It was regarded as essential to demolish this building due to the numerous complaints about working conditions.[180] A note entitled "ways in which the Council of Europe's work is obstructed by inadequate premises" summarised all the arguments for the destruction of the old building. They were the lack of space, the fact that the shabby exterior would affect the European organisation's prestige and that visitors were astonished that a provisional building was still in use after 20 years.[181]

Reacting to the German proposal was the only Bipartite Committee activity regarding the construction. Its involvement gives evidence for that local actors saw the construction of facilities as important to consolidate Strasbourg's position as seat. On the meeting on 29 January 1970, a resolution was adopted that expressed the satisfaction with the French government according a credit sum and stressed that the project needed to be executed immediately, also to the benefit of the EP.[182] Additionally, this statement was supposed to ease communications with the German Foreign minister Walter Scheel, whom Pflimlin intended to contact regarding the issue.[183] Toncic-Sorinj talked to the German permanent representative to the CoE, Ellinor von Puttkamer, about this proposal and she assured him that it had only been made due to financial considerations.[184] Additionally, Daussin proposed to contact Scheel and maybe even the chancellor on the issue to convince them about the construction of the *Palais*, since their suggestion would only slightly relieve the space problem and the French loan would cover the costs for the new building.[185] In April 1970, Scheel answered the letter Pflimlin had sent in February with the Bipartite Committee's resolution, in which the Foreign Minister stated that the German government was now prepared to approve the construction of the *Palais* after an intensive assessment.[186]

---

178 ACE, C156 2/2, *Conclusions du 2.-3.4.1970*, p. 2.

179 ACE, C156 2/2, *Conclusions du 2.-3.4.1970*, p. 2.

180 ACE, C156 2/2, *Memorandum, 6.3.1970*, p. 2.

181 ACE, C156 2/2, *Ways in which the Council of Europe's work is obstructed by inadequate premises, 5.3.1970.*

182 ABR, 1130 W 936/12, *Minutes of the Bipartite Committee session, 29.1.1970*, p. 4.

183 ABR, 1130 W 936/12, *Minutes of the Bipartite Committee session, 29.1.1970*, p. 4.

184 ACE, C156 2/2, *Secrétaire-Général, conversation 2/1970.*

185 ACE, C156 2/2, *Note 4.2.1970.*

186 ACE, C156 2/2, *Lettre de Scheel à Pflimlin, 19.4.1970.*

(i) Temporary office space solutions

Next to accommodating the EP's requirements in the project drafting for the new building, the city sought to ease the housing problem which still remained during this process. In a note to Adam in February 1970, Pflimlin stressed that the assembly's concerns regarding space for their services needed to be addressed without delay, because "[...] la position de Strasbourg à l'égard de cette assemblée reste précaire."[187] As reasons for this circumstance, he cited the inconvenience civil servants encountered when travelling from Luxembourg and that this city was in the process of erecting a building for the EP which would fit quite well to the institution's requirements.[188] The Mayor stressed that if such factors continued to accumulate, the assembly might leave and quoted hearsay that its president, Mario Scelba, was prepared to demand a move to Brussels, should no solution be found in Strasbourg.[189] Thus, a threat situation was added to the process of constructing the *Palais* as well.

The fact that the closest competition Luxembourg and Brussels possessed building infrastructure to house the EP, illustrated the danger Pflimlin assumed that the city was in. It seemed imperative to the municipality to mitigate this circumstance to be able to compete with the other two provisional seats at an at least comparable level.

In order to counter this, Pflimlin proposed to construct another temporary building for office space, modelled on the modalities of previous building projects.[190] He noted that this would not look aesthetically pleasing, but that there was a need to choose between "inconveniences."[191] Incidentally, the EP had come to the same conclusion. On request of Nord, Sforza Galeazzo Sforza, the Deputy Secretary-General of the CoE, stated that the organisation generally had no objections to erect a provisory building until the *Palais* was finished, although he noted that the city's consent was needed for this, since it still owned the site.[192] Nord addressed this request to Pflimlin in February 1970, in which he specified that Monnet created a project for a new wing to the *Maison* that would offer space for 30 additional offices. He added that the financing remained to be assured and asked the city to assist as the Mayor had indicated the city's

187 AS, 752 W 5, *Note pour Adam, 11.2.1970*, p. 1.

188 AS, 752 W 5, *Note pour Adam, 11.2.1970*, p. 1.

189 AS, 752 W 5, *Note pour Adam, 11.2.1970*, p. 1.

190 AS, 752 W 5, *Note pour Adam, 11.2.1970*, p. 2.

191 AS, 752 W 5, *Note pour Adam, 11.2.1970*, p. 2.

192 AS, 752 W 5, *Lettre de Sforza à Nord, 13.1.1970.*

willingness.[193] Pflimlin charged Adam with examining this proposal from the EP as soon as possible, since the city would not have a secure position with Luxembourg constructing a new building for the assembly.[194]

In a meeting in March 1970 with EP officials, the *Société générale alsacienne de banque (Sogenal)*, Fix in his function as Director of the *Habitation Moderne* and Adam, the creation of this wing was decided. The consensus was made to use elements from the Human Rights Court and the C block to finance the project which after an estimate from Monnet amounted to circa 880,000 Francs (930,000€).[195] The EP would contribute by depositing funds in the *Sogenal* which would in turn grant an advance for the construction.[196] The start of works was set for 1 May, as this wing, referred to as D block, needed to be finished for the EP session beginning on 20 September.[197] The *Conférence de la Municipalité* was only informed in June about the project when Adam stated that the same financing scheme as for the addition of a floor to the C block would be used.[198] In sources from the archive of the Council of Europe, the CoE referred to the Human Rights Court building as D block; in this book, the full name of this building will always be used to avoid confusion.

The CoE and EP communicated on housing problems, as well. For instance, Toncic-Sorinj wrote to the President of the EP, Walter Behrendt, in May 1971, because Pflimlin had told him about the conversation with Behrendt regarding the new building and wanted to add his opinion.[199] Toncic-Sorinj stated that there was a difference between the *Palais* as CoE building and the issue of the EP seat, because it was not certain when a definitive solution would be found.[200] Nevertheless, he stated that Behrendt could communicate his building requirements.[201] In his reply the President of the EP stated that the precarious situation with the provisional seats made it impossible for the assembly to commit to any permanent building.[202]

Apart from the threat situation with the three provisional capitals which competed to provide superior facilities, a political uncertainty

193 AS, 752 W 5, *Lettre de Nord à Pflimlin, 6.2.1970.*

194 AS, 97 W 12/1, *Note pour Adam, 11.2.1970.*

195 AS, 752 W 5, *Compte-rendu du 13.3.1970* and *Note pour M. le Maire, 2.3.1970.*

196 AS, 752 W 5, *Compte-rendu du 13.3.1970* and *Note pour M. le Maire, 2.3.1970.*

197 AS, 752 W 5, *Compte-rendu du 13.3.1970*, p. 3.

198 AS, 236 MW 23/7, *Séance de la Conférence Municipal du 8.6.1970.*

199 ACE, C156 1/1, *Lettre de Toncic-Sorinj à Behrendt, 3.5.1971.*

200 ACE, C156 1/1, *Lettre de Toncic-Sorinj à Behrendt, 3.5.1971.*

201 ACE, C156 1/1, *Lettre de Toncic-Sorinj à Behrendt, 3.5.1971.*

202 ACE, C156 1/1, *Lettre de Behrendt à Toncic-Sorinj, 9.6.1971.*

due to the lack of action and definitive decisions was added. Since this hampered both the city and EP to commit to any permanent and custom installations for the assembly, local actors were active in attempting to provide the parliament with the best provisional buildings possible. Next to the C block that was constructed to ease the overcrowding in the *Maison* caused by the sharing of the CoE and EP, the D block included a prime example for this. It constituted a truly temporary building that was constructed to assure adequate housing for the EC assembly until the *Palais* was finished. The threat situation that Luxembourg and Brussels possessed more adequate facilities at the time contributed to this, as well.

(b) Affirming Strasbourg's European mission

Prior to outlining the construction process proper, an overview of several of the ceremonies commemorating different events of the phase will be given. The speeches pronounced at these events give another impression of the symbolic dimension of the erection of the *Palais* and are evidence of local actors' strategies to strengthen their position as seat through this project. The first instance was the ceding of the building site from the city to the CoE on 10 May 1971, when next to speeches of CoE Secretary-General Lujo Toncic-Sorinj and Pierre Pflimlin, the contract was signed, as well.[203] This piece was prefaced by a solemn declaration signed by both parties. Its content bore similarity to the *vocation européenne*-speeches of the city administration. Next to mentioning Ernest Bevin and the city's 1957 resolution for the second seat application round, the text ended with the statement, "Thus the City of Strasbourg's European mission, which has long been rooted in its geography and history, will be confirmed in stone."[204]

It serves as a prime example that the construction of the *Palais*, although largely drafted by the CoE due to lack of office space and a representative building, contained elements of the city's efforts to improve its credentials as seat. Next to the implicit statement that the Strasbourg was Europe-friendly and that the new building expressed that, it can also be characterised as a signal to the EC seat competition. As mentioned above, during the planning phase, the needs of the EP regarding the *Palais* were always emphasised, citing the building efforts of Brussels and Luxembourg for the assembly. Therefore, the new building was employed as an argument for Strasbourg as EP seat as well, even though it was the headquarter of the CoE. The second occasion was the laying

[203] ACE, C156 1/1, *Note pour le Secrétaire-Général, 10.6.1971.*

[204] ACE, C156 1/1, *Solemn declaration.*

of the foundation stone on 15 May 1972 when similar declarations were made, to which the *Conseil Municipal* and *Général*, as well as other local administrative institutions were invited.[205]

(c) Construction phase

In November 1971, the initial project for the new building had been submitted.[206] The construction permit was granted by the *Conférence de la Police du Bâtiment* on 2 February 1972 and delivered in June.[207] The demolition of existing structures on the site, parts of tennis courts and a small building, the *pavillon d'octroi* seemed to have proceeded quickly and without much protest, judging by available archive documents. For example, the demolition and moving of cabins of the swimming club *SNS* seems to have been executed without much controversy.[208]

The final demolition of the *Maison* started in April 1977.[209] According to an article in the *Nouvel Alsacien*, demolitions already started in 1972, after the CoE decided to use the *Pères Oblats* building for temporary office space which the city had placed at the disposition of the CoE as interim housing for services displaced during the construction.[210] Occasionally, the city and the CoE held meetings on building aspects, as well, as for example in March 1972 with Adam, Clamer, city representatives and engineers and architects of the *Communauté Urbaine*, when issues such as parking or access to the building were discussed.[211] Other meetings, with a representative of Bernard discussed building features after the architect's plans and what the CoE, again represented by Clamer, wanted.[212]

The costs seemed to have increased further during the construction process. An article in the regional newspaper *Dernières Nouvelles d'Alsace* stated in 1975 that the costs had passed 220 million Francs (149.6 million €) at that time.[213] Interestingly, archive sources on this circumstance are scarce, the majority of them focussed on the pre-construction process. Therefore, it remains unclear in what way this was financed, since the French government had only offered a 70 million Francs loan, and how

205 ACE, C156 1/1, *Note pour la cérémonie du 27.4.1972.*
206 AS, 782 W 350, *Bernard, 5/1976.*
207 AS, 782 W 348, *Note du 7.2.1972* and 782 W 350, *Bernard, 5/1976.*
208 AS, 173 W 165, *Note du 11.4.1973.*
209 AS, 752 W 4, *Extrait des DNA, 14.4.1977.*
210 AS, 782 W 348, *Extrait du Nouvel Alsacien, 14.3.1972.*
211 AS, 752 W 4, *Compte-rendu du 13.3.1972.*
212 AS, 516 W 101, *Réunion du 22.4.1976.*
213 AS, 752 W 4, *Extrait des DNA, 4.4.1975.*

far the CoE member states shouldered the financial burden. In the initial documents for the construction in the archive of the Council of Europe, a table specified that each member contributed a percentage proportional to its size to the project.[214] It is likely that the CoE states covered additional costs, as well. Although the European organisation and the French state shouldered much of the costs, the willingness of the city administration to institute measures despite additional costs becomes visible again.

(d) Summary

All in all, the *Palais de l'Europe* was the first large permanent building for the European institutions in Strasbourg. The CoE mainly drove its construction process, since the provisional *Maison* became decrepit. Additionally, it and the B and C blocks were insufficient in terms of space. Apart from supporting the regional organisation's endeavours, city administration actors stressed the symbolism of the new building, to the European idea as a whole, but especially as expression of Strasbourg's *vocation européenne*. Although this building was for the CoE, the EP remained an important factor in this process, not just because both institutions shared certain facilities, but also because of implications for Strasbourg in the EC seat question.

This issue continued to be current after the completion of the *Palais*, for instance, a note from 1977 stated that more extensive, immediate facilities needed to be found for the EP, also in light of the approaching direct election.[215] The same document stressed that the rivals Brussels and Luxembourg seemed to possess adequate infrastructure to welcome the EP, and that measures needed to be taken to match at least the other two provisional seat cities.[216] This note specified that further buildings, the F and G blocks, would be finished in 1978. It also considered creating new space for the assembly in Roseraie, where the *Palais des Congrès* was located, but it was finally decided in 1978 to create a *secteur européen* close to the *Palais*.[217] Thus, satisfying infrastructure requirements was not only a strategy to gain the European institutions' appreciation, but also necessary to stay within the competition for the seat of the EP.

---

214 ACE, C156 1/1, *Annexe résolution (71)1.*

215 AS, 331 W 169, *Note du 7.10.1977*, p. 1.

216 AS, 331 W 169, *Note du 7.10.1977*, p. 1.

217 AS, 331 W 169, *Note du 7.10.1977*, p. 2 and *Lettre de Baillard à Delmas, 26.5.1978.*

Section 1.20 The *Immeuble Parlementaire Européenne (IPE)*

The *IPE* was a highly important element in the local actors' efforts to consolidate their position as EP seat. Today, it is named the *Salvador de Madariaga building*, which encompasses the original construction from 1978-1980, as well as several extensions during the 1980s.[218] This sub-chapter will focus on the *IPE's* significance for the city as EP host, rather than its architecture or construction process. Most sources in the municipal archive of Strasbourg covered these matters, but they also allow for inferring information on its importance for the seat question.

Apart from the practical reason of providing more space for a larger EP after the first direct election, it carried several connotations related to the symbolism of this action for Strasbourg's reputation as host. It was a device of the competitive situation between the three provisional seat cities. Luxembourg and Brussels constructed buildings for the EP at the same time which increased this factor. In addition to the competitive situation, an element of uncertainty prevailed regarding an official EC decision about the seat which might have complicated the construction of infrastructure, since the placement was only provisional. Nevertheless, the competition between Brussels, Luxembourg and Strasbourg necessitated both providing facilities for the EP to function and to upgrade holdings accordingly when one city erected a building to attain a superior position over the competition.

As another element, a number of MEPs seemed to have preferred a move to Brussels as the city administration stated in a report on the building infrastructure improvements they already had implemented. "En dépit de tous ces efforts une réticence est ressentie auprès des membres du Parlement qui semblerait accueillir favorablement leur transfert à Bruxelles."[219] Since most of the strategies of local actors aimed at consolidating their position as European institution host through gaining the appreciation of European parliamentarians and civil servants, the seeming preference for Brussels was another serious issue. The construction of the *IPE* was also supposed to alleviate this situation, apart from the fact of keeping up with construction projects in Brussels and Luxembourg.

---

218 "Bâtiment Salvador de Madariaga." <http://www.strasbourg-europe.eu/batiment-salvador-de-madariaga,41337,fr.html> (accessed 24.03.2014).

219 AS, 752 W 12, *Extrait du compte-rendu de la Conférence Municipal du 10.10.1977*, p. 11.

(a) Planning the IPE

Already before the planning phase of the office building for the EP began in 1977, the increasing competition between the three EP seat cities Brussels, Luxembourg and Strasbourg became visible in city administration documents. This rivalry can be separated into two, albeit intertwined aspects; the seeming preference of a number of MEPs for Brussels and construction projects in Luxembourg and the Belgian capital parallel to Strasbourg's efforts. Additionally, an internal working party of the EP to evaluate the infrastructural conditions in the three cities concluded that the facilities the assembly had in the newly-constructed *Palais de l'Europe* would only minimally meet the requirements on the condition that sessions did not last longer than five days and criticised that MEPs did not have single offices.[220] Therefore, there seemed to be a certain threat situation, namely that Strasbourg was in danger of losing its seat status due its infrastructure deficiencies and MEPs' dissatisfaction with them.

The municipality believed that a local plan needed to be formulated by finding a possibility to construct another building for the EP, even before the French government decided on a political strategy on the intergovernmental level in the matter.[221] Regarding this issue, the city administration was aware of the importance a satisfactory building infrastructure had on the rivalry with the other EP host cities. "Il faut donc absolument régler rapidement, de manière favorable, toutes les questions concernant le fonctionnement à Strasbourg du Parlement Européen, pour ne pas fournir des prétextes à ceux qui veulent le transfert à Bruxelles."[222] Hence, constructing a new building for the EP was the central municipal strategy to strengthen the position as seat.

The direct election also increased the currency of the seat question and scrutiny of seat city capabilities. The number of MEPs grew from 198 to 410 and the group of 1,700 civil servants would also grow due to the approaching EC enlargement.[223] In a city document, the reasoning was made that MEPs should have one office each, because the direct election would create a new group of parliamentarians without a dual, national mandate, who could be expected to spend more time in Strasbourg.[224] This circumstance might be a reason why local actors continuously

220 AS, 752 W 12, *Extrait du compte-rendu de la Conférence Municipal du 10.10.1977*, p. 12.

221 AS, 752 W 12, *Extrait du compte-rendu de la Conférence Municipal du 10.10.1977*, p. 12.

222 AS, 752 W 2, *Note pour Hannsler, 17.6.1977.*

223 AS, 752 W 12, *Compte-rendu du 5.12.1977*, p. 2.

224 AS, 752 W 51, *Réponse à Kern*, p. 3.

emphasised the threat from the infrastructure constructions in Brussels and Luxembourg in city documents archived in the municipal archive of Strasbourg.

In order to define the specific needs of the EC assembly, different city-internal and external fora existed, where city administration actors, urban planning agencies and the European institutions met. One example included a round table between the city administration and the EP. One meeting was held in December 1977, in which the CoE was represented, as well.[225] The central topic on the agenda was offices for the EP. Apart from the rooms, the EP already occupied in the *Palais*, it asked for 100 additional offices to fulfil the needs of the larger number of MEPs following the direct election.[226] Pflimlin added that the EP could acquire offices from the municipality should these 100 not be sufficient.[227] This statement again gives evidence for the fact that local actors were anxious to meet any requirement made by the European institutions, which could be characterised as part of the strategies to present the city as an attractive institution host.

In a note to Pflimlin, Adam stated that the needs of the EP remained unclear, since Francesco Pasetti-Bombardella, Director-General of Administration, Personnel and Finances, would name different numbers, depending on who was asked. These specifications ranged from 100-200 extra to one office per MEP.[228] In this connection, Stanley Hunt, Director of Administration and Finances of the CoE, stated that, should the demand rise to over 220, he could not think of anything other than a project established by Henri Bernard that entailed demolishing the C block and constructing a taller building in its stead.[229] Adam added that Hunt had told him, the CoE's relations with the EP would be "variable", while they were excellent with the Commission in Brussels.[230] A reason why the CoE was this cooperative was that the city had given the CoE the site to construct the *Palais* under the condition that the EP could use its plenary hall and be allotted office space in the building.[231] In order to compete successfully with other seat cities or applicants, the local actors mobilised this resource to gain an advantage from the presence of the CoE's facilities.

---

225 AS, 752 W 12, *Procès-verbal du 8.12.1977.*

226 AS, 752 W 12, *Procès-verbal du 8.12.1977*, p. 4.

227 AS, 752 W 12, *Procès-verbal du 8.12.1977*, p. 4.

228 AS, 752 W 2, *Note pour le Président, 4.4.1977*, p. 2.

229 AS, 752 W 2, *Note pour le Président, 4.4.1977*, p. 2.

230 AS, 752 W 2, *Note pour le Président, 4.4.1977*, p. 2.

231 AS, 752 W 12, *Compte-rendu du 5.12.1977*, p. 3.

The CoE played an important role regarding the state of infrastructure for the EP, since it made its facilities available to the assembly and constituted a factor in the status of Strasbourg as parliament seat. In a letter from CoE Secretary-General Georg Kahn-Ackermann to Hans Nord in July 1978, he stated that the regional organisation was prepared to allocate temporarily another 100 offices to the EP until the *IPE* was finished in the "[…] spirit of mutual understanding and cooperation."[232] The offer was made despite the fact that the *Palais* had been intended to group all CoE departments at one place and that this would displace the translation and finance departments from the headquarters.[233] In a CoE ministers' deputies meeting on EP office space in the presence of Pflimlin in May 1978, the point was also made that the accommodation of the EC assembly had led to delays in the construction of the *Palais*.[234] The Mayor added that the city was grateful for the CoE's efforts, since this room allocation would remain outside the city's competence.[235] This was manly achieved by the city stipulation that the regional organisation was obliged to accommodate the requirements of the EC assembly, as well.[236]

These activities and proposals to improve the physical housing situation culminated in the *Conseil Municipal* session of 22 May 1978, when the city officially decided to construct the *IPE*.[237] The decision had been unanimous because of the "extreme importance" for Strasbourg to remain seat of the EP.[238] The reason given by the Mayor during the *Conférence de la Municipalité* meeting in July 1978 to further precise the construction process, hinted at the fact that local actors regarded building infrastructure as a 'weapon' for the competition between Strasbourg, Luxembourg and Brussels. Pflimlin stated that the building was intended to aid the city and that the other two provisional seats were in the process of creating real estate for the EP, as well.[239] This statement included one of the instances where local actors alluded to the threat situation with the other two provisional seats.

Apart from the recurrent effort of providing at minimum comparable facilities, another trend in Strasbourg's strategies became visible. As

232 AS, 752 W 51, *Lettre de Kahn-Ackermann à Nord, 4.7.1978*, p. 2.

233 AS, 752 W 51, *Lettre de Kahn-Ackermann à Nord, 4.7.1978*, p. 1.

234 ACE, 130/01017, *European Parliament, request, 25.-26.5.1978*, p. 74.

235 ACE, 130/01017, *European Parliament, request 25.-26.5.1978*, p. 72.

236 AS, 752 W 51, *Réponse à Kern.*

237 AS, 752 W 12, *Procès-verbal du 31.7.1978*, p. 3.

238 AS, 752 W 37, *Note du 3.8.1979*, p. 3.

239 AS, 752 W 12, *Procès-verbal du 31.7.1978*, p. 3.

analysed in chapter 2, during the second ECSC seat application round from 1957 to 1959, the various hosting arrangements were the principal means, local actors employed, to further Strasbourg's candidature. In contrast, at the end of the 1970s, infrastructure was the central argument, which this statement illustrated. The immediate years leading to the first direct election of the EP in 1979 did not include an application process. However, it gave a currency to the discussion about the assembly's seat which spiked the competitive situation.

(b) Planning the construction

Next to the importance for the seat question, the city administration stressed the symbolism of this construction for Strasbourg. One example was allusions to the European mission. For instance, during the Mayor's budget presentation for 1978 in the *Conseil Municipal*, Pflimlin made such a statement when presenting the possible construction of the *IPE*, on which the assembly had to decide. "Le souvenir du passé, marqué par les tragiques épreuves infligées à notre ville par les discordes de l'Europe, nous inspirera sans doute la volonté de continuer à participer activement, au premier rang, à la construction d'une Europe unie et pacifique."[240] Apart from this reference to the city's alleged European mission, Pflimlin argued with the threat situation derived from the competition. He added that Luxembourg was in the process of constructing a building with a plenary of 750 seats, which could constitute an incentive for the EP to leave Strasbourg.[241]

For the design of the architectural project, Sauer talked to EP officials, his plan was also informed by visits to MP offices in Paris, Brussels, Luxembourg and Bonn.[242] Together with Leissner and Adam, he studied the size and equipment of offices in the German city and the construction modalities and building features of the institution real estate in Brussels.[243] Additionally, these three actors solicited the advice of Belgian architect Paul Noël on how to concept the large meeting rooms and how corresponding structures were designed in the other two provisional seats.[244] These actions might also have had the goal that local actors attempted to anticipate and incorporate wishes of MEPs. Satisfied parliamentarians would eventually

240 AS, 97 W 41/2, *Exposé de Pflimlin, 30.1.1978*, p. 13.

241 AS, 97 W 41/2, *Exposé de Pflimlin, 30.1.1978*, p. 12.

242 AS, 752 W 12, *Procès-verbal du 31.7.1978*, p. 3.

243 AS, 752 W 17, *Note du 21.7.1978* and *Note du 24.7.1978.*

244 AS, 752 W 19, *Note pour M. le Maire, 7.11.1978.*

translate into a good position in the competition with Brussels and Luxembourg.

Regarding the financing of the project, the city choose the Dutch pension fund *SFB* which would subsequently let the building to the city at 6.5 percent of the investment sum per year.[245] In order to organise the construction, the *SERS* and the *SFB* formed the *SCI ERASME.*[246] Subsequently, the city provided the site for the *IPE* to *ERASME* by way of a long-term lease for 45 years, when it could be renewed for another 20 years after which the building became property of the city.[247] The investment of the *SCI* were circa 186 million Francs (87.3 million €) for the building construction only. The expenses for the interior works were covered by the EP which amounted to approximately 55 million Francs (25.8 million €).[248] The city would guarantee the yield of 6.5 percent of the invested capital for 18 years and provide these funds by sub-leasing the *IPE* to the EP.[249] The city leased the building from *ERASME* and sub-let it to the parliament.[250] Thus, the office building was a significant investment in infrastructure for the EP, as well.

(c) Construction phase

For the second aspect of this sub-chapter, the construction of the *IPE*, the symbolism attached to it and how it was employed in the competitive environment of the seat question will form the primary focus. Before the construction, several sports clubs on the future construction site had to be demolished and relocated. This process and the demolition of their structures were not included in the *SFB* financing regime, but were partly financed by the French state.[251]

As correspondence with the *Ill Tennis Club* revealed, these subsidiaries did not seem to cover all the expenses and the sport clubs had to pay

245 AS, 752 W 12, *Procès-verbal du 31.7.1978*, p. 8.

246 AS, 752 W 16, *Protocole du 28.9.1978.*

247 AS, 752 W 26, *Note du 28.7.1980.*

248 AS, 752 W 26, *Note du 28.7.1980.*

249 AS, 752 W 26, *Note du 28.7.1980.*

250 Mulder, Jan. "Working Document on the purchase of WIC and SDM buildings, Committee of Budget, 19.06.2006." <http://www.europarl.europa.eu/meetdocs/2004_2009/documents/dt/620/620567/620567en.pdf> (accessed 15.04.2014), p. 2. This document contains an inaccuracy as it defines the *SCI ERASME* as the Dutch pension fund, although this organisation was the investment company founded by the Dutch *SFB* and *SERS* to execute the construction of the *IPE*.

251 AS, 752 W 20, *Lettre de Barre à Pflimlin, 28.2.1979.*

part of the sums themselves or had to procure other financing options.[252] According to the documents archived in the municipal archive of Strasbourg, this moving operation seemed to have unfolded without any hassles.[253] Most of the activity of the city administration regarding the construction phase itself concentrated itself on this matter. Additionally, especially Pflimlin was involved in promoting the city of Strasbourg.

Files from Pflimlin's private documents in the municipal archive of Strasbourg specify that he actively petitioned Giscard d'Estaing for the support of Strasbourg's plans, especially by naming the dangers that would derive from Brussels' and Luxembourg's construction projects. For instance, in a letter on 19 September 1978, Pflimlin stated that he had learned from a "good source" that Luxembourg had planned an "ambitious" project for the direct election with the plenary construction from November 1979.[254] He added that it would be discussed in the country's chamber of deputies soon and that, although he was not able to verify this information, he thought it urgent to tell the French president should he want to intervene with Luxembourg's government.[255] Pflimlin further analysed that Brussels might presently constitute the bigger threat, but that this building plan in the Grand Duchy was worrying. At the end of the 1970s, half of the EP sessions were already held there and he feared that Luxembourg intended to force this development by their infrastructure improvements.[256] Through this, Luxembourg would have improved its position and simultaneously reduced Strasbourg's standing, which the Alsatian city's actors tried to prevent.

The *IPE* had also sparked one of the few visible (attempted) protests of the local population. Several residents close to the building site tried to cancel the construction permit with a lawsuit, claiming that a building on this particular site would infringe on several laws.[257] In this affair, the city lawyers not only argued with the importance of a European infrastructure for Strasbourg, but also with the *vocation européenne*, argued with EC decisions for Strasbourg as EP seat.[258] In a note to Pflimlin, Adam stated that the residents' lawyer had specified that the excessive height of the building would be the motivation of his clients and that the *IPE* would

252 AS, 752 W 21, *Note pour le Secrétariat Général, 7.12.1979.*

253 AS, 113 W 91, *Lettre de Brun au Maire, 31.3.1978* and *Lettre de Brun au Maire, 31.10.1978.*

254 AS, 9 Z 128/1, *Lettre de Pflimlin à Giscard d'Estaing, 19.9.1978.*

255 AS, 9 Z 128/1, *Lettre de Pflimlin à Giscard d'Estaing, 19.9.1978.*

256 AS, 9 Z 128/1, *Lettre de Pflimlin à Giscard d'Estaing, 19.9.1978.*

257 AS, 752 W 25, *Baumann, 27.11.1979*, pp. 3-7.

258 AS, 752 W 25, *Baumann, 27.11.1979.*

further "denaturalise" the quarter.[259] Thus, it did not necessarily constitute a protest against the presence of the European institutions themselves, but rather one against the types of buildings in the area. It is interesting to note that such a project was executed without drawing significant protest, which might be due to the self-contained nature of the process in the bubble structures of actors.

All in all, the construction of the *IPE* had two principal reasons; a practical one to accommodate a larger EP following the direct election and eliminate a general office shortage, as well as a more important, strategic use in the seat question. Local actors emphasised at every opportunity that the *IPE* was necessary to maintain the seat status in the face that at the same time in Brussels and Luxembourg building activity occurred.

Section 1.21 Concluding Remarks

Providing facilities for the European institutions was the third major theme of local actors' strategies to strengthen Strasbourg's position as seat. Next to the practical need of adequate facilities to assure the organisations' functioning, a symbolic dimension was present. The competitive situation between the three provisional EP seats played a role, as well.

Even in this matter, the CoE was an important factor, since it shared office space in their headquarters. Generally, the construction activity in the city was more aimed towards the EC assembly which could be explained by the provisional nature of its seat. Nevertheless, the local administration did not neglect needs of the CoE if they were approached by it, as the Human Rights Court showed. Likewise, during the planning and construction of the *Palais de l'Europe* which was headed by the organisation itself, the city readily assisted whenever necessary. The majority of aid occurred without state or departmental assistance, and was chiefly assured by local resources.

Until the 1970s, most buildings were provisional like the *Maison de l'Europe*, or intended to ease shortages like the C block, for example. Especially regarding the EP, this development might have been influenced by the uncertainty of the seat situation, because the assembly might still move away from Strasbourg. With these actions local actors attempted to meet requirements of the European institutions despite this situation. In the *plaquette* "Europe in Strasbourg", the city administration had conceptualised in late 1977 to present the real estate possibilities in the

259 AS, 752 W 25, *Note pour M. le Maire, 2.5.1979.*

city, actors emphasised that the publication should express that they were prepared to solve any issues the EP had.[260]

The fact that the *IPE*, which could be regarded as the first permanent EP office building, was constructed, seemed to be a response to the competitive situation with Brussels and Luxembourg. Nevertheless, at a round table meeting about office needs with the CoE and EP, the issue about the provisional nature of the EC parliament's location was raised, as well. Vinci offered the suggestion that the city could be compensated for the custom building it would construct for it should the EP leave.[261]

The overall urban planning measures were governed by political processes which remained generally uncertain due to the continuing nondecision of the EC in seat matters. Hein stresses that a friction was present between architecture and its effectiveness in politics, since their natures, relatively-short term decisions versus long-term existence were not compatible.[262] This aspect could provide a reason why all real estate for the EP until the *IPE* were either smaller solutions to satisfy obvious need or 'loaned' from the CoE. It is feasible that the increased competitive situation with construction activity in all provisional seats had a synergy effect to override this incompatibly.

Additionally, a contributing factor could be that at least in Strasbourg, the emphasis on which type of strategy to use principally had changed. According to documents from the municipal archive of Strasbourg of the 1970s, administration actors employed *accueil des institutions européennes* nearly exclusively in connection with building infrastructure.[263] In contrast, it had been primarily used to encompass hosting arrangements during the 1950s and early 1960s.[264] Moreover, this could also explain why a similar peak in the competitive situation for the EP seat from 1957 to 1959 had not led to a corresponding construction activity as the immediate years surrounding the first direct election of the assembly in 1979.

260 AS, 752 W 12, *Compte-rendu du 5.12.1977*, p. 3.

261 AS, 752 W 12, *Procès-verbal du 8.12.1977*, p. 2.

262 Hein, Carola, "Hauptstadt Europa", Arbeit zur Erlangung des Grades Doktor-Ingenieur am Fachbereich Architektur der Hochschule für bildende Künste Hamburg, 1995, p. 213.

263 E.g. AS, 752 W 11, *Compte-rendu du 13.11.1979*.

264 E.g. AS, 208 MW 267, *Minutes of the Liaison Committee session, 21.1.1957*, p. 1.

Conclusion

In this book, the nature of involvement of local actors in Strasbourg in relation to the seat question of the European institutions has been investigated. This concerned the types of local actors in Strasbourg who were involved in welcoming the European institutions in the city, as well as which kinds of strategies they employed to consolidate the city's position as European institution host. Those strategies principally regarded the institutions located in Strasbourg, but also indirectly the European Communities in the context of the nondecision in seat matters, and the French national government for support of Strasbourg's status. The Council of Europe played an important role in the local actors' efforts. Until 1957, the city administration concentrated on this organisation which was visible in the names of the two Liaison committees. When the Common Assembly of the ECSC was more strongly included in the context of the second seat application round from 1957 onwards, the same measures were applied to it as during PACE sessions and both organisations were dubbed *institutions européennes*. The lavish celebrations for the tenth anniversary of the CoE were exploited for the seat question of the European Communities, as well.

Most European integration literature focuses nearly exclusively on the intergovernmental decision processes of determining the seat. This study fills a lacuna in the discipline with a comprehensive case study of local activity regarding European institutions in Strasbourg. Therefore, it provides an important aspect on the history of European institutions.

The standard narrative in literature on European integration history focuses on intergovernmental processes of determining and consolidating the siting of the various Community institutions.[1] Hardly any scientific attention has been paid to the aspect of local involvement in the processes of siting European Community institutions. For example, a comparison of the building activity in the city administrations of Brussels, Luxembourg and Strasbourg due to the first direct election of the EP in 1979 remains on a general level.[2] During that time, each of the three hosts of the assembly

1 E.g. Dinan, Desmond, *Europe Recast*, Basingstoke, Palgrave, 2004.

2 Clark, Stephen and Priestley, Julian, *Europe's Parliament. People, Places, Politics*, London, John Harper, 2012, pp. 43-72.

competitively constructed buildings in order to improve their position against the other two seats. Although it combines the two important aspects of political activity and urban planning concerning the European institutions, it remains at the surface of local actors' involvement in these matters by only describing key activities. Therefore, this book is an addition to the foundation history of European institutions, by comprehensively investigating decision structures and strategies of local actors towards their presence in Strasbourg.

This study of both local actors and their strategies towards consolidating the position of Strasbourg as host of European institutions nearly exclusively relies on sources from the municipal archive. They detail the actions of the city and departmental administrations, as well as involved other and private associations. Additionally, the documents present a comprehensive story of local efforts regarding the seat question. The overall process remained relatively self-contained from the beginning in 1949 and largely only developed within city limits. Based on these sources, which showed the presence of a widespread, concise local agency, it was possible to analyse several sub-categories of activity within the city. They had in common that their compositions were significantly different to those normally described in European integration literature. In contrast, in most European integration history scholarship, a focus on intergovernmental matters is visible.[3] The only instance of local agency was ascribed to Pflimlin, if at all. Through the mapping of local actors, the following central elements have been identified: highly overlapping internal structures within the overarching bubble of actors and a concentration on local affairs with only a small number of city administration actors directly promoting Strasbourg as seat to the outside.

Section 1.22 Mapping the local group of actors

A bubble of actors within the city administration composed of decision holders such as the mayor or secretary-general together with other ordinary positions and specially created organisations was the driving force with the assistance of a corresponding structure in the departmental administration. Other and private associations which either participated in efforts as part of their general tasks or were purpose-founded supported their actions. The former group was centrally concerned with the improvement of infrastructure, while the latter was most active in hosting measures. Such a division was visible within the involved city administration actors, as well. A characteristic feature was the phenomenon of multipositioned

3 E.g. Dinan, Desmond, *Europe Recast*, Basingstoke, Palgrave, 2004.

actors with two or more posts in the local or regional administrations or membership in associations. This might have been a contributing factor to the relative self-contained nature of local actors' efforts, since different functions were distributed between a small pool of actors. Additionally, the actors involved in hosting arrangements covered the entire spectrum of providing a welcoming atmosphere and distractions. The city and departmental administrations were principally concerned with European parliamentarians and civil servants, the *Cercle des Amitiés Européennes* with spouses, mostly wives of parliamentarians, and the *Cercle européen de Strasbourg* with the diplomatic corps.

Although most activity was concentrated within Strasbourg, the competitive factor from the wider regional and transnational aspects of the seat question influenced the involved local actors, as well. This centrally manifested itself in a competitive element. For example, during the second ECSC seat application round from 1957-1959, the city saw Paris as the main national competition, while the other two French applicants were not seen as serious threats. The policy of the French government was unclear at times, although Strasbourg's actors expressed they were the *seule ville française* that applied. Nevertheless, they considered Paris as superior and therewith in favour of the French and with the other ECSC national governments.[4] To alleviate this perceived threat, they regularly send letters and delegations to the French government to promote Strasbourg.[5] Over the entire period of study, the other two provisional EC seats Luxembourg and Brussels remained the closest competition. When the distribution of institutions between the three cities was again confirmed in the Merger Treaty in 1965, other candidates definitively ceased to be viable options.

A common characteristic of local agency in Strasbourg was that a structured support by the French government came relatively late into the equation or was only indirectly present. One example includes the involvement of the *Département* whose head, the prefect, is the local representative of the national government. Except of somewhat limited political support of the French government regarding the European Communities, the local actors in Strasbourg largely used or acquired their own resources in order to consolidate their status.

Based on empirical sources, a bubble structure of actors has been identified where all activity occurred. In an overarching bubble, the spaces 'local actors' with its umbrella subdivisions municipality and private associations, as well as 'European institutions' were located. The actors in

4 AS, 235 MW 273, *Minutes of the Bipartite Committee session, 27.12.1957*, pp. 2-3.

5 E.g. AS, 208 MW 9, *Lettre du Maire à De Gaulle, 12.6.1958.*

this structure have been further separated into a 'European' and a 'technical' category. The former were mainly city administration politicians and private organisations drafting events. The latter group is composed of city administration civil servants and other actors, who executed measures drafted by the planning organisms or worked to improve infrastructure. The central example for a physical space was the EP and CoE buildings to provide the assemblies with suitable working conditions. Mental spaces were more inherent to hosting activities, for instance the *vocation européenne*-rhetoric signalled the presence of a larger intangible entity. Measures to welcome parliamentarians with receptions and other leisure activities also created such an immaterial 'European' space for them.

A significant protest against the presence of the CoE or the EP was not visible. A reason could be that this self-contained arrangement itself did not present viable premises or opportunities for dissent. As evidence in the two local archives suggests, the population did not pay particular attention to European session periods. For instance, the *Service des Renseignements* noted in the reports of the early 1950s on public opinion during PACE sessions that the citizens remained generally indifferent.[6] The city administration continuously archived a plethora of newspaper articles from local or regional publications mentioning either the CoE or EP, but the majority of them dealt with policy issues that were under discussion during meetings. In the sources, the communist newspaper *L'Humanité* appears to have been the only voice that regularly criticised the presence of the European institutions which seemed to have had no impact. These articles held a general negative view towards European integration which would entail a loss of 'Frenchness'.[7] Likewise, the local actors dealing with welcoming European institutions remained in a self-contained group and only involved ordinary city structures, such as the *Conseil Municipal*, if a decision needed to be made official. Even then, most minutes showed that those occupied with the European presence drove the discussion.

While the bubble structure remained separate from its surroundings, it was highly connected and intertwined on the inside. From 1956 central coordination existed with the four specialised committees, public-private partnerships were common as with the *Cercle des Amitiés* and the city administration co-hosting events or the municipality charging its own construction agency *Habitation Moderne* with effectuating projects intended for the European institutions. Although both the city and the departmental administration participated in consolidating Strasbourg's

6 ABR, 544 D 205/1, *Note du 30.9.1953*, p. 2.

7 208 MW 15, *Extrait de L'Humanité, 18.10.1957.*

position as seat city, the main agency originated from the municipality. Therefore, this formed the main focus of this study.

Nevertheless, the position and personal reputation of certain actors in executive positions in the political arena outside of Strasbourg assisted the city's goal of improving their position as institution host towards these organisations themselves. The prime example for this was Pflimlin, who due to his numerous political posts, engagement in associations and apparently vast political network was a focal point for the outside. Regarding the city's relationship with the European institutions in Strasbourg, such an element was present, as well. As several examples of letters from European civil servants, parliamentarians or their spouses to the city administration, mostly addressed to Mayor Pflimlin, showed, he was often expressly thanked for being a welcoming host.[8]

One major conclusion from the research in regard to local actors is that Pflimlin by no means was the only major actor. Especially before he became mayor in 1959, he was only marginally involved in day-to-day city politics. However, it is recognisable in sources, especially in letters addressed to the city administration that he as the representative of the city might have been the most visible one to the European institutions. He also seemed to have been the most active in lobbying on Strasbourg's behalf with the national government and the European institutions, for example with countermanding rumours as outlined in chapter 2.

Within Strasbourg, the prevalence of multi-positioned actors constituted an important factor which spanned and partly united the different sub-groups of local agency in Strasbourg. They were a quite common and consistent phenomenon in hosting and infrastructure activities over the entire period of study. This form of actors comprised those with membership in private organisations of a European character, technical ones like involved construction firms or both. Thereby, the effect of a self-contained system was reinforced, since it presented the opportunity for single actors to hold several key positions. One example is Albert Fix as secretary-general of the city and director of the *Habitation Moderne*, the constructor of early building projects. In this manner, he held a responsible post in two instances regarding the construction of the C block and other buildings.

Especially the local politicians in the 'European' category of actors were the driving force behind Strasbourg's efforts to consolidate its position as host of international organisations. The multiple positioning of them might have contributed to the fact that the pool of actors remained

8 E.g. AS, 9 Z 110, *Lettre de Balfour à Pflimlin, 5.11.1979.*

relatively stable with an 'inner circle' of long-standing involved actors. Only at the fringes of these actors, minor fluctuations were visible. Within these multi-positioned agents, the 'inner circle' of actors involved over the entire period of study as presented in a table in chapter 2, was supported by those intensively involved in one issue. This small pool of actors might have contributed to the concise development of agency to consolidate Strasbourg's seat status, as well. One example would be the various hosting measures, which after being developed and tested at the end of the 1950s, remained basically the same until the end of the 1970s, when this study ends.

Section 1.23 Strategies to consolidate the seat status

Regarding the kinds of strategies these local actors employed, activities have been partitioned into three major areas – hosting, as well as transport and building infrastructure improvements. The three elements formed in its entirety 'Operation Welcome'. Most of the local strategies to consolidate their seat status were to provide the best facilities possible.

Although hosting, transport and building infrastructure were constantly present in the actors' efforts, each of them enjoyed a decade of principal focus, starting with hosting in the 1950s and the two infrastructure types in the 1960s and 1970s. From 1949 to 1956, the organisation of both local actors and their strategies was unstructured, which caused it not to fully reach its intended audience. Additionally, war damages and housing shortages remained an issue until the mid-1950s, which might have been a contributing factor. A change occurred in the second phase from 1956 to 1959, when a structure was established and activities were intensified to support the city in the second ECSC application round from 1957 onwards. From 1960, a smooth running organisation process had been established, although small adjustments were made in order to function as an incentive for delegates in the long run. Additionally, the 1960s were characterised by transport infrastructure improvements and the 1970s by construction efforts. In the latter decade, a new element, a stronger involvement of the French national government to support local endeavours became apparent. This participation especially regarded expenses generated by the air links.

Next to the strategic activities, the purpose of strengthening Strasbourg's position as seat by proving the city as a capable host, local actors aimed at gaining the upper hand over competing cities. It especially attained currency during times when the EC made efforts to solve the provisional seat situation. The threat that arose from rival seat cities often contained an element of confusion, uncertainty or conflicting information, notably during the two ECSC seat application rounds of the 1950s.

The different local actors played an important role with both directly, openly and secretly influencing decision holders. Efforts to consolidate Strasbourg's position as seat were concentrated on the European institutions in the city to gain their appreciation which could in turn be employed to strengthen the city's positions vis-à-vis the competition. Secondary processes were directly lobbying the national government, other EC member states and the organisation itself. The basic strategy of all efforts of local actors was to accumulate credentials as a host which could be transformed into gaining an advantageous status regarding the deliberations which city should host, or continue to house European institutions.

Apart from concentrating activities within Strasbourg, a small number promoted Strasbourg as seat to the outside. The most prolific example was Pierre Pflimlin, but deputy mayor René Radius was also active in this manner. In a similar function, but only between local actors and the European institutions in the city, several actors were designated as liaisons. These included Alphonse Heitz, Raymond Leissner or Georges Ridoux who communicated both the city's policies towards the organisations, but also collected their demands and wishes. Especially air links had the potential of benefitting those not affiliated with the European institutions, for the special, but regular air links of the 1970s were open to anyone. Another indicator for this bubble structure was that public opinion hardly figured in the relevant documents and did not seem to have had any significant impact on the activities of local actors.

The various strategies in the form of leisure activities and provision of tailored infrastructure for the European institutions aimed at convincing others that Strasbourg would be the best possible host. This mainly occurred through making parliamentarians appreciative so that they would want to stay, upstaging the competition and convincing a general audience with the European mission. This became visible in the founding of the Liaison Committee in 1956 as the first organisational instance of the city administration for welcoming European institutions. It was (implicitly) mentioned whenever new measures, both for hosting and infrastructure, had been introduced.[9]

9 AS, 208 MW 267, *Minutes of the Liaison Committee session, 24.9.1956.*

(a) Keeping it local

As has been shown throughout the chapters, on one part, local strategies to achieve this concentrated on 'wooing' parliamentarians, which had the secondary intention or by-product of the promotion of Strasbourg's qualities as European institutions host. The session frame programme not only had the intention of causing diversions for parliamentarians outside of meetings, but also of furthering the image of Strasbourg as suitable seat.

Each of the three themes of hosting and the two infrastructures that have been analysed enjoyed roughly a decade of principal focus, starting with hosting, and followed by the two infrastructure complexes, transports and constructions. Considering that a trend towards using infrastructure to improve seat candidatures developed during the 1960s and was in full force a decade later, which can be seen in the focus of the city administration on air links and constructions such as the *IPE* for the directly elected parliament. While the 1950s were characterised with many eligible applicants and also unsolicited proposals for European capital cities, the situation had changed by the 1970s, when only the three provisional EC hosts had a realistic chance to become the single seat. Since Brussels, Luxembourg and Strasbourg had already gained credentials as seat during their tenure as institution hosts, making decisions based on which of them could offer the most superior infrastructure could have remained as the singular meaningful criterion.

Regarding the features of the three areas of involvement in Strasbourg, each of them focussed on different elements. Hosting activities had the main purpose of 'seducing' parliamentarians into thinking that Strasbourg was the best possible location and was mostly anticipatory in nature. This mission was also stated in connection to the founding of the Liaison Committee which was supposed to strengthen the ties between the city and the CoE.[10] Especially in the 1950s, on occasions, when the seat question attained more currency, the element of responding to threat situations was present, as well.

Other applicants like Brussels as national capital city could derive status from this or the infrastructure they possessed. During the application phase, only the Placement Study and Bipartite Committees occupied themselves systematically with infrastructure after the application for the single seat had been submitted in July 1957, although the former panel did not meet often and hosting measures remained at the forefront of the other's agenda. In them, different allusions to Europe were present

[10] AS, 208 MW 267, *Minutes of the Liaison Committee session, 24.9.1956*, p. 1.

which manifested themselves in two major categories; a general allusion to some form of Europe and a reference to CoE or EC member states. One of the measures located in both of these areas was the flag decorations throughout the city during session periods to subtly signpost the EP or PACE session period. Since they consisted both of European flags and those of the single member states, they signalled the presence of Europe, but also those of European states in the city.

Such subconscious expressions were geared towards three different audiences with the purpose of furthering Strasbourg's candidature. For the European guests, which included parliamentarians, civil servants, and other European personalities in the city, they contained an implicit message that they were welcome which was mostly achieved by the hosting activities. Both transport and building infrastructure principally responded to concrete demands of the CoE or EP which had the secondary intended effect of 'wooing' their guests. Complying with demands was supposed to generate the effect that European institutions would regard Strasbourg as most suitable candidate.

In this manner, the different local strategies to welcome the European institutions were highly demand oriented in two ways in order to have maximum influencing effect on European parliamentarians and civil servants. The first one was of anticipatory nature, meaning that the various local actors attempted to second-guess preferences of their European guests and implemented ideas of what they thought would be appreciated by parliamentarians and civil servants during sessions. Generally, all hosting events counted among this, but as has been analysed regarding transport infrastructure in chapter 3, city actors also tried to forecast route preference and the comfortableness of airplanes. The other manner based itself on concrete demands made by the European institutions which were usually met assiduously by Strasbourg's actors without any discussion. One of the more prominent examples was the manner in which housing requests of European civil servants or parliamentarians staying (semi-)permanently in the city were fulfilled by the local administration.

In the concentration of activities within the city of Strasbourg, such relations between the local level- actors involved in consolidation efforts- and the supranational level- the European organisations sited in the city- constituted an important element. Apart from being able to implement strategically measures that satisfied the actual demand of the EP and CoE, a good relationship between these two levels also had the secondary effect that it impacted on actors outside of Strasbourg. European institutions appreciative of their current (provisional) host might be liable to influence decision holders not to change the location of their seat.

A second audience were the larger intergovernmental and supranational levels. In this connection, the more technical aspects, such as the presence of an adequate building infrastructure especially designed for the European institutions, signalled this. For instance, the Mayor mentioned this even in 1958, when construction activities remained in the background in comparison to hosting activities. "Nous devons construire, parce que si nous ne construisons pas, ils ne viendront pas."[11] The existence of adequate facilities was seen as important for Strasbourg's ability to improve their chances against other cities and to consolidate their position as seat.

The existence of adequate facilities and the satisfaction of European parliamentarians were secondary intentions of the localised strategies geared towards the outside. Moreover, some form of Strasbourgism was present in this, as well. From 1949 until today, in posters or other material, such as the postmark "Strasbourg, siège du Conseil de l'Europe" from 1957, the city's distinct single spire cathedral was displayed to symbolise the city.

(b) Conditioning elements

Based on this research, different caesuras have been applied to the local activity, than those in the general European integration narrative, because the patterns are different. The political activity of the European Communities was only superficially congruent with those of local actors towards the international institutions in the city. Major decisions, such as the commencement of the second ECSC seat application round in 1957, elicited a corresponding response, but they were not wholly superimposable. An example were city administration activities of the early 1960 to improve lodging possibilities for the permanent staff of the European institutions who required long-term accommodation. During the same period, the efforts of the European Communities finally stalled with continuous postponements of definitive decisions which had prevailed since the end of the 1950s.

Methods of Strasbourg's actors to consolidate their position were embedded in and conditioned by intertwined external processes that originated from the political (non)decisions, the competitive/threat situation with certain other applicant cities, including national alliances and rumours and the question of determining a seat.

---

11 AS, 208 MW 285, *61e séance du Conseil Municipal, 17.11.1958*, p. 23.

The lack of an EC decision on the location of their institutions possibly created a window of opportunity for the different local actors to employ strategies aimed at making parliamentarians feel appreciative of their host city with gifts or receptions in their honour. Numerous thank-you letters archived in the dossiers on the city administration's efforts shows that this strategy might have had some effects on parliamentarians. For instance, British MEP Winifred M. Ewing wrote to Pflimlin after the June 1977 session. "What wonderful hospitality once again. The Reception was a sparkling success. It was most kind of you to send the bouquet of flowers to my bedroom. It made me feel very welcome & my friends from Scotland were also impressed. Sincere thanks."[12]

The use of symbolism, mostly in the form of a European past as necessary prerequisite for the hosting of European institutions was visible in most seat applicants of the 1950s. Of them, Strasbourg constituted an exception, because its actors were the only ones completely relying on this to compete with other cities. They blatantly constructed their city's history as European to use as arguments for the city's suitability to house organisations, while other candidates such as Luxembourg or Brussels were subtler in comparison and only tended to imply their European mission that could be drawn from history.

It is feasible that Strasbourg's local actors pursued an almost exclusively symbolic strategy during the 1950s, because it had been a purely symbolic choice from the start, which was visible in the siting process of the CoE. Additionally, it did not possess adequate infrastructure and still had to struggle with war damages in the early 1950s. The open nature of the seat question during this decade might have contributed to this, as well, since the competition remained largely unclear and undefined. In the 1970s, when this situation had changed and only Brussels, Luxembourg and Strasbourg remained viable candidates, such strategies only occurred in a minor capacity, as support to employing infrastructure improvements in the struggle to be the premier seat choice.

It is possible that such hosting measures, on which the city administration actors spent most of their efforts in the 1950s, thrived due to this. It could have presented an opportunity for local actors to create what they termed a *climat européen* to welcome delegates of the transnational assemblies adequately. It is feasible that items such as welcome gifts, flag decorations or leisure activities would not have had the same apparent effect of furthering the prestige of Strasbourg as good host among European parliamentarians and civil servants, had a definitive decision for the seat been made. The

12 AS, 97 W 10/1, *Lettre de Ewing au Maire.*

hosting efforts can be characterised as a local manifestation of the absence of a final decision by the EC. In minutes of the four specialised committees, the importance of creating a *climat européen* was described as absolutely necessary to signpost that Strasbourg would not have reconsidered its candidature.[13] Additionally, the continuous reservation of housing in anticipation of a definitive choice during the second seat application round at the end of the 1950s had a similar intention.[14]

The second ECSC seat application round from 1957-1959, was one of the first concentrated instances of supranational political activity regarding the seat question that entailed a concretisation of the threat situation surrounding the placement of European institutions. It can be further separated into two strands of action; response of local actors to specific 'danger', such as promotion of the city or individual agency to alleviate such situations caused by events like the French and other ECSC member states governments concretely favouring another city. The second strand of action, which encompassed the bulk of local activities, was a general response to the threat situation, as well as an analysis of the city administration which cities would be the largest rivals to Strasbourg's chances. During the end of the 1950s, this included Paris and Brussels, as well as to a lesser extent Luxembourg. In regard to the latter city, the Bipartite Committee analysed that it was only interested in retaining the High Authority of the ECSC and did not necessarily have ambitions for the single seat and was thus not as dangerous as the other two competitors.[15]

Finding a single capital or seat had most of its currency in the 1950s and early 1960s. During that time, the seat question had been much more open and other proposals for a capital of an entire Europe were present as well. Although hardly any political attention was paid to the capital city for an entire Europe and not just the European Communities aspect, it was a marginal part of the seat question and the fact that the process of determining a host for the European institution had been less confined in the early stages. The ten official candidates of the second ECSC seat application round were an example for this.

(c) The competitive factor

The various strategies contained another intention towards the outside, namely the competitive factor. It can be assumed that strategies of local actors worked in these influencing ways due to the continuing

13 AS, 208 MW 270, *Minutes of the Bipartite Committee session, 7.10.1958*, p. 2.

14 AS, 235 MW 273, *Minutes of the Bipartite Committee session, 12.6.1958.*

15 AS, 235 MW 273, *Minutes of the Bipartite Committee session, 27.12.1957*, p. 3.

climate of indecision of the EC. The fact that its institutions had only been sited provisionally made it possible for such activities of local actors who would not have been doable to the same effect had a definite decision been reached. Especially concerning hosting measures, this might have been the decisive factor in their apparent effectiveness. During the 1950s, the city administration and their cooperating private actors principally relied on this strategy. Ubiquitously directly and indirectly signposting both the European institutions and their member states, with for example flag decorations in the city would not be likely to function as a main strategy to consolidate the seat position or challenge a permanent EC decision for another seat city.

The existence of hosting arrangements and the improvements of transport and building infrastructure for the European institutions was on the one hand a signal to other EC seat cities, generally the other two provisional seats Brussels and Luxembourg in the competitive situation where all three cities vied for the upper hand. On the other hand, these activities were aimed at benefiting European parliamentarians and civil servants. They could be expected to appreciate these actions and likewise constitute positive influences on Strasbourg's seat status with their good opinion of the city. These circumstances were likely to apply to the general political arena, as well, which touched upon national, transnational and supranational levels with the French government, those of other EC member states and the organisation itself.

Concretely, the most promising candidates, which over time were the three provisional EC seats, Brussels, Luxembourg and Strasbourg, entered into a close competition, where any effort or improvement to its prerequisite of one city meant a threat to the chances of the other two contenders. As has been analysed in chapter 4, such processes were especially visible in the immediate years before the direct election when the city administration of Strasbourg closely monitored the construction activities in Brussels and Luxembourg and reacted accordingly in order to remain the best choice for a directly elected EP. An example that this was not only the case for Strasbourg was that Luxembourg's decision and plans to construct a plenary hall on request of MEPs in October 1978, contained a response to the fact that Strasbourg officially decided to build the *IPE* a month later.[16]

16 Soldwisch, Ines, "Die Gebäude des Europäischen Parlaments in Straßburg, Luxemburg und Brüssel als Orte der Kommunikation und Repräsentation 1979-2004", in Schulz, Andreas and Wirsching, Andreas (eds.), *Parlamentarische Kulturen in Europa. Das Parlament als Kommunikationsraum*, Düsseldorf, Droste Verlag, 2012, p. 435.

(d) Promoting Strasbourg

Another set of strategies, direct promotion, existed which prominently contained declaring the European mission of the city of Strasbourg. Measures of this category remained minor to the efforts intended for the European institutions located in Strasbourg. Principally, individual actors from the city administration promoted the city in such a way. To this general advertising of the city's 'Europeanness', averting perceived crises or threats to Strasbourg's success and the dispelling or counteracting of rumours that local actors judged detrimental to the city's chances is counted, as well. Measures against those often contained similar elements as the general promotion. The most important strategy was the historical construction of the European mission in speeches and newspaper articles with the three-step narrative of Bevin recognising it with the siting of the CoE, historic events to prove the *vocation européenne's* existence and the reconciliation symbolism following the Second World War.

All of the strategies to achieve a premier status among the contenders for housing these organisations had the purpose of presenting Strasbourg as European or Europe-friendly. It especially manifested itself in hosting activities and the construction of the alleged *vocation européenne* of the city, but was inherent to infrastructure improvements, as well. However, those speeches and other publications are of a different genre, since they constitute a direct promotion to a certain audience using a standardised argumentation pattern. The local actors appropriated history normatively, selectively and subjectively in a goal-oriented manner to express the city's suitability as institution host through its historic Europeanness.

On one part, city actors expressed this in speeches or other communications, such as the statement by Pflimlin in a publication on occasion of the 25th anniversary of the CoE in 1974. "La flamme européenne ne s'éteindra pas à Strasbourg."[17] As another strategy, local actors employed it in their arguments as supporting statements, such as in a letter to MEPs in 1958, after they had voted Strasbourg as one of their three favourite seat candidates. "Il fait confiance aux Ministres quant à la désignation définitive de Strasbourg, proclament à nouveau sa vocation au triple titre de berceau du Conseil de l'Europe, de symbole de la réconciliation européenne et de carrefour des peuples et des idées."[18]

While Strasbourg's European mission remained the most strongest and ubiquitous example of such a process, general expressions of it

---

17 Pflimlin, Pierre, "La Mission européenne de Strasbourg", in Journal *Développement et Communauté, Numéro spécial, 25 ans d'Europe à Strasbourg*, 1974, p. 3.

18 AS, 208 MW 11, *Scrutin*, pp. 1-2.

occurred, as well. During the second application round for the single seat of ECSC institutions from 1957-1959, the European Communities made it an eligibility criterion for prospective candidates. The urbanism expert committee instituted by them analysed this in the first section of their report. They included the geographic accessibility, but also the European mission of the candidate city. For instance, they counted exchange of ideas and meeting of different cultures among markers for it.[19] On several occasions, the assertion of the nature of an applicant's *vocation européenne* seemed rather constructed. For example, the European qualifications of Stresa listed host for several international conferences and one of the first cities to participate in congresses of the Council of European Municipalities and Regions.[20] The question remains which degree of influence city governments had on the expert committee's assertions. The passage of Strasbourg's European mission in the report was the city administration's own statement without any annotations from the expert committee and contained the local actors' standard three-elements.[21]

Section 1.24 Perspectives

This study showed that a host of different local actors was active in consolidating Strasbourg's seat status and that their strategies to achieve this were essential, even though the formal decision power remained with the EC. The municipal politics of consolidating this placement of European institutions is an important contribution to the history of European integration. This study on the local activities regarding the seat status of the city in Strasbourg could be employed to research similar cases in other cities.[22] It is plausible that apart from political deliberations, strategies within hosting the institutions in the city and providing them with adequate infrastructure in order to assure their functioning are equally important for local agents in other seat cities. Evidence for this circumstance would be findings in studies undertaken mostly in Brussels, for example on the economic impact of the institutions it houses on the city.[23]

---

19 AC, CM1/1958 120, *Bericht*, p. 13.

20 AC, CM1/1958 120, *Bericht*, p. 77.

21 AC, CM1/1958 120, *Bericht*, p. 31 and AS, 9 Z 192, *Vocation européenne-speeches.*

22 For example, a study on Geneva as seat of international organisations using similar parameters is currently being undertaken by Gregory Meyer at the University of Geneva.

23 Degadt, Jan, "The Impact of the Presence of European and International Institutions on the Regional Economic Fabric in Brussels", in De Groof, Roel (ed.), *Brussels and Europe – Bruxelles et l'Europe*, Brussels, ASP, 2008, pp. 219-234.

Another possibility is a comparative study with other seat cities, especially the other two EU host cities, Brussels and Luxembourg, which necessitates the thorough study of each single seats in order to investigate differences, similarities or possible patterns, which has been investigated for Strasbourg with this present book. The competitive moment between the three cities could also present a notable factor in such a comparison. Although the three cases display certain similarities, such as that they hosted European Community institutions, potential differences worth investigating could be the question, whether a European or international organisation other than the EU and its predecessors could be of relevance for local actors.

This study showed that the CoE was the sole focus of local actors in Strasbourg until 1957, when the second ECSC seat application round commenced and the Common Assembly came more strongly to the attention of the city administration. Nevertheless, the CoE remained an important recipient of hosting measures and local actors in Strasbourg generally did not differentiate between the EP and the CoE but employed the equalising term *institutions européennes* to refer to them collectively. Thus, this study potentially allows for research into related issues with its research design.

References

Section 1.25 Unpublished Sources

(a) ABR – Archives Départementales du Bas-Rhin, Strasbourg, France

NB, a number, separated by a slash after the signature proper denotes that the box contained several dossiers on different topics. The number has been assigned by the author in order to be able to discern easily between the different files of the dossier, but is not part of the official dossier code.

544 D 85. Assemblée des nations captives d'Europe 1955-1958.

544 D 205/ 1. Organismes européens. Conseil de l'Europe, fonctionnement: notes de R.G. et coupures de presse, correspondance 1949-1962. Années 1949-1951.

544 D 208. Organismes internationaux. Assemblée des nations captives d'Europe, sessions: notes des R.G., programmes, comptes rendus, brochures, coupures de presse, correspondance 1955-1957.

544 D 209/ 1. Organismes internationaux. Communauté européenne du charbon et de l'Acier (CECA), sessions: notes des R.G., proposition de résolution, affiches, extraits des délibérations du Conseil général, affiches, programme de visites des délégués 1952-1959. Pool Charbon-Acier, Année 1952.

709 D 1. Maison de l'Europe (Palais).

752 D 485. Aérodrome de Strasbourg-Entzheim I-II.

1130 W 894/ 1. Strasbourg, correspondances (Palais de l'Europe, Palais de Congrès, Siège du Parlement Européen) 1975-1981.

1130 W 904/ 1. Contrat Etat – Département – Ville de Strasbourg, réunions des 18.2.1979 et 7.1.1980.

1130 W 904/ 2. Projet de contrat Strasbourg Métropole Européenne.

1130 W 936/ 1. Manifestations organisées de 1964 à 1976.

1130 W 936/ 2. Commission Bipartite Ville-Département charges des Questions Européennes, Réunion du 11 juin 1979.

1130 W 936/ 3. Commission Bipartite Ville-Département pour les affaires européennes, le 8 février 1979.

1130 W 936/ 4. Réunion de la Commission Bipartite Ville-Département chargée des problèmes européens, 16 février 1978.

1130 W 936/ 5. Commission Bipartite pour les affaires européennes 1977.

1130 W 936/ 6. Commission Bipartite Ville-Département pour les affaires européennes, réunion du 26 février 1976.

1130 W 936/ 7. Commission Bipartite, séance du 19 février 1975.

1130 W 936/ 8. Commission bipartite Ville-Département, réunion du 7 février 1974.

1130 W 936/ 9. Commission Bipartite Ville-Département, réunion du 13 décembre 1972.

1130 W 936/ 10. Commission Bipartite Ville-Département, 8 février 1972.

1130 W 936/ 11. Commission Bipartite, séance du 29 janvier 1971.

1130 W 936/ 12. Commission Bipartite Ville-Département, 29 janvier 1970.

1130 W 936/ 13. Commission Bipartite Ville-Département, 15 janvier 1969.

1130 W 936/ 14. Commission Bipartite Ville-Département, 13 mars 1968.

1130 W 936/ 15. Commission Bipartite Ville-Département, 17 janvier 1966.

1130 W 936/ 16. Commission Bipartite Ville-Département, 26 février 1964.

(b) AC – Archive of the Council of the European Union, Brussels, Belgium

CM1/1955 48. Plan Schuman et Conférence des Ministres des 23-24 juillet 1952.

CM1/1958 0120. Siège des Institutions Européennes.

CM1/1958 123. Locaux loués par les institutions communautaires à Luxembourg 1953/1958.

CM1 1961 57.1. Dossier concernant le siège des Institutions des Communautés Européennes, 20 juin 1961.

CM2/1958 0201. Siège des Institutions Communautaires.

CM2/1958 0203. Siège des Institutions Communautaires.

CM2/1958 0204. Siège des Institutions Communautaires.

CM2/1958 0205. Siège des Institutions Communautaires.

CM2 1958 210, Documents divers relatives à l'appréciation des candidatures de Nice, Département de l'Oise, Paris, Strasbourg, mars/mai 1958.

CM2/1958 0221. Siège.

CM2/1958 0222. Siège.

CM2/1959 158. Siège.

CM2 1960 0233ab-b. Note du secrétariat en date du 5 mai 1960, établissant une brève histoire des questions relatives au district européen et au siège. Textes d, i et nl.

CM2 1962 245. Notes sur les conséquences d'un transfert du siège de l'APE.

CM2/1962 0246. Dossier concernant les problèmes relatifs au "district européen" et sur la question du siège, 20 juin 1961-14 mars 1962.

(c) ACE – Archive of the Council of Europe, Strasbourg, France

NB, source signatures only composed of numbers read box/dossier/volume/year

13/16/1/1949. *Rapport.*

17/16/5-6/1949. *Report of the Preparatory Commission of the Council of Europe.*

20/0016/10-12/1949. *Commission préparatoire du C.E., rapport 1re et 2e partie.*

21/0016/1-4/1949. *Commission préparatoire du Conseil de l'Europe, notes du secrétaire exécutif.*

044/00120. *Special Agreement relating to the Seat of the Council of Europe.*

121/0092. *Welfare and Entertainment of Assembly Delegates.*

121/0103/1. *New Council of Europe Building.*

122/0103/2-3. *New Council of Europe Building.*

126/0106. *Hiring of Buildings.*

127/01011. *CE Accommodation – old building.*

130/01017. *Offices allocation for the European Parliament.*

1007/0765. *Air Communications with Strasbourg.*

3068/2009. *Foire européenne de Strasbourg.*

3153/2409. *Seat of the European Institutions (Plan Schuman).*

3153/24010/1-2. *Rationalisation of the Structures of European Organisations.*

3203/2431. *Administrative and Financial Agreement with the European Parliament.*

3262/27118/1. *European Movement (general file).*

3279/27129. *Comité Strasbourgeois pour le Mouvement Européen.*

3358/2981. *Relation avec la Ville de Strasbourg.*

3358/2982. *Cercle européen de Strasbourg.*

3358/2986. *Vitrail Européen, European Window.*

C156 1/2. *Nouveaux bâtiments: 1966-1972; déclaration solennelle du 11 juin 1971; correspondances diverses.*

C156 2/2. *Nouveaux bâtiments: 1966-1972; déclaration solennelle du 11 juin 1971; correspondances diverses.*

C1166/1/1-2. *Strasbourg – Accueil.*

CB(68)19. *Twentieth Anniversary of the Council of Europe, Proposals for celebrating this anniversary, 4.10.1968, Memorandum by the Secretariat.*

COE001872. *Powers and Functions of Monsieur Pierre Pflimlin, Minister of State for Council of Europe Affairs.*

(d) AS – Archives de la Ville de Strasbourg et de la Communauté Urbaine, France

NB, a number separated by a slash after the signature proper denotes that the box contained several dossiers on different topics. The number has been assigned by the author in order to be able to discern easily between the different files of the dossier, but is not part of the official dossier code.

8 MW 667. Exposition "Strasbourg et l'Europe".

8 MW 668. Exposition "Strasbourg et l'Europe".

14 MW 47. Conseil de l'Europe, tricentenaire du rattachement de l'Alsace à la France, organisation de manifestations sportives: correspondance avec Ville, programme de la semaine sportive, rapports à la commission des Sports, notes, carte.

16 MW 11. Cour des Comptes, Compte administratif 1957.

16 MW 93. S.A.R.L. Habitation Moderne.

59 MW 110. Aviation – Liaison aérienne Paris-Strasbourg par Air Inter 1961-1962.

61 MW 4. CTS, 2e tranche de modernisation du réseau des tramways urbains – Lignes 3/13, 9/19 et 20 – 4e avenant à la convention de concession du 11 avril 1930, 1952-1959.

62 MW 99. CTS Ligne d'autobus 3/13 Gare Centrale – Robertsau.

68 MW 37. Taxis, Généralia.

68 MW 38. "Taxis", Augmentation du Nombre.

68 MW 39. Taxis. Réglementation – Tarifs – Stationnement 1953-1973.

68 MW 40. Mauvais fonctionnement du service de taxis et hôtels pendant les sessions du Conseil de l'Europe.

68 MW 88. Aviation, Aéroport de Strasbourg-Entzheim, Correspondance.

68 MW 89. Réunion de la Commission Consultative Economique de l'Aéroport d'Entzheim 1972-1973.

68 MW 98. Liaisons aériennes Paris-Strasbourg.

69 MW 24. Aéroport de Strasbourg-Entzheim, organisation de l'aéronautique civile et des transports aérieux.

198 MW 78. Comité Strasbourgeois pour le Mouvement Européen.

198 MW 82. Installation à Strasbourg.

198 MW 83. Conseil de l'Europe – remerciements.

198 MW 84. Conseil de l'Europe, divers.

198 MW 87. Presse.

198 MW 89. Conseil de l'Europe – guides.

198 MW 90. Conseil de l'Europe, manifestations.

198 MW 91. Conseil de l'Europe, Réunions publiques.

198 MW 93. Installation à Strasbourg des organismes du Plan Schuman.

203 MW 24. Vente des terrains destinés au bâtiment du CoE 1970-71.

208 MW 7. Institutions Européennes candidature 1965.

208 MW 9. Institutions Européennes Candidature.

208 MW 11. Motion de remerciement à l'égard des délégués qui se sont prononcés pour Strasbourg lors du vote du siège à l'APE 1957-58.

208 MW 13. Résolution du Comité d'Action pour les États Unis de l'Europe 1957.

208 MW 15. "Journées Européennes" à Strasbourg, 19-20 octobre 1957.

208 MW 16. Strasbourg, siège du Conseil de l'Europe, articles de journaux janvier 1949 – juin 1949.

208 MW 21. Strasbourg – Siège d'Organismes Européens. Correspondance.

208 MW 267. Rapports entre le Conseil de l'Europe et Ville.

208 MW 270. Xe Anniversaire du Conseil de l'Europe.

208 MW 278. Séances Conseil Municipal, 1957.

208 MW 285. Séances Conseil Municipal, 1957.

208 MW 287. Séances du Conseil Municipal, avril-juin 1969.

209 MW 5. Institutions Européennes, 1957-61.

209 MW 6. Siège des Institutions Européennes.

209 MW 18. Maire, Adjoints, Conseillers, Municipaux. Réunions des Adjoints / Election du Maire et des Adjoints, Désignation des Officiers d'Etat civil mi-juin 1953 / Maire-Adjoints et Conseillers municipaux – Attributions du Maire.

209 MW 39. Affaires internes de l'Administration municipal – Bureaux et salles de l'Hôtel de Ville [1946-1960], Dossier: Flamme d'oblitération. "Strasbourg siège du Conseil de l'Europe".

209 MW 52. Liaisons aériennes, 1964-66.

209 MW 76. Conférence des Adjoints de la Municipalité 1959.

235 MW 26. Réceptions, représentants Conseil de l'Europe, 26 septembre 1952 – 15 janvier 1953.

235 MW 27. Réception du Conseil de l'Europe et de l'Assemblée Commune, 22 juin 1953.

235 MW 135. Comité Strasbourgeois pour le Mouvement Européen, 1949-1952.

235 MW 136. Notes de service relatif aux mesures de sécurité et de protection, sessions du Conseil de l'Europe, 1951-1955.

235 MW 137. Conseil de l'Europe – Wacken, 1949.

235 MW 266. Subventions au Syndicat d'Initiative, 1946-1949.

235 MW 267. Articles de journaux, Syndicat d'Initiative, 1945-1954.

235 MW 268. "Journées Européennes de Strasbourg", 19 et 20 octobre 1957.

235 MW 270. Nouvelle Assemblée Commune - 1re session de l'assemblée des communautés européennes 18 au 23 mars 1958 / Banquet offert par le Maire et le Président du Conseil Général le 18 mars 1958 à l'hôtel de ville.

235 MW 271. PACE et APE 1958.

235 MW 273. Implantation des Institutions Européennes à Strasbourg. Procès-verbal des réunions de la commission bipartite (conseil général - conseil municipal).

236 MW 1/ 1. Conseil de l'Europe, 1re session de l'Assemblée Unique des Communautés Européennes, 19 mars 1958.

236 MW 1/ 2. Conseil de l'Europe, session avril-mai 1958.

236 MW 1/ 3. Session de l'Assemblée Parlementaire Européenne, 21 au 26 juin 1958.

236 MW 1/ 4. Assemblée Européenne: a) Conseil de l'Europe 10-18 octobre 1958, b) Ass. Parlementaire, 21-28 octobre 1958, c) Pouvoirs Locaux, 29-31 octobre 1958.

236 MW 1/ 5. Conseil de l'Europe - Assemblée Consultative et Parlementaire, 7 au 21 janvier 1959.

236 MW 1/ 6. Conseil de l'Europe - Assemblée Parlementaire, 12-15 mai 1959.

236 MW 1/ 7. Session U.E.O. - 15-18 août 1959, Ass. Parl. Europ. - juin 59.

236 MW 1/ 8. Conseil de l'Europe, Assemblée Consultative, 14-19 sept. 1959, Assemblée Parlementaire, du 22 septembre au 1er octobre 1959.

236 MW 2/ 1. Réunions européennes - sessions du mois de janvier 1960.

236 MW 2/ 2. Réunion mixte A.C. et APE 24 et 25 juin 1960, Assemblée Parlementaire Européenne 27 juin au 2 juillet 1960.

236 MW 2/ 3. Assemblée Consultative du 24 au 29 avril 1961.

236 MW 2/ 4. Assemblée Parlementaire Européenne avec la participation de 16 délégués africains et malgaches du 8 au 10 mai 1961.

236 MW 2/ 5. Sessions A.P.E. et C.E. du 19 au 29 septembre 1961.

236 MW 2/ 6. A.P.E.: les 18 et 19 septembre, réunion jointe: les 19 et 20 septembre 1961, A.C.E.: du 21 au 27 septembre 1961.

236 MW 2/ 7. Session de l'APE du 16 au 20 octobre 1961.

236 MW 3/ 6. Sessions Européennes du mois de mai 1963: Conseil de l'Europe du 6 au 10 mai, Parlement Européen les 13 et 14 mai.

236 MW 3/ 8. Sessions européennes juin 1963: a) réunion des délégués des Parlements des Etats associés africains et malgache et du Parlement Européen 20 et 21 juin 1963, b) Parlement Européen 24 au 28 juin 1963.

236 MW 3/ 9. Sessions européennes du mois de septembre 1963: 16 septembre 1963, réunion du Parlement Européen, 17 et 18 septembre 1963, réunion jointe du l'Assemblée Consultative du Conseil de l'Europe et du Parlement Européen, 18 au 24 septembre 1963, session de l'Assemblée Consultative du Conseil de l'Europe.

236 MW 4/ 1. Parlement Européen, session du 20 au 25 mars 1964.

236 MW 4/ 2. Affaires Européennes, sessions, programme des manifestations Commission Bipartite.

236 MW 5/ 3. Session du mois de juin 1965 du Parlement Européen (14 au 18 juin 1965).

236 MW 5/ 6. Sessions des Institutions Européennes en janvier 1966 - 17 au 21 janvier 1966: Parlement Européen: 24 au 28 janvier 1966: Conseil de l'Europe.

236 MW 5/ 7. Session du mois de mars 1966 du Parlement Européen: 7 au 11 mars 1966.

236 MW 6/ 2. Sessions des Institutions Européennes (janvier 1967) - Conseil de l'Europe: 23 au 27 janvier 1967 - Parlement Européen: du 30 janvier au 3 février 1967.

236 MW 6/ 3. Session du mois de mars du Parlement Européen: 13 au 17 mars 1967.

236 MW 9/ 4. Session exceptionnelle du Parlement Européen: du 9 au 12 décembre 1969.

236 MW 10/ 1. Session du mois d'avril 1970 de l'Assemblée Consultative du Conseil de l'Europe (du 17 au 24 avril 1970).

236 MW 10/ 3. Session du Parlement Européen du mois de novembre 1970 (du 16 au 20 novembre 1970).

236 MW 12/ 2. Réception du lundi 11 avril 1960 à 19 heures à l'occasion de la Session de la Cour Européenne des Droits de l'Homme.

236 MW 12/ 3. Réception de l'Assemblée Consultative du C.E., Septembre 1966, le mercredi 28 septembre 1966 à 19 heures, Hôtel de Ville.

236 MW 14/ 1. Dîner offert en l'Hôtel de Ville le lundi 25 mai 1969 en l'honneur de M. Kraft, Président de la Commission Culturelle de l'Assemblée Consultative du Conseil de l'Europe.

236 MW 14/ 2. Dîner donné à l'Hôtel de Ville à l'occasion de la Réunion des Délégués des Ministres du Conseil de l'Europe vendredi 25 novembre 1960.

236 MW 16/ 1. Dîner à l'occasion de la session du Parlement Européen, Hôtel de Ville , 24 mars 1964.

236 MW 19/ 1. Conseil de l'Europe, Excursion dans les Vosges 3 mai 1957.

236 MW 19/ 2. Soirée en l'honneur des membres de l'A.P.E., Orangerie 17 octobre 1960.

236 MW 19/ 3. Soirée donnée par le Cercle des Amitiés Européennes à l'occasion de la session de l'Assemblée Consultative du C.E., Hôtel de la Maison Rouge, 25 avril 1961.

236 MW 19/ 4. Soirée donnée par le Cercle des Amitiés Européennes à l'occasion de la session de l'Assemblée Consultative du C.E., Hôtel de la Maison Rouge, 21 septembre 1961.

236 MW 19/ 5. Fête du Houblon organisée à l'occasion de la IXe Réunion jointe de l'Assemblée Consultative du C.E. et du Parlement Européen, 17 septembre 1962 à Kleinfrankenheim.

236 MW 19/ 6. Invitation à la chasse des Parlementaires européens 1963/64.

236 MW 20/ 1. Assemblée Consultative, Soirée à l'Opéra de Strasbourg suivre d'une réception au Foyer du Théâtre à l'issue de la représentation, 20 septembre 1967, Amitiés Européennes.

236 MW 21/ 1. 10e anniversaire Conseil de l'Europe, Div. VIII, Xe Anniversaire du Conseil de l'Europe, avril 1959.

236 MW 21/ 2. Xe anniversaire du Conseil de l'Europe, Invitations aux manifestations, réponses affirmantes.

236 MW 23/ 1. Relations de la Ville avec le Conseil de l'Europe, du 1er juillet 1956 au 31 décembre 1960.

236 MW 23/ 2. Relations entre la Ville et les Institutions Européennes – Dîners –, du 1er janvier 1961 au 31 décembre 1963.

236 MW 23/ 3. Critique et suggestions des "Européens" – Réunion du 13 février 1963.

236 MW 23/ 4. Logement des membres et fonctionnaires d'Institutions Européennes en cas de transfert du Secrétariat Général du Parlement Européen.

236 MW 23/ 6. Logement des membres et fonctionnaires d'Institutions Européennes – Campagne "Studios".

236 MW 23/ 7. Extension de la Maison de l'Europe pour les besoins des deux institutions.

236 MW 24/ 1. Manifestations à organiser par la Ville à l'occasion de la remise du "Prix de l'Europe", lundi 24 avril 1967; Célébration artistique à la Maison de la Radio à 20 h 30; Réception à l'Hôtel de Ville à 22 heures.

236 MW 25/ 1. Création d'un club européen.

236 MW 26/ 1. No title [10e anniversaire de la fondation du Cercle des Amitiés Européennes].

236 MW 26/ 2. Relations avec le Cercle des Amitiés Européennes – Divers.

236 MW 26/ 3. Conseil de l'Europe – Cercle des Amitiés Européennes, Circulaires 1957-1962.

236 MW 26/ 4. Question du siège du Parlement Européen, Motion du C.M. du 14 septembre 1964, Motion du C.G. du 21 septembre 1964.

236 MW 27/ 1. Réunions à Strasbourg des Assemblées Européennes – Dépenses à partager entre le Département du Bas-Rhin et la Ville de Strasbourg.

236 MW 27/ 2. Liaisons aériennes 1964 (Südflug).

236 MW 27/ 3. Remplacement temporaire des liaisons aériennes par des liaisons routières.

236 MW 27/ 5. Campagne de publicité pour l'avion de la ligne Strasbourg-Paris.

236 MW 27/ 6. Air Inter, Correspondances des liaisons aériennes à Paris.

236 MW 27/ 7. Diffusion des horaires pour les liaisons aériennes à l'occasion des sessions européennes.

236 MW 27/ 8. Pourparlers avec la "Deutsche Nah-Luftverkehr".

236 MW 27/ 9. Etude d'un programme de liaisons aériennes entre Strasbourg et d'autres Villes.

236 MW 27/ 10. Reprise des liaisons aériennes entre Strasbourg-Francfort et Zurich.

236 MW 28/ 1. Coupures de Journaux du 5 août 1957 au 31 décembre 1959.

236 MW 29/ 1. Extraits de presse, Affaires Européennes 1963.

236 MW 31/ 1. Bâtiments Institutions européennes 1959.

236 MW 32/ 1. Célébration du XXe anniversaire du Conseil de l'Europe, Mai 1969 – Généralia.

236 MW 32/ 2. Liaisons aériennes, Mise au point et teste du contrat avec BALAIR, Augmentation du tarif de la Compagnie, passager.

236 MW 32/ 3. Liaisons Aériennes, BALAIR, Correspondances – Factures.

1 W 167. Compagnie des Tramways Strasbourgeoises, Circulation gratuite.

1 W 1599. Conseil de l'Europe, intensification de la desserte jusqu'à 21 heures: rapports, correspondance.

54 W 144. Liaisons aériennes.

54 W 243. Illumination des édifices publics, extension, tranche 1958.

54 W 412. Propagande, Dépliant Spécial pour les Parlementaires Européens Edition 1960.

54 W 413. Dépliant Parlementaires Européens, Edition 1963.

55 W 86. Évacuation Terrain Stade Lenôtre.

97 W 2/ 1. Sessions du Parlement 10 au 14 mars 1975.

97 W 2/ 2. Session du Parlement Européen lundi 12 au vendredi 16 mai 1975.

97 W 10/ 1. Session du Parlement Européen du lundi 13 au vendredi 17 juin 1977.

97 W 12/ 1. Construction d'une nouvelle Maison de l'Europe.

97 W 14/ 1. Relations avec les institutions et organismes européens, Cercle Européen – divers.

97 W 17/ 1. Dîner offert en l'honneur de Messieurs les Représentants permanents auprès du Conseil de l'Europe le lundi 28 avril 1975 à 20 h 00 à l'Hôtel de Ville.

97 W 17/ 2. Session de juillet 1975 du Parlement Européen, Dîner à l'Hôtel de Ville le mercredi 9 juillet 1975 à 20 h 30 en l'honneur de la délégation britannique.

97 W 39/ 1. Parlement Européen, session du mois d'octobre 1978 à Luxembourg, 23 au 25 octobre 1978.

97 W 41/ 2. Affaires diverses, dossier 21-02.

97 W 42/ 1. Gratuité de transport Autobus CTS, Parlementaires Européens, Service Spécial lors des sessions.

113 W 91. Ill Tennis-Club, reconstitution des installations.

114 W 206. Fonctionnement des taxis lors des sessions européennes.

114 W 207. Réservations de taxis à l'approche de l'Aéroport de Strasbourg-Entzheim.

114 W 208. Taxis – Affaires diverses.

114 W 209. Taxis – Généralia.

114 W 216. Navettes de la CTS: notes et correspondance sur l'organisation (notamment les horaires).

114 W 217. Navettes spéciaux de bus entre les Hôtels strasbourgeois et le Palais de l'Europe lors des sessions européennes.

114 W 223. Vols spéciaux, Parlement.

114 W 283. Siège du Parlement Européen, Déclarations de membres.

114 W 284/ 1. Contrat de trois ans "Etat-Département du Bas-Rhin – Ville de Strasbourg" pour Strasbourg, capitale européenne.

114 W 284/ 2. Contrat de trois ans Etat/Département/Ville, Articles de Presse.

168 W 295. Transfert des installations de l'Ill tennis club au quai Jacoutot suite à la construction de l'immeuble pour les parlementaires européens: notes, demande de subvention, convention ville-Ill tennis club, PV de réception, plans.

173 W 165. SNS, Déplacement des Cabines.

223 W 121. Plaintes d'usagers et de parlementaires, PV de réunion entre le Maire et les représentants de taxis de Strasbourg (novembre 1979); relations avec l'Association des taxis: PV de réunions avec la Cellule Technique Spécialisée de Sécurité Routière, correspondance: séparation physique du couloir "taxis" Place de la Gare: note.

331 W 169. Extension du Conseil de l'Europe, habitations pour les fonctionnaires européens, construction du bâtiment des Droits de l'Homme, pont sur l'Ill, déplacement de la passerelle Ducrot.

460 W 1. Office du Tourisme, Convention, Statuts 1968-1978.

481 W 75. Comprenant notamment: groupe scolaire d'application de la Meinau, gendarmerie à la Robertsau, institutions européennes, église protestante Robertsau, église catholique dans les quartiers du Wacken et du Polygone, magasin de décors pour le théâtre municipal.

516 W 101. Aménagement du Quai du Bassin de l'Ill, Aménagement des abords du Palais de l'Europe.

614 W 63. Commerce – Industrie – Artisanat, Horaires d'ouverture et de fermeture des magasins 1977, ouverture des magasins lors des sessions des institutions européennes.

697 W 118. Projet d'extension de l'aérogare, financement: notes au maire, correspondance avec la chambre de commerce et d'industrie, coupures de presse.

752 W 1. Parlement Européen (immeuble du Secrétariat Général).

752 W 2. Bâtiment C.

752 W 3. Construction du premier bâtiment en remplacement de la construction provisoire érigée en 1950: notes, presse, correspondance.

752 W 4. Déplacement du pavillon de l'octroi. Démolition du bâtiment préfabriqué provisoire (1977): notes, coupures de presse.

752 W 5. Extension du Conseil de l'Europe, Bâtiment "D" du Parlement Européen (appelé ultérieurement A bis).

752 W 7. Ancien convent des Pères Oblats 1, rue Boecklin Strasbourg-Robertsau mis à la disposition du Conseil de l'Europe 1972-1986.

752 W 11. Recherche de terrains: notes, comptes rendus des réunions, coupures de presse.

752 W 12. Comptes rendus de réunions et d'entretiens.

752 W 13. Notes, correspondances, comptes rendus des réunions.

752 W 14. Statuts SCI ERASME.

752 W 16. Protocole d'accord entre la SFB et la SERS (Société d'études et d'aménagement de la région de Strasbourg): comptes rendus des réunions, notes, presse.

752 W 17. Financement: analyse des propositions financières des organismes financiers.

752 W 18. Travaux financés par la Ville: documents prévisionnels.

752 W 19. Immeuble pour le Parlement Européen, Intervention de M. Noël, architecte bruxellois au sujet de l'hémicycle.

752 W 20. Transfert des installations sportives de la Robertsau (Ill tennis club, groupement des amis du chien boxer) afin de récupérer les terrains pour la construction de l'immeuble parlementaire européenne, demandes de subvention, correspondance, presse, délibération.

752 W 21. Transfert des installations sportives de la Robertsau (Ill Tennis Club, Groupement des Amis du Chien Boxer) afin de récupérer les terrains pour la construction de l'immeuble parlementaire européen: correspondance, notes, presse.

752 W 25. Recours contre le permis de construire intenté par les riveraines: notes, correspondance.

752 W 26. TVA sur la construction: extraterritorialité d'immeuble: notes, correspondance.

752 W 27. Constructions et financement: compte rendu des réunions, notes, presse.

752 W 37. Travaux au Palais de l'Europe (Passerelles).

752 W 51. Location, notes, comptes rendus de réunions, correspondance.

752 W 63. Travaux financés par la Ville de Strasbourg: originaux des conventions avec la SERS, versements à la SERS.

752 W 80. Bertrand Monnet.

752 W 90. Commission bipartite Ville-Département pour les affaires européennes: notes, correspondance, presse, comptes rendus de réunions.

752 W 98. Liaisons C.T.S. Gare – Palais de l'Europe. Service spécial de l'autobus à l'occasion des sessions du parlement: réunions avec les représentants des taxis, notes, correspondance, coupures de presses, comptes rendus de réunions.

752 W 99. Liaisons ferroviaires Bruxelles-Luxembourg-Strasbourg; projet de TGV Est-européen: notes, coupures de presse.

752 W 108. Institutions européennes, impact économique 1982-1986.

752 W 114. Notes, correspondances, coupures de presse, "affaire" Simone Weil (déclarations de la présidente du Parlement Européen sur les chances de Strasbourg de conserver le siège du parlement).

752 W 115. Notes, correspondances, documents du Parlement Européen.

782 W 343. Conseil de l'Europe, Démolition du BNCP, 1950-1965.

782 W 348. C.E., Avenue de l'Europe 1972-1975.

782 W 350. C.E. Avenue de l'Europe 1972-1992.

958 W 73. Affaires européennes. Dossier pour l'amélioration des conditions de travail des parlementaires européens à Strasbourg.

9 Z 109. Richard de Coudenhove-Kalergi, réalisation d'une enquête parlementaire sur le choix de la capitale européenne: lancement de la candidature de Paris comme capitale européenne: correspondance, extraits de presse, mémorandum, articles.

9 Z 110. Actions de P. P. pour le maintien de Strasbourg comme siège du Parlement Européen; relations entre P. P. et Maurice Schumann notes, extraits de presse, comptes rendus, tableaux, propositions de résolutions, dépêches, motions, procès-verbaux, résolutions, questions écrites et orales, rapport, communiqué de presse.

9 Z 128/ 1. Correspondance avec M. Colombo de juillet 1977 à février 1979.

9 Z 192. Pierre Pflimlin, textes personnels dans lesquels il est question de la vocation européenne de Strasbourg.

9 Z 497. Cercle européen, manifestations.

(e) CARDOC – Archive of the European Parliament, Luxembourg

PE0 AP PV/POLI.1961 POLI-197601190040. European Parliament. Political Affairs Committee, Memorandum on the seat of the Institutions 16 April 1975.

PE0 AP RP/POLI.1961 A0-0064/640040. Aperçu chronologique des débats de l'Assemblée Commune, de l'Assemblée Parlementaire Européenne et du Parlement Européen sur la question du siège.

PE1 AP PR B1-0493/79 0010. Motion on a resolution tabled by Mr. Prag, Mr. Simpson, Mr. Tyrrell, Mr. Seligman and Mr. Price on a single meeting and working place for the European Parliament, 13 November 1979.

PE1 P1 243/EXEM SIEG-1962-0100120. Examen d'une lettre du Maire de la Ville de Strasbourg relative aux lieux de sessions du Parlement Européen.

Section 1.26 Published Sources

Biedermann, Alfred. "Zum Geleit." *Vers l'Europe* 1.1 (1950): 8.

—. "Périr ou s'unir." *Vers l'Europe* 1.6-7 (1950): 5.

—. "Autour de la querelle des capitales. Le véritable en jeu." *Vers l'Europe* 3.24 (1952): 1.

—. "Candidatures Européennes." *Vers l'Europe*, 3.24 (1952): 4-5.

—. "Charles Frey l'Européen." *Un grand Strasbourgeois: Charles Frey.* Eds. Robert Heitz, Paul Casper, and Jean Knittel. Strasbourg: DNA, 1956. 93-99.

Bodson, Victor. "Le Luxembourg et les Communications internationales." *Luxembourg, Ville Européenne.* Ed. Conseil Luxembourgeois du Mouvement Européen. Luxembourg: Imprimerie Hermann, 1957. 40-43.

Cercle européen de Strasbourg. *Cercle européen de Strasbourg 1962-1982*. Strasbourg: Dernières Nouvelles d'Alsace, 1982.

Comité des Amitiés Européennes, ed. *Amitiés Européennes*. Strasbourg: DNA, 1977.

Comité Strasbourgeois pour le Mouvement Européen. "L'Assemblée générale extraordinaire du Comité Strasbourgeois pour le Mouvement Européen." *Vers l'Europe* 1.1 (1950): 6-7.

—. "La vie du Conseil de l'Europe." *Vers l'Europe* 1.3 (1950): 3.

—. "Les réunions de mars." *Vers l'Europe* 1.3 (1950): 8.

—. "Petites nouvelles du Secrétariat." *Vers l'Europe* 1.4 (1950): 8.

—. "Composition du Comité Strasbourgeois pour le Mouvement Européen." *Vers l'Europe* 1.11 (1950): 2.

—. "Voici comment fonctionne le Conseil de l'Europe." *Vers l'Europe* 1.11 (1950): 7.

—. "Nouvelles de notre association." *Vers l'Europe* 2.21 (1951): 2.

—. "Notre enquête des personnalités européennes de tous pays et de toutes tendances se prononcent sur la concentration des autorités spéciales autour du Conseil de l'Europe." *Vers l'Europe* 3.26 (1952): 1-8.

—. "Nouvelles de l'association." *Vers l'Europe* 3.27 (1952): 3.

—. "A quand notre escale aérienne?" *Vers l'Europe* 3.31 (1952): 8.

—. "Réunion du Comité directeur." *Vers l'Europe* 3.32 (1952): 7.

—. *Strasbourg capitale européenne, siège du Conseil de l'Europe, doit devenir le siège des autorités européennes*. Strasbourg: Impressions Strasbourg, 1952.

—. "Réunion de notre Comité directeur." *Vers l'Europe* 4.36 (1953): 7.

—. "Réorganisation." *Vers l'Europe* 5.40 (1954): 8.

—. "Au Comité Strasbourgeois pour le Mouvement Européen, Assemblée Générale." *Vers l'Europe* 5.43 (1954): 4.

Conseil Luxembourgeois du Mouvement Européen, ed. *Luxembourg, Ville Européenne*. Luxembourg: Imprimerie Hermann, 1957.

Conseil Municipal de la Ville de Strasbourg. *Débats du Conseil Municipal de la Ville de Strasbourg en 1952*. Strasbourg: Imprimerie Alsacienne, 1953.

—. *Débats du Conseil Municipal 1957*. Strasbourg: Société d'Édition de la Basse-Alsace, 1958.

—. *Débats du Conseil Municipal 1958*. Strasbourg: Société d'Édition de la Basse-Alsace, 1959.

Cunin, Georges. "Le Palais du Conseil de l'Europe." *Vers l'Europe* 1.3 (1950): 4-5.

Ehret, Albert. "Appel du Trésorier aux membres de notre association." *Vers l'Europe* 1.2 (1950): 8.

Hess, Joseph. "Luxemburgs europäische Berufung." *Luxembourg, Ville Européenne*. Ed. Conseil Luxembourgeois du Mouvement Européen. Luxembourg: Imprimerie Hermann, 1957. 104-111.

L'Huillier, Fernand. "Strasbourg, ville d'Europe." *Extrait de l'Alsace contemporaine, Etudes politiques, économiques, sociales* (1950): 451-452.

Pflimlin, Marie-Odile. "Amitiés Européennes." *Amitiés Européennes*. Ed. Comité des Amitiés Européennes. Strasbourg: DNA, 1977. 3-9.

Schneegans, Suzanne. "1957-1977. Allocution prononcée par Madame Schneegans, présidente des Amitiés Européennes, en présence de Madame Marie-Odile Pflimlin, présidente d'honneur." *Amitiés Européennes*. Ed. Comité des Amitiés Européennes. Strasbourg: DNA, 1977. 18-20.

Stauffer, Charles. *Die europäische Berufung des Elsass (La vocation européenne de l'Alsace)*. Geispolsheim: Imp. Jung, 1978.

Ville de Strasbourg. *Strasbourg invite l'Europe*. Strasbourg: Editions de Calanque, 1957.

—. *Strasbourg invite l'Europe. Complément*. Strasbourg: Editions de Calanque, 1960.

—. *Exposition Strasbourg et l'Europe à l'Hôtel de Ville à partir du 27 Septembre 1979*. Strasbourg: DNA, 1979.

Section 1.27 Literature

Archives de la Ville et de la Communauté de Strasbourg. *Guide des Fonds 2006*. Strasbourg: Imp. Int. C.U., 2006.

Bachofen, Charles. "La reconstruction." *Strasbourg. Chroniques d'urbanisme*. Ed. Francis Cullier. La Tour d'Aigues: Éditions de l'Aube, 1994. 25-48.

Baechler, Christian. "Espoirs et désillusions: l'entre-deux-guerres et l'occupation nazie (1918-1944)", in Livet, Georges and Rapp, Francis (eds.). *Histoire de Strasbourg.* Toulouse: Privé/Dernières Nouvelles d'Alsace, 1987. 405-445.

—. "Les grandes mutations contemporaines et affirmation de la vocation européenne (1945-1986)", in Livet, Georges and Rapp, Francis (eds.). *Histoire de Strasbourg.* Toulouse: Privé/Dernières Nouvelles d'Alsace, 1987. 447-485.

Beers, Marloes. "Hosting Europe. Local Organisation of the Congress of Europe, The Hague." *Le "Congrès de l'Europe" à La Haye (1948-2009).* Eds. Jean-Michel Guieu and Christophe Le Dréau. Brussels: Peter Lang, 2009. 137-149.

Bernard, Nicolas. "L'impact de l'Union européenne sur les prix de l'immobilier à Bruxelles et la configuration spatiale de la ville." *Brussels and Europe – Bruxelles et l'Europe.* Ed. Roel De Groof. Brussels: ASP, 2008. 269-281.

Biesenbender, Jan, and Julia Grösch. "European Identity trough Architecture? Examining the European Parliament Buildings in Brussels and Strasbourg." *Bruxelles l'Européenne. Capitale de qui? Ville de qui?* Ed. Carola Hein. Brussels: La Lettre Volée, 2006. 112-129.

Blumenthal, Daniel. *Alsace-Lorraine; a study of the relations of the two provinces to France and to Germany, and a presentation of the just claims of their people.* New York: G.B. Putnam's Sons, 1917.

Boswell, Laird. "From liberation to purge trials in the 'mythic provinces': Recasting French identities in Alsace and Lorraine, 1918-1920." *French Historical Studies* 23.1 (2000): 129-162.

Brummer, Klaus. *Der Europarat. Eine Einführung.* Wiesbaden: Verlag für Sozialwissenschaften, 2008.

Bullock, Alan. *Ernest Bevin, Foreign Secretary 1945-1951.* London: Heinemann, 1983.

C., F. "Remarques sur le titre X de la Constitution et la réforme de l'Administration départementale." *Revue administrative* 2.8 (1949): 211-214.

Calay, Vincent. "'Capitale de l'Europe' ou 'siège des institutions européennes'? Quels termes pour quels espaces imaginaires?" *Bruxelles l'Européenne. Capitale de qui? Ville de qui?* Ed. Carola Hein. Brussels: La Lettre Volée, 2006. 67-81.

Cercle Pierre Pflimlin, ed. *Pierre Pflimlin: Alsacien & Européen.* Strasbourg: Editions Coprur, 2007.

Clark, Stephen, and Julian Priestley. *Europe's Parliament. People, Places, Politics.* London: John Harper Publishing, 2012.

Corijin, Eric. "Building the Capital of Europe as a Heterotopia." *Bruxelles l'Européenne. Capitale de qui? Ville de qui?* Ed. Carola Hein. Brussels: La Lettre Volée, 2006. 52-66.

Costa, Olivier. *Le Parlement Européen, assemblée délibérante.* Brussels: Ed. de l'Université de Bruxelles, 2001.

Council of Europe. *The Consultative Assembly, Procedure and Practice, Fifth Edition*. Strasbourg, 1965.

—. *The General Agreement on Privileges and Immunities of the Council of Europe of 2nd September 1949, together with the Supplementary Agreement of 18th March 1950, the Protocol to the General Agreement of 6th November 1952, the Second Protocol of 15th December 1956, the Third Protocol of 6th March 1959, and the Fourth Protocol of 16th December 1961 = L'Accord général sur les privilèges et immunités du Conseil de l'Europe du 2 Septembre 1949, avec l'Accord complémentaire du 18 Mars 1950, le Protocole additionnel du 6 Novembre 1952, le Deuxième protocole du 15 Décembre 1956, le Troisième protocole du 6 Mars 1959, et le Quatrième protocole du 16 Décembre 1961*. Strasbourg: Council of Europe, Publications Section, 1983.

Croisé-Schirtz, Edmée. "La bataille des sièges (1950-1958)." *Le Luxembourg face à la construction européenne – Luxemburg und die europäische Einigung*. Eds. Gilbert Trausch, *et al*. Luxembourg: Centre d'études et de recherches européennes Robert Schuman Luxembourg, 1996. 67-104.

Cromback, Lucien, Fernand Guri, and V. Schirrer. "Les bâtiments semi-permanents du Conseil de l'Europe à Strasbourg." *L'architecture d'aujourd'hui*. 22 (1951): 86-9.

Cullier, Francis, ed. *Strasbourg. Chroniques d'urbanisme*. La Tour d'Aigues: Editions de l'Aubé, 1994.

De Groof, Roel. "Promoting Brussels as Political World Capital. From the National Jubilee of 1905 to Expo 58." *Brussels and Europe – Bruxelles et l'Europe*. Ed. Roel De Groof. Brussels: ASP, 2008. 97-126.

Degadt, Jan. "The Impact of the Presence of European and International Institutions on the Regional Economic Fabric in Brussels." *Brussels and Europe – Bruxelles et l'Europe*. Ed. Roel De Groof. Brussels: ASP, 2008. 219-234.

Dinan, Desmond. *Europe Recast*. Basingstoke: Palgrave, 2004.

–. *Ever Closer Union. An Introduction to European Integration*. Basingstoke: Palgrave Macmillan, 2010.

Dussauge Laguna, Mauricio I. "El proceso de integración europea y sus efectos en las administraciones públicas nacionales: ¿hacia la convergencia administrativa?" in *Foro Internacional*, 45.1 (2005): 293-314.

Eckhardt, Carl C. "The Alsace-Lorraine Question." *The Scientific Monthly* 6.5 (1918): 431-443.

English, Jean-Louis, and Daniel Riot. *Itinéraires d'un Européen. Entretiens avec Pierre Pflimlin*. Strasbourg: La Nuée Bleue, 1989.

Featherstone, Kevin and Radaelli, Claudio M. (eds.). *The Politics of Europeanization*. Oxford: Oxford University Press, 2003

Fuchs, René, Georges Livet, and Henri Nonn. "Livre VII. Les grandes mutations contemporaines (1945-1980)." *Histoire de Strasbourg des origines à nos jours*.

Tome 4: Strasbourg de 1815 à nos jours, XIXe et XXe siècles. Eds. Georges Livet and Francis Rapp. Strasbourg: Éditions des Dernières Nouvelles d'Alsace, 1982. 505-600.

Golder, Matthew R. "The Changing Nature of French Dirigisme. A Case Study of Air France." Thesis submitted in partial fulfilment of the requirements for the degree of M. Phil in European Politics and Society in the Faculty of Social Studies at the University of Oxford, 1997 <https://files.nyu.edu/mrg217/public/MA.pdf> (accessed 27 March 2014).

Göldner, Markus. *Politische Symbole der europäischen Integration.* Frankfurt: Peter Lang, 1988.

Grünewald, Irmgard. *Die Elsass-Lothringer im Reich 1918-1933: ihre Organisationen zwischen Integration und "Kampf um Seele der Heimat".* Frankfurt am Main: Peter Lang, 1984.

Harvey, David A. "Lost Children or Enemy Aliens? Classifying the Population of Alsace after the First World War." *Journal of Contemporary History* 34.4 (1999): 537-554.

Hein, Carola. "Hoofdstad Europa: over de vestigingsproblematiek van de Europese Unie/A Capital for Europe: Where to House the European Union", *Archis*, 11, (1995): 62-73.

—. "Hauptstadt Europa." PhD Fachbereich Architektur der Hochschule für bildende Künste Hamburg, 1995.

—. "Choosing a site for the capital of Europe", *Geo Journal*, 51:1-2, (2000): 83-97.

—. *The Capital of Europe. Architecture and Urban Planning for the European Union.* Westport, CT: Praeger, 2004.

—. "Bruxelles et les villes sièges de l'Union Européenne", in Plissart, Marie-Françoise (ed.). *Change. Brussels Capital of Europe.* Brussels: Prisme Editions, 2004. 118-122.

—. "The polycentric and opportunistic capital of Europe: A new model for the siting and reallocation of EU headquarters and the design of European districts in Brussels and other host cities." *Brussels Studies* 2 (2006): 1-8.

—, ed. *Bruxelles l'Européenne. Capitale de qui? Ville de qui?* Brussels: La Lettre Volée, 2006.

—. "Brussels and the Capital of Europe." *Bruxelles l'Européenne. Capitale de qui? Ville de qui?* Ed. Carola Hein. Brussels: La Lettre Volée, 2006. 18-50.

—. "Collaboration for Europe and Brussels." *Bruxelles l'Européenne. Capitale de qui? Ville de qui?* Ed. Carola Hein. Brussels: La Lettre Volée, 2006. 283-294.

—. "Brussels, the unofficial 'capital' of Europe: a motor for European unification." *Brussels: Perspectives on a European Capital.* Eds. Carola Hein and Pierre Laconte. Brussels: Editions Aliter, 2007. 44-57.

Hein, Carola, and Pierre Laconte, eds. *Brussels: Perspectives on a European Capital.* Brussels: Editions Aliter, 2007.

Houdard, Geneviève. "Strasbourg: la vocation européenne." *Moniteur du commerce international* 604 (1984): 37-57.

Hudson, Kenneth, and Julian Pettifer. *Diamonds in the Sky. A Social History of Air Travel*. London: The Bodley Head, 1979.

Jenks, Clarence W. *The headquarters of international institutions: a study of their location and status*. London: The Royal Institute of International Affairs, 1945.

Jung, Louis. "Pierre Pflimlin, l'Europe au cœur." *Pierre Pflimlin: Alsacien & Européen*. Ed. Cercle Pierre Pflimlin. Strasbourg: Editions Coprur, 2007. 7-10.

Kuhk, Annette. "Facilitating the Integration of Discourses about the European Quarter: How Can Inclusive Policies for Complex Urban Issues be More Professional?" *Bruxelles l'Européenne. Capitale de qui? Ville de qui?* Ed. Carola Hein. Brussels: La Lettre Volée, 2006. 155-171.

Leary, Robert M. "Capital on the Ottawa." *Town Planning Review* 41.1 (1970): 3-14.

Levine, Myron A. "The transformation of urban politics in France. The roots of growth politics and urban regimes." *Urban Affairs Quarterly* 29.3 (1994): 383-410.

Moreau, Jacques. *Administration régionale, locale et municipale*. Paris: Editions Dalloz, 1972.

Muller, François. *The European Quarter, Strasbourg*. Schnell & Steiner: Regensburg, 2010.

Nies-Berchem, Martine. "L'administration luxembourgeoise et les débuts de l'administration européenne (1952-1967)." *Le Luxembourg face à la construction européenne – Luxemburg und die europäische Einigung*. Eds. Gilbert Trausch, *et al.* Luxembourg: Centre d'études et de recherches européennes Robert Schuman Luxembourg, 1996. 147-160.

Papadopoulos, Alex G. *Urban Regimes and Strategies; Building Europe's Central Executive District in Brussels, The University of Chicago, Geography Research Paper No. 239*. Chicago: The University of Chicago Press, 1996.

Pflimlin, Pierre. "La mission européenne de Strasbourg." *Journal Développement et Communauté* numéro spécial. 25 ans d'Europe à Strasbourg (1974): 3.

—. "Conclusion: Strasbourg et l'Europe." *Histoire de Strasbourg des origines à nos jours. Tome 4: Strasbourg de 1815 à nos jours, XIXe et XXe siècles*. Eds. Georges Livet and Francis Rapp. Strasbourg: Éditions des Dernières Nouvelles d'Alsace, 1982. 717-735.

—. *Mémoires d'un Européen de la IVe à la Ve République*. Paris: Fayard, 1991.

Pflimlin, Pierre, Édouard Pflimlin, and Carole Monmarché. *Pierre Pflimlin: Les choix d'une vie*. Strasbourg: Editions du Signe, 2001.

Radius, René. "Strasbourg et le Conseil de l'Europe." *Saisons d'Alsace* 60 (1976): 110-112.

Reymund, Phillipe. "La Question du siège de l'Assemblée des Communautés Européennes." Master Université des sciences juridiques, politiques, sociales et de technologie de Strasbourg. Institut des hautes études européennes, 1981.

Ries, Roland. "Vorwort." *L'Eurodistrict Strasbourg-Ortenau: la construction de l'Europe réelle = Der Eurodistrikt Strassburg-Ortenau: Konstruktion eines lebendigen Europa.* Eds. Henri de Grossouvre, Eric Maulin, and Forum Carolus. Vevey: Xenia, 2009. 13-15.

Schröder, Iris. "Der Beton, die Stadt, die Kunst und die Welt. Der Streit um die Pariser UNESCO-Gebäude." *Zeithistorische Forschungen (Online-Ausgabe).* 7 (2010): 1-13.

Soldwisch, Ines. "Die Gebäude des Europäischen Parlaments in Straßburg, Luxemburg und Brüssel als Orte der Kommunikation und Repräsentation 1979-2004." *Parlamentarische Kulturen in Europa. Das Parlament als Kommunikationsraum.* Eds. Andreas Schulz and Andreas Wirsching. Düsseldorf: Droste Verlag, 2012. 423-451.

Starr Jordan, David. "Alsace-Lorraine: a study of conquest", in *Atlantic Monthly* 113 (1914): 688-702.

Thibault, Philippe-Michel. *Air Inter la révolution intérieure.* Paris: Le cherche midi, 2005.

Trausch, Gilbert, *et al.*, eds. *Le Luxembourg face à la construction européenne – Luxemburg und die europäische Einigung.* Luxembourg: Centre d'études et de recherches européennes Robert Schuman Luxembourg, 1996.

Trausch, Gilbert. "Robert Schuman, le Luxembourg et l'Europe." *Le Luxembourg face à la construction européenne – Luxemburg und die europäische Einigung.* Eds. Gilbert Trausch, *et al.* Luxembourg: Centre d'études et de recherches européennes Robert Schuman Luxembourg, 1996. 11-44.

Trunk, Achim. *Europa, ein Ausweg: Politische Eliten und europäische Identität in den 1950er Jahren.* München: Oldenbourg, 2007.

Van Lierde, Claire. "La querelle des sièges des institutions des Communautés Européennes." Mémoire présenté en vue de l'obtention du grade de licenciée en Affaires publiques et internationales, orientation relations internationales Université Catholique de Louvain, 1993.

Villain, Claude. *Rapport sur le renforcement durable du rôle européen de Strasbourg, 31.3.1989.* Ministère des Affaires Européennes, 1989.

Wassenberg, Birte. *Histoire du Conseil de l'Europe.* Brussels: Peter Lang, 2012.

Weiler, Peter. *Ernest Bevin.* Manchester: Manchester University Press, 1993.

Zind, Pierri. *Elsass-Lothringen – Alsace-Lorraine: une nation interdite.* Paris: Copernic, 1979.

Section 1.28 Web sites and online sources

Dehousse, Fernand. "Rationalisation of European Institutions other than those of the Six 1959." <http://www.assembly.coe.int/nw/xml/XRef/X2H-Xref-ViewPDF.asp?FileID=1347&lang=en> (accessed 08.10.2013).

Fainsilber, Denis. "L'adieu à Air Inter. Une saga qui résume trente-sept ans d'histoire de France, No. 17367." <http://www.lesechos.fr/imprimer.php?chemin=/archives/1997/LesEchos/17367-129-ECH.xml> (accessed 09.12.2013, article no longer available online).

François-Poncet, Jean, and Jean-François Le Grand. "Sénat session ordinaire de 2000-2001, Rapport d'Information No. 327 fait au nom de la commission des Affaires économiques et du Plan par le groupe de travail sur l'avenir des dessertes aériennes régionales, ainsi que sur le fonctionnement du fonds d'investissement des aéroports et du transport aérien (FIATA)." <http://senat.fr/rap/r00-327/r00-3271.pdf> (accessed 31.07.2014).

Kennel, Guy-Dominique, "Strasbourg Eurométropole et Collectivité Territoriale d'Alsace: une ambition partagée", Département du Bas-Rhin. <http://www.bas-rhin.fr/eCommunityDocuments/BB9FAA02-A33D-4E64-9176-BA6926CD-4D2B/582/document_communique-presse-bas-rhin-tribune-GDK-eurometrople.pdf> (accessed 3.2.2015).

Kurzok, Jan. "Luftsprünge nach Nordseeinseln. 1.4.1966, No. 14." <http://www.zeit.de/1966/14/luftspruenge-nach-nordseeinseln> (accessed 28.11.2013).

Mulder, Jan. "Working Document on the purchase of WIC and SDM buildings, Committee of Budget, 19.06.2006." <http://www.europarl.europa.eu/meetdocs/2004_2009/documents/dt/620/620567/620567en.pdf> (accessed 15.04.2014).

"Accord conclu entre le gouvernement de la République fédérale d'Allemagne et le gouvernement de la République Française sur le statut de la Sarre 1954." <http://mjp.univ-perp.fr/defense/sarre54.htm> (accessed 09.06.2014).

"Amitiés Européennes. Plus de 50 ans d'accueil", Amitiés Européennes Blog. <http://amities-europeennes.weebly.com/plus-de-50-ans-daccueil.html> (accessed 03.02.2015).

"Annex 6 to Part A, Decision taken by common agreement between the Representatives of the Governments of the member states on the location of the seat of the institutions and of certain bodies and departments of the European Communities, Edinburgh European Council 11-12 December 1992." <http://www.europarl.europa.eu/summits/edinburgh/a6_en.pdf> (accessed 27.6.2014).

"Arrêté du 27 décembre 1966: Aménagement et exploitation commerciale de l'aérodrome de Strasbourg-Entzheim (zone civile) par la Chambre de Commerce et d'Industrie de Strasbourg." <http://www.legifrance.gouv.fr/affichTexte.do?cidTexte=JORFTEXT000000489410&fastPos=1&fastReqId=1714940285&categorieLien=id&oldAction=rechTexte> (accessed 04.02.2014).

"Assembly of Captive European Nations, Records, 1953-1972" Immigration History Research Center University of Minnesota. <http://www.ihrc.umn.edu/research/vitrage/all/am/GENassembly.htm> (accessed 13.02.2015).

"Balair Ltd. 1967." <http://www.flightglobal.com/pdfarchive/view/1967/1967-0574.html> (accessed 29.11.2013).

"Bâtiment B du Conseil de l'Europe." <http://www.strasbourg-europe.eu/batiment-b-du-conseil-de-l-europe,41441,fr.html> (accessed 24.03.2014).

"Bâtiment Salvador de Madariaga." <http://www.strasbourg-europe.eu/batiment-salvador-de-madariaga,41337,fr.html> (accessed 24.03.2014).

"Blog Amitiés Européennes." <http://amitieseuropeennes.weebly.com/> (accessed 15.12.2014).

"Carnets de Ville No. 1, novembre 2013, Le patrimoine, une mémoire pour le futur." <http://www.strasbourg.eu/developpement-rayonnement/urbanisme-logement-amenagement/la-formation-du-territoire/histoire-ville-quartiers-communes/carnets-de-ville> (accessed 19.06.2014).

"C'était en 1877." <http://www.cts-strasbourg.eu/fr/la-cts/c-etait-en-1877/> (accessed 6.2.2014).

"Chambre de Commerce et d'Industrie de Strasbourg et de Bas-Rhin. Présentation Générale." <http://www.strasbourg.cci.fr/cci-pratique/presentation-generale> (accessed 06.02.2014).

"Contrat triennal Strasbourg, capitale européenne 2012-2014 entre l'Etat, la Ville de Strasbourg, la Communauté Urbaine de Strasbourg, le Département du Bas-Rhin, la Région Alsace." <http://www.alsace.pref.gouv.fr/medias/fichiers/Contrat_Triennal_2012_2014.pdf> (accessed 22.05.2014).

"Convertisseur franc-euro: pouvoir d'achat de l'euro et du franc." <http://www.insee.fr/fr/themes/calcul-pouvoir-achat.asp> (accessed 02.06.2014).

"Décision du 24 août 1960 relative au classement de l'aéroport de Strasbourg-Entzheim en ce qui concerne le balisage lumineux." <http://www.legifrance.gouv.fr/affichTexte.do?cidTexte=JORFTEXT000000320039&fastPos=51&fastReqId=700958906&categorieLien=id&oldAction=rechTexte> (accessed 04.02.2014).

"Décret du 6 mai 1955 portant approbation du cahier des charges type applicable aux concessions d'outillage public d'aéroport aux Chambres de Commerce." <http://www.legifrance.gouv.fr/affichTexte.do?cidTexte=JORFTEXT000000850699&fastPos=14&fastReqId=871802162&categorieLien=id&oldAction=rechTexte> (accessed 04.02.2014).

"Depuis 1935, l'aéroport de Strasbourg et la CCI, Le Point éco, No. 224, 2003." <http://www.strasbourg.cci.fr/web/pointeco/pe_dossiers/pe_dos_t7/aeroport_strasbourg1138.php> (accessed 04.02.2014).

"Die saarländische Sonderrolle bis 1955. Sitzverteilung im ersten saarländischen Parlament." <http://www.landtag-saar.de/DerLandtag/langerWeg/Seiten/VTSonderrolle.aspx> (accessed 09.06.2014).

"Dünne Luft. 21.8.1967." <http://www.spiegel.de/spiegel/print/d-46211731.html> (accessed 29.11.2013).

"Fusionsvertrag." <http://eur-lex.europa.eu/LexUriServ/LexUriServ.do?uri=OJ:P:1967:152:FULL:DE:PDF> (accessed 16.11.2013).

"General Agreement on Privileges and Immunities of the Council of Europe 2.IX.1949." <http://conventions.coe.int/Treaty/en/Treaties/Html/002.htm> (accessed 17.03.2014).

Groupement EDR, City Consult, and Médiascope. "Impact économique de la présence des Institutions européennes à Strasbourg." <http://www.alsaeco.com/etudes/impact-economique-de-la-presence-des-institutions-europeennes-a-strasbourg,36941850.html> (accessed 06.02.2014).

"Histoire du Quartier Bourse – Esplanade – Krutenau." <http://www.strasbourg.eu/territoire/les-quartiers/bourse-esplanade-krutenau/decouvrir-quartier-bourse/histoire-quartier-bourse> (accessed 19.06.2014).

"Histoire du Quartier Conseil des XV – Rotterdam." <http://www.strasbourg.eu/territoire/les-quartiers/conseil-des-xv-rotterdam/decouvrir-quartier-rotterdam/histoire-quartier-rotterdam> (accessed 19.06.2014).

"Histoire du Quartier Robertsau, Wacken." <http://www.strasbourg.eu/territoire/les-quartiers/robertsau-wacken/decouvrir-quartier-robertsau/histoire-quartier-robertsau> (accessed 19.06.2014).

"Home page Roland Ries 2014." <http://rolandries2014.eu/pionniere-rayonnante/engagement-total-faveur-vocation-europeenne-strasbourg/> (accessed 06.06.2014).

"Im Lufttaxi zum Baden. 23.6.1961, No. 26." <http://www.zeit.de/1961/26/im-lufttaxi-zum-baden/komplettansicht> (accessed 28.11.2013).

"L'Arménie préside. Strasbourg-Magazine Juillet-August 2013, p. 23." <http://media.strasbourg.eu/alfresco/d/d/workspace/SpacesStore/530334e3-53cf-4494-aca7-dc35afc71550/201307_StrasMag_244.pdf> (accessed 23.08.2013).

"La SERS d'hier à aujourd'hui." <http://www.sers.eu/content/la-sers-dhier-a-aujourdhui> (accessed 14.04.2014).

"Les Anciens Présidents." <http://cercleuropeen.eu/les_anciens_presidents.html> (accessed 20.12.2012).

"Les Maires de Strasbourg." <http://archives.strasbourg.fr/site_maire/index.html> (accessed 20.03.2011).

"Les missions de la Datar." <http://www.datar.gouv.fr/les-missions-de-la-datar> (accessed 26.11.2013).

"Le tram de Strasbourg prend à son tour une allure 'Sooo British!'." <http://www.strasbourg.eu/actus/actus?StartIndex=56&ItemID=2153110598> (accessed 12.03.2012, article no longer available online).

"Lettre de candidature de la ville de Sarrebruck aux institutions communautaires (Sarrebruck, 11 juin 1951)." <http://www.cvce.eu/obj/lettre_de_candidature_de_la_ville_de_sarrebruck_aux_institutions_communautaires_sarrebruck_11_juin_1951-fr-6f8eec29-6f25-4da2-b48a-3eb54c32092e.html> (accessed 13.06.2014).

"Lettre de Roland Ries à Harlem Désir – Strasbourg: Défense du siège du Parlement européen: Roland Ries écrit à Harlem Désir 10.04.2014, Dernières Nouvelles d'Alsace." <http://www.dna.fr/actualite/2014/04/10/defense-du-siege-du-parlement-europeen-roland-ries-ecrit-a-harlem-desir> (accessed 5.06.2014).

"L'histoire du Cercle." <http://cercleuropeen.eu/lhistoire_du_cercle.html> (accessed 20.12.2012).

"Luxembourg siège des Institutions européennes, Considérations proposées à l'attention de la Commission européenne des Experts en matière d'Urbanisme, à l'occasion de leur visite à Luxembourg les 19 et 20 mars 1958." <http://www.ena.lu/luxembourg_seat_european_institutions_luxembourg_19_20_march_1958-2-14296.pdf> (accessed 15.02.2011).

"Luxemburg, Sitz der europäischen Gemeinschaft? d'Letzeburger Land 13/1958." <http://www.eluxemburgensia.lu/BnlViewer/view/index.html?lang=fr#panel:pp|issue:1710141|article:DTL83|query:sitzfrage%20montanunion> (accessed 24.02.2014).

"Missions." <http://lieudeurope.strasbourg.eu/le-lieu-deurope/> (accessed 20.05.2014).

"Note interne du ministère des Affaires étrangères luxembourgeois (14 décembre 1954)." <http://www.ena.lu/internal_note_luxembourg_foreign_ministry_14_december_1954-2-12732.pdf> (accessed 15.02.2011).

"Notre démarche patrimoniale." <http://www.cts-strasbourg.eu/fr/la-cts/notre-demarche-patrimoniale/> (accessed 06.02.2014).

"PACE members, Paul Wach." <http://www.assembly.coe.int/nw/xml/AssemblyList/MP-Details-EN.asp?MemberID=816> (accessed 17.10.2013).

"PACE members, Pierre Pflimlin." <http://www.assembly.coe.int/nw/xml/AssemblyList/MP-Details-EN.asp?MemberID=781> (accessed 17.10.2013).

"PACE members, René Radius." <http://www.assembly.coe.int/nw/xml/AssemblyList/MP-Details-EN.asp?MemberID=391> (accessed 17.10.2013).

"Partenaires." <http://lieudeurope.strasbourg.eu/partenaires/> (accessed 20.05.2014).

"Pierre Pflimlin en quelques dates." <http://www.strasbourg-europe.eu/pierre-pflimlin,14544,fr.html> (accessed 20.03.2013).

"Position du syndicat d'initiative de la ville de Bruxelles sur le siège des institutions communautaires (26 mai 1954)." <http://www.ena.lu/position_city_brussels_tourist_information_office_with_regard_seat_community_institutions_1954-2-12733.pdf> (accessed 15.02.2011).

"Présentation, Fonctionnement." <http://www.strasbourg.eu/fonctionnement-ville-cus/mairie-de-strasbourg/presentation-fonctionnement> (accessed 23.04.2014).

"Qui sommes-nous?" <http://www.datar.gouv.fr/qui-sommes-nous> (accessed 26.11.2013).

"Rapport de Albert Wehrer sur la question du siège des institutions européennes (Luxembourg, 30 octobre 1950)." <http://www.cvce.eu/obj/report_by_albert_wehrer_on_the_question_of_the_seat_of_the_euro pean_institutions_luxembourg_30_october_1950-en-4b115ba2-c37b-423d-9115-a89281e11868.html> (accessed 13.06.2014).

"Répartition du Capital de la SEM." <http://www.sers.eu/content/gouvernance> (accessed 14.04.2014).

"Resolution 1357 (2004) 1: Realising Strasbourg's potential as a European capital." <http://assembly.coe.int/Documents/AdoptedText/ta04/ERES 1357.htm> (last accessed 27.08.2012).

"Secretariat memorandum on the name of the Assembly of the Council of Europe (Strasbourg, 26 February 1975)." <http://www.cvce.eu/content/publication/2005/4/19/f98114c5-8da8-4d43-b7be-daa5b96b3ed2/publishable_en.pdf> (accessed 29.08.2013).

"Seminar, Single Seat Campaign, Towards 2014: A single seat and the European Parliament Election, 10/2012 (Video)." <http://www.youtube.com/watch?v=vDthJzUQxXc> (accessed 12.03.2014).

"Strasbourg et l'Europe." <http://lieudeurope.strasbourg.eu/strasbourg-et-leurope/> (accessed 20.05.2014).

"Südflug unter dem Kranich. 22.12.1967, No. 51." <http://www.zeit.de/1967/51/suedflug-unter-dem-kranich/komplettansicht> (accessed 28.11.2013).

"The European vocation of Strasbourg." <http://en.strasbourg-europe.eu/history,127,en.html> (accessed 05.06.2012).

"The post-war European idea and the first European Movements (1945-1949) – Introduction", Centre Virtuel de la Connaissance sur l'Europe, <http://www.cvce.eu/ obj/the_post_war_european_idea_and_the_first_european_movements_1945_1949_introduction-en-987cf261-b707-4ca1-8de7-d61ab4f445a5.html> (accessed 03.02.2015)

"The price of a multi-seat European Parliament." <http://singleseat.eu/10.html> (accessed 26.06.2014).

"Treaty establishing the European Coal and Steel Community (Paris, 18 April 1951)." <http://www.cvce.eu/content/publication/1997/10/13/11a21305-941e-49d7-a171-ed5be548cd58/publishable_en.pdf> (accessed 24.04.2014).

"Treaty of Amsterdam, Protocol on the location of the seats of the institutions and of certain bodies and departments of the European Communities and of

Europol." <http://old.eur-lex.europa.eu/en/treaties/dat/11997D/htm/11997D.html> (accessed 25.06.2014).

"Une ville en transformation et préservée (depuis 1945)." <http://www.strasbourg.eu/developpement-rayonnement/urbanisme-logement-amenagement/la-formation-du-territoire/histoire-ville-quartiers-communes/etapes-formation-territoire/une-ville-en-transformation-et-preservee-depuis-1945> (accessed 19.06.2014).

"Webpage of the City of Strasbourg." <http://www.strasbourg.eu/> (accessed 09.05.2014).

"Who we are." <http://singleseat.eu/9.html> (accessed 26.06.2014).

Article XI. Appendixes

Section 2.01 Appendix I: Most active multipositioned actors

The following table presents the most involved multipositioned actors – those who were involved in welcoming European parliamentarians and/or securing the European institutions to the city in two or more different capacities. The actors have been collected from the sources in the municipal archive of Strasbourg, the departmental archive of Bas-Rhin and the archive of the Council of Europe. Their posts have been partitioned into four different categories:

- Public European denotes a city or departmental administration office created in response to the European presence in Strasbourg.
- Private European denotes involvement in an association created in response to the European presence in Strasbourg.
- Ordinary administration denotes an ordinary city or departmental administration post involved in an aspect of Operation Welcome.
- Other position/organisation denotes associations and organisations involved in welcoming the institutions, but not ones created for that purpose.

Additionally, membership of the EP or PACE is denoted under "European Institutions".

Several actors with multiple positions not included in this list did not seem to be particularly active in day-to-day business and they only were specified in several member lists of private European organisations.

Name	Public European	Private European	Ordinary administration	Other position/ organisation	European Institutions
Adam, Daniel	1976: Bipartite Committee	Ca. 1982-: *Cercle européen de Strasbourg (Comité de direction, Commission du bâtiment)*	1960s: *Service de Contentieux* (involved in constructions)		
	1978: Working party to study the financing of the *IPE*		1970s: *Secrétaire-Général de la Communauté Urbaine*		
		1962-: *Cercle Européen de Strasbourg*			
Altorffer, Charles	1956-1959: Four specialised committees	1957-1959: *Cercle des Amitiés Européennes (Comité d'honneur)*	1955-1959: Mayor		
Baillard, Robert	28.9.1959: working group meeting reg. hotels/ restaurants for hosting efforts	1962-: *Cercle Européen de Strasbourg (Comité de direction)*	1960s-1970s: *Adjoint au Maire* (involvement in meetings regarding constructions)	1970s: *Président du Conseil d'Administration SERS*	
	7.3.1961: working group meeting reg. lodging for EP functionaries				
	1978: Working party to study the financing of the *IPE*				

Name	Public European	Private European	Ordinary administration	Other position/ organisation	European Institutions
Biedermann, Alfred		1950s: *Congrès du Peuple Européen, section local* 1949-: *CSME* (*Secrétaire-Général*, etc.) 1956-: *Club pan-européen de Strasbourg (membre comité)* Ca. 1957: *Congrès des Peuples Européens, section local – délégué général*			
Feuerstein, Alfred			1960s: *Service des Rélations Publiques* 1970s: *Directeur Adj. Mairie de Strasbourg* (CTS transport, communication with EP) Ca. 1978 – *Directeur Adj. CAB – Relations Publiques/T (Rélations Publiques)* – involved in coordination with taxi associations		

Name	Public European	Private European	Ordinary administration	Other position/ organisation	European Institutions
Fix, Albert	28.9.1959: working group meeting reg. hotels/ restaurants 7.3.1961: working group meeting reg. lodging for EP functionaries	1949-: *CSME (Commission d'Implantation et d'Accueil)*	1960s: *Secrétaire-Général de Strasbourg* (involved in the organisation of building projects)	1950s-1960s: *Directeur Habitation Moderne* (involved in several construction projects)	
Frey, Charles		1949-1955: *Président CSME*	1935-1955: Mayor (suspended during occupation (1940-1944) during the Second World War)		
Grouvel, Monique		1957-: *Cercle des Amitiés Européennes (vice-présidente)*		Ca. 1957-: *Club Europe-Amérique*	
Heitz, Alphonse	7.3.1961: working group meeting reg. lodging for EP civil functionaries	1962-: *Cercle Européen de Strasbourg* (entry card financed by the city administration)	1950s: Head *Division VIII* (implementation of hosting programme) 1960s: *Secrétaire-Général Adjoint* 1970s: *Service des Rélations Publiques*		

Name	Public European	Private European	Ordinary administration	Other position/ organisation	European Institutions
Heitz, Robert	1956-1959: Four specialised committees 1957-1971: Bipartite Committee 28.9.1959: working group meeting reg. hotels/ restaurants 7.3.1961: working group meeting reg. lodging for EP functionaries	1949-: *CSME (Commission du Programme;* new *CSME direction)*	1950s-1960s: *Adjoint au Maire* (involved in Human Rights Court construction – decoration of the interior)	1950s: *Conseiller technique Syndicat d'Initiatives*	
Kien, Léon	1956-1959: four specialised committees 28.9.1959: working group meeting reg. hotels/ restaurants for hosting efforts	1949-: *CSME* (*membre Commission du Programme*)	1950s: *Secrétaire-Général Adjoint de la Mairie* Early 1960s: *Secrétaire-Général de Strasbourg* (involvement with construction)		
Kientzi, Armand	1956-1959: four specialised committees 1957-1977: Bipartite Committee	1949-: *CSME* (*member Commission de Presse;* new *CSME direction*) 1950s: *Congrès du Peuple Européen, section local* 1962-: *Cercle Européen de Strasbourg*	*Conseiller Municipal*		

Name	Public European	Private European	Ordinary administration	Other position/ organisation	European Institutions
Kistler, Michel	1957-1959: Placement Study and Bipartite Committees	1962-: *Cercle Européen de Strasbourg*	*Conseiller Général*	*Président-Directeur SIBAR (Société Immobilière du Bas-Rhin)* – built flats – 1964 – some especially reserved for civil servants of European Institutions	
	1960: Bipartite Committee				
	7.3.1961: working group meeting reg. lodging for EP functionaries				
Leissner, Raymond (Dr.)	1970s: *Adjoint au Maire chargé des affaires européennes*	1973-: founding president of the Lions Club *Strasbourg Metropole Europe* (meets at *CES* location)	1970s-1980s: *Adjoint au Maire*		
	1978-1979: Bipartite Committee				
Lucius, Marc	1956-1959: four specialised committees		*Conseiller Municipal*	early 1950s: *Secrétaire-Général Chambre du Commerce de Strasbourg*	

Name	Public European	Private European	Ordinary administration	Other position/ organisation	European Institutions
Muller, Germain	28.9.1959: working group meeting reg. hotels/ restaurants for hosting efforts 1970-1979: Bipartite Committee 1978/9: working group for the organisation of the exposition '*Strasbourg et l'Europe*' 1978: Working party to study the financing of the *IPE*		*Adjoint au Maire*		He received the *Dannebrog orden* from the Danish consulate in Strasbourg, awarded by Danish President of PACE Per Federspiel in 1963.
Pflimlin, Marie-Odile	1960s-1970s: 'unofficial reception consultant'	1957-: *Présidente (d'honneur) Cercle des Amitiés Européennes* 1962-1985: *Cercle Européen de Strasbourg* (1962 *conseillère, membre du bureau, comité de direction;* 1982 *commission des activités-responsable)*		Ca. 1957-: *Club Europe-Amérique*	She received the *Dannebrog orden* from the Danish consulate in Strasbourg, awarded by Danish President of PACE Per Federspiel in 1963.

Name	Public European	Private European	Ordinary administration	Other position/ organisation	European Institutions
Pflimlin, Pierre	1956-1959: four specialised committees (inofficial member)	1956-: *Club pan-européen de Strasbourg*	1945-1959: *Conseiller Municipal* 1951-1976: *Président du Conseil Général du Bas-Rhin*	1946/1970: *Port Autonome de Strasbourg – Administrateur* (1946); *Président* (1970)	1959-1967: PACE representative (President 1963-1966)
	1957-1983: Bipartite Committee	1962-2000: *Cercle Européen de Strasbourg*	1959-1983: Mayor		1962-1967; 1979-1989: MEP (Vice-president 1979-1984; President 1984-1987)
	28.9.1959: working group meeting reg. hotels/ restaurants for hosting efforts	etc.	1946-1967: Député du Bas-Rhin	National Political offices 1945-1946: *Membre des deux Assemblées Nationales Constituantes* 1946: *Sous-secrétaire d'Etat auprès du ministre de la Santé et de la Population* 1946: *Sous-secrétaire d'Etat auprès du ministre de l'économie nationale* 13.-28.5.1958: *Président du Conseil*	
	7.3.1961: working group meeting reg. lodging for EP functionaries		1951-1970: *Conseiller général du canton de Haguenau* 1951-1960: *Président du Conseil Général du Bas-Rhin*		
	1970s: *Groupe d'Etudes européennes du Conseil Régional d'Alsace*		1967-1983: *Président du conseil de la Communauté urbaine de Strasbourg* 1971-1976: *Conseiller Général du canton de Strasbourg IV*	Government positions – Minister of 1947-1951: *Agriculture* 1951: *Commerce et des relations extérieures* 1952: *France d'Outre-mer*	

Name	Public European	Private European	Ordinary administration	Other position/ organisation	European Institutions
	etc.		1973-1983: *Conseil Régional d'Alsace*	20.1.-8.3.1952: *Ministre d'Etat chargé du Conseil de l'Europe* 1955: *Finances* 1957-1958: *Finances, des affaires économiques et du plan* 1962: *Ministre d'Etat chargé de la coopération*	
Radius, René	1956-1959: Four specialised committees (member)	1949-: *CSME (membre fondateur)*	*Adjoint au Maire*		1952-1978: PACE (substitute 1952-3; 1953-1978 representative; Chair French delegation 1963-; Vice-president ca. 1968)
	1957-1977: Bipartite Committee	1962-: *Cercle Européen de Strasbourg*	*Sénateur du Bas-Rhin*		
	7.3.1961: working group meeting reg. lodging for EP functionaries		etc.		
	28.9.1959: working group meeting reg. hotels/ restaurants for hosting efforts				

Name	Public European	Private European	Ordinary administration	Other position/ organisation	European Institutions
Ridoux, Georges	1957: Placement Study Committee		*Sous-préfet*		
	1957-1964: Bipartite Committee				
	1960-: *Sous-Préfet, chargé de mission pour les affaires européennes*				
	7.3.1961: working group meeting reg. lodging for EP functionaries				
Schmitt, Antoine	1956-1959: Four specialised committees	1950s: *Congrès du Peuple Européen, section local*	*Adjoint au Maire*	Ca. 1968: *Vice-président du Syndicat des Initiatives*	
	1957-1977: Bipartite Committee				
	28.9.1959: working group meeting reg. hotels/ restaurants for hosting efforts				
Schneegans, Suzanne		1957- ca.1962: *Cercle des Amitiés Européennes (Secrétaire)*		ca. 1957-: *Club Europe-Amérique (trésorière)*	
		Ca. 1962-: *Cercle des Amitiés Européennes (Présidente)*			

Name	Public European	Private European	Ordinary administration	Other position/ organisation	European Institutions
Wach, Paul	1956-1959: Four specialised committees (member; Chair of Liaison and Special Liaison Committees)	1949-: *CSME (Président du Commission d'Implantation et d'Accueil)*	1945-1974: *Adjoint au Maire*	1963-1974: *Président Foire Européenne*	1959-1969: PACE representative
	1957-1974: Bipartite Committee	1956-: *Club pan-européen de Strasbourg*	Etc.		
	28.9.1959: working group meeting reg. hotels/ restaurants for hosting efforts	1962-1972: *Cercle Européen de Strasbourg (Vice-président, Comité de Direction)*			
Woehl, Georges	1956-1959: four specialised committees	1953-: new *CSME (membre Comité-directeur)*	*Adjoint au Maire*		
	1957-1971: Bipartite Committee				
	28.9.1959: working group meeting reg. hotels/ restaurants for hosting efforts				

Section 2.02 Appendix II: Examples of Hosting Programme costs

In this appendix, examples of costs and measures of several session periods from 1956 onwards will be presented, which have been compiled from lists and invoices from dossiers from the municipal archive of Strasbourg. As far as present in the dossiers, the expenditures are included in these tables. The expenses were split evenly between the municipal administration and the *Département*. It has to be noted that the information on costs was dispersed throughout the dossiers in the municipal and departmental archive.

The first EP session 19.-21.3.1958

This session period presents an example of a special occasion during the second hosting period, when more effort was made by the two administrations for the frame programme.

Type	Costs (in A. Francs)	Notes
flowers bouquets	180,000 [3,000€]	300 bouquets for each MEP and journalist for their hotel rooms, composed of four white and red carnations each; the colours of the city
promotion brochures	252,000 [4,500€]	300 packages
welcome gifts and alcohol	550-630 per Person [5-10€]	for MEPs and journalists
theatre programme	30,000 [500€]	3000 copies. The costs were originally 150-160,000 Francs [2,600-2,800€], but the earnings from ads reduced the costs, so that just the binding had to be paid for.
hostesses	225,000 [4,000€]	five hostesses, costs for their uniforms
illumination and flags	1,100,000 [19,000€]	for buildings, monuments and central squares
installation of flag poles	205,000 [3,500€] estimated	expense just for Place Brant
flags and country pavilions	126,675 [2,000€]	for placement throughout the city; flags and pavilions for all member states of the European Communities
welcome	750,000 [13,000€]	not specified for what these expenses were exactly incurred
programme of activities	30,000 [500€] estimated	300 copies
luncheon 18.3.	430,500 [7,400€]	"Strasbourg" invited the Committee of Ministers of the European Communities
diversion 18.3.	382,258 [6,600€]	for the Committee of Ministers in the Foyer of the *Théâtre Municipal*
reception 19.3.	220,000 [4,000€]	at the *Hôtel de Ville*
symphonic concert 19.3.		for MEPs
luncheon 21.3.	500,000 [8,700€]	"déjeuner de Strasbourg à l'Europe"
Ballet	173,000 [3,000€]	*divertissement chorégraphique ballet* 18. /20.3.
banquet 20.3.	390,000 [6,800€]	for journalists
miscellaneous	50,000 [900€]	unspecified items in a city administration listing of costs

Type	Costs (in A. Francs)	Notes
brochure *Strasbourg Accueil*	28,711 [500€]	for every MEP; the costs amounted to 220,211 Francs [3,900€], from which the earnings of 191,500 Francs [3,300€] for ads have been deducted
visit of the European committee of urbanism experts	400,000 [7,600€]	costs incurred for the special welcome of the *Comité européen d'experts en urbanisme* which visited the city for its report during this session period

Costs: 5,473,729 Ancien Francs [94,800€]

Source: AS, 236 MW 1/1; 235 MW 270

PACE and EP session 19.-29.9.1961

This session presented an example for a 'normal' session period with common expenses.

Type	Costs (in Francs)	Notes
Surveillance et rondes de nuit	545.70 [800€]	organisation operated parking lots
dinner 19.9.		dinner at *Hôtel de Ville*
Soirée dansante 21.9.	8,050.90 [12,300€]	organised by *CAE*, paid by the city in the Hôtel Maison Rouge, costs for smaller items such as sound installation, artists
excursion 24.9.	6,143.83 [9,400€]	*Vosges du Nord et Palatinat*, costs for bus transport etc., photos
Leinsweiler Hof	2,764.27 [4,200€]	costs for the restaurant during the excursion 24.9.
presentation of films at the cinema 25.9.		with a reception organised by the CAE
lunch 27.9.		at the *Préfecture*
illumination	1,458.90 [2,200€]	special illumination of monuments and important buildings
Nouvel Alsacien	936 [1,400€]	for programme printing
Heiligenstein	26.25 [40€]	cards for parliamentarians
DNA/Novel Alsacien	2,016 [3,000€]	print of 4,000 covers for flight time table brochure *L'Europe vient à Strasbourg'*
flowers	296 [450€]	for accompanying wives and female parliamentarians
installation of flag poles	702.05 [1,100€]	for the flag decorations
flags	424.12 [600€]	for decoration throughout the city
hunting	329.52 [500€]	insurance for hunting for the parlia-mentarians who accepted hunting invitations
stamps	165 [300€]	for mailing invitations

Type	Costs (in Francs)	Notes
CTS	105 [200€]	intensification of service
wine	1,008 [1,500€]	for receptions
taxis	140 [200€]	for journalists

Costs: 25,111.54 Francs [38,300€]

Sources: AS, 236 MW 2/4; 236 MW 2/5; 236 MW 2/6

From the mid-1960s, the expenses for the session frame programme and transport for delegates were not covered by the ordinary budget of the city anymore, but by a special credit that the Bipartite Committee decided on in their annual meetings. If the expenditure exceeded this sum, the organism increased the amount. The following table has been compiled from the annual summaries presented at the Bipartite Committee's meetings. In them, all numbers were listed except for 1965. Expenditure marked with a * denotes that not all expenses were accounted for at the time of the meeting and that this would be an estimation of the Bipartite Committee of total costs made. A # in the transport column denotes that these costs were just for air links and not for all modes of transport. In the case of a raise, the new total amount is given in the column.

Year	Authorised credit sum	Increased to	Total expenditure	For hosting measures	For transport
1963	100,000 [140,000€]	-	152,897.33 [210,000€]	94,622.18 [130,000€]	#58,275.15 [80,000€]
1964	-	-	208,149.46 [280,000€]	158,050.78 [210,000€]	#50,098.68 [70,000€]
1966	200,000 [255,000€]	-	154,977.48 [200,000€]	128,456.13 [165,000€]	26,521.35 [35,000€]
1967	200,000 [250,000€]	-	177,228.60 [220,000€]	150,334.22 [185,000€]	26,894.38 [35,000€]
1968	200,000 [240,000€]	-	147,068.11 [175,000€]	127,694.98 [150,000€]	19,373.23 [25,000€]
1969	180,000 [200,000€]	-	166,022.97 [185,000€]	144,447.84 [160,000€]	21,575.13 [25,000€]
1970	180,000 [190,000€]	-	115,256.55 [120,000€]	98,660.89 [100,000€]	16,595.66 [20,000€]
1971	200,000 [200,000€]	-	*196,178 [195,000€]	178,537.39 [180,000€]	17,640.61 [15,000€]
1972	200,000 [190,000€]	-	138,414.81 [130,000€]	128,231.90 [120,000€]	10,128.91 [10,000€]
1973	250,000 [215,000€]	-	*240,000 [210,000€]	220,090.04 [190,000€]	11,108.30 [10,000€]

Year	Authorised credit sum	Increased to	Total expenditure	For hosting measures	For transport
1974	300,000 [230,000€]	-	*210,900 [160,000€]	185,200.04 [140,000€]	15,700 [10,000€]
1975	300,000 [200,000€]	-	260,270 [180,000€]	233,985 [160,000€]	26,285 [10,000€]
1976	300,000 [190,000€]	350,000 [220,000€]	*335,000 [210,000€]	268,504.41 [170,000€]	50,388.97 [30,000€]
1977	380,000 [215,000€]	-	*375,000 [210,000€]	259,125 [150,000€]	61,400 [35,000€]
1978	420,000 [220,000€]	620,000 [320,000€]	612,777 [318,000€]	498,342 [260,000€]	114,435 [60,000€]
1979	735,000 [350,000€]	2,000,000 [940,000€]	1,447,955.31 [680,000€]	1,070,635.56 [500,000€]	377,319 [180,000€]
1980	850,000 [350,000€]	-	-	-	-

Sources: ABR, 1130 W 936/2-16; AS, 752 W 90

Index

A

Adam, Daniel 57, 101, 181, 228, 229, 230, 233, 234, 255, 256, 258, 262, 264, 266, 312
Adenauer, Konrad 64, 66, 67, 74, 77, 148
Adjedj, Robert 231, 232
Alegria (Colonel) 218, 219
Altorffer, Charles 51, 89, 91, 94, 95, 103, 117, 121, 142, 144, 145, 146, 149, 150, 151, 157, 180, 208, 218, 312
Auberger (Madame) 119
Axelroud, Raymond 125

B

Baby (Madame) 147
Baillard, Robert 125, 229, 230, 231, 233, 244, 247, 312
Balfour, Neil 177
Bauman, Lucien 125
Baumgarten, Georges 125
Bech, Joseph 64, 66, 67, 70
Becker (Madame) 119
Behrendt, Walter 256
Benvenuti, Lodovico 125, 246, 247
Bernard, Henri 228, 232, 250, 258, 262
Bernheim, Hubert 125
Bernheim (Madame) 119
Bevin, Ernest 35, 59, 60, 83, 84, 102, 174, 257, 282
Biedermann, Alfred 107, 111, 112, 313
Bord, André 244
Brusse, Pierre 125
Brousse (Madame) 119
Bure, Victor 72

C

Calsat, Jean-Henri 156, 157, 232
Carcassonne, Roger 205
Carcaterra, Antonio 245
Churchill, Winston 59
Clamer, Roger 239, 258
Coene, René 125
Cottrell, Richard 215
Coudenhove-Kalergi, Richard 21, 131, 136, 138, 148, 149, 150, 177
Cromback, Lucien 237
Cunin, Georges 239, 241
Curtis, Dunstan 117, 122, 124, 125
Cuttoli, Maurice 90, 95

D

Damour, Maurice 125
Darling, George 209
Daussin, Armand 243, 244, 254
De Freitas, Geoffrey 252
De Gasperi, Alcide 64, 66
De Grailly, Michel 205
De Gaulle, Charles 82, 103, 104
Dehousse, Fernand 61, 157, 158
De Nerée tot Babberich, Frits 239
De Pange, Victor 120
De Pange (Madame) 119, 120

Désir, Harlem 31
Douro, Marquis of 221
Dutruel, Georges 125

E

Edwards, John 159
Ehret, Albert 107
Erhard, François 253
Ewing, Winifred M. 279

F

Federspiel, Per 164, 166
Feuerstein, Alfred 92, 179, 181, 185, 210, 217, 229, 313
Fix, Albert 51, 99, 228, 229, 231, 233, 241, 242, 244, 247, 248, 256, 273, 314
Fontaine, René 125
Fox, Ashley 31
Frey, Charles 69, 70, 89, 90, 91, 107, 133, 135, 136, 137, 180, 216, 252, 314

G

Galeazzo Sforza, Sforza 255
Gilliot, Georges 99, 180
Gillmann, Marcel 101
Giscard d'Estaing, Valéry 266
Graff, Jeanne 117, 125
Grandjean, B. 233
Grouvel, Monique 117, 118, 121, 314
Guillmot 163, 164
Guri, Fernand 237

H

Hallstein, Walter 64
Hannsler, Roger 57, 181
Heitz, Alphonse 91, 92, 101, 123, 124, 126, 163, 164, 165, 178, 179, 181, 192, 196, 198, 217, 218, 229, 244, 248, 275, 314
Heitz, Robert 95, 100, 244, 247, 315
Hummelsheim, Walter 241
Hunt, Stanley C. 262

J

Jantkowiak, S. 181

K

Kahn-Ackermann, Georg 263
Kennel, Guy-Dominique 32
Kielholz, Jean-Jacques 125
Kien, Léon 95, 228, 233, 247, 315
Kientzi, Armand 95, 100, 101, 315
Kientzi (Madame) 119, 120, 121
Kistler, Michel 247, 316

L

Labadens, Guillaume 125
Labadens, Odile 119
Leclant, Jean 125
Leissner, Raymond 56, 57, 92, 180, 181, 211, 217, 219, 229, 230, 233, 264, 275, 316
Lévy, Paul 70, 74, 139
Lucius, Marc 95, 316
Luja, A. 72

M

Martino, Gaetano 173
McMillan-Scott, Edward 20
Michaut (Madame) 119
Modinos, Polys 122, 124, 126
Monnet, Bertrand 232, 233, 236, 237, 239, 241, 242, 243, 244, 250, 255, 256
Monnet, Jean 65, 66
Muller, Germain 166, 244, 317

N
Noël, Paul 264
Nord, Hans 185, 216, 218, 228, 248, 255, 263

P
Paludan-Müller, Bent 211
Paris, Jacques Camille 70, 135, 136, 137
Pasetti-Bombardella, Francesco 262
Pautrier, Lucien 107
Peck, John 125
Pflimlin, Marie-Odile 114, 115, 116, 117, 119, 120, 121, 123, 124, 125, 126, 127, 146, 164, 165, 317
Pflimlin, Pierre 15, 16, 22, 23, 24, 35, 45, 46, 47, 49, 50, 55, 57, 69, 77, 81, 82, 84, 89, 91, 95, 96, 100, 101, 102, 103, 104, 114, 120, 121, 124, 125, 127, 137, 147, 148, 149, 150, 157, 158, 159, 161, 165, 168, 170, 171, 172, 177, 180, 181, 183, 192, 193, 197, 199, 201, 202, 204, 205, 215, 218, 223, 224, 228, 232, 241, 242, 243, 244, 247, 250, 252, 254, 255, 256, 257, 262, 263, 264, 266, 270, 273, 275, 279, 282, 318
Precheur, Jean 125, 185

R
Radius, René 95, 100, 101, 102, 103, 104, 108, 120, 121, 125, 144, 149, 150, 192, 209, 241, 244, 247, 252, 275, 319
Radius (Madame) 119, 120, 121
Randet, Pierre 72
Rasmussen, Gustav 60, 63
Ridoux, Georges 90, 92, 101, 124, 127, 163, 164, 165, 178, 179, 180, 181, 196, 197, 198, 206, 217, 241, 245, 246, 247, 248, 275, 320
Ries, Roland 31
Rossig, Johannes 72

S
Sauer, François 232, 234, 264
Scelba, Mario 255
Scheel, Walter 254
Schirer, V. 237
Schmidt, Pierre 92, 124, 165
Schmidt-le-Roi, Pierre 107, 108
Schmitt, Antoine 100, 244, 320
Schneegans, Suzanne 117, 119, 120, 122, 320
Schoff (Madame) 119
Schuman, Robert 24, 59, 60, 62, 64, 66, 67, 135
Sforza, Carlo 64, 255
Simmons, Richard 219
Staub (Madame) 119
Stikker, Dirk 64, 66, 67
Stoskopf, Charles-Gustave 156, 232

T
Thijsse, J.P. 72
Toncic-Sorinj, Lujo 250, 253, 254, 256, 257

U
Uhrich, René 183, 192
Undén, Östen 59, 60, 63

V
Valle, Cesare 72
Van Voorst tot Vorst 136
Van Zeeland, Paul 64, 66, 67
Veil, Simone 171
Verrier (Madame) 119
Vinci, Enrico 268

Voilquin, Albert 252
Von Puttkamer, Ellinor 254
Wach, Paul 50, 95, 96, 100, 101, 102, 103, 104, 107, 108, 120, 125, 144, 146, 159, 164, 209, 241, 244, 321

W

Wach (Madame) 119, 120, 146
Weber, Jean-Julien 130, 131
Weber (Madame) 119
Wehr, Herbert 92, 179, 181, 219
Wehrer, Albert 64
Weill, Axel 125
Weiss, Alfred 125
Wenger-Valentin, Jean 125
Witt, Robert 219
Woehl, Georges 95, 100, 244, 321
Woods, Thomas 247

'Multiple Europes'

The series 'Multiple Europes' is multiple in two ways: it understands Europe in an interdisciplinary manner with a strong historical perspective, and it understands Europe as being inserted in transnational and global contexts. On both levels, the perspectives on Europe and the very role and understanding of Europe is multiple. The special emphasis of the series thus lies in understanding the pasts of Europe as well as its complex present.

The history of Europe and the history of European integration have influenced each other in the past and will continue to do so in the future. There is an inbuilt tension in the relation between European history and the history of European integration. Europe signifies a space and semantics much broader and more complex than the EU. The relations between ideas of Europe, European history, global history and European integration need to be faced more openly. In order to do this, an open dialogue between academic disciplines is just as necessary as critical self-reflection within each discipline. Furthermore, European history was preoccupied with looking at itself and needs to be connected to global relations.

Series Editor: **Hagen Schulz-Forberg**,
Associate Professor for Global and European History

Series Titles

Estonians for Europe. National Activism for European Unification since the 1920s until the End of the Cold War, Pauli HEIKKILÄ, No.54, 2014

Zero Hours. Conceptual Insecurities and New Beginnings in the Interwar Period, Hagen SCHULZ-FORBERG (ed.), No.53, 2013

Globalisation vs Europeanisation. A Human-centric Interaction, Léonce BEKEMANS, No. 52, 2013

The Space of Crisis. Images and Ideas of Europe in the Age of Crisis: 1914-1945, Vittorio DINI & Matthew D'AURIA (eds.), No.51, 2013

EU Enlargement. Current Challenges and Strategic Choices, Finn LAURSEN (ed.), No.50, 2013

Cosmopolitanisms in Enlightenment Europe and Beyond, Mónica GARCÍA-SALMONES and Pamela SLOTTE (eds.), No.49, 2013

The European Public Sphere. From Critical Thinking to Responsible Action, Luciano MORGANTI & Léonce BEKEMANS (eds.), No.48, 2012

Intercultural Dialogue and Multi-level Governance in Europe. A Human Rights Based Approach, Léonce BEKEMANS (ed.), No.47, 2012

Imagining Europe as a Global Player. The Ideological Construction of a New European Identity within the EU, Christoffer KØLVRAA, No.46, 2012

Capital City Cultures. Reconstructing Contemporary Europe in Vienna and Berlin, Monika DE FRANTZ, No.45, 2011

Building a European Public Sphere. From the 1950s to the Present / Un espace public européen en construction. Des années 1950 à nos jours, Robert FRANK, Hartmut KAELBLE, Marie-Françoise LÉVY & Luisa PASSERINI (eds./dir.), No.44, 2010

'We belong to them'. Narratives of Belonging, Homeland and Nationhood in Territorial and Non-territorial Minority Settings, Tünde PUSKÁS, No.43, 2008

Imagining Europe. Europe and European Civilisation as Seen from its Margins and by the Rest of the World, in the Nineteenth and Twentieth Centuries, Michael WINTLE (ed.), No.42, 2008

Figures of Authority. Contributions towards a Cultural History of Governance from the Seventeenth to the Twentieth Century, Peter BECKER & Rüdiger VON KROSIGK (eds.), No.41, 2008

Europe and the Historical Legacies in the Balkans, Raymond DETREZ & Barbara SEGAERT (eds.), No.40, 2008

Histoire économique et sociale de la construction européenne, René LEBOUTTE, n° 39, 2008

Collective Traumas. Memories of War and Conflict in 20th-Century Europe, Conny MITHANDER, John SUNDHOLM & Maria HOLMGREN TROY (eds.), No.38, 2007

Reflections on Europe. Defining a Political Order in Time and Space, Hans-Åke PERSSON & Bo STRÅTH (eds.), No.37, 2007

London – Berlin. Authenticity, Modernity, and the Metropolis in Urban Travel Writing from 1851 to 1939, Hagen SCHULZ-FORBERG, No.36, 2006

(Un)Doing Europe. Discourses and Practices of Negotiating the EU Constitution, Michał KRZYŻANOWSKI & Florian OBERHUBER, No.35, 2007

Developing Cultural Identity in the Balkans. Convergence vs Divergence, Raymond DETREZ & Pieter PLAS (eds.), No.34, 2005

Statehood Before and Beyond Ethnicity. Minor States in Northern and Eastern Europe, 1600-2000, Linas ERIKSONAS & Leos MÜLLER (eds.), No.33, 2005

Berlin en musée. Changements sociopolitiques et usages du patrimoine, Véronique CHARLÉTY, n° 32, 2005

Democratisation in Turkey. The Role of Political Parties, Huri TÜRSAN, No.31, 2004

Unravelling Civilisation. European Travel and Travel Writing, Hagen SCHULZ-FORBERG, No.30, 2005

www.peterlang.com